Contents
Part I

Preface

Subject encyclopedias are among the most valuable components of any library's reference collection. Most libraries have several hundred or more of these publications varying in size from single-volume inexpensive editions to multivolume sets costing several thousand dollars. One library authority states that "Any library, no matter its size, that fails to offer its patrons access to reasonable current editions of at least several hundred (encyclopedias) will likely be considered seriously deficient."[1]

There are subject encyclopedias that focus on a single topic, such as *The Encyclopedia of the Holocaust, The Encyclopedia of Marriage and the Family, The Encyclopedia of Obesity and Eating Disorders,* and *The Encyclopedia of the Environment.* Others can be used for locating articles on a wide variety of topics, such as *The Encyclopedia of Bioethics, The Encyclopedia of Social Work, The Encyclopedia of Social Issues,* and *The Encyclopedia of the Future.*

These publications provide the best source for starting a research paper. A reference librarian at the Library of Congress maintains that the "best way to start many inquiries is to see if someone has already written an overview that outlines the most important facts on the subject and provides a concise list of recommended readings. This is precisely the purpose of an encyclopedia article."[2] Encyclopedia articles, usually written by recognized authorities, provide a systematic overview and summary as well as a list of recommended readings. Other frequently found encyclopedia features that help users locate information are indexes, cross-references, and tables of contents.

Although many library research guides suggest that the library's catalog be searched using a subject heading with the subdivision "Encyclopedias" to find out whether a library has an encyclopedia on a specific subject, more often than not, this approach will not be successful.

Another problem researchers face is the difficulty in finding encyclopedia articles on a specific subject. There is no up-to-date index for articles in subject encyclopedias. Joe Ryan compiled the first such index to articles in subject encyclopedias with *First Stop: The Master Index to Subject Encyclopedias.*[3] This book, published in 1989, provides a keyword index to articles in 430 subject encyclopedias and other standard reference sources.

Yet another obstacle facing the researcher is that the definition of "encyclopedia" is not entirely clear, nor is the term applied consistently across publications. The American Library Association states that an encyclopedia is "A book or set of books containing informational articles on subjects in every field of knowledge, usually arranged in alphabetical order, or a similar work limited to a special field or subject."[4] It is often difficult to identify the differences among dictionaries, encyclopedic dictionaries, and encyclopedias. Sometimes the term "Companion" or "Guide" is used in the titles; for example, *The Blackwell Companion to the Enlightenment; Companion to Literary Myths, Heroes and Archetypes;* and *Johns Hopkins Guide to Literary Theory and Criticism.* In addition, *Civilizations of the Ancient Near East* and *Man, Myth and Magic* are illustrative of publications that are encyclopedic in their coverage but do not include any term to indicate this in their titles.

Subject Encyclopedias: User Guide, Review Citations, and Keyword Index is designed to make subject encyclopedias more accessible. To qualify for inclusion, an encyclopedia must meet the following criteria:

- New or revised edition published since 1990.
- Coverage by subject (not primarily biographical or geographical).
- Intended audience of high school students, college students, and adults.
- Published in the English language.
- Reviewed in one or more professional library journals.

This first edition brings together in one place bibliographic data, reviews and awards information from key library journals, in addition to a keyword index.

NOTES

1. Bailey, Edgar C. "Acquisition and Use of General Encyclopedias in Small Libraries." *RQ,* Winter 1985: 218.
2. Mann, Thomas. *A Guide to Library Research Methods.* New York: Oxford University Press, 1987. p 3.
3. Ryan, Joe. *First Stop: The Master Index to Subject Encyclopedias.* Phoenix: Oryx Press, 1989.
4. *The ALA Glossary of Library and Information Science.* Chicago: American Library Association, 1983. p.85.

How to Use this Guide

This Guide consists of two parts. Part I provides a convenient collection development tool for selecting among 1,129 subject encyclopedias published between 1990 and 1997. Developing a library's collection of subject encyclopedias involves both replacing holdings with revised editions or supplements and purchasing new titles.

The entries in Part I can be checked against entries in the library's catalog to determine which titles are in the collection. Titles in needed subject areas can be identified either by using the encyclopedias section, where they are arranged by partial Library of Congress classification number, or by using the subject heading index. In making the final selection, titles on related subjects can be compared by using the review ratings or by using the review citations to look up and compare the actual reviews.

Part II is a keyword index to article titles for 98 of the subject encyclopedias in Part I. The 98 subject encyclopedias were selected because they are especially suited for college students doing research papers and library patrons performing research.

Every effort was made to ensure the accuracy and currency of the information contained in this *Guide* as well as to identify and select from a large group of encyclopedias for inclusion. In addition, publishers were asked to review and correct their company information for the publisher's index prior to publication. The author welcomes librarians' suggestions and recommendations for titles to include in future editions. These should be sent to Allan Mirwis, in care of The Oryx Press, 4041 N. Central Ave., Phoenix, AZ 85012-3397.

PART I

Encyclopedia entries are arranged by partial Library of Congress classification number. This has the effect of bringing together titles on the same or similar subjects and makes it easier to compare them. Each entry includes a bliographic citation, as well as citations to reviews and awards, a numerical review average, OCLC holdings, and a rating. Title index, Library of Congress subject headings index, Dewey classification index, publisher index, and rating index are also provided.

Encyclopedias

The sample encyclopedia entry on page ix represents the type of information provided for each main entry.

Reviews

Reviews published in professional library journals are frequently used by librarians as a selection tool. Gail Schlachter, former president of the American Library Association's Reference and Adult Services Division, asserts that "Reviews, intrinsically, function as one of the best sources of information in the selection process—more objective than publisher's announcements, more efficient than personal inspection of candidate materials."[1]

There are nine library publications that regularly review reference books—*American Reference Books Annual, Booklist/Reference Books Bulletin, Choice, College & Research Libraries, Guide to Subject Encyclopedias and Dictionaries,*[2] *The Journal of Academic Librarianship, Library Journal, RQ,* and *The Wilson Library Bulletin.*[3] Each review was read to determine (1) whether a subject encyclopedia qualified for inclusion in the *Guide,* and (2) to rate the review.

A five-point scale was used to rate each review based on the recommendation of the reviewer. Unfortunately, there were many reviews that did not have a specific recommendation. These reviews usually received a "2" or "3," based on the overall tone of the review. A title not recommended received a "1"; a title considered "outstanding" or "an essential purchase for all libraries" received a "5"; a "4" was assigned to highly recommended titles; a "3" was assigned to recommended titles; and a "2" was given for no specific recommendation.[4] A Review Average ("Review Avg") was calculated for each title by adding the points for each review and dividing that total by the number of reviews.

Between 1990 and 1997, nearly 4,000 reviews were published in the professional library journals listed below.

Number of Subject Encyclopedias Reviewed in Professional Library Journals (1990-1997)

Number of Individual Titles Reviewed

1070	*The American Reference Books Annual*	(ARBA)
709	*Booklist /Reference Books Bulletin*	(RBB)
738	*Choice*	(Choice)
35	*College and Research Libraries*	(CRL)

SAMPLE ENCYCLOPEDIA ENTRY

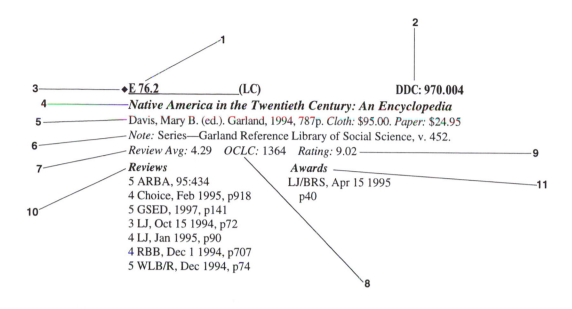

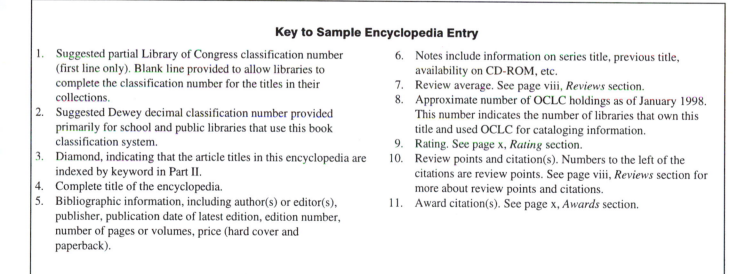

Key to Sample Encyclopedia Entry

1. Suggested partial Library of Congress classification number (first line only). Blank line provided to allow libraries to complete the classification number for the titles in their collections.
2. Suggested Dewey decimal classification number provided primarily for school and public libraries that use this book classification system.
3. Diamond, indicating that the article titles in this encyclopedia are indexed by keyword in Part II.
4. Complete title of the encyclopedia.
5. Bibliographic information, including author(s) or editor(s), publisher, publication date of latest edition, edition number, number of pages or volumes, price (hard cover and paperback).

6. Notes include information on series title, previous title, availability on CD-ROM, etc.
7. Review average. See page viii, *Reviews* section.
8. Approximate number of OCLC holdings as of January 1998. This number indicates the number of libraries that own this title and used OCLC for cataloging information.
9. Rating. See page x, *Rating* section.
10. Review points and citation(s). Numbers to the left of the citations are review points. See page viii, *Reviews* section for more about review points and citations.
11. Award citation(s). See page x, *Awards* section.

556	*Guide to Subject Encyclopedias and Dictionaries*	(GSED)
22	*The Journal of Academic Librarianship*	(JAL)
509	*Library Journal*	(LJ)
79	*RQ*	(RQ)
236	*The Wilson Library Bulletin* and Rettig on Reference	(WLB/R)

3954	Total

Rating

The purpose of the rating in the encyclopedia entry is to provide a method for ranking the publications in the *Guide*. Ratings can be used to select among those publications with the same keyword or subject heading, or among those with the overall highest ratings.

A title's rating is computed in the following way. The number of awards received is multiplied by 2. The review average is calculated by adding the points for each review and dividing that total by the number of reviews. The number of OCLC entries is divided by 500. (The highest number of OCLC holdings is approximately 2200. By dividing this number by 500, the range is between 4.4 and 0, which is similar to the range for the review average.) Two is added to the total of these numbers if the entry in the *Guide* is a revised edition. This is done to compensate for the practice of some journals not reviewing revised editions.

For example, *Native America in the Twentieth Century: An Encyclopedia* has a Rating of 9.02 that was calculated in the following manner:

Number of awards received	=	1*2	=	2.00
Review average	=	4.29	=	4.29
OCLC number	=	1364/500	=	2.73
Revised edition	=	0	=	0.00
Rating			=	9.02

Awards

Those responsible for the purchase of subject encyclopedias do not have the time to read all or most of the reviews. A convenient alternative to reading the reviews is using the various listings of award-winning reference books published annually. They can be used to identify titles that may have been overlooked by librarians during the previous year.

Five award lists are published each year—two by library organizations (the New York Public Library and the American Library Association) and three by library journals.

The most prestigious award, the Dartmouth Prize, is conferred by the American Library Association and announced at its annual midwinter conference.[5] This prize is given by the American Library Association's Reference and Adult Services Division to the one or two "reference works outstanding in quality and significance."[6] Between 1991 and 1998, 19 subject encyclopedias won this prize or received an honorable mention. Page xiii lists all winners of this prize or recipients of an honorable mention since its inauguration in 1975.

Choice and *Library Journal* make their selections based on the recommendations of their subject editors, while *Booklist/Reference Books Bulletin*[7] relies upon the Reference Sources Committee of the American Library Association's Reference and Adult Services Division. Between 1990 and 1997, a total of 457 awards were granted.

Number of Awards Conferred by Each Source (1990 and 1997)

No. of awards	Source of award
111	Reference Books Bulletin *Booklist's* "Outstanding Reference Sources" (RBB/ORS)
155	*Choice's* "Outstanding Academic Books" (Choice/OAB)
104	*Library Journal's* "Best Reference Sources" (LJ/BRS)
19	ALA's "Dartmouth Prize" (Dartmouth)
68	New York Public Library's "Reference Books of the Year" (NYPL)
457	Total awards

Of these awards, 232 were given to subject encyclopedias. Approximately two-thirds (144) received one award, and six appeared on all five lists.

Number of Subject Encyclopedias Receiving One or More Award (1990–1997)

No. of awards	No. of encyclopedias
5	6
4	9
3	20
2	53
1	144
Total	232

Indexes

Five indexes at the end of Part I help to access the information in the encyclopedias section. A diamond (♦) precedes each encyclopedia name for which there are article titles indexed in Part II of this *Guide*. Each entry includes the partial Library of Congress classification number to locate the entire entry in the *Encyclopedias* section.

Title Index

Entries are arranged alphabetically by full title.

The A-to-Z of Pregnancy and Childbirth: A Concise Encyclopedia, RG 525

An A to Z of the Middle East, DS 43

The A-to-Z of Women's Sexuality: A Concise Encyclopedia, HQ 30

The ABC-CLIO Companion to American Reconstruction, 1863–1877, E 668

The ABC-CLIO Companion to the 1960s Counterculture in America, E 169.02

The ABC-CLIO Companion to the American Labor Movement, HD 6508

The ABC-CLIO Companion to the American Peace Movement in the Twentieth Century, JX 1961

The ABC-CLIO Companion to the Civil Rights Movement, E 185.61

Subject Heading Index

Entries are arranged alphabetically by Library of Congress subject headings.

Abnormalities, Human
The Encyclopedia of Genetic Disorders and Birth Defects, RB 155.5

Accounting
The History of Accounting, HF 5605

Acoustics
Encyclopedia of Acoustics, QC 221.5

Adolescence
◆Encyclopedia of Adolescence, HQ 796

Dewey Decimal Classification Number Index

Entries are arranged by Dewey decimal classification number.

001
The Columbia Dictionary of Modern Literary and Cultural Criticism, BH 39

001.1
A Companion to American Thought, E 169.1

001.9
The Encyclopedia of Popular Misconceptions, AZ 999
Encyclopedia of Strange and Unexplained Physical Phenomena, Q 173

Publishers Index

Entries are arranged alphabetically by publisher's code (an abbreviated version of the publisher's name). The entries include the publisher's address, telephone numbers (local, toll-free, and fax), Web site and e-mail addresses (when available), and an alphabetical listing of the publisher's titles.

A L A
American Library Assn.
50 East Huron St
Chicago, IL 60611
312-944-6780; 800-992-7288; fax 212-777-8261
www.allworth.com
pub@allworth.com
Dictionary of Western Church Music, ML 102
World Encyclopedia of Library and Information Services, Z 1006

Rating Index

Entries are arranged in descending order by the encyclopedia's rating. (See page x for an explanation of the rating system.)

18.83
◆Encyclopedia of Bioethics, QH 332
18.44
◆Encyclopedia of American Social History, HN 57
18.31
The Oxford Companion to the English Language, PE 31
18.14
◆Black Women in America: An Historical Encyclopedia, E 185.86
17.83
The Encyclopedia of the Holocaust, D 804

PART II

Keyword Index

The keyword index can be used to locate specific articles from 98 subject encyclopedias, which were selected from the entries in Part I because they are especially well-suited to helping library users begin their research.

Each article title was examined before entering its keywords. Some words were eliminated because they are not usually included in a keyword index, e.g., articles (a, an, the) or prepositions (of, on, in, etc.). Other words were eliminated because the author feels they are not usually meaningful index terms, i.e, they are stopwords. Such stopwords are only indexed when they are germane to the article coverage. The author's stopwords are listed below.

Stopwords

America(n)	Federal	Policy
Aspect(s)	Federation(s)	Principle
Association(s)	Field(s)	Problem(s)
Board	Force	Procedure(s)
Bureau(s)	Foundation	Program(s)
Care	Function(s)	Region(s)
Center(s)	List	State(s)
Company	Meeting	Studies
Congressional	Nation(s)	Study
Corp(s)	National	System(s)
Countries	Office(s)	U.S.
Country	Organization(s)	United States
Criteria	Period(s)	Use(s)
Division(s)	Plan(s)	
Event(s)	Policies	

Keywords were changed, when necessary, to enhance their value as search terms. In so doing, the following occurred:

1. Some hyphens were removed to keep phrases together.
2. Some variant spellings were replaced with their American forms; that is, "behavior," not "behaviour," was used.
3. Abbreviations are not indexed, except when the title of the article is only an abbreviation, such as "AIDS," "UFOs," etc.

A keyword can consist of more than one word. It can be the name of an organization, individual or term, for example, "economic forecasting methods," "civil rights," "United Nations," "freedom of speech," "Roosevelt, Franklin Delano."

To help library researchers locate those subject encyclopedias focusing on one subject, the names of *all* the subject encyclopedias in Part I are also indexed. An encyclopedia whose name is indexed under a particular keyword, but for which no articles are indexed, is preceded by an asterisk (*).

Alphabetically arranged by keyword, then by abbreviated encyclopedia name, and then by article citation, each entry in this index provides the encyclopedia's partial Library of Congress classification number and each article's title, volume, and page numbers. An "S" preceding a citation indicates that a supplemental volume of the encyclopedia was indexed. Keywords that begin with numerals

are at the end of the index. See Abbreviations in Part II, page vi for a key to the abbreviations used in the encyclopedia names.

For example, in the keyword index sample below, there are 13 entries for the keyword "BIOTECHNOLOGY"— 6 encyclopedias and 7 articles.

BIOTECHNOLOGY ——————— KEYWORD

* *Biotechnology from A to Z*, TP248.16 — ABBREVIATED ENCYCLOPEDIA NAMES

■ *E/ Bioethics*, QH332
Biotechnology, 1:283-289 — ARTICLE TITLE

■ *E/ Life Scs.*, QH302.5
Biotechnology, 2:170-176 ——— ARTICLE CITATION

■ *E// Environment*, GE10
Biotechnology: Agricultural, 68-69
Biotechnology, Environmental, 70 — LIBRARY OF CONGRESS CLASSIFICATION NUMBER
Biotechnology, Medical, 70-72

■ *Environmental E.*, GE10
Biotechnology, 98-100

■ *Facts on File D/ Biotechnology and Genetic Engineering*, TP248.16
Biotechnology Genetic Engineering

*A keyword in the full encyclopedia name, rather than in an article title, is indexed.

NOTES

1. Schlachter, Gail. "Reviewing the Reviewers." *RQ,* Summer 1988: 468.
2. Although not a journal, this publication contains reviews in the specialized encyclopedias that appeared in *American Reference Books Annual* between 1987 and 1996 as well as a number of titles not reviewed in this publication.
3. *Wilson Library Bulletin* ceased publication in 1995. Reviews continued to be published on the Internet under Rettig On Reference.
4. See James H. Sweetland, "Reference Book Reviewing Tools: How Well Do They Do the Job?" *Reference Librarian,* 1987: p.66–74, for a good discussion on the problems involved in rating the contents of reviews.
5. All the recipients of this award, both winners and honorable mentions, are listed on page xiii.
6. *Choice,* January 1995. p.696.
7. Also appears each year in the May 1 issue of *American Libraries.*

Dartmouth Medal Award Winners and Recipients of Honorable Mention

This award, given annually by the American Library Association to reference works of outstanding quality, includes many subject encyclopedias.

1975   New England Board of Higher Education for establishing NASIC (Northeast Academic Science Information Center), a regional experiment in the brokerage of information services.

1976   No award presented.

1977   *Atlas of Early American History: The Revolutionary Era, 1760–1790.* (Princeton University Press for the Newberry Library and Institute of Early American History and Culture, 1977).

1978   *International Encyclopedia of Psychiatry, Psychology, Psychoanalysis and Neurology.* (Van Nostrand for Aesculapius, 1977).

1979   *Encyclopedia of Bioethics.* (Free Press, 1978).

1980   No award presented.

1981   *Dictionary of Scientific Biography.* (Scribers, 1981).

1982   *New Grove Dictionary of Music and Musicians.* (Stockton Press, 1980).

1983   Congressional Information Service, Inc., for "The body of its reference works which provide exceptional access to current and retrospective publications of the United States Government and to statistical publications from a wide variety of sources."

1984   *Times Atlas of the Oceans.* (Van Nostrand, 1983).

1985   *Wilsonline.* (H. W. Wilson Co.).

1986   *International Encyclopedia of Education: Research and Studies.* (Pergamon Press, 1985).

1987   *Encyclopedia of the American Constitution.* (Macmillan, 1986).

1988   *Encyclopedia of Religion.* (Macmillan, 1987).

1989   *We the People: An Atlas of America's Diversity.* (Macmillan, 1988).

1990   *Encyclopedia of Southern Culture.* (University of North Carolina Press, 1989).

Honorable Mention: *Dictionary of the Middle Ages.* (Scribners, 1989).

1991   *Encyclopedia of the Holocaust.* (Macmillan, 1989)

Honorable Mention: *Art Across America Two Centuries of Regional Painting, 1710–1920.* (Abbeville Press, 1990).

1992   *Atlas of United States Environmental Issues.* (Macmillan, 1992).

1993   *Encyclopedia of Sociology.* (Macmillan, 1992).

1994   *Black Women in America: An Historical Encyclopedia.* (Carlson, 1993).

Honorable Mention: *Encyclopedia of American Social History.* (Macmillan, 1993).

1995   *Encyclopedia of the American Presidency.* (Simon & Schuster, 1994).

Honorable Mention: *Encyclopedia of the Musical Theatre.* (Schirmer Books, 1994).

1996   *Civilizations of the Ancient Near East.* (Charles Scribner's Sons/Macmillan Library Reference, 1995).

Honorable Mention: *Encyclopedia of New York City.* (Yale University Press, 1995).

Honorable Mention: *Encyclopedia of Bioethics* (rev. ed.). (Macmillan Library Reference/Simon & Schuster Macmillan, 1995).

1997   *Dictionary of Art.* (Grove, 1996).

Honorable Mention: *Encyclopedia of African American Culture and History.* (Macmillan Library Reference, 1996).

Honorable Mention: *Encyclopedia of Latin American History and Culture.* (Charles Scribner's Sons, 1996).

Honorable Mention: *Middle Ages: An Encyclopedia for Students.* (Charles Scribner's Sons, 1996).

1998   *Jewish Women in America: An Historical Encyclopedia.* (Routledge, 1997).

Honorable Mention: *Encyclopedia of Africa South of the Sahara.* (Charles Scribner's Sons, 1996).

Honorable Mention: *Encyclopedia Judaica on CD-ROM.* (Judaica Multimedia).

Honorable Mention: *The Garland Encyclopedia of World Music: Africa.* (Garland, 1996).

Part I

User Guide

Encyclopedias

AE 5_____(LC)　　　DDC: 031

The Oxford Illustrated Encyclopedia of the Universe
Roy, Archie. Oxford Un, 1992. 199p. *Cloth:* $45.00.
Note: Series—Oxford Illustrated Encyclopedia, vol. 8.
Review Avg: 3.00　*OCLC:* 928　*Rating:* 4.86

Reviews
3 ARBA, 94:1944
3 Choice, Oct 1993, p271
3 GSED, 1997, p1001
3 RBB, Dec 1 1993, p716

AE 5_____(LC)　　　DDC: 031

The World Book Encyclopedia of People and Places
World Book, 1995. 2nd ed. 6 vols. *Cloth:* $149.00/set.
Review Avg: 3.60　*OCLC:* 153　*Rating:* 5.91

Reviews
3 ARBA, 93:490
3 GSED, 1997, p12, 182
5 RBB, Sep 1 1992, p91
3 RBB, Mar 15 1997, p1262, 2nd ed.
4 WLB/R, Nov 1992, p97

AG 5_____(LC)　　　DDC: 032

Illustrated Dictionary of Essential Knowledge
McWhirter, Alasdair (ed). Reader's Digest, 1995. 606p. *Cloth:*
$29.95.
Review Avg: 4.00　*OCLC:* 20　*Rating:* 4.04

Reviews
4 RBB, Apr 1 1996, p1389

AG 6_____(LC)　　　DDC: 001.95

Encyclopedia of Hoaxes
Stein, Gordon (ed). Gale Research, 1993. 347p. *Cloth:* $55.00.
Note: There is an abridged paperback version entitled *Hoaxes! Dupes,
Dodges and Other Dastardly Deceptions,* published by Visible Ink
Press.
Review Avg: 3.33　*OCLC:* 434　*Rating:* 6.20

Reviews　　　　　　　　**Awards**
4 Choice, Jan 1994, p763　　NYPL, 1994
3 LJ, Nov 15 1993, p74
3 RBB, Dec 1 1993, p712

AG 105_____(LC)　　　DDC: 031

***From Archetype to Zeitgeist: Powerful Ideas for Powerful
Thinking***
Kohl, Herbert (ed). Little, Brown, 1992. 246p. *Cloth:* $19.95.
Review Avg: 3.00　*OCLC:* 374　*Rating:* 3.75

Reviews
3 ARBA, 93:1060
3 RBB, Oct 15 1992, p452-453

AZ 108_____(LC)　　　DDC: 302.222

The Continuum Encyclopedia of Symbols
Becker, Udo. Continuum, 1994. 345p. *Cloth:* $39.50.
Review Avg: 3.40　*OCLC:* 748　*Rating:* 4.90

Reviews
3 ARBA, 95:1441
4 Choice, Apr 1995, p1268
3 GSED, 1997, p739
3 LJ, Dec 1994, p82
4 WLB/R, Feb 1995, p65

AZ 108_____(LC)　　　DDC: 302.23

***Dictionary of Symbolism: Cultural Icons and the Meanings
Behind Them***
Biedermann, Hans. Facts On File, 1992. 465p. *Cloth:* $45.00.
Review Avg: 3.00　*OCLC:* 1184　*Rating:* 5.37

Reviews
3 ARBA, 94:979
3 Choice, May 1993, p1435
3 GSED, 1997, p508
3 LJ, Sep 1 1992, p166
3 RBB, Feb 1 1993, p1001

AZ 999_____(LC)　　　DDC: 001.9

The Encyclopedia of Popular Misconceptions
Johnsen, Ferris. Carol, 1994. 220p. *Paper:* $9.95.
Review Avg: 3.00　*OCLC:* 99　*Rating:* 3.20

Reviews
3 ARBA, 96:62

B 21_____(LC)　　　DDC: 100

The Blackwell Companion to Philosophy
Bunnin, Nicholas and E. P. Tsui-James (eds). Blackwell, 1996. 786p.
Cloth: $74.95. *Paper:* $24.95.
Review Avg: 3.50　*OCLC:* 489　*Rating:* 4.48

Reviews
3 Choice, Oct 1996, p256
4 LJ, Apr 1 1996, p74

B 41_____(LC)　　　DDC: 103

A Dictionary of Philosophy
Mautner, Thomas (ed). Blackwell, 1996. 482p. *Cloth:* $29.95.
Review Avg: 3.67　*OCLC:* 352　*Rating:* 4.37

Reviews
3 Choice, Jul 1996, p1775
4 LJ, Dec 1995, p90
4 RBB, Feb 1 1996, p950-951

◆ The article titles in this encyclopedia are indexed by keyword in Part II.

B 41 _____(LC)   DDC: 103
A Dictionary of Philosophy
Lacey, A. R. Routledge, 1996. 3rd ed. 386p. *Paper:* $15.95.
Review Avg: 3.00   *OCLC:* 208   *Rating:* 5.42

Reviews
3 ARBA, 97:1164

B 41 _____(LC)   DDC: 103
Dictionary of Philosophy and Religion: Eastern and Western Thought
Reese, William L. Humanities, 1996. 856p. *Paper:* $25.00.
Review Avg: 3.00   *OCLC:* 326   *Rating:* 3.65

Reviews
3 Choice, Feb 1997, p949

◆**B 41** _____(LC)   DDC: 103
Encyclopedia of Philosophy
Macmillan, 1996. 4 vols. *Cloth:* $450.00/set.
Note: Supplement, 775p., 1996, $125.00.
Review Avg: 4.25   *OCLC:* 1345   *Rating:* 8.94

Reviews   **Awards**
4 ARBA, 97:1160, supp.   Choice/OAB, Jan 1997,
5 Choice, Dec 1996, p589,   p740
  supp.
4 LJ, Oct 15 1996, p50,
  supp.
4 RBB, Oct 1 1996, p368,
  supp.

B 41 _____(LC)   DDC: 103
Key Ideas in Human Thought
McLeish, Kenneth (ed). Facts On File, 1993. 789p. *Cloth:* $45.00.
Review Avg: 3.50   *OCLC:* 999   *Rating:* 5.50

Reviews
3 ARBA, 94:1497
4 Choice, Mar 1994, p1098,1100
4 LJ, Oct 15 1993, p60
3 RBB, Mar 1 1994, p1292

B 41 _____(LC)   DDC: 103
The Oxford Dictionary of Philosophy
Blackburn, Simon. Oxford Un, 1994. 408p. *Cloth:* $35.00.
Review Avg: 3.67   *OCLC:* 1439   *Rating:* 6.55

Reviews
3 ARBA, 95:1428
4 Choice, May 1995, p1426
4 GSED, 1997, p733
3 LJ, Nov 1 1994, p66
4 RBB, Jan 15 1995, p962,964
4 WLB/R, Mar 1995, p84,118-119

B 51 _____(LC)   DDC: 103
The Oxford Companion to Philosophy
Honderich, Ted. Oxford Un, 1995. 1009p. *Cloth:* $45.00.
Review Avg: 4.25   *OCLC:* 1508   *Rating:* 13.27

Reviews   **Awards**
4 ARBA, 97:1166   Choice/OAB, Jan 1997,
4 Choice, Jan 1996, p764   p740
5 LJ, Jul 1995, p74-75   NYPL, 1995

4 RBB, Oct 1 1995, p353   RBB/ORS, May 1 1996,
                              p1536

B 105 _____(LC)   DDC: 172.42
An Encyclopedia of War and Ethics
Wells, Donald A. (ed). Greenwood, 1996. 539p. *Cloth:* $95.00.
Review Avg: 3.33   *OCLC:* 248   *Rating:* 3.83

Reviews
4 ARBA, 97:1161
3 Choice, Sep 1996, p96,98
3 RBB, Sep 15 1996, p282

B 105 _____(LC)   DDC: 032
The Hutchinson Dictionary of Ideas
ABC-CLIO, 1994. 583p. *Cloth:* $49.50.
Review Avg: 3.50   *OCLC:* 217   *Rating:* 3.93

Reviews
3 ARBA, 95:56
4 WLB/R, Mar 1995, p83

◆**B 163** _____(LC)   DDC: 180
Encyclopedia of Classical Philosophy
Zeyl, Donald J. (ed). Greenwood, 1997. 614p. *Cloth:* $99.50.
Review Avg: 4.00   *OCLC:* 400   *Rating:* 4.80

Reviews   **Awards**
5 LJ, Jul 1997, p76   LJ/BRS, Apr 15 1998,
3 RBB, Oct 15 1997, p427   p47

B 802 _____(LC)   DDC: 940.25
Encyclopedia of the Enlightenment
Reill, Peter Hanns and Ellen Judy Wilson. Facts On File, 1996. 485p.
Cloth: $50.00.
Review Avg: 3.00   *OCLC:* 504   *Rating:* 4.01

Reviews
3 ARBA, 97:475
3 Choice, Nov 1996, p428
3 RBB, May 1 1996, p1521,1523

B 1031 _____(LC)   DDC: 133
The Paranormal: An Illustrated Encyclopedia
Gordon, Stuart. Headline, 1992. 722p. *Cloth:* $15.95.
Review Avg: 3.00   *OCLC:* 173   *Rating:* 3.35

Reviews
3 RBB, Nov 1 1993, p569

B 1246 _____(LC)   DDC: 192
A Hobbes Dictionary
Martinich, A. P. Blackwell, 1995. 336p. *Cloth:* $22.95.
Review Avg: 4.00   *OCLC:* 240   *Rating:* 4.48

Reviews
4 ARBA, 97:1165
4 Choice, May 1996, p1454

B 2751 _____(LC)   DDC: 193
A Kant Dictionary
Caygill, Howard. Blackwell, 1995. 453p. *Cloth:* $59.95. *Paper:* $22.95.
Note: Series—Philosopher's Dictionaries.

◆ The article titles in this encyclopedia are indexed by keyword in Part II.

Review Avg: 4.00   *OCLC:* 357   *Rating:* 4.71

Reviews
4 ARBA, 96:1428
4 Choice, Jan 1996, p752
4 LJ, May 1 1995, p88

B 3376_____(LC)   **DDC: 192**

A Wittgenstein Dictionary

Glock, Hans-Johann. Blackwell, 1996. 405p. *Cloth:* $54.95.
Review Avg: 3.33   *OCLC:* 354   *Rating:* 4.04

Reviews
3 ARBA, 97:1162
3 Choice, Jul 1996, p1772
4 LJ, Jan 1996, p102

BC 841_____(LC)   **DDC: 282**

The HarperCollins Encyclopedia of Catholicism

McBrien, Richard P. (ed). Harper/San Francisco, 1995. 1353p. *Cloth:* $45.00.
Review Avg: 4.00   *OCLC:* 838   *Rating:* 7.68

Reviews   **Awards**
4 ARBA, 96:1469   NYPL, 1995
4 LJ, Jun 1 1995, p104,106
4 RBB, Sep 1 1995,
  p108-109

BD 111_____(LC)   **DDC: 110**

Handbook of Metaphysics and Ontology

Burkhardt, Hans and Barry Smith. Philosophia Verlag, 1991. 2 vols.
Cloth: $380.00/set.
Review Avg: 4.00   *OCLC:* 247   *Rating:* 4.49

Reviews
4 Choice, Apr 1992, p1208-1209

BD 161_____(LC)   **DDC: 121**

A Companion to Epistemology

Dancy, Jonathan and Ernest Sosa (eds). Blackwell, 1992. 541p. *Cloth:* $74.95.
Review Avg: 5.00   *OCLC:* 378   *Rating:* 5.76

Reviews
5 Choice, Apr 1993, p1292

◆**BD 418.3**_____(LC)   **DDC: 128.2**

A Companion to the Philosophy of Mind

Guttenplan, Samuel (ed). Blackwell, 1994. 642p. *Cloth:* $79.95.
Review Avg: 5.00   *OCLC:* 472   *Rating:* 5.94

Reviews
5 Choice, Sep 1995, p136,138

BF 31_____(LC)   **DDC: 150.3**

Companion Encyclopedia of Psychology

Colman, Andrew M. (ed). Routledge, 1994. 2 vols. (1356p.) *Cloth:* $199.00/set.
Review Avg: 3.75   *OCLC:* 776   *Rating:* 7.30

Reviews   **Awards**
3 ARBA, 95:777   Choice/OAB, Jan 1995,
4 Choice, Jul/Aug 1994,   p719
  p1699

---

4 GSED, 1997, p393
4 LJ, Apr 1 1994, p88

BF 31_____(LC)   **DDC: 150.3**

Concise Encyclopedia of Psychology

Corsini, Raymond J. (ed). Wiley, 1996. 2nd ed. 1035p. *Cloth:* $175.00.
Note: From *Encyclopedia of Psychology.*
Review Avg: 4.25   *OCLC:* 421   *Rating:* 7.09

Reviews
4 ARBA, 97:627
4 Choice, Oct 1996, p249
4 GSED, 1997, p384
5 LJ, May 15 1996, p53

◆**BF 31**_____(LC)   **DDC: 150.3**

Encyclopedia of Human Behavior

Ramachandram, V.S. (ed). Academic, 1994. 4 vols. (2765p.) *Cloth:* $595.00/set.
Review Avg: 4.50   *OCLC:* 1192   *Rating:* 13.93

Reviews   **Awards**
5 ARBA, 95:778   Choice/OAB, Jan 1995,
5 GSED, 1997, p396   p719
4 RBB, Sep 15 1994, p176   LJ/BRS, Apr 15 1995,
4 WLB/R, Sep 1994, p77-78   p39
                   RBB/ORS, May 1 1995,
                   p1603

◆**BF 31**_____(LC)   **DDC: 150.3**

Encyclopedia of Psychology

Corsini, Raymond J. and Bonnie D. Ozaki (eds). Wiley, 1994. 2nd ed. 4 vols. *Cloth:* $475.00/set.
Review Avg: 5.00   *OCLC:* 2056   *Rating:* 13.11

Reviews   **Awards**
5 ARBA, 95:779   Choice/OAB, Jan 1995,
5 Choice, Sep 1994, p68   p719
5 GSED, 1997, p398
5 RBB, Sep 15 1994,
  p176-177

BF 31_____(LC)   **DDC: 150.3**

The Encyclopedic Dictionary of Psychology

Pettijohn, Terry F. (ed). Dushkin, 1991. 4th ed. 298p. *Cloth:* $17.95. *Paper:* $12.95.
Review Avg: 3.00   *OCLC:* 324   *Rating:* 5.65

Reviews
3 ARBA, 93:800
3 GSED, 1997, p403
3 RBB, Apr 15 1992, p1549

BF 31_____(LC)   **DDC: 150.3**

Gale Encyclopedia of Psychology

Gall, Susan (ed). Gale Research, 1996. 435p. *Cloth:* $99.00.
Review Avg: 3.75   *OCLC:* 93   *Rating:* 3.94

Reviews
4 ARBA, 97:628
3 Choice, Apr 1997, p1307
4 LJ, Feb 1 1997, p72
4 RBB, Dec 15 1996, p748

BF 31 _____(LC)   DDC: **150.3**
The International Dictionary of Psychology
Sutherland, Stuart. Crossroad, 1996. 2nd ed. 515p. *Paper:* $29.95.
Review Avg: 3.33   *OCLC:* 248   *Rating:* 5.83

Reviews
3 ARBA, 90:747
3 Choice, Sep 1996, p107
4 RBB, Apr 1 1996, p1389

BF 31 _____(LC)   DDC: **150.3**
A Student's Dictionary of Psychology
Stratton, Peter and Nicky Hayes. Routledge, 1993. 223p. *Paper:*
$15.95.
Review Avg: 3.00   *OCLC:* 348   *Rating:* 3.70

Reviews
2 ARBA, 94:811, 2nd ed.
4 ARBA, 90:747
3 Choice, Feb 1994, p922
3 RBB, Jan 15 1990, p1046

BF 31 _____(LC)   DDC: **150.3**
Survey of Social Science: Psychology Series
Magill, Frank N. (ed). Salem, 1993. 6 vols. (2698p.) *Cloth:* $425.00/
set.
Review Avg: 3.75   *OCLC:* 752   *Rating:* 5.25

Reviews
4 ARBA, 95:782
3 Choice, May 1994, p1422
4 RQ, Fall 1994, p113
4 WLB/R, May 1994, p75

BF 175.4 _____(LC)   DDC: **150.19**
Feminism and Psychoanalysis: A Critical Dictionary
Wright, Elizabeth (ed). Blackwell, 1992. 485p. *Cloth:* $59.95. *Paper:*
$19.95.
Review Avg: 3.33   *OCLC:* 249   *Rating:* 3.83

Reviews
3 ARBA, 93:801
3 Choice, Feb 1993, p938-939
4 GSED, 1997, p406

BF 311 _____(LC)   DDC: **153**
The Blackwell Dictionary of Cognitive Psychology
Eysenck, Michael W. (ed). Blackwell, 1991. 390p. *Cloth:* $69.95.
Paper: $24.95.
Review Avg: 3.50   *OCLC:* 639   *Rating:* 4.78

Reviews
3 ARBA, 93:798
4 Choice, Jul/Aug 1991, p1754

◆**BF 318** _____(LC)   DDC: **153.1**
Encyclopedia of Learning and Memory
Squire, Larry R. Macmillan, 1992. 642p. *Cloth:* $125.00.
Review Avg: 4.00   *OCLC:* 1256   *Rating:* 6.51

Reviews
4 ARBA, 94:809
4 Choice, Apr 1993, p1294
4 GSED, 1997, p106,397

3 LJ, Feb 15 1993, p158,160
5 RBB, Apr 15 1993, p1533-1534

BF 371 _____(LC)   DDC: **153.12**
The Encyclopedia of Memory and Memory Disorders
Noll, Richard and Carol Turkington. Facts On File, 1994. 265p. *Cloth:*
$45.00.
Review Avg: 2.25   *OCLC:* 531   *Rating:* 3.31

Reviews
2 ARBA, 96:780
1 Choice, Apr 1995, p1280
3 LJ, Mar 15 1995, p62
3 RBB, Feb 15 1995, p1109

◆**BF 431** _____(LC)   DDC: **153.9**
Encyclopedia of Human Intelligence
Sternberg, Robert J. (ed). Macmillan, 1994. 2 vols. (1234p.) *Cloth:*
$190.00/set.
Review Avg: 4.40   *OCLC:* 1147   *Rating:* 8.69

Reviews   *Awards*
5 Choice, Feb 1995, p915   Choice/OAB, Jan 1996,
3 LJ, Jan 1995, p85   p724
5 RBB, Feb 15 1995, p1109
4 RQ, Spr 1995, p392-393
5 WLB/R, Dec 1994, p71-72

BF 637 _____(LC)   DDC: **361.3**
Dictionary of Counseling
Biggs, Donald A. Greenwood, 1994. 229p. *Cloth:* $59.95.
Review Avg: 3.00   *OCLC:* 608   *Rating:* 4.22

Reviews
3 ARBA, 95:775
3 Choice, Dec 1994, p572
3 GSED, 1997, p389
3 RBB, Nov 1 1994, p536,538

BF 713 _____(LC)   DDC: **155**
The Encyclopedia of Human Development and Education:
Theory, Research, and Studies
Thomas, R. Murray (ed). Pergamon, 1990. 519p. *Cloth:* $160.00.
Note: Series—Advances in Education.
Review Avg: 4.50   *OCLC:* 389   *Rating:* 5.28

Reviews
5 ARBA, 91:793
4 GSED, 1997, p405

BF 721 _____(LC)   DDC: **155.4**
The Family Encyclopedia of Child Psychology and Develop-
ment
Bruno, Frank J. Wiley, 1992. 420p. *Cloth:* $27.95.
Review Avg: 3.00   *OCLC:* 367   *Rating:* 3.73

Reviews
3 ARBA, 94:807
3 GSED, 1997, p390

◆**BF 724.5** _____(LC)   DDC: **155.6**
Encyclopedia of Adult Development
Kastenbaum, Robert. Oryx, 1993. 574p. *Cloth:* $95.00.

◆ The article titles in this encyclopedia are indexed by keyword in Part II.

Review Avg: 4.00   *OCLC:* 1069   *Rating:* 8.14

Reviews   **Awards**
4 ARBA, 95:781   LJ/BRS, Apr 15 1994,
5 Choice, May 1994, p1506   p39
4 GSED, 1997, p400,461
3 RBB, Dec 1 1993, p712
4 WLB/R, Feb 1994, p79

BF 1025 _____(LC)   **DDC: 133**
The Encyclopedia of Parapsychology and Psychical Research
Berger, Arthur S. and Joyce Berger. Paragon, 1991. 554p.
Review Avg: 2.75   *OCLC:* 666   *Rating:* 4.08

Reviews
3 ARBA, 92:761
2 Choice, Apr 1991, p1284
3 RBB, Feb 15 1991, p1246,1248
3 WLB/R, May 1991, p140-141

BF 1025 _____(LC)   **DDC: 133**
The Encyclopedia of the Paranormal
Stein, Gordon (ed). Prometheus, 1996. 859p. *Cloth:* $149.95.
Review Avg: 3.33   *OCLC:* 460   *Rating:* 4.25

Reviews
3 ARBA, 97:634
4 Choice, Oct 1996, p250,252
3 RBB, Jun 1996, p1772

◆**BF 1031** _____(LC)   **DDC: 133.8**
Alternative Realities: The Paranormal, the Mystic and Transcendent in Human Experience
George, Leonard. Facts On File, 1995. 360p. *Cloth:* $35.00. *Paper:* $18.95.
Review Avg: 3.00   *OCLC:* 486   *Rating:* 3.97

Reviews
3 RBB, May 1 1995, p1589

◆**BF 1078** _____(LC)   **DDC: 154.6**
Encyclopedia of Sleep and Dreaming
Carskadon, Mary A. (ed). Macmillan, 1993. 703p. *Cloth:* $125.00.
Review Avg: 3.33   *OCLC:* 1286   *Rating:* 9.90

Reviews   **Awards**
3 ARBA, 94:808   NYPL, 1994
4 Choice, Sep 1993, p80   RBB/ORS, May 1 1994,
4 GSED, 1997, p391,925   p1627
2 LJ, Aug 1990, p108
4 RBB, Oct 15 1993, p472
3 WLB/R, Apr 1991, p117

BF 1091 _____(LC)   **DDC: 154.6**
The Dream Encyclopedia
Lewis, James R. Gale Research, 1995. 416p. *Cloth:* $49.95. *Paper:* $16.95.
Review Avg: 3.00   *OCLC:* 547   *Rating:* 4.09

Reviews
3 ARBA, 96:779
3 Choice, Dec 1995, p596
3 RBB, Nov 15 1995, p579

BF 1311 _____(LC)   **DDC: 133.9**
Encyclopedia of Afterlife Beliefs and Phenomena
Lewis, James R. Gale Research, 1994. 420p. *Cloth:* $37.95.
Review Avg: 2.50   *OCLC:* 257   *Rating:* 3.01

Reviews
3 ARBA, 96:1445
2 RBB, Apr 15 1995, p1522

BF 1407 _____(LC)   **DDC: 133**
Encyclopedia of Occultism and Parapsychology: A Compendium of Information on the Occult Sciences, Magic, Demonology, Superstitions, Spiritualism, Mysticism, Metaphysics, Psychical Science, and Parapsychology
Shepard, Leslie (ed). Gale Research, 1991. 3rd ed. 2 vols. *Cloth:* $295.00/set.
Review Avg: 4.40   *OCLC:* 584   *Rating:* 7.57

Reviews
5 ARBA, 92:762, 3rd ed.
4 ARBA, 97:633, 4th ed.
5 Choice, Jun 1991, p1615
4 GSED, 1997, p423
4 RBB, Sep 1 1991, p79

BF 1407 _____(LC)   **DDC: 133**
Harper's Encyclopedia of Mystical and Paranormal Experience
Guiley, Rosemary E. Harper/ San Francisco, 1991. 666p. *Cloth:* $35.95. *Paper:* $19.95.
Review Avg: 3.20   *OCLC:* 846   *Rating:* 4.89

Reviews
3 ARBA, 92:765
3 Choice, Dec 1991, p574
3 GSED, 1997, p417
3 LJ, Aug 1991, p86
4 RBB, Oct 1 1991, p364

◆**BF 1411** _____(LC)   **DDC: 133.4**
Man, Myth, and Magic: The Illustrated Encyclopedia of Mythology, Religion, and the Unknown
Cavendish, Richard and Brian Innes (eds). Cavendish, 1995. Revised edition. 21 vols. (3201p.) *Cloth:* $549.95/set.
Review Avg: 4.00   *OCLC:* 676   *Rating:* 7.35

Reviews
3 ARBA, 96:1348
3 Choice, Jul/Aug 1995, p1710
4 GSED, 1997, p684
4 LJ, Jun 15 1995, p62
4 RBB, Jun 1 1995, p1826-1827
5 RQ, Fall 1995, p124-125
5 WLB/R, May 1995, p75

BF 1461 _____(LC)   **DDC: 133.1**
The Encyclopedia of Ghosts and Spirits
Spencer, John and Anne Spencer. Trafalgar Square, 1992. 408p. *Cloth:* $39.95.
Review Avg: 4.00   *OCLC:* 1165   *Rating:* 6.33

Reviews
4 ARBA, 93:810

4 GSED, 1997, p424
4 RBB, Oct 15 1993, p470

BF 1588 _____(LC)   DDC: 133.4

Wizards and Sorcerers: From Abracadabra to Zoroastrianism

Ogden, Tom. Facts On File, 1997. 246p. *Cloth:* $40.00. *Paper:* $19.95.
Review Avg: 3.50   *OCLC:* 121   *Rating:* 3.74

Reviews
4 ARBA, 98:716
3 RBB, Dec 1 1997, p659-660

BF 1655 _____(LC)   DDC: 133.5

The Astrology Encyclopedia

Lewis, James R. Gale Research, 1994. 603p. *Cloth:* $45.00. *Paper:* $19.95.
Review Avg: 3.83   *OCLC:* 549   *Rating:* 8.93

Reviews	**Awards**
3 ARBA, 95:790	NYPL, 1994
4 Choice, Oct 1994, p263	RBB/ORS, May 1 1995,
3 GSED, 1997, p420	p1603
4 LJ, Mar 1 1995, p64	
4 RBB, Aug 1994,	
p2065-2066	
5 RQ, Fall 1994, p100-101	

BF 1751 _____(LC)   DDC: 133

Divining the Future: Prognostication from Astrology to Zoomancy

Shaw, Eva. Facts On File, 1995. 293p. *Cloth:* $35.00.
Review Avg: 2.50   *OCLC:* 169   *Rating:* 2.84

Reviews
3 ARBA, 96:791
2 RBB, Aug 1995, p1969

BF 1751 _____(LC)   DDC: 133.3

The Illustrated Encyclopedia of Divination: A Practical Guide to the Systems That Can Reveal Your Destiny

Karcher, Stephen L. Penguin, 1997. 256p. *Paper:* $21.95.
Review Avg: 3.00   *OCLC:* 177   *Rating:* 3.35

Reviews
3 ARBA, 98:714
3 LJ, Jul 1997, p77

BH 39 _____(LC)   DDC: 001

The Columbia Dictionary of Modern Literary and Cultural Criticism

Childers, Joseph and Gary Hontzi (eds). Columbia Un, 1995. 352p.
Cloth: $49.50. *Paper:* $19.50.
Review Avg: 3.00   *OCLC:* 571   *Rating:* 4.14

Reviews
3 ARBA, 96:960
3 LJ, Apr 1 1995, p86
3 RBB, Jun 1 1995, p1819,1821

BH 56 _____(LC)   DDC: 111.85

A Companion to Aesthetics

Cooper, David E. Blackwell, 1995. Revised edition. 466p. *Cloth:* $74.95.
Review Avg: 3.00   *OCLC:* 367   *Rating:* 5.73

Reviews
3 ARBA, 94:1492
3 Choice, Jul/Aug 1993, p1745
3 LJ, Dec 1992, p120

BJ 31 _____(LC)   DDC: 200.1

The Oxford Dictionary of World Religions

Bowker, John. Oxford Un, 1997. 1111p. *Cloth:* $45.00.
Review Avg: 3.33   *OCLC:* 586   *Rating:* 4.50

Reviews	**Awards**
4 Choice, Oct 1997, p273	Choice/OAB, Jan 1998,
3 LJ, May 1 1997, p94	p760
3 RBB, Jul 1997, p1837	

BJ 63 _____(LC)   DDC: 170

Dictionary of Ethics, Theology and Society

Clarke, Paul Barry and Andrew Linzey (eds). Routledge, 1996. 926p.
Cloth: $150.00.
Review Avg: 3.67   *OCLC:* 282   *Rating:* 4.23

Reviews
3 ARBA, 97:73, p41
4 Choice, Nov 1996, p427
4 RBB, Jul 1996, p1841-1842

◆ BJ 63 _____(LC)   DDC: 170

Encyclopedia of Ethics

Becker, Lawrence C. and Charlotte B. Becker. Garland, 1992. 2 vols. (1462p.) *Cloth:* $150.00/set.
Review Avg: 4.33   *OCLC:* 1734   *Rating:* 11.80

Reviews	**Awards**
3 ARBA, 93:1395	Choice/OAB, Jan 1993,
4 Choice, Nov 1992, p440	p734
5 GSED, 1997, p732	LJ/BRS, Apr 15 1993,
5 LJ, Jun 15 1992, p68	p58-59
4 RBB, Oct 1 1992,	
p366-367	
5 WLB/R, Jun 1992, p110	

◆ BJ 63 _____(LC)   DDC: 170

Encyclopedia of Values and Ethics

Hester, Joseph P. ABC-CLIO, 1996. 376p. *Cloth:* $60.00.
Review Avg: 2.50   *OCLC:* 322   *Rating:* 3.14

Reviews
3 ARBA, 97:1163
3 Choice, Jun 1997, p1640
2 LJ, Apr 15 1997, p68
2 RBB, Apr 1 1997, p1354

BJ 63 _____(LC)   DDC: 170

Ready Reference, Ethics

Roth, John K. (ed). Salem, 1994. 3 vols. (1150p.) *Cloth:* $270.00/set.
Review Avg: 3.17   *OCLC:* 778   *Rating:* 4.73

Reviews
3 ARBA, 95:1429

◆ The article titles in this encyclopedia are indexed by keyword in Part II.

3 Choice, Oct 1994, p258
3 LJ, Sep 1 1994, p173
4 RBB, Sep 1 1994, p68-70
3 RQ, Win 1994, p250-251
3 WLB/R, Sep 1994, p78-79

BJ 1199 _____(LC)   DDC: **241**

Encyclopedia of Biblical and Christian Ethics
Harrison, R. K. (ed). Nelson, 1992. Revised edition. 472p. *Paper:* $14.95.
Review Avg: 4.00   *OCLC:* 228   *Rating:* 6.46

Reviews
3 ARBA, 93:1419
5 GSED, 1997, p765

BJ 1199 _____(LC)   DDC: **241**

New Dictionary of Christian Ethics and Pastoral Theology
Atkinson, David J. and David H. Field (eds). InterVarsity, 1995. 678p. *Cloth:* $39.99.
Review Avg: 3.00   *OCLC:* 39   *Rating:* 3.08

Reviews
3 ARBA, 97:1209

BJ 1285 _____(LC)   DDC: **296**

The Jewish Encyclopedia of Moral and Ethical Issues
Amsel, Nachum. Aronson, 1994. 505p. *Cloth:* $30.00.
Review Avg: 3.00   *OCLC:* 134   *Rating:* 3.27

Reviews
3 ARBA, 95:1475
3 GSED, 1997, p776

BL 31 _____(LC)   DDC: **200**

Concise Dictionary of Religion
Hexham, Irving. InterVarsity, 1993. 245p. *Paper:* $15.99.
Review Avg: 3.00   *OCLC:* 213   *Rating:* 3.43

Reviews
3 GSED, 1997, p743

BL 31 _____(LC)   DDC: **291**

Contemporary Religions: A World Guide
Harris, Ian and others. Gale Research, 1992. 511p. *Cloth:* $175.00.
Review Avg: 2.00   *OCLC:* 195   *Rating:* 2.39

Reviews
3 ARBA, 94:1516
1 RBB, Jun 1993, p1894

BL 31 _____(LC)   DDC: **291**

Continuum Dictionary of Religion
Pye, Michael (ed). Continuum, 1994. 319p. *Cloth:* $34.95.
Note: Also called *Macmillan Dictionary of Religion* (London, 1994).
Review Avg: 3.00   *OCLC:* 584   *Rating:* 6.17

Reviews   **Awards**
3 ARBA, 95:1440   Choice/OAB, Jan 1995,
3 Choice, May 1994, p1410   p719
3 RBB, Aug 1990, p2200
3 RBB, May 1 1994,
  p1617-1618

BL 31 _____(LC)   DDC: **200**

Dictionary of Cults, Sects, Religions and the Occult
Mather, George A. and Larry A. Nichols. Zondervan, 1993. 384p. *Cloth:* $27.99.
Review Avg: 2.40   *OCLC:* 596   *Rating:* 3.59

Reviews
3 ARBA, 94:1513
3 Choice, Sep 1993, p84
3 GSED, 1997, p746
1 LJ, Jun 1 1993, p106,108
2 RBB, Jul 1993, p2001

BL 31 _____(LC)   DDC: **291**

The HarperCollins Dictionary of Religion
Smith, Jonathan Z. Harper/San Francisco, 1995. 1154p. *Cloth:* $45.00.
Review Avg: 4.00   *OCLC:* 1092   *Rating:* 6.18

Reviews
4 Choice, May 1996, p1448,1450
4 LJ, Apr 1 1996, p74

BL 31 _____(LC)   DDC: **200**

Larousse Dictionary of Beliefs and Religions
Goring, Rosemary (ed). Larousse, 1994. 605p. *Cloth:* $30.00.
Review Avg: 3.40   *OCLC:* 319   *Rating:* 4.04

Reviews
3 ARBA, 95:1443
3 GSED, 1997, p745
3 LJ, Nov 1 1994, p66
4 RBB, Dec 1 1994, p703
4 RQ, Spr 1995, p400-401

BL 31 _____(LC)   DDC: **291**

A New Dictionary of Religions
Hinnells, John R. (ed). Blackwell, 1995. 760p. *Cloth:* $74.95.
Review Avg: 3.67   *OCLC:* 401   *Rating:* 4.47

Reviews
4 ARBA, 97:1179
4 Choice, May 1996, p1455
3 LJ, Nov 15 1995, p68

BL 80.2 _____(LC)   DDC: **291**

Eliade Guide to World Religions
Eliade, Mircea. Harper/San Francisco, 1991. 301p. *Cloth:* $22.95.
Review Avg: 3.00   *OCLC:* 1046   *Rating:* 5.09

Reviews
3 ARBA, 93:1409
3 LJ, Nov 15 1991, p73
3 RBB, May 15 1992, p1715

BL 80.2 _____(LC)   DDC: **291**

The Illustrated Encyclopedia of Active New Religions, Sects, and Cults
Beit-Hallahmi, Benjamin. Rosen, 1993. 341p. *Cloth:* $49.95.
Review Avg: 3.00   *OCLC:* 592   *Rating:* 4.18

Reviews
3 ARBA, 94:1529
3 Choice, Oct 1994, p256
4 GSED, 1997, p734
2 RBB, Nov 1 1993, p566-567

BL 80.2 _____(LC)   **DDC: 291**

Longman Guide to Living Religions
Harris, Ian and others. Stockton, 1994. 278p. _Cloth:_ $29.95.
Review Avg: 4.00   _OCLC:_ 116   _Rating:_ 6.23

Reviews   **Awards**
4 Choice, Feb 1996, p930   Choice/OAB, Jan 1997,
                                  p740

BL 80.2 _____(LC)   **DDC: 200**

Religion: A Cross-Cultural Encyclopedia
Levinson, David. ABC-CLIO, 1996. 288p. _Cloth:_ $49.50.
Note: Series—Encyclopedias of the Human Experience.
Review Avg: 3.50   _OCLC:_ 323   _Rating:_ 4.15

Reviews
4 ARBA, 97:1178
3 Choice, Jun 1997, p1642

BL 311 _____(LC)   **DDC: 291.1**

World Mythology
Willis, Roy (ed). Holt, 1996. 320p. _Paper:_ $22.50.
Review Avg: 3.00   _OCLC:_ 812   _Rating:_ 6.62

Reviews   **Awards**
3 ARBA, 94:1398   NYPL, 1994
3 LJ, Feb 1 1994, p73

BL 325 _____(LC)   **DDC: 291.2**

Encyclopedia of Creation Myths
Leeming, David Adams. ABC-CLIO, 1994. 330p. _Cloth:_ $60.00.
Review Avg: 1.67   _OCLC:_ 621   _Rating:_ 2.91

Reviews
1 ARBA, 96:1444
1 RBB, Mar 1 1995, p1269-1270
3 WLB/R, Feb 1995, p67

BL 473 _____(LC)   **DDC: 291.2**

Encyclopedia of Gods: Over 2,500 Deities of the World
Jordan, Michael. Facts On File, 1993. 337p. _Cloth:_ $40.00.
Review Avg: 3.33   _OCLC:_ 914   _Rating:_ 5.16

Reviews
3 ARBA, 94:1395
4 Choice, Dec 1993, p587
3 GSED, 1997, p691
4 LJ, Jul 1993, p70
3 RBB, Oct 15 1993, p470-472
3 RQ, Spr 1994, p416

BL 473 _____(LC)   **DDC: 291.2**

Guide to the Gods
Leach, Marjorie. ABC-CLIO, 1992. 995p. _Cloth:_ $150.00.
Review Avg: 3.50   _OCLC:_ 846   _Rating:_ 7.19

Reviews   **Awards**
2 ARBA, 93:1305   RBB/ORS, May 1 1993,
4 Choice, Jul/Aug 1992,   p1620
  p1658
4 RBB, Mar 15 1992,
  p1402-1403
4 WLB/R, May 1992,
  p124,126

BL 477 _____(LC)   **DDC: 291.2**

Angels A to Z
Lewis, James R. and others (eds). Gale Research, 1996. 485p. _Cloth:_
$49.95.
Review Avg: 3.40   _OCLC:_ 460   _Rating:_ 4.32

Reviews
4 ARBA, 97:1176
3 Choice, Oct 1996, p249
3 RBB, Dec 15 1995, p723
4 RQ, Sum 1996, p545-546
3 WLB/R, 1995

BL 477 _____(LC)   **DDC: 291.2**

Encyclopedia of Angels
Guiley, Rosemary E. Facts On File, 1996. 214p. _Cloth:_ $40.00.
Review Avg: 3.00   _OCLC:_ 359   _Rating:_ 3.72

Reviews
3 Choice, Sep 1997, p99-100
3 LJ, Nov 15 1996, p54
3 RBB, May 15 1997, p1612

BL 603 _____(LC)   **DDC: 291.13**

An Encyclopedia of Archetypal Symbolism
Moon, Beverly (ed). Shambhala, 1991. 510p. _Cloth:_ $125.00.
Review Avg: 5.00   _OCLC:_ 365   _Rating:_ 7.73

Reviews   **Awards**
5 Choice, Mar 1992, p1037   Choice/OAB, Jan 1993,
                                  p734

BL 715 _____(LC)   **DDC: 292**

The Encyclopedia of Mythology
Cotterell, Arthur. Smithmark, 1996. 256p. _Cloth:_ $19.98.
Review Avg: 3.50   _Rating:_ 3.50

Reviews
4 GSED, 1997, p686
3 RBB, Sep 15 1996, p282

BL 715 _____(LC)   **DDC: 292**

_The Encyclopedia of Mythology: Gods, Heroes, and Legends
of the Greeks and Romans_
Flaum, Eric and David Pandy. Courage, 1993. 176p. _Cloth:_ $22.98.
Review Avg: 3.67   _OCLC:_ 459   _Rating:_ 4.59

Reviews
3 ARBA, 95:1321
4 GSED, 1997, p690
4 LJ, Sep 1 1993, p170

BL 795 _____(LC)   **DDC: 292**

_Cassell's Encyclopedia of Queer Myth, Symbol, and Spirit:
Gay, Lesbian, Bisexual, and Transgender Lore_
Conner, Randy P. and others. Sterling, 1997. 382p. _Cloth:_ $29.95.
Review Avg: 3.00   _OCLC:_ 119   _Rating:_ 3.24

Reviews
3 LJ, Sep 1 1997, p172

BL 900 _____(LC)   **DDC: 299**

Dictionary of Celtic Religion and Culture
Maier, Bernhard. Boydell, 1997. 338p. _Cloth:_ $71.00.

◆ The article titles in this encyclopedia are indexed by keyword in Part II.

Review Avg: 4.00   *OCLC:* 103   *Rating:* 4.21

Reviews
4 Choice, Dec 1997, p614,616

BL 900 _____(LC)   DDC: **299.16**
The Encyclopedia of Celtic Wisdom
Matthews, Caitlin. Element, 1994. 456p. *Cloth:* $39.95.
Review Avg: 2.00   *OCLC:* 59   *Rating:* 2.12

Reviews
2 ARBA, 96:788

BL 1005 _____(LC)   DDC: **291.095**
The Encyclopedia of Eastern Philosophy and Religion: Buddhism, Hinduism, Taoism, Zen
Fischer-Schreiber, Ingrid. Shambhala, 1994. 468p. *Cloth:* $39.95.
Paper: $22.50.
Review Avg: 3.50   *OCLC:* 537   *Rating:* 4.57

Reviews
3 ARBA, 96:1483
4 RBB, Sep 15 1994, p178-179

BL 1060 _____(LC)   DDC: **299.2**
Dictionary of Ancient Near Eastern Mythology
Leick, Gwendolyn. Routledge, 1991. 199p. *Cloth:* $55.00.
Review Avg: 2.33   *OCLC:* 495   *Rating:* 3.32

Reviews
2 ARBA, 92:1323
2 Choice, Oct 1991, p262
3 RBB, Nov 1 1991, p560

BL 1060 _____(LC)   DDC: **291.13**
The Encyclopaedia of Middle Eastern Mythology and Religion
Knappert, Jan. Element, 1993. 309p. *Cloth:* $29.95.
Review Avg: 3.33   *OCLC:* 550   *Rating:* 4.43

Reviews
3 ARBA, 95:1442
4 LJ, Dec 1993, p112,114
3 RBB, Mar 1 1994, p1289

BL 1105 _____(LC)   DDC: **294.5**
Encyclopaedia of the Hindu World
Garg, Ganga Ram (ed). Concept, 1992-. 3 vols. *Cloth:* $45.00.
Review Avg: 4.00   *OCLC:* 86   *Rating:* 4.17

Reviews
4 Choice, Oct 1992, p271

BL 1105 _____(LC)   DDC: **294.5**
Historical Dictionary of Hinduism
Sullivan, Bruce M. Scarecrow, 1997. 345p. *Cloth:* $49.00.
Review Avg: 4.00   *OCLC:* 127   *Rating:* 4.25

Reviews
4 RBB, Dec 1 1997, p654,656

BL 1238.52 _____(LC)   DDC: **181.45**
Shambhala Encyclopedia of Yoga
Feuerstein, Georg. Shambhala, 1997. 304p. *Cloth:* $30.00.

Note: Revision of *Encyclopedic Dictionary of Yoga.*
Review Avg: 3.40   *OCLC:* 550   *Rating:* 6.50

Reviews
3 ARBA, 91:1405
4 Choice, Jan 1991, p754,756
4 Choice, Nov 1997, p452,454
3 LJ, Jun 1 1990, p116
3 RBB, Jul 1990, p2114

Awards
Choice/OAB, May 1992, p1342

BL 2003 _____(LC)   DDC: **294.5**
Popular Dictionary of Hinduism
Werner, Karel. Humanities, 1994. 185p. *Paper:* $18.00.
Review Avg: 3.50   *OCLC:* 347   *Rating:* 4.19

Reviews
3 ARBA, 95:1472
4 GSED, 1997, p774

BL 2017.3 _____(LC)   DDC: **294.6**
Encyclopaedia of Sikh Religion and Culture
Dogra, Ramesh Chander and Gobind Singh Mansukhani. South Asian Publications, 1995. 511p. *Cloth:* $44.00.
Review Avg: 3.50   *OCLC:* 125   *Rating:* 3.75

Reviews
3 ARBA, 97:1225
4 Choice, Jul/Aug 1995, p1705

BL 2017.3 _____(LC)   DDC: **294.6**
A Popular Dictionary of Sikhism
Cole, W. Owen and Piara Sigh Sambhi. NTC, 1990. 163p. *Paper:* $14.95.
Review Avg: 3.00   *OCLC:* 38   *Rating:* 3.08

Reviews
3 GSED, 1997, p782

BL 2520 _____(LC)   DDC: **291.0973**
Encyclopedia of Religions in the United States: One Hundred Religious Groups Speak for Themselves
Williamson, William Bedford. Crossroad, 1992. 352p. *Cloth:* $35.00.
Review Avg: 3.75   *OCLC:* 465   *Rating:* 4.68

Reviews
5 ARBA, 93:1407
4 GSED, 1997, p751
3 LJ, Feb 1 1992, p78,80
3 RBB, Mar 1 1992, p1305-1306

BL 2525 _____(LC)   DDC: **291.0973**
The Encyclopedia of American Religious History
Queen, Edward L. and others. Facts On File, 1996. 2 vols. *Cloth:* $110.00/set.
Review Avg: 4.00   *OCLC:* 82   *Rating:* 10.16

Reviews
4 Choice, Jul 1996, p1776
4 LJ, Jan 1996, p90
4 RBB, Mar 1 1996, p1206

Awards
Choice/OAB, Jan 1997, p740
LJ/BRS, Apr 15 1997, p39
NYPL, 1996

BL 2525 _____(LC)   DDC: 291.0973
Encyclopedic Handbook of Cults in America
Melton, J. Gordon. Garland, 1992. Revised edition. 407p. *Cloth:*
$65.00. *Paper:* $18.95.
Note: Series—Garland Reference Library of Social Science, vol. 797.
Review Avg: 3.00   *OCLC:* 1092   *Rating:* 7.18
Reviews
3 ARBA, 93:1410

BL 2525 _____(LC)   DDC: 291.0973
Handbook of Denominations in the United States
Mead, Frank S. Abingdon, 1995. 10th ed. 352p. *Cloth:* $15.95.
Review Avg: 4.00   *OCLC:* 424   *Rating:* 6.85
Reviews
4 ARBA, 91:1445

BL 2530 _____(LC)   DDC: 291.0973
Encyclopedia of American Religions
Melton, J. Gordon. Gale Research, 1996. 5th ed. 1150p. *Cloth:*
$175.00.
Review Avg: 5.00   *OCLC:* 577   *Rating:* 8.15
Reviews
5 ARBA, 94:1518, 4th ed.
5 ARBA, 91:1415
5 GSED, 1997, p747

BM 5 _____(LC)   DDC: 296.4
Encyclopedia of Jewish Symbols
Frankel, Ellen and Betsy Platin Teutsch. Aronson, 1992. 234p. *Cloth:*
$35.00.
Review Avg: 3.50   *OCLC:* 168   *Rating:* 3.84
Reviews
3 ARBA, 93:443
4 GSED, 1997, p152

BM 50 _____(LC)   DDC: 296
The Blackwell Dictionary of Judaica
Cohn-Sherbok, Dan. Blackwell, 1992. 597p. *Cloth:* $74.95. *Paper:*
$24.95.
Review Avg: 3.00   *OCLC:* 409   *Rating:* 3.82
Reviews
3 ARBA, 94:1554
4 Choice, May 1993, p1436
3 GSED, 1997, p777
2 RBB, Mar 1 1993, p1250

BM 50 _____(LC)   DDC: 296
A Dictionary of Judaism and Christianity
Cohn-Sherbok, Dan. Trinity, 1991. 181p. *Paper:* $15.95.
Review Avg: 3.00   *OCLC:* 186   *Rating:* 3.37
Reviews
3 ARBA, 93:1405
3 GSED, 1997, p738

BM 50 _____(LC)   DDC: 296
Dictionary of Judaism in the Biblical Period: 450 B.C.E. to
600 C.E.
Green, William Scott (ed). Macmillan, 1996. 2 vols. (693p.) *Cloth:*
$190.00/set.
Review Avg: 4.00   *OCLC:* 348   *Rating:* 6.70
Reviews   **Awards**
4 Choice, Sep 1996, p94-95   Choice/OAB, Jan 1997,
                                    p740

BM 50 _____(LC)   DDC: 296
The Jewish Religion: A Companion
Jacobs, Louis. Oxford Un, 1995. 641p. *Cloth:* $39.95.
Review Avg: 5.00   *OCLC:* 448   *Rating:* 7.90
Reviews   **Awards**
5 Choice, May 1996, p1450   Choice/OAB, Jan 1997,
                                    p740

BM 50 _____(LC)   DDC: 296
The Oxford Dictionary of the Jewish Religion
Werblowsky, R. I. Zwi and Geoffrey Wigoder (eds). Oxford Un, 1997.
764p. *Cloth:* $95.00.
Review Avg: 4.50   *OCLC:* 1109   *Rating:* 6.72
Reviews   **Awards**
4 ARBA, 98:1396   Choice/OAB, Jan 1998,
5 Choice, Sep 1997, p102   p760
5 LJ, Apr 15 1997, p70,72   NYPL, 1997
4 RBB, Jul 1997,
   p1836-1837

BM 50 _____(LC)   DDC: 296
A Popular Dictionary of Judaism
Cohn-Sherbok, Lavinia and Dan Cohn-Sherbok. Curzon, 1995. 199p.
Paper: $18.50.
Review Avg: 2.00   *OCLC:* 85   *Rating:* 2.17
Reviews
2 Choice, Apr 1996, p1282

BM 660 _____(LC)   DDC: 296.4
The Encyclopedia of Jewish Prayer: Ashkenazic and
Sephardic Rites
Nulman, Macy. Aronson, 1993. 429p. *Cloth:* $50.00.
Review Avg: 3.00   *OCLC:* 116   *Rating:* 3.23
Reviews
3 ARBA, 94:1556
3 GSED, 1997, p779

BP 10 _____(LC)   DDC: 297
Islam and Islamic Groups: A Worldwide Reference Guide
Shaikh, Farzana (ed). Gale Research, 1992. 316p. *Cloth:* $155.00.
Review Avg: 3.00   *OCLC:* 41   *Rating:* 3.08
Reviews
3 ARBA, 94:1553
3 Choice, Jun 1993, p1604
3 LJ, May 15 1993, p62,64
3 RBB, Jul 1993, p2003

◆ The article titles in this encyclopedia are indexed by keyword in Part II.

BP 40_____(LC)   DDC: 297

The Concise Encyclopedia of Islam
Glasse, Cyril. Harper/San Francisco, 1991. 472p. *Paper:* $24.95.
Review Avg: 3.50   *OCLC:* 284   *Rating:* 4.07

Reviews
2 ARBA, 91:1448
5 GSED, 1997, p775

◆**BP 605**_____(LC)   DDC: 130.3

New Age Encyclopedia
Melton, J. Gordon. Gale Research, 1990. 586p. *Cloth:* $65.00.
Review Avg: 3.83   *OCLC:* 482   *Rating:* 10.79

Reviews	**Awards**
5 ARBA, 91:1451	Choice/OAB, May 1991,
4 Choice, Nov 1990, p464	p1430
4 GSED, 1997, p421,781	NYPL, 1991
3 LJ, Aug 1990, p106	RBB/ORS, May 1 1991,
3 RBB, Sep 15 1990, p194	p1735
4 WLB/R, Oct 1990,	
p130-131	

BQ 130_____(LC)   DDC: 294.3

Historical Dictionary of Buddhism
Prebish, Charles S. Scarecrow, 1993. 387p. *Cloth:* $42.50.
Note: Series—Historical Dictionaries of Religions, Philosophies, and Movements, no. 1.
Review Avg: 3.80   *OCLC:* 648   *Rating:* 5.10

Reviews
3 ARBA, 94:1519
4 Choice, Dec 1993, p589
4 GSED, 1997, p773
4 LJ, Oct 15 1993, p62
4 RBB, Nov 1 1993, p566

BR 66.5_____(LC)   DDC: 270.1

Encyclopedia of the Early Church
Di Berardino, Angelo (ed). Oxford Un, 1992. 2 vols. *Cloth:* $175.00/set.
Review Avg: 3.83   *OCLC:* 947   *Rating:* 5.72

Reviews
3 ARBA, 93:1406
4 CRL, Sep 1992, p418-419
4 Choice, Sep 1992, p76
4 GSED, 1997, p742
4 LJ, Jun 1 1992, p110
4 WLB/R, Jun 1992, p110-111

BR 95_____(LC)   DDC: 203.21

The Blackwell Encyclopedia of Modern Christian Thought
McGrath, Alister E. (ed). Blackwell, 1993. 701p. *Cloth:* $99.95.
Review Avg: 3.00   *OCLC:* 533   *Rating:* 4.07

Reviews
3 ARBA, 95:1465
3 Choice, Jun 1994, p1548
3 GSED, 1997, p759
3 RBB, Jun 1 1994, p1866,1868

BR 95_____(LC)   DDC: 203.21

Concise Dictionary of Christian Theology
Erickson, Millard J. Baker, 1994. 187p. *Paper:* $8.99.
Review Avg: 4.00   *OCLC:* 442   *Rating:* 4.88

Reviews
4 ARBA, 96:1453

BR 95_____(LC)   DDC: 203.21

Evangelical Dictionary of Theology
Elwell, Walter A. (ed). Baker, 1996. 2nd ed. 933p. *Cloth:* $44.99.
Review Avg: 4.00   *OCLC:* 69   *Rating:* 6.14

Reviews
4 Choice, Dec 1996, p589

BR 95_____(LC)   DDC: 230

New Twentieth-Century Encyclopedia of Religious Knowledge
Douglas, J. D. (ed). Baker, 1991. 2nd ed. 896p. *Cloth:* $39.95.
Review Avg: 3.00   *OCLC:* 455   *Rating:* 5.91

Reviews
3 ARBA, 92:1417
3 RBB, Sep 15 1991, p195

BR 95_____(LC)   DDC: 203

The Oxford Dictionary of the Christian Church
Cross, Frank Leslie and Elizabeth A. Livingstone (eds). Oxford Un, 1997. 3rd ed. 1786p. *Cloth:* $125.00.
Review Avg: 5.00   *OCLC:* 1084   *Rating:* 9.17

Reviews
5 Choice, Nov 1997, p455
5 RBB, Oct 1 1997, p356-357

BR 118_____(LC)   DDC: 230.01

Companion Encyclopedia of Theology
Houlden, Leslie and Peter Byrne. Routledge, 1995. 1092p. *Cloth:* $125.00.
Review Avg: 5.00   *OCLC:* 305   *Rating:* 5.61

Reviews
5 LJ, Jun 15 1995, p60

BR 130.5_____(LC)   DDC: 232.9

Jesus and His World: An Archaeological and Cultural Dictionary
Rousseau, John J. and Rami Arav. Fortress Press, 1995. 392p. *Cloth:* $48.00. *Paper:* $25.00.
Review Avg: 3.00   *OCLC:* 424   *Rating:* 3.85

Reviews
3 ARBA, 97:1213

BR 162.2_____(LC)   DDC: 270.1

Encyclopedia of Early Christianity
Ferguson, Everett and others (eds). Garland, 1997. 2nd ed. 1213p. *Cloth:* $150.00.
Note: Series— Garland Reference Library of the Humanities, No. 1839.
Review Avg: 3.63   *OCLC:* 580   *Rating:* 8.79

Reviews
4 ARBA, 91:1442
3 Choice, Sep 1990, p74,76
4 Choice, Sep 1997, p99,
  2nd ed.
4 GSED, 1997, p763
4 LJ, May 1 1990, p82
4 LJ, May 1 1997, p96, 2nd
  ed.
3 RBB, Aug 1990, p2202
3 RBB, Oct 1 1997, p352,
  2nd ed.

Awards
LJ/BRS, Apr 15 1991,
  p42

BR 302.8 _____(LC)   DDC: 270.6
The Oxford Encyclopedia of the Reformation
Hillerbrand, Hans I. (ed). Oxford Un, 1996. 4 vols. _Cloth:_ $450.00/
set.
Review Avg: 4.60   _OCLC:_ 1106   _Rating:_ 10.81

Reviews
5 ARBA, 97:1211
5 CRL, Mar 1997, p173-174
4 Choice, Jul 1996, p1776
4 LJ, May 15 1996, p54
5 RBB, Mar 1 1996,
  p1206-1207

Awards
Choice/OAB, Jan 1997,
  p740
LJ/BRS, Apr 15 1997,
  p39

BR 515 _____(LC)   DDC: 277
Concise Dictionary of Christianity in America
Reid, Daniel G. and others (eds). InterVarsity, 1995. 378p. _Paper:_
$16.99.
Note: Condensed version of _Dictionary of Christianity in America,_
1990.
Review Avg: 2.50   _OCLC:_ 74   _Rating:_ 2.65

Reviews
2 ARBA, 96:1466
3 Choice, Mar 1996, p1090

BR 515 _____(LC)   DDC: 277
Dictionary of Christianity in America: A Comprehensive
Resource on the Religious Impulse That Shaped a Continent
Reid, David G. and others (eds). InterVarsity, 1990. 1305p. _Cloth:_
$39.95.
Review Avg: 4.40   _OCLC:_ 1179   _Rating:_ 8.76

Reviews
5 ARBA, 91:1444
5 GSED, 1997, p772
4 LJ, Mar 15 1990, p84
4 RBB, May 15 1990, p1838
4 WLB/R, Jun 1990,
  p144,146

Awards
RBB/ORS, May 1 1991,
  p1734

BR 515 _____(LC)   DDC: 273
Encyclopedia of Religious Controversies in the United States
Sriver, George H. and Bill J. Leonard (eds). Greenwood, 1997. 542p.
Cloth: $99.50.
Review Avg: 4.00   _OCLC:_ 39   _Rating:_ 4.08

Reviews
4 LJ, Dec 1997, p90,92

BR 563 _____(LC)   DDC: 200.8996
Encyclopedia of African American Religions
Murphy, Larry G. and others (eds). Garland, 1993. 926p. _Cloth:_
$125.00.
Note: Series—Religious Information Systems, vol. 9.
Review Avg: 4.60   _OCLC:_ 1015   _Rating:_ 8.63

Reviews
5 ARBA, 94:1514
4 Choice, Mar 1994, p1094
5 GSED, 1997, p749
4 RBB, Jan 15 1994,
  p960-961
5 WLB/R, Dec 1993, p77-78

Awards
NYPL, 1994

BR 782 _____(LC)   DDC: 274.11
Dictionary of Scottish Church History and Theology
Cameron, Nigel M. de S. (ed). InterVarsity, 1993. 906p. _Cloth:_
$79.99.
Review Avg: 4.50   _OCLC:_ 163   _Rating:_ 4.83

Reviews
5 ARBA, 95:1466
4 GSED, 1997, p736

BS 80.2 _____(LC)   DDC: 291
Religions of the World: The Illustrated Guide to Origins,
Beliefs, Traditions and Festivals
Breuilly, Elizabeth and others. Facts On File, 1997. 160p. _Cloth:_
$29.95.
Review Avg: 4.00   _OCLC:_ 501   _Rating:_ 5.00

Reviews
4 ARBA, 98:1348

BS 440 _____(LC)   DDC: 220
The Anchor Bible Dictionary
Freedman, David Noel and others. Doubleday, 1992. 6 vols. _Cloth:_
$360.00/set.
Note: Available on CD-ROM.
Review Avg: 5.00   _OCLC:_ 1465   _Rating:_ 7.93

Reviews
5 GSED, 1997, p754
5 LJ, Jan 1993, p92
5 RBB, Feb 15 1993, p1076

BS 440 _____(LC)   DDC: 220
Mercer Dictionary of the Bible
Mills, Watson E. (ed). Mercer Un, 1990. 993p. _Cloth:_ $50.00.
Review Avg: 3.50   _OCLC:_ 598   _Rating:_ 6.70

Reviews
3 ARBA, 91:1430
4 Choice, Dec 1990, p611

Awards
RBB/ORS, May 1 1991,
  p1735

BS 440 _____(LC)   DDC: 220.3
New Bible Dictionary
Douglas, J. D. (ed). InterVarsity, 1996. 3rd ed. 1298p. _Cloth:_ $39.99.
Review Avg: 4.00   _OCLC:_ 238   _Rating:_ 6.48

Reviews
4 ARBA, 98:1373

◆ The article titles in this encyclopedia are indexed by keyword in Part II.

BS 440 _____(LC)   DDC: 220

The Oxford Companion to the Bible
Metzger, Bruce M. and Michael D. Coogan (eds). Oxford Un, 1993. 874p. _Cloth:_ $55.00.
Note: Available on CD-ROM.
Review Avg: 3.83   _OCLC:_ 1903   _Rating:_ 13.64

Reviews   **Awards**
3 ARBA, 94:1545   Choice/OAB, Jan 1995,
4 Choice, Jul/Aug 1994,   p720
   p1705   LJ/BRS, Apr 15 1994,
4 GSED, 1997, p756   p42
4 LJ, Sep 15 1993, p69   RBB/ORS, May 1 1994,
4 RBB, Dec 15 1993, p780   p1627
4 WLB/R, Jan 1994, p91

BS 440 _____(LC)   DDC: 220

Revell Bible Dictionary
Revell, 1990. 1156p. _Cloth:_ $39.99. _Paper:_ $29.99.
Review Avg: 3.25   _OCLC:_ 234   _Rating:_ 3.72

Reviews
3 ARBA, 91:1432
4 GSED, 1997, p757
3 LJ, Dec 1990, p122
3 RBB, Dec 15 1990, p883

BS 500 _____(LC)   DDC: 220.6

A Dictionary of Biblical Interpretation
Coggins, R. J. Trinity, 1990. 751p. _Cloth:_ $49.95.
Review Avg: 3.00   _OCLC:_ 398   _Rating:_ 3.80

Reviews
3 ARBA, 91:1425
3 GSED, 1997, p753

BS 533 _____(LC)   DDC: 220.6

The Encyclopedia of Biblical Errancy
McKinsey, C. Dennis. Prometheus, 1995. 533p. _Cloth:_ $49.95.
Review Avg: 2.00   _OCLC:_ 98   _Rating:_ 2.20

Reviews
2 ARBA, 96:1456

BS 622 _____(LC)   DDC: 913.031

Archaeological Encyclopedia of the Holy Land
Negev, Avraham (ed). Prentice-Hall, 1990. 3rd ed. 419p. _Cloth:_ $29.95.
Review Avg: 4.00   _OCLC:_ 480   _Rating:_ 6.96

Reviews
4 GSED, 1997, p191
4 RBB, Apr 15 1991, p1662

BS 680 _____(LC)   DDC: 220.8

And Adam Knew Eve: A Dictionary of Sex in the Bible
Ecker, Ronald L. Hodge, 1995. 192p. _Cloth:_ $35.00.
Review Avg: 2.00   _OCLC:_ 18   _Rating:_ 2.04

Reviews
2 ARBA, 96:1452

BS 2555.2 _____(LC)   DDC: 226

Dictionary of Jesus and the Gospels: A Compendium of Contemporary Biblical Scholarship
Green, Joel B. and Scot McKnight (eds). InterVarsity, 1992. 933p. _Cloth:_ $39.99.
Review Avg: 4.00   _OCLC:_ 421   _Rating:_ 4.84

Reviews
4 ARBA, 93:1428
4 GSED, 1997, p755

BT 83.55 _____(LC)   DDC: 230.082

Dictionary of Feminist Theologies
Russell, Letty M. and J. Shannon Clarkson (eds). Westminster John Knox, 1996. 351p. _Cloth:_ $39.00.
Review Avg: 4.00   _OCLC:_ 358   _Rating:_ 4.72

Reviews
4 ARBA, 97:1177
4 GSED, 1997, p750
4 RBB, Aug 1996, p1922

BT 1102 _____(LC)   DDC: 239

Dictionary of Fundamental Theology
Latourelle, Rene and Rino Fisichella (eds). Crossroad, 1994. 1222p. _Cloth:_ $75.00.
Review Avg: 4.00   _OCLC:_ 249   _Rating:_ 4.50

Reviews
4 ARBA, 95:1470
4 RBB, Feb 1 1995, p1025

BT 1315.2 _____(LC)   DDC: 273

Crimes of Perception: An Encyclopedia of Heresies and Heretics
George, Leonard. Paragon, 1995. 358p. _Cloth:_ $29.95.
Review Avg: 3.00   _OCLC:_ 344   _Rating:_ 3.69

Reviews
3 ARBA, 96:1468
3 Choice, Dec 1995, p594
3 LJ, May 15 1995, p64

BT 1315.2 _____(LC)   DDC: 273

Encyclopedia of Heresies and Heretics
Clifton, Charles S. ABC-CLIO, 1992. 156p. _Cloth:_ $50.00.
Review Avg: 3.00   _OCLC:_ 566   _Rating:_ 4.13

Reviews
2 ARBA, 94:1530
3 Choice, May 1993, p1436
3 GSED, 1997, p737
3 RBB, Feb 1 1997, p1001
4 WLB/R, May 1993, p116-117

BV 150 _____(LC)   DDC: 246

Dictionary of Christian Art
Apostolos-Cappadona, Diane. Continuum, 1994. 376p. _Cloth:_ $39.50.
Review Avg: 4.67   _OCLC:_ 620   _Rating:_ 5.91

Reviews
5 ARBA, 96:1028

4 LJ, Jan 1995, p82
5 RBB, Apr 1 1995, p1442

BV 656 _____ (LC) **DDC: 269**

Prime-Time Religion: An Encyclopedia of Religious Broadcasting

Melton, J. Gordon. Oryx, 1997. 413p. *Cloth:* $64.95.
Review Avg: 3.67　*OCLC:* 522　*Rating:* 4.71

Reviews
4 ARBA, 98:1366
3 Choice, Jul 1997, p1782
4 RBB, Dec 1 1996, p686

BV 1461 _____ (LC) **DDC: 268**

Harper's Encyclopedia of Religious Education

Cully, Iris V. and Kendig Brubaker (eds.). HarperCollins, 1990. 717p. *Cloth:* $34.95.
Review Avg: 3.00　*OCLC:* 460　*Rating:* 3.92

Reviews
3 ARBA, 91:1413
3 Choice, Oct 1990, p283
3 RBB, Oct 1 1990, p388

BX 6.3 _____ (LC) **DDC: 270.82**

Dictionary of the Ecumenical Movement

Lossky, Nicholas and others (eds). Eerdmans, 1991. 1196p. *Cloth:* $69.95.
Review Avg: 4.14　*OCLC:* 635　*Rating:* 7.41

Reviews	**Awards**
4 ARBA, 92:1417	RBB/ORS, May 1 1992,
3 Choice, Dec 1991, p572	p1625
5 GSED, 1997, p766	
5 LJ, Aug 1991, p85	
4 RBB, Sep 15 1991, p192	
4 RQ, Spr 1992, p415-416	
4 WLB/R, Nov 1991, p110	

BX 6.3 _____ (LC) **DDC: 270.82**

Historical Dictionary of Ecumenical Christianity

Van der Bent, Ans Joachim. Scarecrow, 1994. 599p. *Cloth:* $69.50.
Note: Series—Historical Dictionaries of Religions, Philosophies, and Movements, No. 3.
Review Avg: 3.00　*OCLC:* 186　*Rating:* 3.37

Reviews
4 ARBA, 96:1473
2 Choice, May 1995, p1434-1435

BX 130.5 _____ (LC) **DDC: 281.7**

The Coptic Encyclopedia

Atiya, Aziz S. Macmillan, 1991. 8 vols. *Cloth:* $1000.00/set.
Review Avg: 4.50　*OCLC:* 273　*Rating:* 5.05

Reviews
5 ARBA, 92:1414
4 CRL, Sep 1992, p417-418
4 Choice, Apr 1992, p1205
5 GSED, 1997, p740

BX 230 _____ (LC) **DDC: 281.9**

Historical Dictionary of the Orthodox Church

Prokurat, Michael and others. Scarecrow, 1996. 439p. *Cloth:* $89.00.
Note: Series—Religions, Philosophies, and Movements, no. 9.
Review Avg: 3.00　*OCLC:* 263　*Rating:* 3.53

Reviews
3 ARBA, 97:1212

BX 841 _____ (LC) **DDC: 282**

The Modern Catholic Encyclopedia

Glazier, Michael and Monika K. Hellwig. Liturgical, 1995. 976p. *Cloth:* $69.95.
Review Avg: 4.00　*OCLC:* 363　*Rating:* 4.73

Reviews
4 ARBA, 95:1469
4 GSED, 1997, p764

BX 841 _____ (LC) **DDC: 282**

Our Sunday Visitor's Catholic Encyclopedia

Stravinskas, Peter M. J. Our Sunday Visitor, 1992. 1008p. *Cloth:* $22.95. *Paper:* $11.95.
Note: Available on CD-ROM, 1994, $49.95.
Review Avg: 3.50　*OCLC:* 95　*Rating:* 3.69

Reviews
4 ARBA, 96:1471-2
3 RBB, Sep 1 1995, p109

BX 955.2 _____ (LC) **DDC: 262.13**

The Pope Encyclopedia: An A to Z of the Holy See

Bunson, Matthew. Crown, 1995. 390p. *Paper:* $17.00.
Review Avg: 2.00　*OCLC:* 249　*Rating:* 2.50

Reviews
1 LJ, Nov 1 1995, p58
3 RBB, Sep 1 1995, p109

BX 1753 _____ (LC) **DDC: 261.8**

The New Dictionary of Catholic Social Thought

Dwyer, Judith A. (ed). Liturgical, 1994. 1019p. *Paper:* $79.50.
Review Avg: 4.00　*OCLC:* 342　*Rating:* 4.68

Reviews
4 ARBA, 96:1470

BX 8211 _____ (LC) **DDC: 287**

Historical Dictionary of Methodism

Yrigoyen, Charles, Jr., and Susan E. Warrick. Scarecrow, 1996. 299p. *Cloth:* $47.00.
Note: Series—Historical Dictionaries, Philosophies and Movements, no. 8.
Review Avg: 4.00　*OCLC:* 283　*Rating:* 4.57

Reviews
4 ARBA, 97:1214
4 Choice, Feb 1997, p952

◆ The article titles in this encyclopedia are indexed by keyword in Part II.

BX 8605.5 _____ (LC)   DDC: 289

Encyclopedia of Mormonism: The History, Scripture, Doctrine, and Procedure of the Church of Jesus Christ of Latter-Day Saints
Ludlow, Daniel H. (ed). Macmillan, 1992. 5 vols. _Cloth:_ $450.00/set.
Note: Available on CD-ROM, 1992, $195.00.
Review Avg: 4.14   _OCLC:_ 493   _Rating:_ 5.13

Reviews
3 ARBA, 93:1420
3 Choice, Jul/Aug 1992, p1654
5 GSED, 1997, p766
5 LJ, Feb 15 1992, p156,158
4 RBB, May 1 1992, p1620
5 RQ, Fall 1992, p111-112
4 WLB/R, Apr 1992, p121-122

BX 8605.5 _____ (LC)   DDC: 289.3

Historical Dictionary of Mormonism
Bitton, Davis. Scarecrow, 1994. 338p. _Cloth:_ $39.50.
Note: Series—Historical Dictionaries of Religions, Philosophies, and Movements, no. 2.
Review Avg: 3.67   _OCLC:_ 342   _Rating:_ 4.35

Reviews
4 ARBA, 95:1464
3 Choice, Jul/Aug 1994, p1697
4 GSED, 1997, p758

BX 9406 _____ (LC)   DDC: 284.2

Encyclopedia of the Reformed Faith
McKim, Donald K. (ed). John Knox, 1992. 414p. _Cloth:_ $42.00.
Review Avg: 3.20   _OCLC:_ 392   _Rating:_ 3.98

Reviews
3 ARBA, 93:1422
3 Choice, Jul/Aug 1992, p1655
4 GSED, 1997, p769
3 LJ, Mar 1 1992, p82
3 RBB, Jun 1 1992, p1775

◆**CB 158** _____ (LC)   DDC: 303.49

Encyclopedia of the Future
Molitor, Graham T. and George Thomas Kurian (eds). Macmillan, 1996. 2 vols. (1115p.) _Cloth:_ $190.00/set.
Review Avg: 3.60   _OCLC:_ 501   _Rating:_ 4.60

Reviews
4 ARBA, 97:42
3 Choice, Jun 1996, p1614,1616
4 GSED, 1997, p463
3 LJ, Jun 1 1994, p94,96
4 RBB, Jun 1996, p1770-1772

CB 311 _____ (LC)   DDC: 930

Visual Dictionary of Ancient Civilizations
Houghton, 1994. 64p. _Cloth:_ $15.95.
Note: Series—Eyewitness visual dictionaries.
Review Avg: 4.00   _OCLC:_ 424   _Rating:_ 4.85

Reviews
3 ARBA, 95:584
5 GSED, 1997, p253

CB 411 _____ (LC)   DDC: 940.25

The Blackwell Companion to the Enlightenment
Yolton, John. Blackwell, 1992. 581p. _Cloth:_ $74.95.
Review Avg: 4.00   _OCLC:_ 554   _Rating:_ 5.11

Reviews
5 ARBA, 93:555
4 Choice, Nov 1992, p437-438
3 LJ, Dec 1991, p132

CC 70 _____ (LC)   DDC: 930.1

Dictionary of Concepts in Archaeology
Mignon, Molly Raymond. Greenwood, 1993. 364p. _Cloth:_ $85.00.
Note: Series—Reference Sources for the Social Sciences and Humanities, no. 13.
Review Avg: 3.50   _OCLC:_ 276   _Rating:_ 4.05

Reviews
3 ARBA, 94:487
4 Choice, Feb 1994, p917

CC 78 _____ (LC)   DDC: 930.1

The Oxford Companion to Archaeology
Fagan, Brian M. and others (eds). Oxford Un, 1997. 844p. _Cloth:_ $55.00.
Review Avg: 4.00   _OCLC:_ 942   _Rating:_ 5.88

Reviews	**Awards**
4 ARBA, 98:428	Choice/OAB, Jan 1998,
4 Choice, Jul 1997	p760
4 LJ, Feb 15 1997, p129	NYPL, 1997
4 RBB, Mar 15 1997, p1260	

CE 6 _____ (LC)   DDC: 529

Religious Holidays and Calendars: An Encyclopedic Handbook
Kelly, Aidan and others. Omnigraphics, 1993. 163p. _Cloth:_ $64.00.
Review Avg: 3.25   _OCLC:_ 559   _Rating:_ 4.37

Reviews
3 ARBA, 94:1517
3 JAL, May 1993, p131
3 RBB, Jul 1993, p2004-2005
4 WLB/R, Jun 1993, p130

CJ 67 _____ (LC)   DDC: 737

The International Encyclopaedic Dictionary of Numismatics
Carlton, R. Scott. Krause, 1996. 444p. _Cloth:_ $39.95.
Review Avg: 3.00   _OCLC:_ 155   _Rating:_ 3.31

Reviews
3 Choice, Sep 1997, p95
3 RBB, May 15 1997, p1613

CS 9 _____ (LC)   DDC: 929.1

The Oxford Companion to Local and Family History
Hey, David (ed). Oxford Un, 1996. 517p. _Cloth:_ $49.95.
Review Avg: 3.67   _OCLC:_ 349   _Rating:_ 4.37

Reviews
4 ARBA, 97:352
4 LJ, Aug 1996, p64
3 RBB, Oct 1 1996, p372

CS 21_____(LC)   **DDC: 919.1**

The Encyclopedia of Jewish Genealogy
Kurzweil, Arthur and Miriam Weiner (eds). Aronson, 1991. 3 vols.
Cloth: $30.00/vol.
Review Avg: 3.33   *OCLC:* 180   *Rating:* 3.69

Reviews
3 ARBA, 92:384
4 GSED, 1997, p151
3 RBB, Jun 15 1991, p2001

D 9_____(LC)   **DDC: 903**

Dictionary of Historical Terms
Cook, Chris. Bedrick, 1990. 2nd ed. 350p. *Paper:* $14.95.
Review Avg: 3.00   *OCLC:* 415   *Rating:* 5.83

Reviews
3 RBB, Jun 15 1990, p2028

D 9_____(LC)   **DDC: 903**

The Hutchinson Dictionary of World History
ABC-CLIO, 1994. 699p. *Cloth:* $49.50.
Review Avg: 4.50   *OCLC:* 814   *Rating:* 8.13

Reviews   **Awards**
4 ARBA, 95:581   Choice/OAB, Jan 1995,
5 Choice, Apr 1994, p1272   p720
4 GSED, 1997, p244
5 LJ, Mar 15 1994, p64

D 9_____(LC)   **DDC: 903**

The Illustrated Encyclopedia of World History
Van Heel, K. Donker (ed). Sharpe, 1997. 414p. *Cloth:* $99.00.
Review Avg: 2.00   *OCLC:* 84   *Rating:* 2.17

Reviews
2 LJ, Jun 1 1997, p90

D 9_____(LC)   **DDC: 903**

Larousse Dictionary of World History
Lenman, Bruce P. (ed). Larousse, 1994. 996p. *Cloth:* $40.00.
Note: Revision of *Chambers Dictionary of World History*.
Review Avg: 3.60   *OCLC:* 382   *Rating:* 4.36

Reviews
5 ARBA, 95:582
3 Choice, Nov 1994, p430
4 GSED, 1997, p247
3 LJ, Sep 1 1994, p174
3 RBB, Nov 1 1994, p543-545

D 9_____(LC)   **DDC: 903**

*World History: A Dictionary of Important People, Places, and
Events from Ancient Times to the Present*
Wetterau, Bruce. Holt, 1995. 1173p. *Paper:* $25.00.
Review Avg: 4.00   *OCLC:* 785   *Rating:* 5.57

Reviews
5 Choice, Oct 1994, p266-267
3 RBB, Sep 1 1994, p77
4 WLB/R, Oct 1994, p89

D 21.3_____(LC)   **DDC: 909.08**

*The Encyclopedia of Revolutions and Revolutionaries: From
Anarchism to Zhou Enlai*
Van Crevald, Martin. Facts On File, 1996. 494p. *Cloth:* $75.00.
Review Avg: 3.00   *OCLC:* 393   *Rating:* 5.79

Reviews   **Awards**
3 Choice, Jun 1996, p1614   NYPL, 1996
3 RBB, May 15 1996, p1620

D 25_____(LC)   **DDC: 355**

*The Battle Book: Crucial Conflicts in History from 1469 BC
to the Present*
Perrett, Bryan. Sterling, 1992. 349p. *Cloth:* $24.95. *Paper:* $19.95.
Review Avg: 3.00   *OCLC:* 194   *Rating:* 3.39

Reviews
3 ARBA, 94:695
3 RBB, Apr 1 1996, p1386-1387

D 25_____(LC)   **DDC: 355**

*Encyclopedia of Invasions and Conquests from Ancient
Times to the Present*
Davis, Paul K. ABC-CLIO, 1996. 443p. *Cloth:* $60.00.
Review Avg: 3.25   *OCLC:* 275   *Rating:* 3.80

Reviews
4 ARBA, 97:564
4 Choice, Jun 1997, p1638
2 LJ, Jan 1997, p84,86
3 RBB, Jun 1 1997, p1756

D 25_____(LC)   **DDC: 355**

Encyclopedia of Twentieth Century Conflict: Land Warfare
Forty, George. Sterling, 1997. 320p. *Cloth:* $34.95.
Review Avg: 2.50   *OCLC:* 0   *Rating:* 2.50

Reviews
2 ARBA, 98:613
3 RBB, Oct 15 1997, p427-428

D 25_____(LC)   **DDC: 355**

*The Harper Encyclopedia of Military History: From 3500
B.C. to the Present*
Dupuy, R. Ernest and Trevor N. Dupuy (eds). HarperCollins, 1993.
4th ed. 1654p. *Cloth:* $65.00.
Note: Revision of *Encyclopedia of Military History*.
Review Avg: 4.00   *OCLC:* 828   *Rating:* 7.66

Reviews
4 ARBA, 94:687
4 Choice, Nov 1993, p428,430
5 GSED, 1997, p325
3 RBB, Nov 1 1993, p564-565

D 114_____(LC)   **DDC: 909.07**

The Encyclopedia of the Middle Ages
Bunson, Matthew. Facts On File, 1995. 498p. *Cloth:* $50.00.
Review Avg: 2.50   *OCLC:* 520   *Rating:* 3.54

Reviews
4 ARBA, 96:565
1 Choice, Apr 1996, p1282

◆ The article titles in this encyclopedia are indexed by keyword in Part II.

D 114 _____(LC)   DDC: 909.07
The Middle Ages: An Encyclopedia for Students
Jordan, William Chester (ed). Scribner's, 1996. 4 vols. (940p.) *Cloth:*
$299.00.
Note: Abridged version of *The Dictionary of the Middle Ages.*
Review Avg: 3.50   *OCLC:* 40   *Rating:* 7.58

Reviews	*Awards*
4 ARBA, 97:471	Dartmouth, 1997
3 RBB, Sep 1 1996, p168	NYPL, 1996

D 205 _____(LC)   DDC: 903
The New Penguin Dictionary of Modern History, 1789-1945
Townson, Duncan. Penguin, 1994. Revised edition. 941p. *Paper:*
$13.95.
Note: Revision of *The Penguin Dictionary of Modern History, 1789-
1945,* 1983.
Review Avg: 4.00   *OCLC:* 179   *Rating:* 6.36

Reviews
4 WLB/R, Mar 1995, p84

D 214 _____(LC)   DDC: 904.7
*Warfare and Armed Conflicts: A Statistical Reference to
Casualty and Other Figures, 1618-1991*
Clodfelter, Michael. McFarland, 1991. 2 vols. (1414p.) *Cloth:*
$125.00/set.
Review Avg: 3.60   *OCLC:* 394   *Rating:* 4.39

Reviews
3 ARBA, 94:692
3 Choice, Apr 1993, p1292
4 RBB, Feb 1 1993, p1005
4 RQ, Fall 1993, p137-138
4 WLB/R, Mar 1993, p115

D 286 _____(LC)   DDC: 909.7
A Dictionary of Eighteenth-Century World History
Black, Jeremy and Roy Porter (eds). Blackwell, 1994. 880p. *Cloth:*
$59.95.
Review Avg: 3.50   *OCLC:* 366   *Rating:* 4.23

Reviews
4 Choice, May 1995, p1426,1428
3 LJ, May 1 1994, p94

D 356 _____(LC)   DDC: 909.81
A Dictionary of Nineteenth-Century World History
Belchem, John and Richard Price (ed). Blackwell, 1994. 746p. *Cloth:*
$59.95.
Review Avg: 3.33   *OCLC:* 336   *Rating:* 4.00

Reviews
3 ARBA, 95:578
3 GSED, 1997, p235
4 WLB/R, Nov 1994, p90

D 359.7 _____(LC)   DDC: 909.8103
*The ABC-CLIO World History Companion to the Industrial
Revolution*
Stearns, Peter N. and John H. Hinshaw. ABC-CLIO, 1996. 328p.
Cloth: $60.00.
Review Avg: 3.00   *OCLC:* 656   *Rating:* 4.31

Reviews
3 Choice, Jan 1997, p776
3 RBB, Sep 1 1996, p164

D 419 _____(LC)   DDC: 909.82
Dictionary of Twentieth-Century History
Brownstone, David M. and Irene M. Franck. Prentice-Hall, 1990.
444p. *Cloth:* $24.95.
Review Avg: 3.33   *OCLC:* 710   *Rating:* 4.75

Reviews
3 ARBA, 91:553
3 GSED, 1997, p236
4 LJ, Aug 1990, p102
5 RBB, Nov 15 1990, p681
2 RBB, Dec 15 1992, p762
3 WLB/R, Nov 1992, p92

D 419 _____(LC)   DDC: 909.82
Dictionary of Twentieth Century History: 1914-1990
Teed, Peter. Oxford Un, 1992. 520p. *Cloth:* $30.00.
Review Avg: 3.00   *OCLC:* 636   *Rating:* 4.27

Reviews
3 ARBA, 93:557
3 GSED, 1997, p213
3 WLB/R, Nov 1992, p92

D 419 _____(LC)   DDC: 909.82
The Facts On File Encyclopedia of the Twentieth Century
Drexel, John (ed). Facts On File, 1991. 1046p. *Cloth:* $79.95.
Review Avg: 3.40   *OCLC:* 1119   *Rating:* 5.64

Reviews
3 ARBA, 92:507
3 Choice, May 1992, p1366
3 LJ, Nov 15 1991, p74
3 RBB, Dec 15 1991, p785
5 WLB/R, Mar 1992, p114-115

D 419 _____(LC)   DDC: 909.82
*The Global Village Companion: An A-to-Z Guide to Under-
standing Current World Affairs*
Levinson, David and Karen Christensen. ABC-CLIO, 1996. 438p.
Cloth: $60.00.
Review Avg: 3.00   *OCLC:* 247   *Rating:* 3.49

Reviews
3 ARBA, 97:470
3 Choice, Jun 1997, p1641-1642
3 LJ, Apr 15 1997, p70
3 RBB, May 1 1997, p1530

D 419 _____(LC)   DDC: 909.82
Larousse Dictionary of Twentieth Century History
Lee, Min (ed). Larousse, 1994. 767p. *Paper:* $12.95.
Review Avg: 3.00   *OCLC:* 43   *Rating:* 3.09

Reviews
3 ARBA, 96:566

D 421 _____(LC)   **DDC: 909.82**

Great Events from History: Worldwide Twentieth Century Series

Magill, Frank N. (ed). Salem, 1992. 10 vols. (1431p.) _Cloth:_ $250.00/set.

Review Avg: 3.00   _OCLC:_ 731   _Rating:_ 4.46

Reviews
3 ARBA, 94:539
3 WLB/R, Apr 1993, p121

D 421 _____(LC)   **DDC: 909.82**

A History of the World in the Twentieth Century

Grenville, J. A. S. Belknap, 1994. Revised edition. 973p. _Cloth:_ $39.95.

Review Avg: 4.00   _OCLC:_ 616   _Rating:_ 7.23

Reviews
5 ARBA, 95:589
3 LJ, Jul 1994, p85

D 424 _____(LC)   **DDC: 940.28**

The Columbia Dictionary of European Political History Since 1914

Stevenson, John (ed). Columbia Un, 1992. 437p. _Cloth:_ $69.50.

Note: Originally entitled _Dictionary of British and European History Since 1914_ (Macmillan, 1991).

Review Avg: 3.40   _OCLC:_ 459   _Rating:_ 4.32

Reviews
3 ARBA, 93:529
4 Choice, Sep 1992, p74
4 GSED, 1997, p224
3 RBB, Jul 1992, p1957-1958
3 RQ, Fall 1992, p108-109

D 431 _____(LC)   **DDC: 355**

The Penguin Encyclopedia of Modern Warfare: 1850 to the Present Day

Macksey, Kenneth and William Woodhouse. Penguin, 1991. 373p. _Cloth:_ $29.95.

Review Avg: 3.25   _OCLC:_ 525   _Rating:_ 4.30

Reviews
3 ARBA, 93:701
4 Choice, Jun 1992, p1522
3 LJ, Nov 1 1991, p90
3 RBB, Feb 15 1992, p1132

D 510 _____(LC)   **DDC: 940.3**

The European Powers in the First World War: An Encyclopedia

Tucker, Spencer C. (ed). Garland, 1996. 783p. _Cloth:_ $95.00.

Review Avg: 3.00   _OCLC:_ 195   _Rating:_ 3.39

Reviews
3 ARBA, 97:467
3 Choice, Nov 1996, p428
3 GSED, 1997, p252,334
3 RBB, Jul 1996, p1843-1844

D 510 _____(LC)   **DDC: 940.3**

The United States in the First World War: An Encyclopedia

Venzon, Anne Cipriano and Paul L. Miles. Garland, 1995. 830p. _Cloth:_ $95.00.

Review Avg: 3.67   _OCLC:_ 565   _Rating:_ 4.80

Reviews
5 ARBA, 96:685
3 Choice, Feb 1996, p935
3 RBB, Feb 1 1996, p953

D 522.7 _____(LC)   **DDC: 940.3**

The Grolier Library of World War I

Grolier, 1997. 8 vols. _Cloth:_ $249.00.

Review Avg: 4.00   _OCLC:_ 144   _Rating:_ 4.29

Reviews
4 ARBA, 98:614

D 740 _____(LC)   **DDC: 940.53**

Dictionary of the Second World War

Wheal, Elizabeth-Anne and others. Bedrick, 1990. 541p. _Cloth:_ $39.95.

Note: Now called _The Meridian Encyclopedia of the Second World War_.

Review Avg: 3.60   _OCLC:_ 614   _Rating:_ 4.83

Reviews
3 ARBA, 91:554
4 Choice, Jan 1991, p764-765
4 LJ, Sep 15 1990, p74
3 RBB, Nov 1 1990, p564
4 WLB/R, Nov 1990, p148-149

D 740 _____(LC)   **DDC: 940.53**

The Historical Encyclopedia of World War II

Baudot, Marcel and others (eds). Fine Communications, 1996. 550p. _Cloth:_ $12.98.

Review Avg: 4.00   _OCLC:_ 11   _Rating:_ 4.02

Reviews
4 GSED, 1997, p234

D 740 _____(LC)   **DDC: 940.53**

The Oxford Companion to World War II

Dear, I. C. B. (ed). Oxford Un, 1995. 1343p. _Cloth:_ $49.95.

Review Avg: 4.40   _OCLC:_ 1436   _Rating:_ 9.27

Reviews	**Awards**
5 ARBA, 97:571	LJ/BRS, Apr 15 1996,
3 CRL, Mar 1996, p185	p40
5 Choice, Dec 1995, p598	
5 LJ, Jun 15 1995, p62,64	
4 RBB, Aug 1995, p1973	

D 743.5 _____(LC)   **DDC: 940.53**

The New Grolier Encyclopedia of World War II

Cooke, Tim and Sarah Halliwell (eds). Grolier, 1995. 8 vols. _Cloth:_ $229.00/set.

Review Avg: 2.50   _OCLC:_ 154   _Rating:_ 2.81

Reviews
4 ARBA, 96:684
1 RBB, Oct 1 1995, p352

◆ The article titles in this encyclopedia are indexed by keyword in Part II.

D 743.5 _____(LC)   DDC: 940.53

World War II: The Encyclopedia of the War Years, 1941-1945
Polmar, Norman and Thomas B. Allen. Random House, 1996. 940p.
Paper: $20.00.
Note: Originally entitled _World War II: America at War, 1941-1945._
Review Avg: 3.67   _OCLC:_ 758   _Rating:_ 7.19

Reviews   **Awards**
3 ARBA, 93:556   NYPL, 1992
5 LJ, Feb 1 1992, p82
3 RBB, Jan 15 1992, p980

D 756.5 _____(LC)   DDC: 940.5421

D-Day Encyclopedia
Chandler, David G. and James Lawton Collins, Jr. Simon & Schuster,
1994. 665p. _Cloth:_ $105.00.
Note: Available on CD-ROM, $105.00.
Review Avg: 4.00   _OCLC:_ 560   _Rating:_ 5.12

Reviews
4 ARBA, 95:686
4 ARBA, 95:689, Review of CD-Rom
4 Choice, Mar 1994, p1090
4 GSED, 1997, p333, Review of CD-ROM
4 LJ, Jan 1994, p100,104
4 RBB, Jan 1 1994, p849-850
4 WLB/R, Feb 1994, p78-79

D 804 _____(LC)   DDC: 940.5318

The Encyclopedia of the Holocaust
Gutman, Israel (ed). Macmillan, 1990. 2 vols. _Cloth:_ $360.00/set.
Review Avg: 4.57   _OCLC:_ 1629   _Rating:_ 17.83

Reviews   **Awards**
5 ARBA, 91:520   Choice/OAB, May 1991,
4 CRL, Sep 1990, p441-442   p1429
4 Choice, Jun 1990,   Dartmouth, 1991
  p1650-1652   LJ/BRS, Apr 15 1991,
5 GSED, 1997, p242   p43
4 LJ, Apr 15 1990, p82   NYPL, 1991
5 RBB, Mar 1 1990,   RBB/ORS, May 1 1991,
  p1375-1378   p1734
5 WLB/R, Apr 1990,
  p119-120

D 804.25 _____(LC)   DDC: 940.53

The Holocaust: A Grolier Student Library
Wigoder, Geoffrey (ed). Grolier, 1997. 4 vols. _Cloth:_ $169.00.
Review Avg: 4.00   _OCLC:_ 229   _Rating:_ 4.46

Reviews
4 ARBA, 98:501
4 LJ, Mar 15 1997, p54,56
4 RBB, Feb 15 1997, p1042

D 840 _____(LC)   DDC: 909.825

The Cold War Encyclopedia
Parrish, Thomas. Holt, 1996. 516p. _Cloth:_ $60.00.
Review Avg: 3.67   _OCLC:_ 237   _Rating:_ 4.14

Reviews
5 ARBA, 97:473
3 LJ, Dec 1995, p94
3 RBB, Feb 1 1996, p952

D 842 _____(LC)   DDC: 909.82

_International Conflict: A Chronological Encyclopedia of
Conflicts and Their Management_
Bercovitch, Jacob and Richard Jackson. Congressional Quarterly,
1997. 372p. _Cloth:_ $85.00.
Review Avg: 4.00   _OCLC:_ 184   _Rating:_ 4.37

Reviews
4 ARBA, 98:696

D 843 _____(LC)   DDC: 909.82

Encyclopedia of the Cold War
Arms, Thomas S. Facts On File, 1994. 628p. _Cloth:_ $70.00.
Review Avg: 3.86   _OCLC:_ 1023   _Rating:_ 5.91

Reviews
3 ARBA, 95:577
3 Choice, Dec 1994, p571-572
3 GSED, 1997, p233
5 LJ, Oct 15 1994, p50
4 RBB, Oct 1 1994, p355
4 RQ, Spr 1995, p393-394
5 WLB/R, Nov 1994, p90-91

D 847 _____(LC)   DDC: 909.09

Encyclopedia of the Second World
Kurian, George Thomas (ed). Facts On File, 1991. 614p. _Cloth:_
$95.00.
Review Avg: 2.60   _OCLC:_ 579   _Rating:_ 3.76

Reviews
3 ARBA, 92:509
1 Choice, Sep 1991, p64
3 GSED, 1997, p246
3 RBB, Aug 1991, p217
3 WLB/R, Jun 1991, p134

D 1051 _____(LC)   DDC: 940.55

Dictionary of European History and Politics Since 1945
Unwin, Derek. Addison-Wesley, 1996. 423p. _Paper:_ $24.95.
Review Avg: 4.50   _OCLC:_ 227   _Rating:_ 4.95

Reviews
4 Choice, Nov 1996, p438
5 RBB, Oct 1 1996, p368

DA 16 _____(LC)   DDC: 941

_The British Empire: An Encyclopedia of the Crown's Hold-
ings, 1493 through 1995_
Stewart, John. McFarland, 1996. 384p. _Cloth:_ $65.00.
Review Avg: 3.00   _OCLC:_ 187   _Rating:_ 3.37

Reviews
3 ARBA, 97:444
3 Choice, Oct 1996, p258
3 LJ, Aug 1996, p66

DA 16 _____(LC)   DDC: 909.097

Dictionary of the British Empire and Commonwealth
Palmer, Alan. Trafalgar Square, 1996. 395p. _Cloth:_ $35.00.
Review Avg: 4.00   _OCLC:_ 166   _Rating:_ 4.33

Reviews
4 Choice, Oct 1996, p256
4 LJ, Aug 1996, p64

DA 27.5 _____(LC)   DDC: **941**
The Encyclopedia of Britain
Gascoigne, Bamber. Macmillan, 1993. 720p. *Cloth:* $110.00.
Review Avg: 3.50   *OCLC:* 454   *Rating:* 4.41

Reviews
3 ARBA, 94:133
4 CRL, Sep 1996, p471-472
3 Choice, Feb 1994, p914
3 GSED, 1997, p39
4 RQ, Sum 1994, p549
4 WLB/R, Feb 1994, p79-80

DA 34 _____(LC)   DDC: **941**
The Columbia Companion to British History
Gardiner, Juliet and Neil Wenborn (eds). Columbia Un, 1997. 840p.
Cloth: $40.00.
Note: Originally entitled *The History Today Companion to British History*. London, Collins & Brown, 1995.
Review Avg: 3.00   *OCLC:* 264   *Rating:* 3.53

Reviews   *Awards*
3 Choice, Dec 1997, p620   Choice/OAB, Jan 1998,
3 RBB, Mar 15 1997,   p759
   p1254,1256

DA 152 _____(LC)   DDC: **809.9351**
The New Arthurian Encyclopedia
Lacy, Norris J. and others (eds). Garland, 1991. 615p. *Cloth:* $65.00.
Paper: $29.95/1996 ed.
Review Avg: 3.50   *OCLC:* 729   *Rating:* 4.96

Reviews
3 ARBA, 92:1190
4 LJ, May 15 1991, p78

DA 152.5 _____(LC)   DDC: **809.9351**
The Encyclopaedia of Arthurian Legends
Coghlan, Ronan. Natl Book Network, 1991. 234p. *Cloth:* $18.95.
Review Avg: 3.00   *OCLC:* 168   *Rating:* 3.34

Reviews
3 ARBA, 93:1190

DA 225 _____(LC)   DDC: **942**
The Plantagenet Encyclopedia: An Alphabetical Guide to 400 Years of English History
Hallam, Elizabeth (ed). Grove/Atlantic, 1990. 224p. *Cloth:* $32.95.
Review Avg: 3.00   *OCLC:* 139   *Rating:* 3.28

Reviews
3 ARBA, 91:525

DA 375 _____(LC)   DDC: **941.06**
Historical Dictionary of Stuart England, 1603-1689
Fritze, Ronald H. and William B. Robinson (eds). Greenwood, 1996.
611p. *Cloth:* $95.00.
Review Avg: 4.00   *OCLC:* 292   *Rating:* 6.58

Reviews   *Awards*
4 Choice, Sep 1996, p99   LJ/BRS, Apr 15 1997,
                   p39

DA 529 _____(LC)   DDC: **941.09**
Encyclopedia of Romanticism: Culture in Britain, 1780-1830
Dabundo, Laura (ed). Garland, 1992. 662p. *Cloth:* $95.00.
Review Avg: 4.00   *OCLC:* 683   *Rating:* 5.37

Reviews
5 ARBA, 93:531
5 CRL, Sep 1993, p430
2 Choice, Oct 1992, p271-272
5 LJ, Jul 1992, p74
3 RBB, Nov 1 1992, p545-546
4 WLB/R, Sep 1992, p112

DA 550 _____(LC)   DDC: **941.081**
The Encyclopedia of the Victorian World: A Reader's Companion to the People, Places, Events, and Everyday Life of the Victorian Era
Corey, Melinda and George Ochoa (eds). Holt, 1996. 544p. *Cloth:* $50.00.
Review Avg: 3.33   *OCLC:* 412   *Rating:* 4.15

Reviews
3 GSED, 1997, p239
4 LJ, May 1 1996, p86,88
3 RBB, Sep 15 1996, p282-282

DA 560 _____(LC)   DDC: **941.081**
The 1890s: An Encyclopedia of British Literature, Art, and Culture
Cevasco, G. A. (ed). Garland, 1993. 714p. *Cloth:* $95.00.
Note: Series— Garland Reference Library of the Humanities, vol. 1237.
Review Avg: 4.00   *OCLC:* 441   *Rating:* 4.88

Reviews
5 ARBA, 94:981
4 Choice, Dec 1993, p579
5 GSED, 1997, p510
3 LJ, Aug 1993, p92
3 RBB, Oct 1 1993, p382-382

DA 566 _____(LC)   DDC: **941.082**
Twentieth-Century Britain: An Encyclopedia
Leventhal, F. M. (ed). Garland, 1995. 902p. *Cloth:* $95.00.
Review Avg: 2.60   *OCLC:* 369   *Rating:* 3.34

Reviews
3 ARBA, 96:543
3 CRL, Sep 1996, p471
2 Choice, Feb 1996, p935
2 LJ, Nov 1 1995, p60
3 RBB, Feb 1 1996, p956

DA 757.9 _____(LC)   DDC: **941.1**
A Companion to Scottish History: From the Reformation to the Present
Donnachie, Ian and George Hewitt. Facts On File, 1990. 245p. *Cloth:* $27.50.
Review Avg: 3.00   *OCLC:* 453   *Rating:* 3.91

◆ The article titles in this encyclopedia are indexed by keyword in Part II.

Reviews
3 ARBA, 91:533
3 Choice, Sep 1990, p74
3 RBB, Aug 1990, p2198,2200

DA 772 _____(LC)   DDC: 422.3

Collins Encyclopaedia of Scotland
Keay, John and Julia Keay (eds). HarperCollins, 1994. 1046p. _Cloth:_
$60.00.
Review Avg: 3.33   _OCLC:_ 381   _Rating:_ 4.09

Reviews
3 ARBA, 96:148
4 Choice, Mar 1996, p1090
3 RBB, Jan 1 1996, p880

DA 890 _____(LC)   DDC: 941.3

Edinburgh Encyclopedia
Mullay, Sandy. Trafalgar Square, 1997. 384p. _Cloth:_ $39.95.
Review Avg: 3.00   _OCLC:_ 14   _Rating:_ 3.03

Reviews
3 ARBA, 98:137
3 Choice, Jul 1997, p1782

DA 912 _____(LC)   DDC: 941.5

Companion to Irish History, 1603-1921: From the Submission of Tyrone to Partition
Newman, Peter R. Facts On File, 1991. 244p. _Cloth:_ $27.95.
Review Avg: 3.33   _OCLC:_ 437   _Rating:_ 4.20

Reviews
4 ARBA, 93:539
3 Choice, Apr 1992, p1211
3 LJ, Oct 1 1991, p90

DC 33.2 _____(LC)   DDC: 944

Medieval France: An Encyclopedia
Kibler, William W. and others (eds). Garland, 1995. 1047p. _Cloth:_
$95.00.
Review Avg: 4.67   _OCLC:_ 589   _Rating:_ 5.85

Reviews
5 Choice, Nov 1995, p440
4 LJ, Jun 15 1995, p62
5 RQ, Win 1995, p259

DC 147 _____(LC)   DDC: 940.27

Dictionary of the Napoleonic Wars
Chandler, David G. Simon & Schuster, 1993. 570p. _Cloth:_ $60.00.
Review Avg: 3.00   _OCLC:_ 72   _Rating:_ 3.14

Reviews
3 ARBA, 94:521

DC 401 _____(LC)   DDC: 944.082

Historical Dictionary of the French Fourth and Fifth Republics, 1946-1990
Northcutt, Wayne. Greenwood, 1992. 527p. _Cloth:_ $89.50.
Review Avg: 3.50   _OCLC:_ 336   _Rating:_ 4.17

Reviews
3 Choice, Nov 1992, p442
4 LJ, Feb 15 1992, p160

DD 256.5 _____(LC)   DDC: 943.086

Encyclopedia of German Resistance to the Nazi Movement
Benz, Wolfgang and Walter H. Pehle (eds). Continuum, 1997. 354p.
Cloth: $39.50.
Review Avg: 3.33   _OCLC:_ 455   _Rating:_ 4.24

Reviews
2 ARBA, 98:470
4 Choice, May 1997, p1474
4 LJ, Dec 1996, p84

DD 256.5 _____(LC)   DDC: 943.086

The Encyclopedia of the Third Reich
Zentner, Christian and Friedemann Bedurftig. Macmillan, 1991. Revised edition. 2 vols. (1150p.) _Cloth:_ $200.00/set.
Review Avg: 4.33   _OCLC:_ 1009   _Rating:_ 12.35

Reviews	**Awards**
3 ARBA, 92:493	Choice/OAB, May 1992,
5 Choice, Jun 1991, p1615	p1341
4 GSED, 1997, p228	RBB/ORS, May 1 1992,
4 LJ, Apr 15 1991, p82	p1625
5 RBB, Jun 1 1991, p1891	
5 WLB/R, May 1991, p140	

DE 5 _____(LC)   DDC: 930

A Dictionary of Ancient History
Speake, Graham (ed). Blackwell, 1994. 758p. _Cloth:_ $59.95.
Review Avg: 3.00   _OCLC:_ 235   _Rating:_ 3.47

Reviews
3 ARBA, 95:583

DE 5 _____(LC)   DDC: 938

An Encyclopedia of the History of Classical Archaeology
De Grummond, Nancy Thomson. Greenwood, 1996. 2 vols. (1330p.)
Cloth: $225.00.
Review Avg: 3.50   _OCLC:_ 269   _Rating:_ 4.04

Reviews
3 Choice, May 1997, p1474-1475
4 RBB, Feb 1 1997, p964-965

DE 5 _____(LC)   DDC: 938

The Oxford Classical Dictionary
Hornblower, Simon and Antony Spawforth (eds). Oxford Un, 1996.
3rd ed. 1640p. _Cloth:_ $99.95.
Review Avg: 5.00   _OCLC:_ 1371   _Rating:_ 9.74

Reviews	**Awards**
5 Choice, May 1997, 3rd ed.	Choice/OAB, Jan 1998, p760
5 RBB, May 1 1997, p1533, 3rd ed.	

DF 16 _____(LC)   DDC: 938

Dictionary of the Ancient Greek World
Sacks, David. Oxford Un, 1995. 306p. _Cloth:_ $45.00.
Note: Originally entitled _Encyclopedia of the Ancient Greek World._
Review Avg: 3.75   _OCLC:_ 80   _Rating:_ 3.91

Reviews
4 ARBA, 97:450
3 Choice, Feb 1996, p932,934

4 LJ, Apr 15 1996, p74
4 RBB, Nov 1 1995, p502

DF 521 _____(LC) DDC: 949.5
The Oxford Dictionary of Byzantium
Kazhdan, Alexander P. and others. Oxford Un, 1991. 3 vols. *Cloth:* $275.00/set.
Review Avg: 4.00   *OCLC:* 1148   *Rating:* 10.30

Reviews	**Awards**
3 ARBA, 92:510	Choice/OAB, May 1992,
4 Choice, Oct 1991, p263	p1342
3 GSED, 1997, p249	LJ/BRS, Apr 15 1992,
5 LJ, Aug 1991, p88	p45-46
5 RBB, Sep 15 1991,	
p189-190	

DG 270 _____(LC) DDC: 937.06
Encyclopedia of the Roman Empire
Bunson, Matthew. Facts On File, 1994. 494p. *Cloth:* $50.00.
Review Avg: 3.00   *OCLC:* 869   *Rating:* 4.74

Reviews
3 ARBA, 95:579
3 Choice, Oct 1994, p256
3 GSED, 1997, p238
3 RBB, Jun 1 1994, p1874,1876

DJK 50 _____(LC) DDC: 947.08
Dictionary of East European History Since 1945
Held, Joseph. Greenwood, 1994. 509p. *Cloth:* $59.95.
Review Avg: 3.20   *OCLC:* 574   *Rating:* 4.35

Reviews
3 ARBA, 95:560
3 Choice, Apr 1995, p1276
3 GSED, 1997, p226
3 RBB, Feb 1 1995, p1024
4 WLB/R, Mar 1995, p84

DK 36 _____(LC) DDC: 947
Encyclopedia of Russian History: From the Christianization of Kiev to the Breakup of the USSR
Paxton, John. ABC-CLIO, 1993. 484p. *Cloth:* $65.00.
Note: Originally entitled *Companion to Russian History,* 1983.
Review Avg: 2.50   *OCLC:* 812   *Rating:* 4.12

Reviews
2 ARBA, 94:524
2 Choice, Feb 1994, p920
3 LJ, Dec 1993, p116
3 RBB, Jan 15 1994, p964

DK 286 _____(LC) DDC: 947.085
Russia and the Commonwealth A to Z
Wilson, Andrew and Nina Bachkatov. HarperCollins, 1992. 258p.
Cloth: $30.00. *Paper:* $15.00.
Review Avg: 3.00   *OCLC:* 536   *Rating:* 4.07

Reviews
3 ARBA, 94:525
3 Choice, Mar 1994, p1122,1124
3 RBB, Feb 1 1993, p1005

DL 30 _____(LC) DDC: 948.02
Medieval Scandinavia: An Encyclopedia
Pulsiano, Phillip (ed). Garland, 1993. 768p. *Cloth:* $95.00.
Note: Series—Garland Encyclopedias of the Middle Ages, vol. 1.
Review Avg: 3.75   *OCLC:* 348   *Rating:* 4.45

Reviews
3 ARBA, 94:526
4 Choice, Nov 1993, p437
4 GSED, 1997, p229
4 RQ, Spr 1994, p422

DP 56 _____(LC) DDC: 946
Historical Dictionary of the Spanish Empire, 1402-1975
Olson, James S. and others (eds). Greenwood, 1992. 701p. *Cloth:* $89.50.
Review Avg: 3.50   *OCLC:* 550   *Rating:* 6.60

Reviews	**Awards**
3 ARBA, 93:540	Choice/OAB, Jan 1993,
3 Choice, Apr 1992, p1209	p734
3 GSED, 1997, p230	
4 LJ, Jan 1992, p108	
4 RBB, Mar 15 1992, p1403	
4 WLB/R, Apr 1992, p125	

DP 192 _____(LC) DDC: 946
Historical Dictionary of Modern Spain, 1700-1988
Kern, Robert W. (ed). Greenwood, 1990. 697p. *Cloth:* $95.00.
Review Avg: 4.25   *OCLC:* 643   *Rating:* 5.54

Reviews
4 Choice, Jul/Aug 1990, p1806
4 GSED, 1997, p42
5 LJ, Feb 15 1990, p178,180
4 RBB, Jun 15 1990, p2030-2031

DS 33.4 _____(LC) DDC: 303.48
United States in Asia: A Historical Dictionary
Shavit, David. Greenwood, 1990. 620p. *Cloth:* $75.00.
Review Avg: 3.00   *OCLC:* 289   *Rating:* 3.58

Reviews
3 ARBA, 92:746
3 Choice, Apr 1991, p1293

DS 35.53 _____(LC) DDC: 909.976
The Oxford Encyclopedia of the Modern Islamic World
Esposito, John L. (ed). Oxford Un, 1995. 4 vols. *Cloth:* $395.00/set.
Review Avg: 4.25   *OCLC:* 1294   *Rating:* 10.84

Reviews	**Awards**
4 ARBA, 96:1477	LJ/BRS, Apr 15 1996,
4 CRL, Mar 1996, p187	p40
4 LJ, Mar 15 1995, p62	RBB/ORS, May 1 1996,
5 RBB, May 1 1995, p1588	p1536

DS 43 _____(LC) DDC: 956
An A to Z of the Middle East
Gresh, Alain and Dominique Vidal. Humanities, 1990. 261p. *Paper:* $15.00.
Note: Translation of *Les Cent Portes du Proche-Orient.*
Review Avg: 3.00   *OCLC:* 273   *Rating:* 3.55

◆ The article titles in this encyclopedia are indexed by keyword in Part II.

Reviews
3 ARBA, 92:118
3 Choice, May 1991, p1456,1458

DS 43 _____ (LC) **DDC: 956**
The Encyclopedia of the Modern Middle East, 1800-1994
Simon, Reeva S. and others (eds). Macmillan, 1996. 4 vols. (2182p.)
Cloth: $375.00/set.
Review Avg: 3.60   *OCLC:* 874   *Rating:* 5.35

Reviews	*Awards*
2 ARBA, 97:136	Choice/OAB, Jan 1998,
4 Choice, Feb 1997, p943	p760
4 GSED, 1997, p232	
4 LJ, Apr 15 1997, p64,66	
4 RBB, Nov 15 1996, p605	

DS 56 _____ (LC) **DDC: 939**
The Oxford Encyclopedia of Archaeology in the Near East
Meyers, Eric M. (ed). Oxford Un, 1997. 5 vols. (2608p.) *Cloth:*
$575.00.
Review Avg: 4.67   *OCLC:* 559   *Rating:* 5.79

Reviews	*Awards*
4 ARBA, 98:429	Choice/OAB, Jan 1998,
5 Choice, May 1997,	p760
p1478-1479	LJ/BRS, Apr 15 1998,
5 RBB, Mar 15 1997, p1260	p49

DS 61 _____ (LC) **DDC: 956**
The Middle East: A Political Dictionary
Ziring, Lawrence. ABC-CLIO, 1992. 401p. *Paper:* $29.95.
Review Avg: 3.33   *OCLC:* 650   *Rating:* 4.63

Reviews
3 ARBA, 93:776
4 Choice, Feb 1993, p948
3 GSED, 1997, p375
3 LJ, Jul 1992, p79
3 RBB, Sep 1 1992, p87
4 WLB/R, Dec 1992, p110

DS 63.1 _____ (LC) **DDC: 956**
The Middle East
Diller, Daniel C. and John L. Moore (eds). Congressional Quarterly,
1995. 8th ed. 432p. *Cloth:* $42.95.
Review Avg: 3.00   *OCLC:* 576   *Rating:* 6.15

Reviews
3 ARBA, 96:764

DS 102.8 _____ (LC) **DDC: 909**
The New Standard Jewish Encyclopedia
Wigoder, Geoffrey (ed). Facts On File, 1992. 7th ed. 1001p. *Cloth:*
$59.95.
Review Avg: 3.00   *OCLC:* 678   *Rating:* 6.36

Reviews
3 ARBA, 93:448
3 Choice, Apr 1993, p1298
3 GSED, 1997, p154,778
3 RBB, Jan 1 1993, p826

DS 111 _____ (LC) **DDC: 933**
*The New Encyclopedia of Archaeological Excavations in the
Holy Land*
Stern, Ephraim (ed). Macmillan, 1993. Revised edition. 4 vols. *Cloth:*
$375.00/set.
Note: Revision of *Encyclopedia of Archaeological Excavations in the
Holy Land.*
Review Avg: 4.50   *OCLC:* 560   *Rating:* 7.62

Reviews
5 ARBA, 94:489
5 Choice, Nov 1993, p437
3 GSED, 1997, p192
5 LJ, Sep 1 1993, p172,174
4 RBB, Dec 1 1993, p707
5 WLB/R, Oct 1993, p92-93

DS 119.7 _____ (LC) **DDC: 327.5694**
An Historical Encyclopedia of the Arab-Israeli Conflict
Reich, Bernard (ed). Greenwood, 1996. 655p. *Cloth:* $105.00.
Review Avg: 4.50   *OCLC:* 416   *Rating:* 5.33

Reviews
4 ARBA, 97:455
5 LJ, Jan 1996, p88

DS 126.5 _____ (LC) **DDC: 956.94**
Historical Dictionary of Israel
Reich, Bernard. Scarecrow, 1992. 353p. *Cloth:* $55.00.
Review Avg: 2.33   *OCLC:* 414   *Rating:* 3.16

Reviews
1 Choice, Apr 1993, p1299
3 LJ, Jan 1993, p104,105
3 RBB, Jan 1 1993, p825-826

DS 126.5 _____ (LC) **DDC: 956.94**
Political Dictionary of the State of Israel
Rolef, Susan Hattis (ed). Macmillan, 1993. 2nd ed. 417p. *Cloth:*
$75.00.
Review Avg: 3.50   *OCLC:* 210   *Rating:* 5.92

Reviews
3 ARBA, 94:785
3 Choice, Nov 1993, p437-438
4 GSED, 1997, p374
4 RQ, Spr 1994, p424

DS 149 _____ (LC) **DDC: 320.5**
New Encyclopedia of Zionism and Israel
Wigoder, Geoffrey (ed). Associated Un Presses, 1994. 2 vols. *Cloth:*
$185.00/set.
Review Avg: 3.33   *OCLC:* 275   *Rating:* 3.88

Reviews
3 ARBA, 96:164
4 Choice, Apr 1995, p1280
3 RBB, Feb 15 1995, p1111

DS 518.1 _____ (LC) **DDC: 959.05**
Dictionary of the Modern Politics of South-East Asia
Leifer, Michael. Routledge, 1995. 271p. *Cloth:* $59.95.
Review Avg: 4.00   *OCLC:* 359   *Rating:* 4.72

Reviews
4 ARBA, 96:747

DS 557 _____(LC)   **DDC: 939**
Civilizations of the Ancient Near East
Sasson, Jack M. (ed). Scribner's, 1995. 4 vols. *Cloth:* $449.00/set.
Review Avg: 4.33   *OCLC:* 861   *Rating:* 10.05

Reviews   *Awards*
5 ARBA, 96:159   Choice/OAB, Jan 1997,
4 RBB, Apr 15 1996,   p739
  p1456-1457   Dartmouth, 1996
4 WLB/R, 1995

DS 557.7 _____(LC)   **DDC: 959.704**
Encyclopedia of the Vietnam War
Kutler, Stanley I. (ed). Scribner's, 1996. 711p. *Cloth:* $99.00.
Review Avg: 4.20   *OCLC:* 914   *Rating:* 8.03

Reviews   *Awards*
3 ARBA, 97:433   NYPL, 1997
3 Choice, Jul 1996,   RBB/ORS, May 1 1997,
  p1771-1772   p1524
5 GSED, 1997, p327
5 LJ, Jan 1997, p86
5 RBB, May 1 1996, p1524

DS 740.2 _____(LC)   **DDC: 951**
Historical Dictionary of Revolutionary China, 1839-1976
Long, Edwin Pak-wah (ed). Greenwood, 1992. 566p. *Cloth:* $85.00.
Review Avg: 4.00   *OCLC:* 478   *Rating:* 6.96

Reviews   *Awards*
3 ARBA, 93:523   Choice/OAB, Jan 1993,
5 Choice, Oct 1992, p274   p734
4 RBB, Oct 1 1992, p369

DS 805 _____(LC)   **DDC: 952**
The Encyclopedia of Japan: Japanese History and Culture,
from Abacus to Zori
Perkins, Dorothy (ed). Facts On File, 1991. 410p. *Cloth:* $40.00.
Review Avg: 3.75   *OCLC:* 189   *Rating:* 4.13

Reviews
5 ARBA, 92:95
3 Choice, Sep 1991, p66
4 LJ, Nov 1 1990, p84
3 RBB, Feb 15 1991, p1246

DS 805 _____(LC)   **DDC: 952**
Japan: An Illustrated Encyclopedia
Macmillan, 1993. 2 vols. (1924p.) *Cloth:* $300.00/set.
Note: Revision of *Kodansha Encyclopedia of Japan.*
Review Avg: 4.33   *OCLC:* 939   *Rating:* 10.21

Reviews   *Awards*
5 ARBA, 94:115   LJ/BRS, Apr 15 1994,
4 Choice, Nov 1993, p436   p39
4 GSED, 1997, p30   RBB/ORS, May 1 1994,
5 LJ, Oct 1 1993, p86,89   p1627
4 RBB, Dec 15 1993, p778
4 RQ, Fall 1994, p108-109

DS 805 _____(LC)   **DDC: 952**
Japan Encyclopedia
De Mente, Boye Lafayette. Passport, 1995. 558p. *Cloth:* $27.95.
Note: Revision of *Passport's Japan Almanac.*
Review Avg: 3.00   *OCLC:* 264   *Rating:* 3.53

Reviews
4 ARBA, 97:109
1 Choice, Jan 1996, p754
4 RBB, Jan 1 1996, p884

DS 909 _____(LC)   **DDC: 951.9**
Historical Dictionary of the Republic of Korea
Nahm, Andrew C. Scarecrow, 1993. 272p. *Cloth:* $45.00.
Review Avg: 3.50   *OCLC:* 396   *Rating:* 4.29

Reviews
4 Choice, Nov 1993, p437
3 LJ, Jun 15 1993, p64

DS 918 _____(LC)   **DDC: 951.904**
Historical Dictionary of the Korean War
Matray, James (ed). Greenwood, 1991. 626p. *Cloth:* $85.00.
Review Avg: 3.60   *OCLC:* 755   *Rating:* 9.11

Reviews   *Awards*
3 ARBA, 92:648   Choice/OAB, Jan 1993,
4 Choice, Feb 1992,   p734
  p874,876   LJ/BRS, Apr 15 1992,
4 GSED, 1997, p329   p44
3 RBB, Nov 15 1991, p644
4 WLB/R, Jan 1992,
  p127-128

DS 918 _____(LC)   **DDC: 951.904**
The Korean War: An Encyclopedia
Sandler, Stanley (ed). Garland, 1995. 416p. *Cloth:* $85.00.
Note: Series—Military History of the United States.
Review Avg: 3.60   *OCLC:* 610   *Rating:* 4.82

Reviews
3 ARBA, 96:538
4 Choice, May 1996, p1452
3 GSED, 1997, p332
4 LJ, Feb 1 1996, p70
4 RBB, Mar 1 1996, p1212

DT 58 _____(LC)   **DDC: 932**
The Encyclopedia of Ancient Egypt
Bunson, Margaret. Facts On File, 1991. 291p. *Cloth:* $45.00.
Review Avg: 3.00   *OCLC:* 872   *Rating:* 4.74

Reviews
3 ARBA, 92:450
3 Choice, Mar 1992, p1040
3 GSED, 1997, p237
3 RBB, Sep 15 1991, p192-193

DU 90 _____(LC)   **DDC: 994**
Historical Dictionary of Australia
Docherty, James C. Scarecrow, 1992. 300p. *Cloth:* $35.00.
Review Avg: 3.00   *OCLC:* 287   *Rating:* 3.57

Reviews
3 ARBA, 94:124

◆ The article titles in this encyclopedia are indexed by keyword in Part II.

3 Choice, Jul/Aug 1993, p1748
3 RBB, Mar 15 1993, p1376-1377

DU 90 _____(LC)   **DDC: 994**

The Oxford Illustrated Dictionary of Australian History
Bassett, Jan. Oxford Un, 1993. 304p. *Cloth:* $49.95.
Review Avg: 4.00   *OCLC:* 186   *Rating:* 4.37

Reviews
5 ARBA, 94:516
4 Choice, Oct 1993, p262
3 GSED, 1997, p222

DU 112.3 _____(LC)   **DDC: 355**

The Oxford Companion to Australian Military History
Dennis, Peter and others. ABC-CLIO, 1995. 692p. *Cloth:* $75.00.
Review Avg: 4.00   *OCLC:* 84   *Rating:* 4.17

Reviews
4 ARBA, 97:563

E 20 _____(LC)   **DDC: 978**

The Cowboy Encyclopedia
Slatta, Richard W. ABC-CLIO, 1994. 474p. *Cloth:* $60.00.
Review Avg: 4.00   *OCLC:* 603   *Rating:* 9.21

Reviews   **Awards**
3 ARBA, 96:510   LJ/BRS, Apr 15 1995,
5 RBB, Apr 1 1995, p1440   p41
4 WLB/R, Apr 1995, p84   RBB/ORS, May 1 1995,
                        p1603

◆**E 45** _____(LC)   **DDC: 940**

Encyclopedia of the North American Colonies
Cooke, Jacob Ernest (ed). Scribner's, 1993. 3 vols. *Cloth:* $330.00/
set.
Review Avg: 4.63   *OCLC:* 1226   *Rating:* 15.08

Reviews   **Awards**
5 ARBA, 95:540   Choice/OAB, Jan 1995,
4 CRL, May 1994, p249-250   p719
5 Choice, May 1994, p1412   LJ/BRS, Apr 15 1994,
4 GSED, 1997, p197   p39
5 LJ, Jan 1994, p104   NYPL, 1994
5 RBB, Apr 1 1994, p1472   RBB/ORS, May 1 1995,
5 RQ, Sum 1994, p549-550   p1602
4 WLB/R, Feb 1994, p80

E 45 _____(LC)   **DDC: 970**

Great Events from History: North American Series
Magill, Frank N. and John L. Loos (eds). Salem, 1997. Revised
edition. 4 vols. *Cloth:* $300.00.
Review Avg: 4.00   *OCLC:* 463   *Rating:* 6.93

Reviews
4 ARBA, 98:497

E 46.5 _____(LC)   **DDC: 970**

*Colonial Wars of North America, 1512-1763: An Encyclope-
dia*
Gallay, Alan (ed). Garland, 1996. 2 vols. *Cloth:* $150.00.
Review Avg: 4.00   *OCLC:* 187   *Rating:* 4.37

Reviews
4 GSED, 1997, p323

E 61 _____(LC)   **DDC: 970.01**

*Legend and Lore of the Americas Before 1492: An Encyclo-
pedia of Visitors, Explorers and Immigrants*
Fritze, Ronald H. ABC-CLIO, 1993. 319p. *Cloth:* $65.00.
Review Avg: 4.00   *OCLC:* 555   *Rating:* 5.11

Reviews
5 ARBA, 94:417
3 Choice, Dec 1993, p584
5 GSED, 1997, p142
3 RBB, Nov 1 1993, p568
4 WLB/R, Nov 1993, p105

E 76.2 _____(LC)   **DDC: 970**

American Indians
Dawson, Dawn P. Salem, 1995. 3 vols. *Cloth:* $270.00/set.
Review Avg: 3.75   *OCLC:* 683   *Rating:* 7.12

Reviews   **Awards**
3 ARBA, 96:417   RBB/ORS, May 1 1996,
4 Choice, Oct 1995, p259   p1536
4 RBB, Sep 1 1995, p100
4 RQ, Win 1995, p249

E 76.2 _____(LC)   **DDC: 970.004**

The Encyclopedia of North American Indians
Hoxie, Frederick (ed.). Cavendish, 1997. 11 vols. (1540p.) *Cloth:*
$459.95.
Review Avg: 3.75   *OCLC:* 335   *Rating:* 4.42

Reviews
5 ARBA, 98:354
3 Choice, Sep 1997, p106
3 LJ, May 1 1997, p96
4 RBB, Sep 1 1997, p164

E 76.2 _____(LC)   **DDC: 970.004**

*Encyclopedia of North American Indians: Native American
History, Culture, and Life from Paleo-Indians to the Present*
Hoxie, Frederick E. Houghton, 1996. 756p. *Cloth:* $45.00.
Review Avg: 4.00   *OCLC:* 282   *Rating:* 6.56

Reviews   **Awards**
4 ARBA, 98:353   Choice/OAB, Jan 1998,
4 Choice, Apr 1997, p1307   p759
5 LJ, Dec 1996, p84   LJ/BRS, Apr 15 1997,
3 RBB, Dec 15 1996, p747   p39

◆**E 76.2** _____(LC)   **DDC: 970.004**

Native America in the Twentieth Century: An Encyclopedia
Davis, Mary B. (ed). Garland, 1994. 787p. *Cloth:* $95.00. *Paper:*
$24.95.
Note: Series—Garland Reference Library of Social Science, vol. 452.
Review Avg: 4.29   *OCLC:* 1364   *Rating:* 9.02

Reviews   **Awards**
5 ARBA, 95:434   LJ/BRS, Apr 15 1995,
4 Choice, Feb 1995, p918   p40
5 GSED, 1997, p141
3 LJ, Oct 15 1994, p72
4 LJ, Jan 1995, p90

4 RBB, Dec 1 1994, p707
5 WLB/R, Dec 1994, p74

E 76.2 _____(LC)   **DDC: 970.004**
The Native Tribes of North America: A Concise Encyclopedia
Johnson, Michael G. Macmillan, 1994. 210p. *Cloth:* $70.00.
Review Avg: 2.75   *OCLC:* 807   *Rating:* 4.36

Reviews
3 ARBA, 95:435
3 Choice, Jun 1994, p1556
2 GSED, 1997, p145
3 RBB, May 1 1994, p1634

E 76.2 _____(LC)   **DDC: 970.004**
Scholastic Encyclopedia of the North American Indian
Ciment, James. Scholastic, 1996. 224p. *Cloth:* $17.95.
Review Avg: 4.00   *OCLC:* 534   *Rating:* 5.07

Reviews
4 ARBA, 98:355

E 76.2 _____(LC)   **DDC: 970.004**
World Dance: The Language of Native American Culture
Waldman, Carl. Facts On File, 1994. 290p. *Cloth:* $25.95.
Review Avg: 3.50   *OCLC:* 0   *Rating:* 3.50

Reviews
4 ARBA, 95:437
3 LJ, Oct 15 1994, p72

E 77 _____(LC)   **DDC: 970.004**
The Native North American Almanac
Champagne, Duane (ed). Multiculture, 1994. 4 vols. *Cloth:* $95.00.
Review Avg: 3.25   *OCLC:* 77   *Rating:* 3.40

Reviews
4 Choice, May 1994, p1419
3 LJ, May 1 1994, p96
3 RBB, May 1 1994, p1634
3 RBB, Feb 1 1995, p1023-1024

E 83.876 _____(LC)   **DDC: 973.8**
Custer and the Battle of the Little Bighorn: An Encyclopedia of the People, Places, Events, Indian Culture and Customs, Information Sources, Art and Films
Hatch, Thom. McFarland, 1997. 229p. *Cloth:* $45.00.
Review Avg: 4.00   *OCLC:* 194   *Rating:* 4.39

Reviews
4 ARBA, 98:441
4 LJ, Feb 15 1997, p127-128

E 98 _____(LC)   **DDC: 391.0089**
Encyclopedia of American Indian Costume
Paterek, Josephine. ABC-CLIO, 1994. 516p. *Cloth:* $79.50.
Review Avg: 3.60   *OCLC:* 1243   *Rating:* 12.09

Reviews   **Awards**
3 ARBA, 95:442   Choice/OAB, Jan 1995,
4 Choice, Sep 1994, p76   p721
3 GSED, 1997, p147   LJ/BRS, Apr 15 1995,
3 RBB, Sep 1 1994, p68   p40-41

5 RQ, Win 1994, p238   RBB/ORS, May 1 1995,
                                p1603

E 98 _____(LC)   **DDC: 615.8**
Encyclopedia of Native American Healing
Lyon, William S. ABC-CLIO, 1996. 373p. *Cloth:* $55.00.
Review Avg: 3.33   *OCLC:* 387   *Rating:* 4.10

Reviews
4 ARBA, 97:340
3 Choice, Jul 1997, p1780
3 LJ, Mar 15 1997, p56

E 98 _____(LC)   **DDC: 299.7**
The Encyclopedia of Native American Religions: An Introduction
Hirschfelder, Arlene and Paulette Molin. Facts On File, 1992. 367p. *Cloth:* $50.00.
Review Avg: 3.63   *OCLC:* 1473   *Rating:* 8.58

Reviews   **Awards**
3 ARBA, 93:432   NYPL, 1994
4 Choice, Oct 1992, p274
4 GSED, 1997, p144
3 JAL, May 1993, p130-131
4 LJ, Jul 1992, p76,78
3 RBB, May 15 1992, p1716
3 RBB, Jun 1993,
  p1879-1880
5 RQ, Win 1992, p278-279

◆**E 111** _____(LC)   **DDC: 970.015**
The Christopher Columbus Encyclopedia
Bedini, Silvio A. (ed). Simon & Schuster, 1992. 2 vols. (787p.) *Cloth:* $175.00/set.
Review Avg: 4.00   *OCLC:* 1164   *Rating:* 10.33

Reviews   **Awards**
3 ARBA, 92:415   LJ/BRS, Apr 15 1992,
3 Choice, Feb 1992, p872   p42
4 GSED, 1997, p171   NYPL, 1992
5 LJ, Oct 1 1991, p88
5 WLB/R, Jan 1992, p126

E 111 _____(LC)   **DDC: 970.015**
Columbus Dictionary
Provost, Foster. Omnigraphics, 1991. 142p. *Cloth:* $54.00.
Review Avg: 3.33   *OCLC:* 347   *Rating:* 4.02

Reviews
3 ARBA, 93:517
3 GSED, 1997, p199
4 WLB/R, Mar 1992, p114

E 156 _____(LC)   **DDC: 973**
Worldmark Encyclopedia of the States
Cal, Timothy L. Gale Research, 1995. 3rd ed. 758p. *Cloth:* $135.00.
Review Avg: 3.00   *OCLC:* 917   *Rating:* 6.83

Reviews
3 Choice, Jun 1995, p1581-1582

◆ The article titles in this encyclopedia are indexed by keyword in Part II.

E 169.02 _____ (LC)   DDC: 973.923

The ABC-CLIO Companion to the 1960s Counterculture in America

Hamilton, Neil A. ABC-CLIO, 1997. 386p. *Cloth:* $60.00.
Note: Series—Companions to Key Issues in American History and Life.
Review Avg: 3.50   *OCLC:* 175   *Rating:* 3.85

Reviews
3 ARBA, 98:437
4 LJ, Nov 15 1997, p52

E 169.1 _____ (LC)   DDC: 001.1

A Companion to American Thought

Fox, Richard Wrightman and James T. Kloppenberg (eds). Blackwell, 1995. 804p. *Cloth:* $39.95.
Review Avg: 4.25   *OCLC:* 848   *Rating:* 5.95

Reviews
4 CRL, Sep 1996, p472
4 Choice, Mar 1996, p1090
5 LJ, Nov 1 1995, p58
4 RBB, Feb 1 1996, p952

E 169.1 _____ (LC)   DDC: 973.8

The Gay Nineties in America: A Cultural Dictionary of the 1890s

Gale, Robert L. Greenwood, 1992. 457p. *Cloth:* $75.00.
Review Avg: 3.00   *OCLC:* 439   *Rating:* 3.88

Reviews
3 ARBA, 93:518
3 LJ, Sep 1 1992, p166,168
3 RBB, Oct 15 1992, p453

E 169.12 _____ (LC)   DDC: 306.09

Dictionary of Twentieth Century Culture: American Culture After World War II

Rood, Karen L. (ed). Gale Research, 1994. 393p. *Cloth:* $60.00.
Review Avg: 3.33   *OCLC:* 71   *Rating:* 3.47

Reviews
3 ARBA, 95:927
4 Choice, Feb 1995, p914
4 GSED, 1997, p514
3 LJ, Jan 1995, p82,84
3 RBB, Dec 1 1994, p701
3 WLB/R, Dec 1994, p71

E 169.12 _____ (LC)   DDC: 306

The Encyclopedia of Bad Taste

Stern, Jane and Michael Stern. Harper Perennial, 1991. 331p. *Paper:* $29.99.
Review Avg: 2.00   *OCLC:* 684   *Rating:* 3.37

Reviews
1 Choice, Mar 1991, p1108
1 LJ, Nov 1 1990, p86
4 WLB/R, Feb 1991, p138-139

E 169.12 _____ (LC)   DDC: 973

Encyclopedia of Rural America: The Land and People

Goreham, Gary A. (ed). ABC-CLIO, 1997. 2 vols. (861p.) *Cloth:* $175.00.
Review Avg: 3.00   *OCLC:* 204   *Rating:* 3.41

Reviews
3 ARBA, 98:98

E 169.12 _____ (LC)   DDC: 973.9

Jane and Michael Stern's Encyclopedia of Pop Culture

Stern, Jane and Michael Stern. Harper Perennial, 1992. 593p. *Cloth:* $35.00. *Paper:* $17.50.
Review Avg: 3.00   *OCLC:* 691   *Rating:* 4.38

Reviews
2 LJ, Oct 15 1992, p64
4 WLB/R, Feb 1993, p105-106

◆**E 174** _____ (LC)   DDC: 973

Dictionary of American History

Adams, James T. (ed). Macmillan, 1996. 8 vols. *Cloth:* $525.00/set.
Note: Supplement, 2 vols., 1996, $180.00.
Review Avg: 4.00   *OCLC:* 2129   *Rating:* 8.26

Reviews
4 ARBA, 97:414
4 Choice, May 1996, p1455-1456
4 Choice, Jan 1997, p768, supp.
4 RBB, Nov 1 1996, p534

E 174 _____ (LC)   DDC: 973

The Encyclopedic Dictionary of American History

Faragher, John Mack (ed). Dushkin, 1991. 4th ed. 344p. *Cloth:* $17.95. *Paper:* $12.95.
Note: Series—Encyclopedic Dictionary Reference Set, vol. 2.
Review Avg: 3.00   *OCLC:* 212   *Rating:* 5.42

Reviews
3 RBB, Apr 15 1992, p1549

◆**E 174** _____ (LC)   DDC: 973

The Reader's Companion to American History

Foner, Eric and John Garraty. Houghton, 1991. 1226p. *Cloth:* $35.00.
Review Avg: 3.60   *OCLC:* 1794   *Rating:* 13.19

Reviews	**Awards**
3 ARBA, 92:468	Dartmouth, 1992
3 Choice, Feb 1992, p878	LJ/BRS, Apr 15 1992,
4 LJ, Nov 1 1991, p90	p46
4 RBB, Jan 1 1992,	NYPL, 1992
p851-852	
4 WLB/R, Jan 1992, p129	

E 174.5 _____ (LC)   DDC: 973

Encyclopedia of American History

Morris, Richard B. and Jeffrey B. Morris. HarperCollins, 1996. 7th ed. 1278p. *Cloth:* $50.00/O.P.
Review Avg: 3.00   *OCLC:* 560   *Rating:* 6.12

Reviews
3 GSED, 1997, p209

E 176.1 _____(LC)   DDC: 923.173

American Presidents

Whitney, David C. Reader's Digest, 1996. 7th ed. 562p. _Cloth:_ $17.50.

Review Avg: 2.50   _OCLC:_ 178   _Rating:_ 4.86

Reviews
2 ARBA, 91:496
3 RBB, Jun 1 1990, p1875

E 178 _____(LC)   DDC: 973

Great Events from History: American Series

Magill, Frank N. (ed). Salem, 1997. 4 vols. _Cloth:_ $300.00/set.

Review Avg: 3.67   _OCLC:_ 1072   _Rating:_ 5.81

Reviews
3 ARBA, 92:1465
5 Choice, Oct 1997, p276,278
3 RBB, Aug 1997, p1925-1926

E 180 _____(LC)   DDC: 973

Facts About the States

Kane, Joseph Nathan. Wilson, 1993. 2nd ed. 624p. _Cloth:_ $60.00.

Review Avg: 3.67   _OCLC:_ 925   _Rating:_ 7.52

Reviews
5 ARBA, 90:706
3 Choice, Feb 1990, p932
3 RBB, Aug 1994, p2070, 2nd ed.

E 181 _____(LC)   DDC: 973

Reference Guide to United States Military History

Shrader, Charles R. (ed). Facts On File, 1991. 5 vols. _Cloth:_ $60.00/vol.

Review Avg: 3.63   _OCLC:_ 667   _Rating:_ 4.96

Reviews
4 ARBA, 94:501-2
3 Choice, Nov 1993, p438, v. 2-3
3 Choice, Jul/Aug 1994, p1706, v. 4
4 LJ, Apr 1 1993, p94, v. 2-3
4 LJ, May 1 1994, p97, v. 4
4 LJ, Apr 15 1991, p86, v. 1
4 RBB, Nov 1 1993, p569, v. 2-3
3 RBB, Jul 1991, p2071, v. 1

E 183.7 _____(LC)   DDC: 327.73

Dictionary of American Foreign Affairs

Flanders, Stephen A. and Carl N. Flanders. Macmillan, 1993. 833p. _Cloth:_ $100.00.

Review Avg: 3.50   _OCLC:_ 726   _Rating:_ 4.95

Reviews
3 ARBA, 94:731
3 Choice, Oct 1993, p266
4 GSED, 1997, p360
4 LJ, Sep 1 1993, p170
3 RBB, Dec 1 1993, p709-710
4 WLB/R, Oct 1993, p86-88

E 183.7 _____(LC)   DDC: 327.73

Encyclopedia of U.S. Foreign Relations

Jentleson, Bruce W. and Thomas G. Paterson (eds). Oxford Un, 1997. 4 vols. (1936p.) _Cloth:_ $450.00.

Review Avg: 4.50   _OCLC:_ 865   _Rating:_ 6.23

Reviews	_Awards_
4 ARBA, 98:660	Choice/OAB, Jan 1998, p760
5 Choice, Sep 1997, p106	LJ/BRS, Apr 15 1998, p47
5 LJ, Apr 1 1997, p82	RBB/ORS, May 1 1998, p1538
4 RBB, Oct 1 1997, p353	

E 184 _____(LC)   DDC: 973.0495

The Asian American Encyclopedia

Ng, Franklin (ed). Cavendish, 1995. 6 vols. _Cloth:_ $459.95/set.

Review Avg: 4.20   _OCLC:_ 509   _Rating:_ 7.22

Reviews	_Awards_
5 ARBA, 96:394	Choice/OAB, Jan 1996, p723
4 Choice, May 1995, p1422	
3 RBB, May 1 1995, p1590,1592	
4 RQ, Fall 1995, p109	
5 WLB/R, Apr 1995, p83	

E 184 _____(LC)   DDC: 306.4

Encyclopedia of Multiculturalism

Auerbach, Susan (ed). Cavendish, 1994. 6 vols. _Cloth:_ $459.95/set.

Review Avg: 3.80   _OCLC:_ 865   _Rating:_ 7.53

Reviews	_Awards_
3 ARBA, 95:396	Choice/OAB, Jan 1995, p719
5 Choice, Jul/Aug 1994, p1700	
3 GSED, 1997, p135	
4 LJ, Apr 15 1994, p64	
4 RBB, May 1 1994, p1618-1620	

◆**E 184** _____(LC)   DDC: 305.8

Gale Encyclopedia of Multicultural America

Galens, Judy and others (eds). Gale Research, 1995. 2 vols. (1477p.) _Cloth:_ $125.00/set.

Review Avg: 4.33   _OCLC:_ 1515   _Rating:_ 15.36

Reviews	_Awards_
4 ARBA, 96:387	Choice/OAB, Jan 1997, p740
4 Choice, Apr 1996, p1286	LJ/BRS, Apr 15 1996, p40
5 LJ, Apr 15 1996	NYPL, 1995
4 LJ, Nov 1 1995, p58	RBB/ORS, May 1 1996, p1536
5 RBB, Dec 1 1995, p658	
4 WLB/R, 1996	

E 184 _____(LC)   DDC: 973.0468

The Hispanic-American Almanac: A Reference Work on Hispanics in the United States

Kanellos, Nicolas (ed). Gale Research, 1993. 780p. _Cloth:_ $29.00.

Review Avg: 4.33   _OCLC:_ 400   _Rating:_ 7.13

Reviews	_Awards_
3 Choice, Jul/Aug 1993, p1752	NYPL, 1993
5 LJ, Apr 15 1993, p86	
5 RBB, Apr 15 1993, p1536	

◆ The article titles in this encyclopedia are indexed by keyword in Part II.

E 184 _____(LC)   DDC: 973.0495

Japanese American History: An A-to-Z Reference from 1868 to the Present

Niiya, Brian (ed). Facts On File, 1993. 386p. *Cloth:* $50.00.

Review Avg: 4.20   *OCLC:* 1141   *Rating:* 10.48

Reviews	Awards
4 ARBA, 94:423	Choice/OAB, Jan 1995,
4 Choice, Feb 1994, p916	p719
5 LJ, Jul 1993, p71	RBB/ORS, May 1 1994,
3 RBB, Nov 1 1993,	p1627
p567-568	
5 RQ, Sum 1994, p555-556	

E 184 _____(LC)   DDC: 973.04924

Jewish-American History and Culture: An Encyclopedia

Fischel, Jack and Sanford Pinsker (eds). Garland, 1992. 710p. *Cloth:* $95.00.

Review Avg: 3.80   *OCLC:* 786   *Rating:* 7.37

Reviews	Awards
3 ARBA, 93:442	RBB/ORS, May 1 1993,
4 CRL, Sep 1992, p419-420	p1620
4 Choice, May 1992, p1370	
4 LJ, Aug 1992, p90	
4 RBB, May 1 1992, p1629	

E 184 _____(LC)   DDC: 973.0468

Latino Encyclopedia

Chabran, Richard and Rafael Chabran. Cavendish, 1996. 6 vols. *Cloth:* $459.95/set.

Review Avg: 3.50   *OCLC:* 328   *Rating:* 4.16

Reviews
4 ARBA, 97:337
2 Choice, Sep 1996, p100
3 LJ, Mar 1 1996, p74
5 RBB, Apr 15 1996, p1461-1462

E 185 _____(LC)   DDC: 973.0496

The African American Encyclopedia

Williams, Michael W. (ed). Cavendish, 1997. 6 vols. (1818p.) *Cloth:* $459.95/set.

Note: Supplement, 2 vols., 1997, $149.95.

Review Avg: 3.80   *OCLC:* 1052   *Rating:* 7.90

Reviews	Awards
4 ARBA, 94:402	NYPL, 1994
4 ARBA, 98:336, supp.	
3 Choice, Nov 1993, p423	
3 Choice, May 1997, p1471,	
supp.: v.7, v.8	
4 GSED, 1997, p137	
4 JAL, Sep 1993, p274	
3 LJ, Sep 1 1993, p168	
4 LJ, Jan 1997, p82, supp.	
5 RBB, Jul 1993,	
p1998,2000	
4 WLB/R, Oct 1993, p85	

E 185 _____(LC)   DDC: 305.896

Encyclopedia of African-American Civil Rights: From Emancipation to the Present

Lowery, Charles D. and John F. Marszalek. Greenwood, 1992. 658p. *Cloth:* $59.95.

Review Avg: 4.00   *OCLC:* 1663   *Rating:* 11.33

Reviews	Awards
5 ARBA, 93:616	LJ/BRS, Apr 15 1993,
4 Choice, Dec 1992, p600	p58
4 GSED, 1997, p365	NYPL, 1993
4 LJ, May 1 1992, p74	
4 RBB, Aug 1992, p2036	
3 RQ, Win 1992, p278	
4 WLB/R, Oct 1992, p107	

◆**E 185** _____(LC)   DDC: 973.0496

The Encyclopedia of African-American Culture and History

Salzman, Jack and others (eds). Macmillan, 1996. 5 vols. (3203p.) *Cloth:* $475.00/set.

Review Avg: 4.80   *OCLC:* 1485   *Rating:* 17.77

Reviews	Awards
5 ARBA, 97:332	Choice/OAB, Jan 1997,
4 Choice, Sep 1996, p95	p740
5 GSED, 1997, p200	Dartmouth, 1997
5 LJ, Jul 1996, p100,102	LJ/BRS, Apr 15 1997,
5 RBB, Feb 15 1996, p1037	p37
	NYPL, 1996
	RBB/ORS, May 1 1997,
	p1524

E 185 _____(LC)   DDC: 973.0496

The Encyclopedia of African-American Heritage

Altman, Susan. Facts On File, 1997. 308p. *Cloth:* $37.95.

Review Avg: 3.33   *OCLC:* 201   *Rating:* 3.73

Reviews
4 ARBA, 98:338
3 Choice, Oct 1997, p263
3 RBB, Mar 15 1997, p1256

E 185.61 _____(LC)   DDC: 305.896

The ABC-CLIO Companion to the Civil Rights Movement

Grossman, Mark. ABC-CLIO, 1993. 263p. *Cloth:* $55.00.

Note: Series—ABC-CLIO Companions to Key Issues in American History and Life.

Review Avg: 2.75   *OCLC:* 561   *Rating:* 3.87

Reviews
3 ARBA, 95:627
2 Choice, Jun 1994, p1554,1556
3 RBB, Mar 1 1994, p1278
3 WLB/R, Apr 1994, p87

E 185.61 _____(LC)   DDC: 323.1

Historical Dictionary of the Civil Rights Movement

Luker, Ralph E. Scarecrow, 1997. 331p. *Cloth:* $68.00.

Note: Series—Historical Dictionaries of Religions, Philosophies, and Movements.

Review Avg: 2.50   *OCLC:* 350   *Rating:* 3.20

Reviews
2 Choice, Nov 1997, p461
3 RBB, Feb 15 1997, p1042

◆**E 185.86**_____(LC)   **DDC: 920.7208**
Black Women in America: An Historical Encyclopedia
Hine, Darlene Clark Hine (ed). Carlson, 1993. 2 vols. *Cloth:* $195.00/set.
Review Avg: 4.25   *OCLC:* 1943   *Rating:* 18.14

Reviews	*Awards*
5 ARBA, 94:965	Choice/OAB, Jan 1994,
4 Choice, Jun 1993, p1596	p712
4 GSED, 1997, p500	Dartmouth, 1994
3 JAL, Jul 1993, p200	LJ/BRS, Apr 15 1994,
5 LJ, Feb 15 1993, p156	p38
5 RBB, May 1 1993,	NYPL, 1994
p1614,1616	RBB/ORS, May 1 1994,
4 RQ, Sum 1993, p561	p1627
4 WLB/R, May 1993, p113	

E 185.96_____(LC)   **DDC: 920.7208**
The Facts On File Encyclopedia of Black Women
Hine, Darlene Clark and Kathleen Thompson. Facts On File, 1997. 11 vols. *Cloth:* $296.50.
Review Avg: 3.00   *OCLC:* 288   *Rating:* 3.58

Reviews
3 ARBA, 98:343
3 LJ, Apr 15 1997, p66,68

E 208_____(LC)   **DDC: 973.3**
The American Revolution, 1775-1783: An Encyclopedia
Blanco, Richard L. Garland, 1993. 2 vols. (1896p.) *Cloth:* $175.00/set.
Note: Series—Military History of the United States, vol. 1.
Review Avg: 3.38   *OCLC:* 943   *Rating:* 9.27

Reviews	*Awards*
3 ARBA, 94:503	Choice/OAB, Jan 1994,
3 CRL, Sep 1993, p433-434	p711
4 Choice, Oct 1993, p261	LJ/BRS, Apr 15 1994,
3 GSED, 1997, p194	p38
3 GSED, 1997, p320	
4 LJ, Jul 1993, p66	
3 RBB, Oct 15 1993, p465	
4 WLB/R, Sep 1993, p114	

E 208_____(LC)   **DDC: 973.3**
The Blackwell Encyclopedia of the American Revolution
Greene, Jack P. and J. R. Pole (eds). Blackwell, 1991. 845p. *Cloth:* $54.95. *Paper:* $26.95.
Review Avg: 3.75   *OCLC:* 505   *Rating:* 4.76

Reviews
3 ARBA, 92:470
3 GSED, 1997, p193
5 LJ, Oct 1 1991, p88
4 RBB, Nov 15 1991, p640

E 208_____(LC)   **DDC: 973.3**
Encyclopedia of the American Revolution
Boatner, Mark Mayo. Stackpole, 1994. 3rd ed. 1290p. *Cloth:* $9.98.
Review Avg: 3.00   *OCLC:* 774   *Rating:* 6.55

Reviews
3 ARBA, 96:506

E 342_____(LC)   **DDC: 973.4**
James Madison and the American Nation, 1751-1836: An Encyclopedia
Rutland, Robert A. (ed). Simon & Schuster, 1994. 509p. *Cloth:* $99.00.
Review Avg: 4.00   *OCLC:* 508   *Rating:* 5.02

Reviews
4 ARBA, 96:507
4 LJ, Mar 15 1995, p61
4 RBB, Mar 15 1995, p1350-1351
4 WLB/R, May 1995, p75

E 354_____(LC)   **DDC: 973.5**
Encyclopedia of the War of 1812
Heidler, David S. and Jeanne T. Heidler (eds). ABC-CLIO, 1997. 636p. *Cloth:* $95.00.
Review Avg: 3.00   *OCLC:* 166   *Rating:* 3.33

Reviews
3 ARBA, 98:612

◆**E 441**_____(LC)   **DDC: 305.5**
Dictionary of Afro-American Slavery
Miller, Randall and John David Smith. Praeger, 1997. Revised edition. 892p. *Cloth:* $99.50. *Paper:* $35.00.
Review Avg: 3.50   *OCLC:* 1369   *Rating:* 8.24

Reviews
3 ARBA, 90:493
4 GSED, 1997, p208

E 456_____(LC)   **DDC: 973.7**
The American Civil War: A Multicultural Encyclopedia
Civil War Society. Grolier, 1994. 7 vols. *Cloth:* $169.00/set.
Review Avg: 3.00   *OCLC:* 283   *Rating:* 3.57

Reviews
3 ARBA, 96:504
3 RBB, Feb 1 1995, p1021

E 487_____(LC)   **DDC: 973.713**
Encyclopedia of the Confederacy
Current, Richard N. and others (eds). Scribner's, 1993. 4 vols. *Cloth:* $365.00/set.
Review Avg: 4.17   *OCLC:* 1083   *Rating:* 12.34

Reviews	*Awards*
5 ARBA, 94:506	Choice/OAB, Jan 1995,
4 CRL, Sep 1994, p420-421	p719
4 Choice, Feb 1994, p913	LJ/BRS, Apr 15 1994,
4 GSED, 1997, p202	p39
4 LJ, Jan 1994, p100	RBB/ORS, May 1 1994,
4 RBB, Feb 1 1994, p1021	p1627

E 668_____(LC)   **DDC: 973.8**
The ABC-CLIO Companion to American Reconstruction, 1863-1877
Richter, William L. ABC-CLIO, 1996. 505p. *Cloth:* $60.00.

◆ The article titles in this encyclopedia are indexed by keyword in Part II.

Note: Series—ABC-CLIO Companions to Key Issues in American History and Life.
Review Avg: 4.67   *OCLC:* 432   *Rating:* 5.53

Reviews
5 ARBA, 97:420
5 Choice, Jun 1997, p1644
4 LJ, Mar 15 1997, p58

Awards
Choice/OAB, Jan 1998,
  p760

E 668   (LC)   DDC: 973.8
Historical Dictionary of Reconstruction
Trefousse, Hans L. Greenwood, 1991. 284p. *Cloth:* $65.00.
Review Avg: 3.60   *OCLC:* 573   *Rating:* 4.75

Reviews
3 ARBA, 92:469
3 Choice, Jan 1992, p728
4 GSED, 1997, p215
5 LJ, Sep 1 1991, p186
3 RBB, Dec 1 1991, p721

E 715   (LC)   DDC: 973.8
Historical Dictionary of the Spanish American War
Dyal, Donald H. Greenwood, 1996. 378p. *Cloth:* $89.50.
Review Avg: 3.00   *OCLC:* 292   *Rating:* 3.58

Reviews
3 Choice, Dec 1996, p589

◆**E 740.7**   (LC)   DDC: 973
Encyclopedia of the United States in the Twentieth Century
Kutler, Stanley I. and others (ed). Macmillan, 1996. 4 vols. *Cloth:* $385.00/set.
Review Avg: 4.20   *OCLC:* 635   *Rating:* 9.47

Reviews
4 ARBA, 97:416
5 Choice, Apr 1996, p1284
4 GSED, 1997, p206
4 RBB, Mar 1 1996,
  p1205-1206
4 RQ, Sum 1996, p556-557

Awards
Choice/OAB, Jan 1997,
  p740
LJ/BRS, Apr 15 1997,
  p39

E 743.5   (LC)   DDC: 973.918
Encyclopedia of the McCarthy Era
Klingaman, William K. Facts On File, 1996. 502p. *Cloth:* $50.00.
Review Avg: 3.67   *OCLC:* 531   *Rating:* 6.73

Reviews
4 ARBA, 97:591
4 LJ, Sep 1 1996, p168,170
3 RBB, Sep 1 1996, p165

Awards
RBB/ORS, May 1 1997,
  p1524

E 745   (LC)   DDC: 973.8
The War of 1898 and U.S. Interventions 1898-1934: An Encyclopedia
Beede, Benjamin R. (ed). Garland, 1994. 751p. *Cloth:* $95.00.
Note: Series—Military History of the United States, vol. 2; Garland Reference Library of the Humanities, vol. 933.
Review Avg: 3.00   *OCLC:* 214   *Rating:* 3.43

Reviews
3 ARBA, 95:685
3 GSED, 1997, p319

E 838.6   (LC)   DDC: 973.9
A Dictionary of Contemporary American History: 1945 to the Present
Hochman, Stanley and Eleanor Hochman. NAL, 1993. 624p. *Paper:* $7.99.
Note: Originally entitled *Yesterday and Today: A Dictionary of Recent American History.*
Review Avg: 4.00   *OCLC:* 513   *Rating:* 5.03

Reviews
4 LJ, Oct 1 1993, p86

E 839.5   (LC)   DDC: 320.973
Encyclopedia of American Political Reform
Clucas, Richard A. ABC-CLIO, 1996. 346p. *Cloth:* $60.00.
Review Avg: 4.00   *OCLC:* 369   *Rating:* 4.74

Reviews
4 ARBA, 98:657
4 Choice, Jun 1997,
  p1636-1637

Awards
Choice/OAB, Jan 1998,
  p759

E 876   (LC)   DDC: 973.927
The Reagan Years A to Z: An Alphabetical History of Ronald Reagan's Presidency
Kurz, Kenneth Franklin. Lowell House, 1996. 288p. *Cloth:* $30.00.
Review Avg: 3.00   *OCLC:* 72   *Rating:* 3.14

Reviews
3 ARBA, 97:592

F 128.3   (LC)   DDC: 974.71
The Encyclopedia of New York City
Jackson, Kenneth T. (ed). Yale Un, 1995. 1350p. *Cloth:* $60.00.
Review Avg: 4.50   *OCLC:* 811   *Rating:* 14.12

Reviews
3 ARBA, 96:107
5 CRL, Mar 1996, p186
5 Choice, Sep 1996, p96
5 LJ, Sep 1 1995, p160
5 RBB, Nov 1 1995,
  p502-503
4 WLB/R, 1995

Awards
Dartmouth, 1996
LJ/BRS, Apr 15 1996,
  p40
NYPL, 1995
RBB/ORS, May 1 1996,
  p1536

F 128.65   (LC)   DDC: 974.71
Broadway: An Encyclopedic Guide to the History, People and Places of Times Square
Bloom, Ken. Facts On File, 1991. 442p. *Cloth:* $50.00.
Review Avg: 3.75   *OCLC:* 507   *Rating:* 6.76

Reviews
3 ARBA, 92:467
4 Choice, Sep 1991, p52
4 LJ, Nov 1 1990, p80
4 RBB, Apr 15 1991, p1663

Awards
NYPL, 1992

F 351   (LC)   DDC: 977
The Encyclopedia of the Central West
Carpenter, Allan. Facts On File, 1990. 544p. *Cloth:* $35.00.
Review Avg: 3.00   *OCLC:* 354   *Rating:* 3.71

Reviews
3 ARBA, 91:502

3 Choice, Oct 1990, p278
3 GSED, 1997, p195
3 LJ, Aug 1990, p102

F 451　　　　　　　　　　　(LC)　　　　DDC: 976.9
The Kentucky Encyclopedia
Kleber, John E. (ed). Un Press of Kentucky, 1992. 1088p. *Cloth:* $35.00.
Review Avg: 3.50　*OCLC:* 386　*Rating:* 4.27

Reviews
3 Choice, Dec 1992, p602
4 LJ, Jun 1 1992, p112

F 534　　　　　　　　　　　(LC)　　　　DDC: 977.2
The Encyclopedia of Indianapolis
Bodenhamer, David J. and Robert G. Barrows. Indiana Un, 1994. 1600p. *Cloth:* $49.95.
Review Avg: 3.50　*OCLC:* 175　*Rating:* 3.85

Reviews
3 ARBA, 96:929
4 LJ, Nov 1 1994, p66

F 591　　　　　　　　　　　(LC)　　　　DDC: 978
The American West: A Multicultural Encyclopedia
Utley, Robert M. Grolier, 1995. 10 vols. (1819p.) *Cloth:* $269.00/set.
Review Avg: 3.00　*OCLC:* 182　*Rating:* 3.36

Reviews
3 ARBA, 96:505

F 591　　　　　　　　　　　(LC)　　　　DDC: 978
Encyclopedia of the American West
Phillips, Charles and Alan Axelrod (eds). Macmillan, 1996. 4 vols. (1935p.) *Cloth:* $375.00/set.
Review Avg: 3.60　*OCLC:* 401　*Rating:* 4.40

Reviews
4 ARBA, 97:415
3 Choice, Feb 1997, p943
4 LJ, Nov 1 1996, p58
3 RBB, Dec 1 1996, p680,682
4 RQ, Spr 1997, p451-452

F 591　　　　　　　　　　　(LC)　　　　DDC: 973
The Encyclopedia of the Far West
Carpenter, Allan. Facts On File, 1991. 544p. *Cloth:* $40.00.
Review Avg: 2.33　*OCLC:* 321　*Rating:* 2.97

Reviews
1 ARBA, 92:84
3 Choice, Jun 1991, p1612
3 RBB, Mar 15 1991, p1518

F 596　　　　　　　　　　　(LC)　　　　DDC: 978
Cowboys and the Wild West: An A-Z Guide from the Chisholm Trail to the Silver Screen
Cusic, Don. Facts On File, 1994. 356p. *Cloth:* $40.00.
Review Avg: 3.00　*OCLC:* 365　*Rating:* 3.73

Reviews
3 ARBA, 95:541
3 RBB, Jan 1 1995, p840

F 826　　　　　　　　　　　(LC)　　　　DDC: 979.2
Utah History Encyclopedia
Powell, Allan Kent (ed). Un of Utah, 1994. 674p. *Cloth:* $50.00.
Review Avg: 4.00　*OCLC:* 140　*Rating:* 4.28

Reviews
4 ARBA, 96:511

F 869　　　　　　　　　　　(LC)　　　　DDC: 979.4
Los Angeles A to Z: An Encyclopedia of the City and County
Pitt, Leonard and Dale Pitt. Un of California, 1997. 605p. *Paper:* $34.95.
Review Avg: 3.67　*OCLC:* 267　*Rating:* 4.20

Reviews
3 Choice, Dec 1997, p610-612
4 LJ, May 15 1997, p73
4 RBB, Sep 1 1997, p165-166

F 1210　　　　　　　　　　　(LC)　　　　DDC: 972
Encyclopedia of Mexico: History, Society and Culture
Werner, Michael S. (ed). Fitzroy, 1997. 1749p. *Cloth:* $250.00.
Review Avg: 5.00　*OCLC:* 207　*Rating:* 5.41

Reviews
5 ARBA, 98:141

F 1219　　　　　　　　　　　(LC)　　　　DDC: 972
Encyclopedia of Ancient Mesoamerica
Bunson, Margaret and Stephen M. Bunson. Facts On File, 1996. 322p. *Cloth:* $45.00.
Review Avg: 2.50　*OCLC:* 334　*Rating:* 3.17

Reviews
3 ARBA, 97:453
2 LJ, Aug 1996, p62

F 1406　　　　　　　　　　　(LC)　　　　DDC: 980
Encyclopedia of Latin American History and Culture
Tenenbaum, Barbara A. (ed). Scribner's, 1996. 5 vols. *Cloth:* $449.00/set.
Review Avg: 4.50　*OCLC:* 1356　*Rating:* 17.21

Reviews	**Awards**
4 ARBA, 97:349	Choice/OAB, Jan 1997, p740
4 CRL, Sep 1996, p473	Dartmouth, 1997
5 Choice, Jul 1996, p1771	LJ/BRS, Apr 15 1997, p39
5 GSED, 1997, p231	NYPL, 1996
5 LJ, Jul 1996, p102	RBB/ORS, May 1 1997, p1524
4 RBB, Jul 1996, p1839-1840	

F 1410　　　　　　　　　　　(LC)　　　　DDC: 327
Encyclopedia of the Inter-American System
Atkins, G. Pope. Greenwood, 1997. 561p. *Cloth:* $115.00.
Review Avg: 4.00　*OCLC:* 165　*Rating:* 4.33

Reviews
4 ARBA, 98:695
4 RBB, May 15 1997, p1612

◆ The article titles in this encyclopedia are indexed by keyword in Part II.

F 1410 _____(LC)   DDC: 320.098

Political and Economic Encyclopaedia of South America and the Caribbean
Calvert, Peter (ed). Gale Research, 1991. 363p. *Cloth:* $85.00.
Review Avg: 2.67   *OCLC:* 165   *Rating:* 3.00

Reviews
3 ARBA, 93:774
2 Choice, May 1992, p1374
3 LJ, Mar 15 1992, p80

F 1418 _____(LC)   DDC: 303.48

The United States in Latin America: A Historical Dictionary
Shavit, David. Greenwood, 1992. 471p. *Cloth:* $79.50.
Review Avg: 2.75   *OCLC:* 290   *Rating:* 3.33

Reviews
3 ARBA, 93:786
2 Choice, Nov 1992, p450
3 GSED, 1997, p383
3 RBB, Jun 15 1992, p1890-1891

F 1434 _____(LC)   DDC: 972.8

Indians of Central and South America: An Ethnohistorical Dictionary
Olson, James S. Greenwood, 1991. 515p. *Cloth:* $75.00.
Review Avg: 3.25   *OCLC:* 487   *Rating:* 4.22

Reviews
3 ARBA, 92:371
3 Choice, Jan 1992, p724
4 LJ, Jun 1 1991, p128
3 RBB, Dec 1 1991, p721-722

F 1435 _____(LC)   DDC: 299.792

The Gods and Symbols of Ancient Mexico and the Maya: An Illustrated Dictionary of Mesoamerican Religion
Miller, Mary and Karl Taube. Thames & Hudson, 1993. 216p. *Cloth:* $34.95.
Review Avg: 4.00   *OCLC:* 738   *Rating:* 5.48

Reviews
4 ARBA, 95:1444

F 2183 _____(LC)   DDC: 972.8

The Dictionary of Contemporary Politics of Central America and Caribbean
Gunson, Phil and Greg Chamberlain. Simon & Schuster, 1991. 397p. *Cloth:* $60.00.
Review Avg: 3.25   *OCLC:* 749   *Rating:* 6.75

Reviews   **Awards**
3 ARBA, 92:723   LJ/BRS, Apr 15 1992,
4 Choice, Mar 1992, p1046   p43-44
3 LJ, Oct 15 1991, p72
3 RBB, Nov 15 1991, p641

FC 2154 _____(LC)   DDC: 971.8

Encyclopedia of Newfoundland and Labrador
Smallwood, Joseph R. (ed). Greenwood, 1991. 687p. *Cloth:* $90.00.
Review Avg: 3.00   *OCLC:* 80   *Rating:* 3.16

Reviews
3 ARBA, 93:133

G 63 _____(LC)   DDC: 910

The Concise Oxford Dictionary of Geography
Mayhew, Susan and Anne Penny. Oxford Un, 1992. 247p. *Paper:* $8.95.
Review Avg: 3.00   *OCLC:* 227   *Rating:* 3.45

Reviews
3 ARBA, 93:489

G 63 _____(LC)   DDC: 910

Encyclopedia of the First World
Kurian, George Thomas (ed). Facts On File, 1990. 2 vols. (1436p.) *Cloth:* $145.00/set.
Review Avg: 3.00   *OCLC:* 697   *Rating:* 4.39

Reviews
4 ARBA, 91:85
3 Choice, Mar 1991, p1100
3 GSED, 1997, p10
3 LJ, Aug 1990, p106
2 RBB, Sep 1 1990, p82,84

G 63 _____(LC)   DDC: 910

Exploring Your World: The Adventure of Geography
Crump, Donald J. (ed). Natl Geographic Society, 1993. Revised edition. 608p. *Cloth:* $29.95.
Review Avg: 3.33   *OCLC:* 154   *Rating:* 5.64

Reviews
3 ARBA, 91:446
3 ARBA, 95:494, Rev. ed.
4 GSED, 1997, p174

G 63 _____(LC)   DDC: 910

Modern Geography: An Encyclopedic Survey
Dunbar, Gary S. Garland, 1991. 219p. *Cloth:* $50.00.
Review Avg: 4.00   *OCLC:* 718   *Rating:* 7.44

Reviews   **Awards**
3 ARBA, 92:416   Choice/OAB, May 1992,
5 Choice, Apr 1991, p1292   p1342
4 GSED, 1997, p173
4 WLB/R, Mar 1991,
 p129-131

G 63 _____(LC)   DDC: 910

World Geographical Encyclopedia
Parker, Sybil P. (ed). McGraw-Hill, 1995. 5 vols. *Cloth:* $500.00/set.
Review Avg: 3.67   *OCLC:* 539   *Rating:* 6.75

Reviews   **Awards**
3 ARBA, 96:456   Choice/OAB, Jan 1997,
5 Choice, Jan 1996, p770   p741
3 RBB, Oct 15 1995, p430

G 63 _____(LC)   DDC: 903

Worldmark Encyclopedia of the Nations
Henderson, Andrea Kovacs. Gale Research, 1995. 8th ed. 5 vols. *Cloth:* $335.00/set.
Review Avg: 3.25   *OCLC:* 930   *Rating:* 7.11

Reviews
3 ARBA, 96:106
2 Choice, Jun 1995, p1581

4 GSED, 1997, p13
4 RBB, Apr 1 1995, p1445

G 116   (LC)   DDC: 910
Companion Encyclopedia of Geography: The Environment and Humankind
Douglas, Ian and others (eds). Routledge, 1996. 1021p. *Cloth:* $150.00.
Review Avg: 5.00   *OCLC:* 354   *Rating:* 5.71

Reviews   **Awards**
5 Choice, Feb 1997, p940   Choice/OAB, Jan 1998, p759

G 133   (LC)   DDC: 910
Encyclopedia of World Geography
Haggett, Peter and others (ed). Cavendish, 1994. 24 vols. *Cloth:* $499.95/set.
Review Avg: 3.50   *OCLC:* 393   *Rating:* 4.29

Reviews
3 LJ, Mar 15 1994, p62
4 RBB, May 1 1994, p1620,1622

G 141   (LC)   DDC: 911
Encyclopedia of Geographical Features in World History: Europe and the Americas
Penn, James R. ABC-CLIO, 1997. 317p. *Cloth:* $55.00.
Note: Series—Europe and the Americas.
Review Avg: 2.00   *OCLC:* 134   *Rating:* 2.27

Reviews
2 ARBA, 98:399

G 175   (LC)   DDC: 910.9
Marshall Cavendish Illustrated Encyclopedia of Discovery and Exploration
Cavendish, 1991. 17 vols. *Cloth:* $449.95/set.
Review Avg: 5.00   *OCLC:* 270   *Rating:* 5.54

Reviews
5 ARBA, 92:417
5 GSED, 1997, p178

G 855   (LC)   DDC: 919.89
Antarctica: An Encyclopedia
Stewart, John. McFarland, 1990. 2 vols. (1193p.) *Cloth:* $135.00/set.
Review Avg: 4.00   *OCLC:* 447   *Rating:* 6.89

Reviews   **Awards**
5 ARBA, 92:92   LJ/BRS, Apr 15 1991, p46
4 Choice, Apr 1991, p1294-1295
4 LJ, Jan 1991, p96,98
3 WLB/R, Mar 1991, p126-127

GC 9   (LC)   DDC: 551.46
Encyclopedia of Marine Sciences
Baretta-Bekker, J.G. and others (eds). Springer-Verlag, 1992. 311p. *Cloth:* $39.00.
Review Avg: 3.33   *OCLC:* 335   *Rating:* 4.00

Reviews
4 ARBA, 94:1744
3 Choice, Feb 1993, p938
3 GSED, 1997, p857

GE 10   (LC)   DDC: 628
Concise Encyclopedia of Environmental Systems
Young, Peter C. (ed). Pergamon, 1993. 769p. *Cloth:* $340.00.
Note: Series—Advances in Systems, Control, and Information Engineering.
Review Avg: 3.00   *OCLC:* 86   *Rating:* 3.17

Reviews
3 ARBA, 95:1768
3 GSED, 1997, p1044

◆GE 10   (LC)   DDC: 363.7
Conservation and Environmentalism: An Encyclopedia
Paehlke, Robert (ed). Garland, 1995. 771p. *Cloth:* $95.00.
Review Avg: 3.33   *OCLC:* 855   *Rating:* 9.04

Reviews   **Awards**
3 ARBA, 97:1426   LJ/BRS, Apr 15 1996, p40
4 LJ, Dec 1995, p88   RBB/ORS, May 1 1996, p1536
3 RBB, Feb 15 1996, p1040,1042

GE 10   (LC)   DDC: 363.7
Dictionary of Environment and Development: People, Places, Ideas, and Organizations
Crump, Andy. MIT, 1993. 272p. *Cloth:* $40.00. *Paper:* $10.95.
Review Avg: 3.00   *OCLC:* 326   *Rating:* 5.65

Reviews   **Awards**
3 ARBA, 94:1995   Choice/OAB, Jan 1993, p734
3 Choice, Mar 1992, p1042
3 GSED, 1997, p1032

◆GE 10   (LC)   DDC: 363.7
The Encyclopedia of the Environment
Eblen, Ruth A. and William R. Eblen (eds). Houghton, 1994. 846p. *Cloth:* $49.95.
Review Avg: 3.40   *OCLC:* 752   *Rating:* 4.90

Reviews
3 ARBA, 95:1765
3 Choice, Jan 1995, p748
4 GSED, 1997, p1034
3 LJ, Feb 1 1995, p70
4 RBB, Oct 1 1994, p355-356

◆GE 10   (LC)   DDC: 363.7
Environmental Encyclopedia
Cunningham, William P. and others (eds). Gale Research, 1994. 981p. *Cloth:* $195.00.
Review Avg: 3.80   *OCLC:* 1052   *Rating:* 9.90

Reviews   **Awards**
3 ARBA, 95:1764   Choice/OAB, Jan 1995
4 Choice, Sep 1994, p68   RBB/ORS, May 1 1995, p1603
4 GSED, 1997, p1033
5 LJ, Jun 1 1994, p96
3 RBB, May 15 1994, p1714

◆ The article titles in this encyclopedia are indexed by keyword in Part II.

GE 10 _____(LC)   DDC: 363.7

The Green Encyclopedia
Franck, Irene and David Brownstone. Prentice-Hall, 1992. 486p.
Paper: $20.00.
Review Avg: 2.71   _OCLC:_ 869   _Rating:_ 6.45

Reviews	**Awards**
3 ARBA, 94:1996	NYPL, 1994
2 Choice, Jun 1993, p1602	
3 GSED, 1997, p1036	
3 JAL, May 1993, p131	
2 LJ, Nov 15 1992, p70	
3 RBB, Dec 15 1992, p762	
3 RQ, Sum 1993, p568-569	

GE 10 _____(LC)   DDC: 333.7

Macmillan Encyclopedia of the Environment
Kellert, Stephen R. Macmillan, 1997. 6 vols. _Cloth:_ $150.00.
Review Avg: 4.33   _OCLC:_ 290   _Rating:_ 4.91

Reviews	**Awards**
4 ARBA, 97:1410	RBB/ORS, May 1 1998,
5 LJ, Jul 1997, p78	p1538
4 RBB, Aug 1997,	
p1926-1927	

GE 10 _____(LC)   DDC: 628

McGraw-Hill Encyclopedia of Environmental Science and Engineering
Parker, Sybil P. McGraw-Hill, 1993. 3rd ed. 749p. _Cloth:_ $85.50.
Note: From _McGraw-Hill Encyclopedia of Science and Technology._
Review Avg: 3.00   _OCLC:_ 485   _Rating:_ 5.97

Reviews
3 ARBA, 94:1999
3 Choice, Oct 1993, p268
3 JAL, Sep 1993, p275
3 RQ, Win 1993, p290-291
3 WLB/R, Sep 1993, p119,121

GE 150 _____(LC)   DDC: 363.7

Great Events from History II: Ecology and the Environment Series
Magill, Frank N. (ed). Salem, 1995. 5 vols. (2123p.) _Cloth:_ $375.00/set.
Review Avg: 4.50   _OCLC:_ 405   _Rating:_ 5.31

Reviews
4 Choice, Apr 1996, p1286
5 LJ, Feb 1 1996, p68

GE 197 _____(LC)   DDC: 363.7

The ABC-CLIO Companion to the Environmental Movement
Grossman, Mark. ABC-CLIO, 1994. 445p. _Cloth:_ $55.00.
Review Avg: 3.00   _OCLC:_ 577   _Rating:_ 4.15

Reviews
3 ARBA, 96:1869
3 Choice, May 1995, p1428
3 LJ, Mar 15 1995, p60

GF 4 _____(LC)   DDC: 304.2

Dictionary of Human Geography
Johnston, R. J. and others (eds). Blackwell, 1994. 3rd ed. 724p. _Cloth:_ $89.95. _Paper:_ $22.95.
Review Avg: 4.00   _OCLC:_ 467   _Rating:_ 6.93

Reviews
4 Choice, Jun 1994, p1550,1552
4 GSED, 1997, p493

◆**GF 4** _____(LC)   DDC: 304.2

Human Environments: A Cross-Cultural Encyclopedia
Levinson, David. ABC-CLIO, 1995. 284p. _Cloth:_ $49.50.
Note: Series—Encyclopedias of the Human Experience.
Review Avg: 3.00   _OCLC:_ 280   _Rating:_ 3.56

Reviews
3 ARBA, 96:1798

GF 11 _____(LC)   DDC: 363.7

The HarperCollins Dictionary of Environmental Science
Jones, Gareth and others. Harper Perennial, 1992. 453p. _Paper:_ $13.00.
Review Avg: 3.33   _OCLC:_ 472   _Rating:_ 4.27

Reviews
3 ARBA, 93:1753
3 Choice, Jun 1992, p1520
4 GSED, 1997, p1037

GN 11 _____(LC)   DDC: 032

The Oxford Illustrated Encyclopedia of Peoples and Cultures
Hoggart, Richard (ed). Oxford Un, 1992. 392p. _Cloth:_ $49.95.
Note: Series—Oxford Illustrated Encyclopedia, vol. 7.
Review Avg: 4.67   _OCLC:_ 426   _Rating:_ 5.52

Reviews
5 ARBA, 94:397
5 Choice, Jul/Aug 1993, p1753
4 RBB, Jul 1993, p2004

GN 25 _____(LC)   DDC: 301

Companion Encyclopedia of Anthropology
Ingold, Tim (ed). Routledge, 1994. 1127p. _Cloth:_ $99.95.
Review Avg: 3.67   _OCLC:_ 524   _Rating:_ 4.72

Reviews
3 ARBA, 95:392
4 GSED, 1997, p131
4 LJ, Feb 1 1994, p68

GN 50.3 _____(LC)   DDC: 573

Dictionary of Concepts in Physical Anthropology
Stevenson, Joan C. Greenwood, 1991. 432p. _Cloth:_ $89.50.
Review Avg: 3.33   _OCLC:_ 265   _Rating:_ 3.86

Reviews
3 ARBA, 93:415
3 Choice, Mar 1992, p1056
4 GSED, 1997, p132

GN 50.3 _____(LC)   DDC: 573
History of Physical Anthropology: An Encyclopedia
Spencer, Frank (ed). Garland, 1996. 2 vols (1195p.) *Cloth:* $175.00/set.
Note: Series—Garland Reference Library of Social Sciences, vol. 677.
Review Avg: 4.00   *OCLC:* 38   *Rating:* 4.08

Reviews	Awards
4 ARBA, 98:320	Choice/OAB, Jan 1998,
4 Choice, Jun 1997	p760
4 LJ, Mar 15 1997, p54	LJ/BRS, Apr 15 1998,
4 RBB, Jun 1 1997,	p47
p1760,1762	

◆GN 281 _____(LC)   DDC: 573.2
The Encyclopedia of Evolution: Humanity's Search for Its Origins
Milner, Richard (ed). Holt, 1993. 481p.
Review Avg: 4.00   *OCLC:* 173   *Rating:* 8.35

Reviews	Awards
5 ARBA, 92:1523	NYPL, 1992
4 Choice, Jun 1991, p1619	RBB/ORS, May 1 1992,
5 GSED, 1997, p845	p1625
3 LJ, Dec 1990, p120	
4 RBB, Jan 1 1991, p950	
3 WLB/R, Mar 1991, p128	

GN 307 _____(LC)   DDC: 306
Dictionary of Concepts in Cultural Anthropology
Winthrop, Robert H. Greenwood, 1991. 347p. *Cloth:* $65.00.
Review Avg: 3.40   *OCLC:* 531   *Rating:* 6.46

Reviews	Awards
3 ARBA, 93:418	Choice/OAB, Jan 1993,
5 Choice, May 1992,	p735
p1376,1378	
3 GSED, 1997, p133	
3 LJ, Feb 15 1992, p162	
3 RBB, May 15 1992, p1714	

GN 307 _____(LC)   DDC: 306
Dictionary of Twentieth Century Culture: French Culture 1900-1975
Rood, Karen L. Gale Research, 1994. 449p. *Cloth:* $60.00.
Review Avg: 4.00   *OCLC:* 68   *Rating:* 4.14

Reviews
4 ARBA, 96:545

GN 307 _____(LC)   DDC: 306
Encyclopedia of Cultural Anthropology
Levinson, David and Melvin Ember (eds). Holt, 1996. 4 vols. *Cloth:* $395.00/set.
Review Avg: 4.50   *OCLC:* 1043   *Rating:* 10.59

Reviews	Awards
5 ARBA, 97:315	Choice/OAB, Jan 1997,
4 Choice, Sep 1996, p96	p740
5 LJ, May 15 1996, p53-54	RBB/ORS, May 1 1997,
4 RBB, Jun 1 1996, p1760	p1524

◆GN 307 _____(LC)   DDC: 306
Encyclopedia of Social and Cultural Anthropology
Barnard, Alan and Jonathan Spencer (eds). Routledge, 1996. 658p. *Cloth:* $120.00.
Review Avg: 3.67   *OCLC:* 532   *Rating:* 4.73

Reviews	Awards
3 ARBA, 97:317	Choice/OAB, Jan 1998,
4 Choice, Mar 1997, p1136	p759
4 LJ, Feb 1 1997, p70,72	

GN 307 _____(LC)   DDC: 306
Encyclopedia of World Cultures
Levinson, David (ed). Hall, 1991. 10 vols. *Cloth:* $1100.00/set.
Review Avg: 4.43   *OCLC:* 1793   *Rating:* 16.02

Reviews	Awards
4 ARBA, 94:395, vol. 4	Choice/OAB, Jan 1993,
5 ARBA, 97:320	p734
5 ARBA, 97:319	Choice/OAB, Jan 1997,
5 ARBA, 97:318	p740
4 ARBA, 91:505, vol. 1	NYPL, 1992
5 ARBA, 92:335, vol. 2	NYPL, 1996
5 ARBA, 92:334, vol. 1	
4 ARBA, 95:397, vol. 6-7	
4 ARBA, 94:396, vol. 5	
4 ARBA, 93:413, vol. 3	
5 Choice, Apr 1992, p1208	
5 Choice, Dec 1992, p601,	
vol. 2	
4 Choice, Feb 1995, p916	
4 Choice, Oct 1991, p256,	
vol. 6	
5 GSED, 1997, p127-130	
3 LJ, Mar 15 1991, p84,	
vol. 6	
4 LJ, Jan 1992, p106,108,	
vol. 2	
4 RBB, Jul 1991,	
p2061-2062, vol. 1	
4 RBB, Jun 1 1996,	
p1760,1762, vol. 8-10	
5 RQ, Spr 1992, p416-417	
5 WLB/R, Jun 1991, p134	

◆GN 480 _____(LC)   DDC: 306.8
Marriage, Family, and Relationships: A Cross-Cultural Encyclopedia
Broude, Gwen J. ABC-CLIO, 1994. 372p. *Cloth:* $49.50.
Note: Series—Encyclopedias of the Human Experience.
Review Avg: 3.50   *OCLC:* 1216   *Rating:* 7.93

Reviews	Awards
3 ARBA, 96:862	Choice/OAB, Jan 1996,
4 Choice, Jun 1995, p1566	p723
3 LJ, Feb 1 1995, p66	
4 WLB/R, May 1995, p75-76	

GN 495.4 _____(LC)   DDC: 305.8
The Encyclopedia of the Peoples of the World
Gonen, Amiram (ed). Holt, 1993. 703p.
Review Avg: 3.86   *OCLC:* 1059   *Rating:* 7.98

Reviews	Awards
5 ARBA, 95:399	LJ/BRS, Apr 15 1994, p39

3 Choice, Apr 1994, p1270
4 GSED, 1997, p136
4 LJ, Apr 1 1994, p88,90
3 RBB, Mar 15 1994, p1390
4 RQ, Fall 1994, p105-106
4 WLB/R, Mar 1994, p92

GN 496 _____ (LC)   DDC: 305.8

Dictionary of Race and Ethnic Relations

Cashmore, E. Ellis (ed). Routledge, 1994. 3rd ed. 370p. *Cloth:* $40.00.
Review Avg: 4.00   *OCLC:* 445   *Rating:* 6.89

Reviews
3 ARBA, 90:363, 2nd ed.
5 ARBA, 95:394, 3rd ed.
4 GSED, 1997, p134

◆**GN 496** _____ (LC)   DDC: 305.8

Ethnic Relations: A Cross-Cultural Encyclopedia

Levinson, David. ABC-CLIO, 1994. 293p. *Cloth:* $49.50.
Review Avg: 3.33   *OCLC:* 918   *Rating:* 5.17

Reviews
3 ARBA, 96:389
3 Choice, Jun 1995, p1576
4 RBB, Apr 15 1995, p1523

◆**GR 72** _____ (LC)   DDC: 808.5

Storytelling Encyclopedia: Historical, Cultural, and Multi-ethnic Approaches to Oral Traditions Around the World

Leeming, David Adams (ed). Oryx, 1997. 543p. *Cloth:* $69.95.
Review Avg: 3.50   *OCLC:* 192   *Rating:* 3.88

Reviews
3 ARBA, 98:1256
4 LJ, Oct 1 1997, p76

◆**GR 101** _____ (LC)   DDC: 398.2

American Folklore: An Encyclopedia

Brunvand, Jan Harold (ed). Garland, 1996. 816p. *Cloth:* $95.00.
Note: Series—Reference Library of the Humanities, vol. 1551.
Review Avg: 4.00   *OCLC:* 1406   *Rating:* 12.81

Reviews   **Awards**
3 ARBA, 97:1088   Choice/OAB, Jan 1997,
4 Choice, Oct 1996, p247   p739
4 GSED, 1997, p676   LJ/BRS, Apr 15 1997,
4 LJ, Jan 1997, p82   p37
5 RBB, Aug 1996,   RBB/ORS, May 1 1997,
 p1920-1921   p1524

GR 365 _____ (LC)   DDC: 398.2

The Oxford Companion to Australian Folklore

Davey, Gwenda Beed and Graham Seal (eds). Oxford Un, 1993. 381p.
Cloth: $49.95.
Review Avg: 4.50   *OCLC:* 251   *Rating:* 7.00

Reviews   **Awards**
4 ARBA, 94:1390   Choice/OAB, Jan 1994,
5 Choice, Nov 1993, p437   p714

GR 549 _____ (LC)   DDC: 398

American Elves: An Encyclopedia of Little People from the Lore of 300 Ethnic Groups of the Western Hemisphere

Roth, John E. McFarland, 1997. 329p. *Cloth:* $68.50.
Review Avg: 2.00   *OCLC:* 113   *Rating:* 2.23

Reviews
2 ARBA, 98:1255
3 Choice, Sep 1997, p107
1 LJ, Apr 15 1997, p72,74

GR 549 _____ (LC)   DDC: 398.21

Spirits, Fairies, Gnomes, and Goblins: An Encyclopedia of the Little People

Rose, Carol. ABC-CLIO, 1996. 369p. *Cloth:* $49.50.
Review Avg: 3.67   *OCLC:* 514   *Rating:* 4.70

Reviews
3 ARBA, 97:1090
5 LJ, Mar 1 1997, p70
3 RBB, May 1 1997, p1534

GR 830 _____ (LC)   DDC: 700

The Vampire Book: The Encyclopedia of the Undead

Melton, J. Gordon. Gale Research, 1994. 852p. *Cloth:* $39.95. *Paper:* $16.95.
Review Avg: 3.00   *OCLC:* 333   *Rating:* 3.67

Reviews
3 ARBA, 95:1328
3 Choice, Apr 1995, p1279
3 GSED, 1997, p698
3 RBB, Mar 1 1995, p1257,1267

GR 830 _____ (LC)   DDC: 700

The Vampire Encyclopedia

Bunson, Matthew. Random House, 1993. 303p. *Paper:* $16.00.
Review Avg: 3.50   *OCLC:* 623   *Rating:* 4.75

Reviews
3 ARBA, 95:1325
4 LJ, Jun 1 1993, p102
3 RBB, Oct 1 1993, p387
4 WLB/R, Oct 1993, p96,98

GT 580 _____ (LC)   DDC: 391

The Illustrated Encyclopaedia of Costume and Fashion: From 1066 to the Present

Cassin-Scott, Jack. Sterling, 1994. Revised edition. 192p. *Cloth:* $24.95.
Review Avg: 3.00   *OCLC:* 865   *Rating:* 6.73

Reviews
3 ARBA, 95:986
3 LJ, Oct 1 1994, p68
3 WLB/R, Dec 1994, p73

GT 2853 _____ (LC)   DDC: 394.1

Encyclopedia of North American Eating and Drinking Traditions, Customs, and Rituals

Gay, Kathlyn and Martin K. Gay. ABC-CLIO, 1996. 289p. *Cloth:* $65.00.
Review Avg: 3.33   *OCLC:* 497   *Rating:* 4.32

Reviews
3 ARBA, 97:1250
4 Choice, Apr 1997, p1307-1308
3 RBB, Feb 15 1997, p1041

GV 11 _____(LC)   DDC: 790
Dictionary of Concepts in Recreation and Leisure Studies
Smith, Stephen L. J. Greenwood, 1990. 372p. *Cloth:* $59.50.
Review Avg: 3.50   *OCLC:* 427   *Rating:* 4.35

Reviews
3 ARBA, 91:807
4 Choice, Mar 1991, p1108
3 GSED, 1997, p431
4 RBB, Dec 1 1990, p774,776

GV 17 _____(LC)   DDC: 796
Greek and Roman Sport: A Dictionary of Athletes and Events from the Eighth Century B.C. to the Third Century
Matz, David. McFarland, 1991. 169p. *Cloth:* $32.50.
Review Avg: 3.40   *OCLC:* 429   *Rating:* 4.26

Reviews
4 ARBA, 92:772
3 Choice, Nov 1991, p418
4 GSED, 1997, p427
3 LJ, Jun 15 1991, p70
3 WLB/R, Sep 1991, p123

GV 199.85 _____(LC)   DDC: 796.522
Encyclopaedia of Mountaineering
Unsworth, Walt. Penguin, 1992. 384p. *Cloth:* $24.99.
Review Avg: 3.00   *OCLC:* 10   *Rating:* 3.02

Reviews
3 GSED, 1997, p452

GV 200 _____(LC)   DDC: 796.522
Climbing: The Complete Reference
Child, Greg. Facts On File, 1995. 304p. *Cloth:* $40.00. *Paper:* $19.95.
Review Avg: 3.00   *OCLC:* 414   *Rating:* 5.83

Reviews   *Awards*
3 ARBA, 96:829   LJ/BRS, Apr 15 1996,
3 LJ, Oct 1 1995, p75   p39

◆GV 558 _____(LC)   DDC: 613.7
Encyclopedia of Sports Science
Zumerchik, John. Macmillan, 1996. 2 vols. (943p.) *Cloth:* $200.00.
Review Avg: 4.00   *OCLC:* 872   *Rating:* 5.74

Reviews
4 ARBA, 98:720
4 Choice, Nov 1997, p457
4 RBB, Aug 1997, p1925

GV 567 _____(LC)   DDC: 796
The Encyclopedia of North American Sports History
Hickok, Ralph. Facts On File, 1992. 516p. *Cloth:* $55.00.
Review Avg: 3.60   *OCLC:* 916   *Rating:* 5.43

Reviews
3 ARBA, 93:819
4 Choice, Jul/Aug 1992, p1657

4 GSED, 1997, p426
3 LJ, Jan 1992, p108
4 RBB, Feb 15 1992, p1130

◆GV 567 _____(LC)   DDC: 796
Encyclopedia of World Sport: From Ancient Times to the Present
Levinson, David and Karen Christensen (eds). ABC-CLIO, 1996. 3 vols. (1317p.) *Cloth:* $225.00.
Review Avg: 4.33   *OCLC:* 521   *Rating:* 9.37

Reviews   *Awards*
3 Choice, Jul 1997, p1779   LJ/BRS, Apr 15 1997,
5 LJ, Apr 15 1997, p66   p39
5 RBB, May 1 1997,   NYPL, 1997
   p1526-1528   RBB/ORS, May 1 1997,
                p1524

GV 675 _____(LC)   DDC: 796
The Oxford Companion to Australian Sport
Vamplew, Wray (ed). Oxford Un, 1994. 2nd ed. 575p. *Cloth:* $45.00.
Review Avg: 4.00   *OCLC:* 95   *Rating:* 6.19

Reviews
4 GSED, 1997, p428

GV 709 _____(LC)   DDC: 796
Encyclopedia of Women and Sports
Sherrow, Victoria. ABC-CLIO, 1996. 382p. *Cloth:* $60.00.
Review Avg: 3.33   *OCLC:* 624   *Rating:* 4.58

Reviews
4 ARBA, 97:644
3 Choice, Jun 1997, p1644
3 LJ, Jan 1997, p91

GV 731 _____(LC)   DDC: 796
Sports Rules Encyclopedia
White, Jess R. Human Kinetics, 1990. 2nd ed. 732p. *Cloth:* $44.95. *Paper:* $19.95.
Review Avg: 3.00   *OCLC:* 1220   *Rating:* 7.44

Reviews
3 ARBA, 91:808
3 Choice, Apr 1990, p1305
3 GSED, 1997, p432

GV 847.8 _____(LC)   DDC: 796.962
Complete Encyclopedia of Hockey
Hollander, Zander and Hal Bock. Gale Research, 1993. 4th ed. 604p. *Cloth:* $55.00. *Paper:* $22.95.
Note: Paperback available from Visible Ink Press.
Review Avg: 5.00   *OCLC:* 165   *Rating:* 7.33

Reviews
5 ARBA, 94:852
5 GSED, 1997, p448

GV 862.3 _____(LC)   DDC: 796.357
The Cultural Encyclopedia of Baseball
Light, Jonathan Fraser. McFarland, 1997. 888p. *Cloth:* $75.00.
Review Avg: 4.67   *OCLC:* 160   *Rating:* 4.99

Reviews
5 ARBA, 98:733
5 Choice, Dec 15 1997, p712
4 LJ, Sep 15 1997, p62

GV 863 _____(LC)   DDC: 796.357
Total Baseball: The Ultimate Encyclopedia of Baseball
Thorn, John and Peter Palmer. Penguin, 1997. 5th ed. 2458p. *Cloth:* $64.95.
Review Avg: 4.33   *OCLC:* 472   *Rating:* 9.27

Reviews   *Awards*
5 ARBA, 92:786, 4th ed.   Choice/OAB, Jan 1994,
4 ARBA, 98:737, 5th ed.   p714
4 Choice, Jul/Aug 1993,
  p1756

GV 875 _____(LC)   DDC: 796.357
Encyclopedia of Major League Baseball Teams
Dewey, Donald and Nicholas Ecocella. HarperCollins, 1993. 594p. *Cloth:* $35.00.
Review Avg: 3.50   *OCLC:* 90   *Rating:* 3.68

Reviews
5 ARBA, 94:831
3 ARBA, 92:779, National League
3 ARBA, 92:778, American League
3 GSED, 1997, p434
4 LJ, Oct 15 1993, p58
3 RBB, Oct 15 1991, p458-459

GV 875 _____(LC)   DDC: 796.357021
The Encyclopedia of Minor League Baseball: The Official Record of Minor League Baseball
Johnson, Lloyd and others (eds). Baseball America, 1997. 2nd ed. 666p. *Cloth:* $48.95. *Paper:* $39.95.
Review Avg: 5.00   *OCLC:* 19   *Rating:* 7.04

Reviews
5 ARBA, 98:729

GV 875 _____(LC)   DDC: 796.357
Former Major League Teams: An Encyclopedia
Jones, Donald D. McFarland, 1995. 233p. *Cloth:* $35.00.
Review Avg: 3.00   *OCLC:* 175   *Rating:* 3.35

Reviews
3 ARBA, 97:646
3 Choice, Oct 1995, p266
3 RQ, Win 1995, p256-257

GV 875 _____(LC)   DDC: 796.357
Professional Baseball Franchises: From the Abbeville Athletics to the Zanesville Indians
Filichia, Peter. Facts On File, 1993. 290p. *Cloth:* $25.95.
Review Avg: 3.33   *OCLC:* 309   *Rating:* 3.93

Reviews
3 ARBA, 94:832
4 Choice, Jul/Aug 1993, p1748
3 RBB, Mar 1 1993, p1267

GV 877 _____(LC)   DDC: 796.357
The Baseball Encyclopedia: The Complete and Official Record of Major League Baseball
Reichler, Joseph L. Macmillan, 1996. 10th ed. 280p. *Cloth:* $49.95.
Note: Includes CD-ROM.
Review Avg: 3.57   *OCLC:* 196   *Rating:* 5.96

Reviews
3 ARBA, 94:830
4 ARBA, 90:764
3 Choice, Sep 1993, p74
4 Choice, May 1997, p1482, CD-ROM version
4 GSED, 1997, p433
3 LJ, Sep 1 1990, p210
4 RBB, Nov 15 1990, p680-681

GV 885.515 _____(LC)   DDC: 796.323
The Encyclopedia of Pro Basketball Team Histories
Bjarkman, Peter. Carroll & Graf, 1994. 533p. *Cloth:* $24.00.
Review Avg: 3.67   *OCLC:* 461   *Rating:* 4.59

Reviews
3 LJ, Dec 1994, p99
3 RBB, Dec 1 1994, p650
5 WLB/R, Feb 1995, p67

GV 885.7 _____(LC)   DDC: 796.323
The Encyclopedia of College Basketball
Douchant, Mike. Gale Research, 1995. 615p. *Cloth:* $42.95. *Paper:* $19.95.
Note: Paperback available from Visible Ink Press.
Review Avg: 4.00   *OCLC:* 454   *Rating:* 4.91

Reviews
4 ARBA, 96:809
3 Choice, Apr 1995, p1270,1272
4 LJ, Feb 1 1995, p60
4 RBB, Feb 1 1995, p1025-1026
5 RBB, May 1 1996, p1536

GV 885.7 _____(LC)   DDC: 796.323
The Official NBA Basketball Encyclopedia: The Complete History and Statistics of Professional Basketball
Sachare, Alex. Random House, 1994. 2nd ed. 842p. *Cloth:* $29.95.
Review Avg: 3.00   *OCLC:* 511   *Rating:* 6.02

Reviews
3 RBB, Mar 1 1990, p1386-1387
3 RBB, Mar 1 1995, p1273, 2nd ed.

GV 891 _____(LC)   DDC: 794.72
The Illustrated Encyclopedia of Billiards
Shamos, Michael Ian. Lyons & Burford, 1993. 308p. *Cloth:* $35.00.
Review Avg: 4.00   *OCLC:* 181   *Rating:* 4.36

Reviews
5 ARBA, 95:813
4 GSED, 1997, p438
3 RBB, Feb 15 1994, p1109

GV 943 _____(LC)   DDC: 796.334
The World Encyclopedia of Soccer
LeBlanc, Michael and Richard Henshaw (eds). Gale Research, 1994. 430p. *Cloth:* $39.95. *Paper:* $14.95.

Review Avg: 3.20   *OCLC:* 390   *Rating:* 3.98

Reviews
3 ARBA, 95:824
1 Choice, Apr 1994, p1273
4 GSED, 1997, p455
4 RBB, Apr 15 1994, p1557
4 WLB/R, Apr 1994, p93

GV 943.49 _____ (LC)   DDC: 796.334

The Encyclopedia of World Cup Soccer
Duarte, Orlando. McGraw-Hill, 1994. 435p. *Paper:* $24.95.
Review Avg: 3.00   *OCLC:* 115   *Rating:* 3.23

Reviews
3 ARBA, 95:822
3 GSED, 1997, p454

GV 955 _____ (LC)   DDC: 796.332

The Sports Encyclopedia: Pro Football, The Modern Era 1972-1996
Neft, David S. and others (eds). St Martin's, 1997. 6th ed. 623p. *Paper:* $19.99.
Review Avg: 3.00   *OCLC:* 169   *Rating:* 5.34

Reviews
3 ARBA, 98:746

GV 955.5 _____ (LC)   DDC: 796.332

Total Football: The Official Encyclopedia of the National Football League
Carroll, Bob and others. HarperCollins, 1997. 1652p. *Cloth:* $55.00.
Review Avg: 4.00   *OCLC:* 283   *Rating:* 4.57

Reviews
4 ARBA, 98:747

GV 956.8 _____ (LC)   DDC: 796.332

College Football Encyclopedia: The Authoritative Guide to 124 Years of College Football
Ours, Robert M. Prima, 1994. 501p. *Cloth:* $29.95. *Paper:* $19.95.
Review Avg: 3.00   *OCLC:* 415   *Rating:* 3.83

Reviews
3 LJ, Nov 1 1993, p78
3 RBB, Jan 1 1994, p848

GV 965 _____ (LC)   DDC: 796.352

The Encyclopedia of Golf
Campbell, Malcolm. Random House, 1991. 336p. *Cloth:* $60.00.
Review Avg: 3.50   *OCLC:* 4   *Rating:* 3.51

Reviews
4 ARBA, 93:832
3 GSED, 1997, p447n

GV 965 _____ (LC)   DDC: 796.352

Golf Magazine's Encyclopedia of Golf
Peper, George and the editors of Golf Magazine. HarperCollins, 1993. 2nd ed. 518p. *Cloth:* $55.00.
Review Avg: 3.00   *OCLC:* 235   *Rating:* 5.47

Reviews
3 ARBA, 94:850
3 GSED, 1997, p447

GV 992 _____ (LC)   DDC: 796.342

Bud Collins' Modern Encyclopedia of Tennis
Collins, Bud and Zander Hollander (eds). Visible Ink, 1997. 3rd ed. 698p. *Paper:* $19.95.
Review Avg: 3.75   *OCLC:* 356   *Rating:* 6.46

Reviews
5 ARBA, 95:825
2 ARBA, 98:750
4 GSED, 1997, p457
4 RBB, Jan 1 1994, p847

GV 1061.2 _____ (LC)   DDC: 629.228

National Road Race Encyclopedia
Weddington, Michael and Barry Perilli (eds). Griffin, 1997. 1 vol. (Unpaged) *Paper:* $24.95.
Review Avg: 3.00   *OCLC:* 15   *Rating:* 3.03

Reviews
3 ARBA, 98:751

GV 1101 _____ (LC)   DDC: 796.8

The Original Martial Arts Encyclopedia: Tradition, History, Pioneers
Corcoran, John. Pro-Action, 1993. 410p. *Cloth:* $29.95.
Note: Originally entitled *Martial Arts: Traditions, History, People* (Gallery Books, 1988).
Review Avg: 4.00   *OCLC:* 367   *Rating:* 4.73

Reviews
5 GSED, 1997, p451
3 RBB, Sep 1 1993, p90

GV 1143.2 _____ (LC)   DDC: 796.8

The Encyclopedia of the Sword
Evangelista, Nick. Greenwood, 1995. 690p. *Cloth:* $79.50.
Review Avg: 3.50   *OCLC:* 167   *Rating:* 3.83

Reviews
4 ARBA, 96:816
3 RQ, Win 1995, p255-256

GV 1198.12 _____ (LC)   DDC: 796.812

Encyclopedia of American Wrestling
Chapman, Mike. Books on Demand, 1990. 533p. *Paper:* $25.95.
Review Avg: 4.00   *OCLC:* 317   *Rating:* 4.63

Reviews
5 ARBA, 91:840
3 Choice, Mar 1990, p1108

GV 1314.5 _____ (LC)   DDC: 794.1

The Chess Encyclopedia
Divinsky, Nathan. Facts On File, 1991. 247p. *Cloth:* $35.00.
Note: Originally published by Batsford, London, 1990.
Review Avg: 3.00   *OCLC:* 354   *Rating:* 3.71

Reviews
3 ARBA, 92:789

◆ The article titles in this encyclopedia are indexed by keyword in Part II.

3 Choice, Jan 1992, p718
3 RBB, Aug 1991, p2171

GV 1445 _____(LC)   DDC: 794.1
The Oxford Companion to Chess
Hooper, David and Kenneth Whyld. Oxford Un, 1992. 2nd ed. 483p.
Cloth: $35.00.
Review Avg: 3.00   *OCLC:* 374   *Rating:* 5.75

Reviews
3 ARBA, 94:842
3 GSED, 1997, p441

GV 1585 _____(LC)   DDC: 792.8
International Dictionary of Ballet
Bremser, Martha and Larraine Nicholas (eds). St James, 1993. 2 vols.
Cloth: $230.00/set.
Review Avg: 3.67   *OCLC:* 549   *Rating:* 6.77

Reviews   **Awards**
3 ARBA, 94:1423   RBB/ORS, May 1 1994,
4 CRL, Sep 1994, p415-416   p1627
4 GSED, 1997, p703
3 JAL, Jan 1994, p419
4 LJ, Apr 1 1994, p90
4 RQ, Sum 1994, p554-555

GV 1815 _____(LC)   DDC: 791.3
*Two Hundred Years of the American Circus: From Aba-
Daba to the Zoppe-Zavatta Troupe*
Ogden, Tom. Facts On File, 1993. 402p. *Cloth:* $50.00.
Review Avg: 3.75   *OCLC:* 666   *Rating:* 9.08

Reviews   **Awards**
3 ARBA, 94:1419   NYPL, 1994
4 Choice, Mar 1994, p1102   RBB/ORS, May 1 1994,
4 LJ, Aug 1993, p96   p1627
4 RBB, Dec 1 1993, p717

◆**H 41** _____(LC)   DDC: 300
*The Blackwell Dictionary of Twentieth-Century Social
Thought*
Outhwaite, William and Tom Bottomore. Blackwell, 1993. 864p.
Cloth: $59.95. *Paper:* $26.95.
Review Avg: 3.80   *OCLC:* 597   *Rating:* 4.99

Reviews
4 ARBA, 94:73
3 CRL, Sep 1994, p419
4 Choice, Jul/Aug 1993, p1744
4 GSED, 1997, p1
4 RBB, Jun 1993, p1890,1892

◆**H 41** _____(LC)   DDC: 303
The Social Science Encyclopedia
Kuper, Adam and Jessica Kuper (eds). Routledge, 1996. 2nd ed. 923p.
Cloth: $89.95.
Review Avg: 4.00   *OCLC:* 924   *Rating:* 7.85

Reviews
4 ARBA, 97:75
4 Choice, Oct 1996, p258
4 RBB, Apr 1 1996, p1390

HB 61 _____(LC)   DDC: 330
The Encyclopedic Dictionary of Economics
Cole, Don (ed). Dushkin, 1991. 4th ed. 270p. *Paper:* $12.95.
Note: Series—Encyclopedic Dictionary Reference Set, vol. 3.
Review Avg: 4.00   *OCLC:* 240   *Rating:* 6.48

Reviews
5 ARBA, 93:180
3 RBB, Apr 15 1992, p1549

◆**HB 61** _____(LC)   DDC: 330
The Fortune Encyclopedia of Economics
Henderson, David R. (ed). Warner, 1993. 876p. *Cloth:* $49.95.
Review Avg: 3.75   *OCLC:* 1083   *Rating:* 7.92

Reviews   **Awards**
3 ARBA, 95:184   NYPL, 1994
4 GSED, 1997, p56
5 LJ, Aug 1993, p94
3 RBB, Jan 15 1994, p964

HB 61 _____(LC)   DDC: 330
The HarperCollins Dictionary of Economics
Pass, Christopher and others. Harper Perennial, 1991. 562p. *Cloth:*
$25.00. *Paper:* $12.95.
Review Avg: 3.00   *OCLC:* 383   *Rating:* 3.77

Reviews
3 ARBA, 92:126
3 RBB, May 15 1991, p1833-1834

◆**HB 61** _____(LC)   DDC: 330
McGraw-Hill Encyclopedia of Economics
Greenwald, Douglas (ed). McGraw-Hill, 1994. 2nd ed. 1093p. *Cloth:*
$99.50.
Note: Revision of *Encyclopedia of Economics,* 1982.
Review Avg: 4.00   *OCLC:* 983   *Rating:* 7.97

Reviews
5 ARBA, 96:179, 2nd ed.
4 Choice, Mar 1994, p1096, 2nd ed.
3 RBB, Jan 15 1994, p964, 2nd ed.
4 WLB/R, Jan 1994, p89-90, 2nd ed.

HB 61 _____(LC)   DDC: 330
The MIT Dictionary of Modern Economics
Pearce, David W. MIT, 1992. 4th ed. 474p. *Cloth:* $42.00. *Paper:*
$18.50.
Review Avg: 5.00   *OCLC:* 447   *Rating:* 7.89

Reviews
5 ARBA, 93:183
5 GSED, 1997, p59

HB 61 _____(LC)   DDC: 330
The Penguin Dictionary of Economics
Bannock, Graham and others. Penguin, 1992. 5th ed. 448p. *Paper:*
$13.00.
Review Avg: 3.00   *OCLC:* 200   *Rating:* 5.40

Reviews
3 ARBA, 94:159

<u>**HB 61**</u>   **(LC)**   **DDC: 330**

Survey of Social Science: Economics Series

Magill, Frank N. (ed). Salem, 1991. 5 vols. (2494p.) *Cloth:* $375.00/set.

Review Avg: 3.75   *OCLC:* 637   *Rating:* 5.02

Reviews
3 ARBA, 92:127
4 Choice, Jun 1992, p1529
4 RBB, Mar 15 1992, p1404
4 WLB/R, Feb 1992, p112

<u>**HB 99.7**</u>   **(LC)**   **DDC: 330.15**

An Encyclopedia of Keynesian Economics

Cate, Thomas and others (eds). Elgar, 1997. 638p. *Cloth:* $235.00.

Review Avg: 5.00   *OCLC:* 94   *Rating:* 5.19

Reviews
5 ARBA, 98:152

<u>**HB 139**</u>   **(LC)**   **DDC: 330**

A Dictionary of Econometrics

Darnell, Adrian C. Elgar, 1994. 458p. *Cloth:* $112.95.

Review Avg: 4.00   *OCLC:* 322   *Rating:* 4.64

Reviews
4 ARBA, 95:182
4 Choice, Dec 1994, p573

◆<u>**HB 3711**</u>   **(LC)**   **DDC: 338.5**

Business Cycles and Depressions: An Encyclopedia

Glasner, David (ed). Garland, 1997. 779p. *Cloth:* $95.00.

Review Avg: 4.00   *OCLC:* 462   *Rating:* 4.92

Reviews   **Awards**
4 Choice, Jul 1997, p1776   RBB/ORS, May 1 1998,
                               p1538

<u>**HC 55**</u>   **(LC)**   **DDC: 330**

Great Events from History II: Business and Commerce

Magill, Frank N. (ed). Salem, 1994. 5 vols. *Cloth:* $375.00/set.

Review Avg: 3.80   *OCLC:* 443   *Rating:* 4.69

Reviews
3 ARBA, 95:209
4 Choice, Apr 1995, p1276
4 LJ, Feb 15 1995, p150
3 RBB, May 1 1995, p1596
5 WLB/R, Mar 1995, p79-80

<u>**HC 59.7**</u>   **(LC)**   **DDC: 909.0972**

Dictionary of Third World Terms

Hadjor, Buenor. Tauris, 1992. 303p. *Cloth:* $49.95.

Review Avg: 3.33   *OCLC:* 163   *Rating:* 3.66

Reviews
3 ARBA, 93:136
3 Choice, Dec 1992, p602
4 GSED, 1997, p37

<u>**HC 59.7**</u>   **(LC)**   **DDC: 909.0972**

The Encyclopedia of the Third World

Kurian, George Thomas (ed). Facts On File, 1992. 4th ed. 3 vols. (2432p.) *Cloth:* $225.00/set.

Review Avg: 3.50   *OCLC:* 995   *Rating:* 7.49

Reviews
3 ARBA, 93:167
4 GSED, 1997, p10

<u>**HC 94**</u>   **(LC)**   **DDC: 382**

Encyclopedia of the North American Free Trade Agreement, the New American Community, and Latin-American Trade

Rosenberg, Jerry M. Greenwood, 1995. 562p. *Cloth:* $79.95.

Review Avg: 3.50   *OCLC:* 559   *Rating:* 4.62

Reviews
3 Choice, May 1995, p1433
4 WLB/R, Apr 1995, p86

<u>**HC 102**</u>   **(LC)**   **DDC: 330.973**

Dictionary of United States Economic History

Olson, James S. and Susan Wladaver-Morgan. Greenwood, 1992. 667p. *Cloth:* $85.00.

Review Avg: 3.60   *OCLC:* 672   *Rating:* 4.94

Reviews
4 ARBA, 94:158
4 Choice, Mar 1993, p1118
3 GSED, 1997, p58
4 LJ, Oct 15 1992, p62
3 RBB, Jan 15 1993, p936,938

<u>**HC 102**</u>   **(LC)**   **DDC: 338.0973**

Encyclopedia of American Industries

Hillstrom, Kevin (ed). Gale Research, 1994. 2 vols. *Cloth:* $250.00/set.

Note: Vol 1: Manufacturing Industries.

Review Avg: 4.29   *OCLC:* 559   *Rating:* 5.41

Reviews
5 ARBA, 95:236
3 Choice, Apr 1994, p1272
4 GSED, 1997, p73
4 LJ, Feb 15 1995, p150
5 RBB, Apr 15 1995, p1522
4 RQ, Fall 1995, p114-115
5 WLB/R, Mar 1995, p77-78

<u>**HC 106.8**</u>   **(LC)**   **DDC: 338.0973**

Inside U.S. Business: A Concise Encyclopedia of Leading Industries

Mattera, Philip. Irwin, 1994. 1994 ed. 629p. *Cloth:* $47.50.

Review Avg: 3.00   *OCLC:* 279   *Rating:* 5.56

Reviews
3 ARBA, 92:205
3 Choice, Jul/Aug 1991, p1762
3 RBB, Apr 1 1991, p1590
3 WLB/R, May 1991, p143

<u>**HC 241.2**</u>   **(LC)**   **DDC: 940.559**

European Communities Encyclopedia and Directory

Gale Research, 1992. 390p. *Cloth:* $325.00.

Review Avg: 2.80   *OCLC:* 203   *Rating:* 3.21

Reviews
3 ARBA, 92:711
3 ARBA, 97:607

◆ The article titles in this encyclopedia are indexed by keyword in Part II.

2 Choice, Mar 1992, p1042
3 LJ, Dec 1991, p134
3 RBB, Feb 1 1992, p1054

HC 254.5 _____(LC)   DDC: 338.0941
Companion to the Industrial Revolution
Lines, Clifford. Facts On File, 1990. 262p. _Cloth:_ $27.50.
Review Avg: 3.00   _OCLC:_ 489   _Rating:_ 3.98

Reviews
3 ARBA, 91:159
3 Choice, Jan 1991, p758-759

HC 435 _____(LC)   DDC: 338.5
India 2001: Reference Encyclopedia
South Asian Publications, 1995. 1 vol. _Cloth:_ $125.00.
Review Avg: 4.00   _OCLC:_ 29   _Rating:_ 4.06

Reviews
4 ARBA, 96:132

HC 462.9 _____(LC)   DDC: 330.952
The MIT Encyclopedia of the Japanese Economy
Hsu, Robert C. MIT, 1994. 406p. _Cloth:_ $50.00.
Review Avg: 3.00   _OCLC:_ 380   _Rating:_ 3.76

Reviews
3 ARBA, 95:273
3 Choice, Feb 1995, p917

HD 62.15 _____(LC)   DDC: 658.5
The McGraw-Hill Encyclopedia of Quality Terms and Concepts
Cortada, James W. and John A. Woods. McGraw-Hill, 1995. 392p.
Cloth: $34.95.
Review Avg: 3.00   _OCLC:_ 616   _Rating:_ 4.23

Reviews
3 ARBA, 96:284
3 Choice, Jan 1996, p752,754
3 RBB, Jan 1 1996, p886

HD 62.7 _____(LC)   DDC: 658.022
The Entrepreneur and Small Business Problem Solver: An Encyclopedic Reference and Guide
Cohen, William A. Wiley, 1990. 2nd ed. 565p. _Paper:_ $24.95.
Review Avg: 3.50   _OCLC:_ 591   _Rating:_ 6.68

Reviews
3 ARBA, 91:152
4 GSED, 1997, p53

HD 1365 _____(LC)   DDC: 333.33
Arnold Encyclopedia of Real Estate
Arnold, Alvin L. Wiley, 1993. 2nd ed. 610p. _Cloth:_ $129.95.
Review Avg: 4.00   _OCLC:_ 261   _Rating:_ 6.52

Reviews
4 GSED, 1997, p95

HD 2324 _____(LC)   DDC: 338
Encyclopedia of Global Industries
Sawinski, Diane M. and Wendy H. Mason. Gale Research, 1996.
1034p. _Cloth:_ $395.00.
Note: Companion to _The Encyclopedia of American Industries._
Review Avg: 3.25   _OCLC:_ 185   _Rating:_ 3.62

Reviews
4 ARBA, 97:204
3 Choice, Oct 1996, p250
3 RBB, Aug 1996, p1924
3 RQ, Win 1996, p290

HD 2954 _____(LC)   DDC: 334
Cooperative-Credit Union Dictionary and Reference (including Encyclopedic Materials)
McLanahan, Jack and Connie McLanahan. Cooperative Alumni Assn,
1990. 410p. _Cloth:_ $23.50.
Review Avg: 3.50   _OCLC:_ 270   _Rating:_ 6.04

Reviews   **_Awards_**
3 ARBA, 91:134   Choice/OAB, May 1991,
4 Choice, Nov 1990, p454   p1429

HD 5324 _____(LC)   DDC: 331.8929
Labor Conflict in the United States: An Encyclopedia
Filippelli, Ronald L. Garland, 1990. 609p.
Review Avg: 4.00   _OCLC:_ 1012   _Rating:_ 8.02

Reviews   **_Awards_**
3 ARBA, 92:215   LJ/BRS, Apr 15 1991,
4 Choice, Mar 1991, p1100   p44-45
5 LJ, Aug 1990, p106
4 RBB, Feb 1 1991,
 p1153-1154

HD 6095 _____(LC)   DDC: 331.4
The ABC-CLIO Companion to Women in the Workplace
Schneider, Dorothy and Carl J. Schneider. ABC-CLIO, 1993. 371p.
Cloth: $55.00.
Note: Series—ABC-CLIO Companions to Key Issues in American
History and Life.
Review Avg: 3.60   _OCLC:_ 810   _Rating:_ 5.22

Reviews
3 ARBA, 95:913
4 Choice, May 1994, p1420
3 LJ, Mar 1 1994, p82
5 RBB, Mar 1 1994, p1278
3 WLB/R, Apr 1994, p87

HD 6508 _____(LC)   DDC: 331.88
The ABC-CLIO Companion to the American Labor Movement
Taylor, Paul F. ABC-CLIO, 1993. 237p. _Cloth:_ $55.00.
Review Avg: 3.00   _OCLC:_ 445   _Rating:_ 3.89

Reviews
5 ARBA, 95:294
1 Choice, May 1994, p1422
3 WLB/R, Apr 1994, p87

HD 6657   (LC)   DDC: 331.88

European Labor Unions
Campbell, Joan (ed). Greenwood, 1992. 648p. *Cloth:* $135.00.
Review Avg: 4.00   *OCLC:* 210   *Rating:* 4.42

Reviews
4 Choice, May 1993, p1512
4 LJ, Jan 1993, p96

HD 9515   (LC)   DDC: 338.4

Iron and Steel in the Twentieth Century
Seely, Bruce E. (ed). Facts On File, 1994. 512p. *Cloth:* $95.00.
Note: Series—Encyclopedia of American Business History and Biography.
Review Avg: 4.00   *OCLC:* 423   *Rating:* 4.85

Reviews
4 ARBA, 95:238

HD 9560.1   (LC)   DDC: 338.2

International Petroleum Encyclopedia
West, Jim (ed). PennWell, 1995. 359p. *Cloth:* $130.00.
Review Avg: 4.50   *OCLC:* 0   *Rating:* 4.50

Reviews
5 ARBA, 93:1744
3 ARBA, 90:1783
5 ARBA, 95:1744
5 GSED, 1997, p1026, 1994 volume

◆**HE 203**   (LC)   DDC: 388.0973

The ABC-CLIO Companion to Transportation in America
Richter, William L. ABC-CLIO, 1995. 653p. *Cloth:* $55.00.
Note: Series—ABC-CLIO Companions to Key Issues in American History and Life.
Review Avg: 3.50   *OCLC:* 375   *Rating:* 4.25

Reviews
4 Choice, Mar 1996, p1104
3 WLB/R, 1996

HE 745   (LC)   DDC: 387.5

A Historical Dictionary of the U.S. Merchant Marine and Shipping Industry Since the Introduction of Steam
de la Pedraja, Rene. Greenwood, 1994. 754p. *Cloth:* $99.95.
Review Avg: 4.00   *OCLC:* 203   *Rating:* 4.41

Reviews
4 Choice, Jan 1995, p746
4 GSED, 1997, p337
4 LJ, Aug 1994, p73
4 WLB/R, Jan 1995, p80-81

HF 1001   (LC)   DDC: 650.1

Encyclopedia of Business
Maurer, John G. and others. Gale Research, 1995. 2 vols. (1584p.) *Cloth:* $395.00/set.
Review Avg: 3.60   *OCLC:* 200   *Rating:* 6.00

Reviews   **Awards**
3 ARBA, 97:155   Choice/OAB, Jan 1997,
4 Choice, Sep 1996, p96   p740
5 GSED, 1997, p55

3 LJ, Mar 1 1996, p72
3 RBB, Jun 1996, p1769

◆**HF 1001**   (LC)   DDC: 650

International Encyclopedia of Business and Management
Warner, Malcolm (ed). Routledge, 1996. 6 vols. (5523p.) *Cloth:* $1295.00/set.
Review Avg: 4.00   *OCLC:* 233   *Rating:* 4.47

Reviews   **Awards**
4 Choice, Feb 1997, p946   Choice/OAB, Jan 1998,
4 RBB, Nov 15 1996,   p760
  p606-607

HF 1359   (LC)   DDC: 338.9

The International Business Dictionary and Reference
Presner, Lewis A. Wiley, 1991. 486p. *Cloth:* $45.00.
Review Avg: 3.33   *OCLC:* 635   *Rating:* 4.60

Reviews
3 ARBA, 93:255
4 Choice, Jul/Aug 1992, p1660
3 RBB, Mar 1 1992, p1307

HF 1359   (LC)   DDC: 338.9

The International Development Dictionary
Fry, Gerald M. and Galen R. Martin. ABC-CLIO, 1991. 445p. *Cloth:* $65.00.
Review Avg: 4.25   *OCLC:* 476   *Rating:* 7.20

Reviews   **Awards**
5 ARBA, 92:125   Choice/OAB, May 1992,
3 Choice, Dec 1991,   p1342
  p573-574
4 LJ, Sep 15 1991, p68
5 RBB, Oct 1 1991,
  p364-365

HF 5381   (LC)   DDC: 650.1

Encyclopedia of Career Change and Work Issues
Jones, Lawrence K. (ed). Oryx, 1992. 379p. *Cloth:* $67.50.
Review Avg: 4.00   *OCLC:* 972   *Rating:* 7.94

Reviews   **Awards**
5 ARBA, 93:409   RBB/ORS, May 1 1993,
4 Choice, Jan 1993, p766   p1620
4 GSED, 1997, p87,125
3 JAL, Mar 1993, p56
4 RBB, Oct 1 1992, p366

HF 5381   (LC)   DDC: 650.1

The Encyclopedia of Careers and Vocational Guidance
Hopke, William E. (ed). Ferguson, 1997. 11th ed. 4 vols. *Cloth:* $149.95/set.
Note: Available on CD-ROM, $199.95.
Review Avg: 3.56   *OCLC:* 708   *Rating:* 6.98

Reviews
3 ARBA, 94:386, 9th ed.
3 ARBA, 91:374, 8th ed.
4 Choice, Mar 1991, p1094, 8th ed.
4 GSED, 1997, p123
4 LJ, Mar 15 1991, p84, 8th ed.
3 RBB, Jan 15 1994, p963-964, 9th ed.

◆ The article titles in this encyclopedia are indexed by keyword in Part II.

3 RBB, May 1 1997, Review of CD-ROM
4 WLB/R, Mar 1991, p128
4 WLB/R, Jan 1994, p87

HF 5381.2   (LC)   DDC: 650.1
Career Discovery Encyclopedia
Cosgrove, Holli (ed). Ferguson, 1997. 6 vols. *Cloth:* $129.95/set.
Review Avg: 3.33   *OCLC:* 357   *Rating:* 4.04

Reviews
4 ARBA, 91:371
3 ARBA, 98:213, 1997 ed.
3 GSED, 1997, p121
3 RBB, May 15 1990, p1836,1838
4 RBB, Aug 1997, p1923-1924, 1997 ed.
3 WLB/R, Apr 1990, p117-118

HF 5382.5   (LC)   DDC: 650.1
Cassell Careers Encyclopedia
Segal, Audrey and Katherine Lea. Mansell, 1992. 13th ed. 768p.
Cloth: $80.00.
Review Avg: 3.50   *OCLC:* 35   *Rating:* 5.57

Reviews
3 ARBA, 94:385
4 GSED, 1997, p122

HF 5382.5   (LC)   DDC: 331.7
VGM's Careers Encyclopedia
VGM Career Horizons (eds). VGM, 1997. 4th ed. 456p. *Cloth:* $39.95.
Review Avg: 3.00   *OCLC:* 613   *Rating:* 6.23

Reviews
3 RBB, Aug 1997, p1923

HF 5383   (LC)   DDC: 650.1
The Encyclopedia of Career Choices for the 1990s: A Guide to Entry Level Jobs
Career Associates. Walker, 1991. 862p. *Paper:* $19.95.
Review Avg: 4.00   *OCLC:* 246   *Rating:* 4.49

Reviews
5 ARBA, 93:309
4 Choice, Mar 1993, p1126
3 RBB, Dec 1 1991, p718,720

HF 5415.3   (LC)   DDC: 658.8343
Encyclopedia of Consumer Brands
Jorgensen, Janice (ed). St James, 1994. 3 vols. *Cloth:* $195.00/set.
Review Avg: 4.50   *OCLC:* 864   *Rating:* 10.23

Reviews   **Awards**
5 ARBA, 95:324   LJ/BRS, Apr 15 1995,
5 Choice, Jul/Aug 1994,   p38-39
   p1700   RBB/ORS, May 1 1995,
5 GSED, 1997, p93   p1603
4 LJ, Mar 1 1994, p78
3 RBB, Feb 15 1994, p1107
5 WLB/R, Jun 1994, p94,97

HF 5605   (LC)   DDC: 657
The History of Accounting: An International Encyclopedia
Chatfield, Michael and Richard Vangermeersch (eds). Garland, 1996. 649p. *Cloth:* $95.00.
Review Avg: 3.00   *OCLC:* 225   *Rating:* 3.45

Reviews
3 ARBA, 97:179
3 Choice, Oct 1996, p253
3 RBB, Jul 1996, p1845

HG 151   (LC)   DDC: 332.1
Encyclopedia of Banking and Finance
Garcia, F. L. and Charles J. Woelfel. St James, 1994. 10th ed. 1219p.
Cloth: $115.00. *Paper:* $49.95.
Note: Available on CD-ROM, 225.00.
Review Avg: 4.20   *OCLC:* 393   *Rating:* 6.99

Reviews
5 ARBA, 94:208, 10th ed.
5 ARBA, 92:186, 9th ed.
4 Choice, Jul/Aug 1991, p1762
3 GSED, 1997, p68
4 RBB, May 15 1991, p1832-1833

HG 151   (LC)   DDC: 332
The Fitzroy Dearborn Encyclopedia of Banking and Finance
Woelfel, Charles J. Fitzroy, 1994. 10th ed. 1219p. *Cloth:* $125.00.
Review Avg: 3.33   *OCLC:* 247   *Rating:* 5.82

Reviews
3 ARBA, 95:230
3 Choice, Oct 1994, p260
4 GSED, 1997, p64

HG 151   (LC)   DDC: 332
The New Palgrave Dictionary of Money and Finance
Newman, Peter and others (eds). Stockton, 1992. 3 vols. *Cloth:* $595.00/set.
Review Avg: 4.40   *OCLC:* 1132   *Rating:* 12.66

Reviews   **Awards**
5 ARBA, 93:242   Choice/OAB, Jan 1994,
4 Choice, Feb 1993,   p712
   p942-943   LJ/BRS, Apr 15 1993,
5 GSED, 1997, p69   p62
4 RBB, Feb 15 1993, p1082   RBB/ORS, May 1 1993,
4 WLB/R, Jan 1993, p111   p1620

HG 2461   (LC)   DDC: 332
Banking and Finance to 1913
Schweikart, Larry (ed). Facts On File, 1990. 528p. *Cloth:* $99.00.
Note: Series—Encyclopedia of American Business and History and Biography.
Review Avg: 3.00   *OCLC:* 658   *Rating:* 4.32

Reviews
3 ARBA, 91:213

HG 2481   (LC)   DDC: 332
Banking and Finance, 1913-1989
Schweikart, Larry (ed). Facts On File, 1990. 505p. *Cloth:* $99.00.
Note: Series—Encyclopedia of American Business History and Biography.

Review Avg: 3.75   *OCLC:* 777   *Rating:* 5.30

Reviews
3 ARBA, 92:185
5 Choice, Apr 1991, p1283-1284
4 LJ, Mar 15 1991, p83
3 RBB, May 15 1991, p1832-1833

HG 4530 _____(LC)   DDC: 332.63
The Mutual Fund Encyclopedia
Perritt, Gerald W. Dearborn, 1995. 1995-1996 565p. *Paper:* $35.95.
Review Avg: 3.33   *OCLC:* 178   *Rating:* 5.69

Reviews
3 ARBA, 91:184
3 Choice, Apr 1993, p1298
4 GSED, 1997, p70
3 LJ, Nov 1 1990, p84,86
4 LJ, May 15 1993, p64
3 RBB, Feb 15 1991, p1250

HM 17 _____(LC)   DDC: 301
The Blackwell Dictionary of Sociology: A User's Guide to Sociological Language
Johnson, Allan G. Blackwell, 1995. 378p. *Cloth:* $49.95.
Review Avg: 3.00   *OCLC:* 211   *Rating:* 3.42

Reviews
3 RBB, Dec 1 1996, p683-684

HM 17 _____(LC)   DDC: 301
The Concise Oxford Dictionary of Sociology
Marshall, Gordon (ed). Oxford Un, 1994. 571p. *Cloth:* $29.95. *Paper:* $13.95.
Review Avg: 3.50   *OCLC:* 470   *Rating:* 4.44

Reviews
3 ARBA, 96:834
4 Choice, Nov 1994, p422,424

◆**HM 17** _____(LC)   DDC: 301
Encyclopedia of Sociology
Borgatta, Edgar F. and Marie L. Borgatta. Macmillan, 1992. 4 vols. (2359p.) *Cloth:* $400.00/set.
Review Avg: 4.86   *OCLC:* 2118   *Rating:* 17.10

Reviews	**Awards**
5 ARBA, 93:847	Choice/OAB, Jan 1993, p734
5 Choice, Jul/Aug 1992, p1654-1655	Dartmouth, 1993
5 GSED, 1997, p458	LJ/BRS, Apr 15 1993, p60
5 LJ, Jul 1992, p76	RBB/ORS, May 1 1993, p1620
5 RBB, May 1 1992, p1619	
5 RQ, Fall 1992, p112-113	
4 WLB/R, May 1992, p123	

HM 17 _____(LC)   DDC: 301
The Encyclopedic Dictionary of Sociology
Lachmann, Richard (ed). Dushkin, 1991. 4th ed. 321p. *Cloth:* $17.95. *Paper:* $12.95.
Review Avg: 4.00   *OCLC:* 366   *Rating:* 6.73

Reviews
5 ARBA, 93:849

4 GSED, 1997, p462
3 RBB, Apr 15 1992, p1549

HM 17 _____(LC)   DDC: 301
The HarperCollins Dictionary of Sociology
Jary, David and Julia Jary. Harper Perennial, 1991. 601p. *Paper:* $13.00.
Review Avg: 3.50   *OCLC:* 791   *Rating:* 5.08

Reviews
3 ARBA, 93:848
3 Choice, Jun 1992, p1520
4 LJ, Mar 15 1992, p76
4 WLB/R, May 1992, p123

HM 17 _____(LC)   DDC: 301
Survey of Social Science: Sociology Series
Magill, Frank N. (ed). Salem, 1994. 5 vols. (2244p.) *Cloth:* $375.00/set.
Review Avg: 3.75   *OCLC:* 596   *Rating:* 4.94

Reviews
4 ARBA, 96:836
3 Choice, May 1995, p1434
4 LJ, May 15 1995, p66
4 WLB/R, Apr 1995, p90

HM 101 _____(LC)   DDC: 306
A Dictionary of Cultural and Critical Theory
Payne, Michael and others. Blackwell, 1996. 644p. *Cloth:* $74.95.
Review Avg: 3.00   *OCLC:* 328   *Rating:* 3.66

Reviews
3 Choice, Jul 1997, p1771

◆**HM 132** _____(LC)   DDC: 302
Encyclopedia of Relationships Across the Lifespan
Turner, Jeffrey S. Greenwood, 1996. 495p. *Cloth:* $100.00.
Review Avg: 3.00   *OCLC:* 343   *Rating:* 3.69

Reviews
3 ARBA, 97:631
3 Choice, Sep 1996, p107
3 LJ, Dec 1995, p97

HM 136 _____(LC)   DDC: 303.6
Aggression and Conflict: A Cross-Cultural Encyclopedia
Levinson, David. ABC-CLIO, 1994. 234p. *Cloth:* $49.50.
Review Avg: 3.67   *OCLC:* 874   *Rating:* 5.42

Reviews
3 ARBA, 96:835
4 Choice, Jun 1995, p1576
4 WLB/R, May 1995, p75-76

HM 251 _____(LC)   DDC: 302
The Blackwell Encyclopedia of Social Psychology
Manstead, Antony S. and Milles Hewstone (eds). Blackwell, 1995. 694p. *Cloth:* $125.00.
Review Avg: 4.00   *OCLC:* 563   *Rating:* 5.13

Reviews
3 Choice, Jan 1996, p752
5 LJ, Apr 15 1995, p62

◆ The article titles in this encyclopedia are indexed by keyword in Part II.

◆**HM 278**_____(LC)   DDC: 303.61
Protest, Power and Change: Encyclopedia of Nonviolent Action from ACT-UP to Woman's Suffrage
Powers, Roger S. and William B. Vogele (eds). Garland, 1996. 610p. *Cloth:* $75.00.
Review Avg: 4.00   *OCLC:* 419   *Rating:* 4.84

Reviews   **Awards**
4 ARBA, 98:692   RBB/ORS, May 1 1998,
4 Choice, Sep 1997, p107   p1538
4 RBB, Jun 1 1997,
  p1764-1765

◆**HM 291**_____(LC)   DDC: 303.6
The Encyclopedia of Violence: Origins, Attitudes, Consequences
DiCanio, Margaret. Facts On File, 1993. 404p. *Cloth:* $45.00.
Review Avg: 3.00   *OCLC:* 880   *Rating:* 4.76

Reviews
4 ARBA, 94:586
2 Choice, Apr 1994, p1268
3 GSED, 1997, p285
4 LJ, Nov 1 1993, p72
2 RBB, Dec 15 1993, p776

HN 1_____(LC)   DDC: 304
Encyclopedia of World Problems and Human Potential
Union of International Associations. Saur, 1994. 4th ed. 3 vols. *Cloth:* $725.00/set.
Review Avg: 3.75   *OCLC:* 170   *Rating:* 6.09

Reviews
3 ARBA, 98:43, CD-Rom version
3 ARBA, 92:803, 3rd ed.
4 ARBA, 95:828, 4th ed.
5 GSED, 1997, p459

HN 28_____(LC)   DDC: 306.09
Encyclopedia of Social History
Stearns, Peter N. (ed). Garland, 1994. 856p. *Cloth:* $95.00.
Note: Series— Garland Reference Library of Social Science, vol. 1780.
Review Avg: 3.50   *OCLC:* 776   *Rating:* 7.05

Reviews   **Awards**
3 ARBA, 95:96   Choice/OAB, Jan 1995,
4 Choice, Jun 1994,   p719
  p1552,1554
3 GSED, 1997, p6
4 RBB, May 15 1994, p1714

◆**HN 57**_____(LC)   DDC: 301.973
Encyclopedia of American Social History
Clayton, Mary Kupiec and others (eds). Scribner's, 1993. 3 vols. (2652p.) *Cloth:* $360.00/set.
Review Avg: 4.88   *OCLC:* 1782   *Rating:* 18.44

Reviews   **Awards**
5 ARBA, 94:505   Choice/OAB, Jan 1994,
5 CRL, Sep 1993, p434   p712
5 Choice, Sep 1993, p78,80   Dartmouth, 1994
5 GSED, 1997, p201   LJ/BRS, Apr 15 1994,
5 LJ, Jun 1 1993, p102,104   p39

4 RBB, Aug 1993, p2082   NYPL, 1994
5 RQ, Fall 1993, p123-124   RBB/ORS, May 1 1994,
5 WLB/R, May 1993, p116   p1627

◆**HN 57**_____(LC)   DDC: 306
Encyclopedia of Social Issues
Roth, John K. (ed). Cavendish, 1997. 6 vols. (1830p.) *Cloth:* $459.95.
Review Avg: 3.67   *OCLC:* 273   *Rating:* 4.22

Reviews
3 Choice, Jul 1997, p1779
4 LJ, Jun 15 1997, p60,62
4 RBB, Jun 1 1997, p1758,1760

◆**HQ 9**_____(LC)   DDC: 306.7
Dr. Ruth's Encyclopedia of Sex
Westheimer, Ruth K. and others (eds). Continuum, 1994. 319p. *Cloth:* $29.50.
Review Avg: 4.20   *OCLC:* 660   *Rating:* 5.52

Reviews
4 ARBA, 95:878
4 GSED, 1997, p478
5 LJ, Jul 1994, p84
4 RBB, Sep 1 1994, p66-67
4 WLB/R, Sep 1994, p77

◆**HQ 9**_____(LC)   DDC: 306.7
Encyclopedia of Marriage and the Family: The Definitive Guide to the Challenges and Realities Facing the Modern Family
Levinson, David (ed). Macmillan, 1995. 2 vols. *Cloth:* $190.00/set.
Review Avg: 3.60   *OCLC:* 1236   *Rating:* 6.07

Reviews
4 ARBA, 96:863
4 Choice, Apr 1996, p1284
4 GSED, 1997, p469
2 LJ, Dec 1995, p92
4 RBB, Feb 1 1996, p954

◆**HQ 9**_____(LC)   DDC: 306.7
Human Sexuality: An Encyclopedia
Bullough, Vern L. and Bonnie Bullough (eds). Garland, 1994. 643p. *Cloth:* $95.00.
Review Avg: 4.40   *OCLC:* 1098   *Rating:* 10.60

Reviews   **Awards**
5 ARBA, 95:872   LJ/BRS, Apr 15 1995,
4 Choice, Jun 1994, p1556   p40
5 GSED, 1997, p473   NYPL, 1994
4 RBB, May 1 1994, p1631
4 WLB/R, Apr 1994, p89-90

HQ 9_____(LC)   DDC: 306.7
Language of Sex: An A to Z Guide
Carrera, Michael A. Facts On File, 1992. 180p. *Cloth:* $24.95.
Review Avg: 3.25   *OCLC:* 337   *Rating:* 3.92

Reviews
3 ARBA, 93:883
3 GSED, 1997, p474
3 RBB, Jun 15 1992, p1884
4 WLB/R, Jun 1992, p112-114

HQ 12 _____(LC)   DDC: 306.7

The Encyclopedia of Erotic Wisdom: A Reference Guide to the Symbolism, Techniques, Rituals, Sacred Texts, Psychology, Anatomy, and History of Sexuality

Camphausen, Rufus C. Inner Traditions, 1991. 269p. *Paper:* $19.95.

Review Avg: 3.00   *OCLC:* 73   *Rating:* 3.15

Reviews
3 Choice, Apr 1992, p1205

HQ 21 _____(LC)   DDC: 306.7

The International Encyclopedia of Sexuality

Francoeur, Robert T. (ed). Continuum, 1996. 3 vols. (1737p.) *Cloth:* $255.00.

Review Avg: 2.50   *OCLC:* 69   *Rating:* 2.64

Reviews   **Awards**
3 ARBA, 98:797   LJ/BRS, Apr 15 1998,
2 LJ, Jun 15 1997, p62   p47

HQ 30 _____(LC)   DDC: 306.7

The A-to-Z of Women's Sexuality: A Concise Encyclopedia

Kahn, Ada P. and Linda Hughey Holt. Hunter House, 1992. Revised edition. 362p. *Paper:* $14.95.

Review Avg: 2.33   *OCLC:* 136   *Rating:* 4.60

Reviews
1 Choice, Nov 1990, p460
3 LJ, Apr 15 1990, p86,88
3 RBB, Sep 1 1990, p79

HQ 75 _____(LC)   DDC: 305.9

Completely Queer: The Gay and Lesbian Encyclopedia

Hogan, Steve and Lee Hudson. Holt, 1997. 672p. *Cloth:* $50.00.

Note: Series—Henry Holt Reference Book.

Review Avg: 4.00   *OCLC:* 19   *Rating:* 4.04

Reviews
4 LJ, Nov 15 1997, p52

◆**HQ 76** _____(LC)   DDC: 306.766

Encyclopedia of Homosexuality

Dynes, Wayne R. and others (eds). Garland, 1990. 2 vols. *Cloth:* $150.00/set.

Review Avg: 4.57   *OCLC:* 1364   *Rating:* 15.30

Reviews   **Awards**
5 ARBA, 91:870   Choice/OAB, May 1991,
5 Choice, Jun 1990, p1650   p1429
4 GSED, 1997, p476   LJ/BRS, Apr 15 1991,
5 LJ, Jan 1990, p100   p42-43
4 RBB, May 15 1990,   NYPL, 1991
   p1840-1841   RBB/ORS, May 1 1991,
5 RQ, Fall 1990, p16-18   p1734
4 WLB/R, May 1990,
   p127-128

HQ 767.84 _____(LC)   DDC: 305.23

Growing Up: A Cross-Cultural Encyclopedia

Broude, Gwen J. ABC-CLIO, 1995. 376p. *Cloth:* $49.50.

Review Avg: 2.00   *OCLC:* 253   *Rating:* 2.51

Reviews
1 ARBA, 97:708
3 Choice, May 1996, p1446

HQ 769 _____(LC)   DDC: 649.1

Parenting A to Z: A Guide to Everything from Conception to College

Franck, Irene and David Brownstone. HarperCollins, 1996. 2nd ed. 728p. *Cloth:* $32.50.

Review Avg: 4.00   *OCLC:* 465   *Rating:* 6.93

Reviews
3 ARBA, 98:803
5 LJ, Mar 15 1997, p54

HQ 769 _____(LC)   DDC: 649.1

The Parent's Desk Reference: The Ultimate Family Encyclopedia from Conception to College

Franck, Irene and David Brownstone. Prentice-Hall, 1991. 615p. *Cloth:* $29.95.

Review Avg: 4.00   *OCLC:* 720   *Rating:* 7.44

Reviews   **Awards**
4 ARBA, 92:842   RBB/ORS, May 1 1992,
4 RBB, Aug 1991,   p1625
   p2173-2174

◆**HQ 796** _____(LC)   DDC: 305.23

Encyclopedia of Adolescence

Lerner, Richard M. and others. Garland, 1991. 2 vols. (1222p.) *Cloth:* $150.00/set.

Note: Series—Garland Reference Library of the Social Sciences, vol. 495.

Review Avg: 3.86   *OCLC:* 1310   *Rating:* 8.48

Reviews   **Awards**
4 ARBA, 92:843   Choice/OAB, May 1992,
5 Choice, Sep 1991, p56   p1341
4 GSED, 1997, p485
4 LJ, May 15 1991, p77
3 RBB, Feb 15 1992, p128
3 RBB, Jun 15 1991, p2000
4 WLB/R, May 1991, p139

◆**HQ 1061** _____(LC)   DDC: 305.2

Encyclopedia of Aging: A Comprehensive Resource in Gerontology and Geriatrics

Maddox, George L. (ed). Springer-Verlag, 1995. 2nd ed. 1216p. *Cloth:* $159.00.

Review Avg: 4.00   *OCLC:* 1481   *Rating:* 8.96

Reviews
5 ARBA, 96:850
4 GSED, 1997, p464
3 WLB/R, Oct 1992, p104

HQ 1061 _____(LC)   DDC: 305.26

The Encyclopedia of Aging and the Elderly

Roy, F. Hampton and Charles Russell. Facts On File, 1992. 308p. *Cloth:* $50.00.

Review Avg: 3.00   *OCLC:* 812   *Rating:* 4.62

Reviews
3 ARBA, 93:858

◆ The article titles in this encyclopedia are indexed by keyword in Part II.

3 Choice, Dec 1992, p604-605
3 GSED, 1997, p466
3 LJ, Oct 15 1992, p62,64
3 RBB, Aug 1992, p2036-2037
3 WLB/R, Oct 1992, p104

HQ 1061 _____(LC)   DDC: 305.26
Encyclopedia of Financial Gerontology
Vitt, Lois A. and Jurg K. Siegenthaler (eds). Greenwood, 1996. 600p.
Cloth: $99.50.
Review Avg: 4.00   *OCLC:* 42   *Rating:* 4.08

Reviews
4 Choice, Oct 1996, p250

HQ 1064 _____(LC)   DDC: 305.26
The Graying of America: An Encyclopedia of Aging, Health, Mind, and Behavior
Kausler, Donald H. and Barry C. Kausler. Un of Ill, 1996. 356p. *Cloth:*
$39.95.
Review Avg: 3.00   *OCLC:* 208   *Rating:* 3.42

Reviews
2 ARBA, 97:668
4 Choice, Jan 1997, p770
3 RBB, Jul 1996, p1844-1845

HQ 1064 _____(LC)   DDC: 305.26
Older Americans Almanac: A Reference Work on Seniors in the United States
Manheimer, Ronald J. (ed). Gale Research, 1994. 881p. *Cloth:* $99.50.
Review Avg: 4.00   *OCLC:* 782   *Rating:* 5.56

Reviews
5 Choice, Nov 1994, p434
3 LJ, Oct 1 1994, p71

HQ 1115 _____(LC)   DDC: 305.4
American Women's History: An A to Z of People, Organizations, Issues, and Events
Weatherford, Doris. Prentice-Hall, 1994. 396p. *Cloth:* $30.00. *Paper:*
$18.00.
Review Avg: 4.00   *OCLC:* 805   *Rating:* 5.61

Reviews
4 RBB, Jun 1 1994, p1863-1864
4 WLB/R, Sep 1994, p77

HQ 1115 _____(LC)   DDC: 305.4
The Dictionary of Feminist Theory
Humm, Maggie. Ohio State Un, 1995. 2nd ed. 354p. *Cloth:* $59.50.
Paper: $20.00.
Review Avg: 3.86   *OCLC:* 478   *Rating:* 8.82

Reviews	*Awards*
3 ARBA, 91:925	Choice/OAB, May 1991,
2 ARBA, 96:948, 2nd ed.	p1430
5 Choice, Sep 1990, p78	
5 Choice, Nov 1995,	
p436,438, 2nd ed.	
5 GSED, 1997, p501	
2 LJ, Jan 1990, p102	
5 RBB, Apr 1 1990, p1575	

◆**HQ 1115** _____(LC)   DDC: 305.4
Women's Issues
Mc Fadden, Margaret (ed). Salem, 1997. 3 vols. (1041p.) *Cloth:*
$270.00.
Note: Series—Ready Reference.
Review Avg: 4.00   *OCLC:* 501   *Rating:* 5.00

Reviews	*Awards*
4 Choice, Sep 1997, p98	RBB/ORS, May 1 1998,
4 RBB, Jun 1 1997, p1765	p1538

◆**HQ 1410** _____(LC)   DDC: 305.4
The ABC-CLIO Companion to Women's Progress in America
Frost-Knappman, Elizabeth. ABC-CLIO, 1994. 389p. *Cloth:* $55.00.
Note: Series—ABC-CLIO Companions to Key Issues in American
History and Life.
Review Avg: 4.33   *OCLC:* 821   *Rating:* 7.97

Reviews	*Awards*
4 ARBA, 95:914	Choice/OAB, Jan 1995,
5 Choice, Dec 1994,	p719
p573-574	
4 WLB/R, Nov 1994, p98,139	

HQ 1410 _____(LC)   DDC: 305.4
The Encyclopedia of Women's History in America
Cullen-DuPont, Kathryn. Facts On File, 1996. 336p. *Cloth:* $45.00.
Review Avg: 3.00   *OCLC:* 927   *Rating:* 6.85

Reviews	*Awards*
3 ARBA, 97:736	NYPL, 1996
3 Choice, Sep 1996, p94	
3 LJ, Dec 1995, p88,90	
3 RBB, Mar 15 1996, p1313	

HQ 1410 _____(LC)   DDC: 305.4
Handbook of American Women's History
Zophy, Angela Howard (ed). Garland, 1990. 763p. *Cloth:* $95.00.
Review Avg: 3.25   *OCLC:* 1534   *Rating:* 10.32

Reviews	*Awards*
3 ARBA, 91:929	Choice/OAB, May 1991,
4 Choice, Sep 1990, p76	p1429
2 LJ, Mar 1 1990, p88	RBB/ORS, May 1 1991,
4 RBB, Mar 15 1990, p1500	p1735

HQ 1410 _____(LC)   DDC: 303.4
Scholastic Encyclopedia of Women in the United States
Kennan, Sheila. Scholastic, 1996. 206p. *Cloth:* $17.95.
Review Avg: 3.00   *OCLC:* 475   *Rating:* 3.95

Reviews
3 ARBA, 98:836

HS 119 _____(LC)   DDC: 366
The International Encyclopedia of Secret Societies and Fraternal Orders
Axelrod, Alan. Facts On File, 1996. 287p. *Cloth:* $40.00.
Review Avg: 3.00   *OCLC:* 626   *Rating:* 4.25

Reviews
3 ARBA, 98:764

3 LJ, May 15 1997, p70
3 RBB, Sep 1 1997, p164

4 LJ, Jan 1992, p104
3 RBB, Feb 15 1992, p1128

HS 2330 _____(LC)   DDC: 322.4209

The Ku Klux Klan: An Encyclopedia
Newton, Michael. Garland, 1991. 639p. *Cloth:* $80.00.
Review Avg: 2.83   *OCLC:* 848   *Rating:* 4.53

Reviews
2 ARBA, 92:730
3 Choice, Jul/Aug 1991, p1763
2 LJ, Feb 15 1991, p188
3 RBB, Jun 1 1991, p1900
3 RQ, Spr 1992, p420
4 WLB/R, Apr 1991, p119

HT 108.5 _____(LC)   DDC: 307.76

World Encyclopedia of Cities
Kurian, George Thomas (ed). ABC-CLIO, 1994. 2 vols. *Cloth:*
$150.00/vol.
Review Avg: 3.83   *OCLC:* 803   *Rating:* 7.44

Reviews   **Awards**
5 ARBA, 95:900   LJ/BRS, Apr 15 1994,
3 Choice, May 1994, p1418   p40
4 GSED, 1997, p11,494
3 LJ, Apr 1 1994, p90
4 RBB, May 1 1994, p1637
4 WLB/R, May 1994, p77

HV 12 _____(LC)   DDC: 361.7

International Encyclopedia of Foundations
Kiger, Joseph C. (ed). Greenwood, 1990. 355p. *Cloth:* $89.50.
Review Avg: 3.67   *OCLC:* 383   *Rating:* 4.44

Reviews
4 Choice, Oct 1990, p284
4 GSED, 1997, p471
3 LJ, Apr 15 1990, p86

◆**HV 35** _____(LC)   DDC: 361.3

Encyclopedia of Social Work
Edwards, Richard L. (ed). Natl Assn of Social Workers, 1995. 19th
ed. 3 vols. (2746p.) *Cloth:* $150.00/set. *Paper:* $120.00.
Note: Available on CD-ROM, $275.00.
Review Avg: 4.50   *OCLC:* 422   *Rating:* 7.34

Reviews
4 ARBA, 96:893, 19th ed.
4 Choice, Nov 1995, p432, 19th ed.
5 GSED, 1997, p480, 19th ed.
5 RBB, Jul 1995, p1897, 19th ed.

◆**HV 875.55** _____(LC)   DDC: 362.7

The Encyclopedia of Adoption
Adamec, Christine A. and William L. Pierce. Facts On File, 1991.
382p. *Cloth:* $45.00.
Review Avg: 3.80   *OCLC:* 978   *Rating:* 5.76

Reviews
3 ARBA, 93:866
4 Choice, Sep 1992, p71
5 GSED, 1997, p469

◆**HV 1461** _____(LC)   DDC: 362.6

Encyclopedia of Home Care for the Elderly
Romaine-Davis, Ada and others (eds). Greenwood, 1995. 436p.
Cloth: $85.00.
Review Avg: 3.20   *OCLC:* 532   *Rating:* 4.26

Reviews
3 ARBA, 96:1681
4 Choice, Oct 1995, p262
3 LJ, Jan 1995, p84-85
3 RBB, Jun 1 1995, p1821,1823
3 RQ, Win 1995, p255

HV 1553 _____(LC)   DDC: 323.3

The ABC-CLIO Companion to the Disability Rights Move-
ment
Pelka, Fred. ABC-CLIO, 1997. 422p. *Cloth:* $60.00.
Note: Series—ABC-CLIO Companions to Key Issues in American
History and Life.
Review Avg: 4.00   *OCLC:* 299   *Rating:* 4.60

Reviews
4 ARBA, 98:776

◆**HV 1568** _____(LC)   DDC: 362.4

Encyclopedia of Disability and Rehabilitation
Dell Orto, Arthur E. and Robert P. Marinelli (eds). Macmillan, 1995.
820p. *Cloth:* $125.00.
Review Avg: 3.60   *OCLC:* 902   *Rating:* 7.40

Reviews   **Awards**
4 ARBA, 97:670   Choice/OAB, Jan 1997,
4 Choice, Sep 1996, p96   p740
3 GSED, 1997, p922
3 LJ, May 1 1996, p86
4 RBB, Jun 1996,
 p1769-1770

HV 5017 _____(LC)   DDC: 362.29

The Encyclopedia of Alcoholism
O'Brien, Robert and Morris Chafetz. Facts On File, 1991. 2nd ed.
346p. *Cloth:* $50.00.
Review Avg: 3.75   *OCLC:* 1188   *Rating:* 8.13

Reviews
4 ARBA, 92:839
4 GSED, 1997, p483
3 RBB, Nov 1 1991, p564
4 WLB/R, Nov 1991, p110

HV 5804 _____(LC)   DDC: 362.29

The Encyclopedia of Drug Abuse
Evans, Glen and others. Facts On File, 1992. 2nd ed. 370p. *Cloth:*
$50.00.
Review Avg: 4.67   *OCLC:* 1244   *Rating:* 9.16

Reviews
5 ARBA, 93:890, 2nd ed.
5 GSED, 1997, p484, 2nd ed.
4 RBB, Feb 15 1992, p1130, 2nd ed.

◆ The article titles in this encyclopedia are indexed by keyword in Part II.

◆**HV 5804** _____(LC)   DDC: 362.29

Encyclopedia of Drugs and Alcohol
Jaffe, Jerome (ed). Macmillan, 1995. 4 vols. (1861p.) _Cloth:_ $375.00/set.
Review Avg: 4.67   _OCLC:_ 1597   _Rating:_ 11.86

Reviews   **_Awards_**
5 ARBA, 97:707   Choice/OAB, Jan 1996,
4 Choice, Dec 1995, p592   p724
5 GSED, 1997, p481   LJ/BRS, Apr 15 1996,
4 RBB, Oct 1 1995, p337   p40
5 RBB, May 1 1996, p1536
5 RQ, Spr 1996, p408-409

HV 5822 _____(LC)   DDC: 362.294

Psychedelics Encyclopedia
Stafford, Peter. Ronin, 1992. 3rd ed. 512p. _Paper:_ $29.95.
Review Avg: 4.50   _OCLC:_ 463   _Rating:_ 7.43

Reviews
4 GSED, 1997, p956
5 LJ, Nov 15 1992, p72

HV 6017 _____(LC)   DDC: 364

Crime: An Encyclopedia
Cyriax, Oliver. Trafalgar Square, 1994. 468p. _Cloth:_ $29.95. _Paper:_ $16.95.
Review Avg: 3.50   _OCLC:_ 22   _Rating:_ 3.54

Reviews
3 Choice, Apr 1995, p1270
4 RBB, Apr 15 1995, p1522

HV 6017 _____(LC)   DDC: 364

Crime and Justice System in America: An Encyclopedia
Schmalleger, Frank (ed). Greenwood, 1997. 299p. _Cloth:_ $65.00.
Review Avg: 4.00   _Rating:_ 4.00

Reviews
4 ARBA, 98:550

HV 6017 _____(LC)   DDC: 364

World Encyclopedia of Organized Crime
Nash, Jay Robert. Paragon, 1992. 624p.
Note: From _Encyclopedia of World Crime._
Review Avg: 3.00   _OCLC:_ 377   _Rating:_ 3.75

Reviews
3 ARBA, 93:610
3 LJ, Mar 15 1992, p78
3 RBB, Apr 15 1992, p1556

HV 6278 _____(LC)   DDC: 364.1524

Encyclopedia of Assassinations
Sifakis, Carl. Facts On File, 1991. 228p. _Cloth:_ $35.00.
Review Avg: 3.00   _OCLC:_ 683   _Rating:_ 6.37

Reviews   **_Awards_**
3 ARBA, 92:558   NYPL, 1992
3 Choice, Jul/Aug 1991,
  p1766
3 GSED, 1997, p295
3 LJ, May 15 1991, p80
3 RBB, Jun 1 1991,
  p1898-1899
3 WLB/R, May 1991, p140

HV 6431 _____(LC)   DDC: 909.82

Almanac of Modern Terrorism
Shafritz, Jay M. and others. Facts On File, 1991. 290p. _Cloth:_ $35.00.
Review Avg: 3.00   _OCLC:_ 581   _Rating:_ 4.16

Reviews
3 ARBA, 92:557

HV 6431 _____(LC)   DDC: 303.6

Encyclopedia of World Terrorism
Creenshaw, Matha and John Pimlott (eds). Sharpe, 1997. 3 vols. (768p.) _Cloth:_ $299.00.
Review Avg: 3.00   _OCLC:_ 282   _Rating:_ 3.56

Reviews
3 Choice, Jul 1997, p1779
3 GSED, 1997, p382

HV 6431 _____(LC)   DDC: 909.82

Historical Dictionary of Terrorism
Anderson, Sean and Stephen Sloan. Scarecrow, 1995. 452p. _Cloth:_ $57.50.
Note: Series— Historical Dictionaries of Religions, Philosophies, Movements. No. 4.
Review Avg: 3.00   _OCLC:_ 526   _Rating:_ 4.05

Reviews
3 LJ, May 1 1995, p88

HV 6439 _____(LC)   DDC: 364.1066

National Gangs Resource Handbook: An Encyclopedic Reference
Knox, George W. Wyndham Hall, 1994. 240p. _Cloth:_ $24.95.
Review Avg: 4.00   _OCLC:_ 389   _Rating:_ 4.78

Reviews
4 Choice, Oct 1995, p268

HV 6515 _____(LC)   DDC: 364

World Encyclopedia of Twentieth Century Murder
Nash, Jay Robert. Marlow, 1992. 693p. _Cloth:_ $49.95.
Note: From _Encyclopedia of World Crime._
Review Avg: 3.00   _OCLC:_ 350   _Rating:_ 3.70

Reviews
3 ARBA, 93:611
3 Choice, Jul/Aug 1992, p1659
3 GSED, 1997, p292
3 RBB, Jan 15 1992, p964
3 RBB, Oct 1 1992, p367-368
3 RBB, Apr 15 1992, p1556

HV 6545 _____(LC)   DDC: 362.2

An Encyclopedia of Famous Suicides
Lester, David. Nova Science, 1996. 149p. _Cloth:_ $59.00.
Review Avg: 1.00   _OCLC:_ 26   _Rating:_ 1.05

Reviews
1 ARBA, 98:768

HV 6710 _____ (LC) DDC: 306.482

The Encyclopedia of Gambling

Sifakis, Carl. Facts On File, 1990. 340p. *Cloth:* $40.00.

Review Avg: 3.50 *OCLC:* 674 *Rating:* 4.85

Reviews
5 ARBA, 91:806
3 Choice, Sep 1991, p70
3 RBB, Mar 15 1990, p1498,1500
3 RQ, Fall 1990, p115-116

HV 6789 _____ (LC) DDC: 364.973

The Encyclopedia of American Crime

Sifakis, Carl (ed). Smithmark, 1992. Revised edition. 832p. *Cloth:* $19.98.

Review Avg: 3.00 *OCLC:* 446 *Rating:* 5.89

Reviews
3 GSED, 1997, p295n

◆**HV 7901** _____ (LC) DDC: 363.2

The Encyclopedia of Police Science

Bailey, William G. (ed). Garland, 1995. 2nd ed. 865p. *Cloth:* $95.00.

Review Avg: 3.75 *OCLC:* 834 *Rating:* 7.42

Reviews
5 ARBA, 96:599
3 Choice, Oct 1995, p262
3 GSED, 1997, p283
4 RBB, Sep 1 1995, p106

HV 9304 _____ (LC) DDC: 365

Dictionary of American Penology: An Introductory Guide

Williams, Vergil L. Greenwood, 1996. Revised edition. 530p. *Cloth:* $89.50.

Review Avg: 4.00 *OCLC:* 379 *Rating:* 6.76

Reviews
4 ARBA, 97:506
4 Choice, Jun 1997, p1647

◆**HV 9471** _____ (LC) DDC: 365

Encyclopedia of American Prisons

McShane, Marilyn D. and Frank P. Williams III (eds). Garland, 1996. 532p. *Cloth:* $95.00.

Note: Series—Garland Reference Library of the Humanities, 1748.

Review Avg: 3.75 *OCLC:* 743 *Rating:* 11.24

Reviews   *Awards*
4 Choice, Sep 1996, p95-96   Choice/OAB, Jan 1997,
4 GSED, 1997, p288   p740
3 LJ, Jun 1 1996, p94   LJ/BRS, Apr 15 1997,
4 RBB, Jul 1996,   p37
  p1842-1843   RBB/ORS, May 1 1997,
                                     p1524

◆**HX 86** _____ (LC) DDC: 335.00973

Encyclopedia of the American Left

Buhle, Mari Jo and others (eds). Garland, 1990. 928p. *Cloth:* $95.00.

Paper: $29.95.

Note: Series—Garland Reference Library of the Social Sciences, vol. 502.

Review Avg: 4.20 *OCLC:* 1020 *Rating:* 10.24

Reviews   *Awards*
5 ARBA, 91:763   Choice/OAB, May 1991,
4 Choice, Oct 1990, p281   p1429
5 GSED, 1997, p378   LJ/BRS, Apr 15 1991,
3 LJ, Jun 15 1990, p108   p43
4 RBB, Aug 1990,
  p2202-2203

JA 61 _____ (LC) DDC: 320.5

Dictionary of Conservative and Libertarian Thought

Ashford, Nigel and Stephen Davies (eds). Routledge, 1992. 288p. *Cloth:* $49.95.

Review Avg: 3.67 *OCLC:* 269 *Rating:* 4.21

Reviews
3 ARBA, 92:727
4 GSED, 1997, p377
4 WLB/R, Nov 1991, p110

JA 61 _____ (LC) DDC: 320

The Dictionary of Twentieth-Century World Politics

Shafritz, Jay M. and others. Holt, 1993. 756p. *Cloth:* $60.00. /O.P.

Review Avg: 3.86 *OCLC:* 847 *Rating:* 7.55

Reviews   *Awards*
3 ARBA, 94:718   Choice/OAB, Jan 1995,
4 CRL, Sep 1994, p418-419   p721
4 Choice, Jan 1994, p762
4 GSED, 1997, p353
4 LJ, Sep 1 1993, p177
4 RBB, Jan 1 1994,
  p850-851
4 WLB/R, Jan 1994, p86

JA 61 _____ (LC) DDC: 320

Dictionary of World Politics: A Reference Guide to Concepts, Ideas and Institutions

Evans, Graham and Jeffrey Newnham. Simon & Schuster, 1990. 449p. *Cloth:* $60.00.

Review Avg: 3.00 *OCLC:* 673 *Rating:* 4.35

Reviews
3 ARBA, 92:673
1 Choice, May 1991, p1456
3 GSED, 1997, p346
5 LJ, Dec 1990, p116
3 RBB, Mar 15 1991, p1522

◆**JA 61** _____ (LC) DDC: 320

Encyclopedia of Government and Politics

Hawkesworth, Mary and Maurice Kogan. Routledge, 1992. 2 vols. (1404p.) *Cloth:* $230.00/set.

Review Avg: 4.00 *OCLC:* 422 *Rating:* 4.84

Reviews
4 Choice, Mar 1993, p1110

JA 61 _____ (LC) DDC: 321.8

Illustrated Dictionary of Constitutional Concepts

Maddex, Robert L. Congressional Quarterly, 1996. 335p. *Cloth:* $84.95.

Review Avg: 4.00 *OCLC:* 280 *Rating:* 4.56

◆ The article titles in this encyclopedia are indexed by keyword in Part II.

Reviews
4 RBB, Apr 15 1997, p1450-1451

◆**JA 61** _____(LC)   DDC: 320

The Oxford Companion to Politics of the World

Krieger, Joel (ed). Oxford Un, 1993. 1088p. *Cloth:* $49.95.
Review Avg: 4.14   *OCLC:* 1537   *Rating:* 9.21

Reviews	*Awards*
5 ARBA, 94:717	NYPL, 1994
4 CRL, Sep 1994, p418-419	
4 Choice, Sep 1993, p86	
4 GSED, 1997, p350	
5 LJ, Mar 15 1993, p72	
3 RBB, May 1 1993,	
p1628,1630	
4 WLB/R, Jun 1993, p129	

◆**JA 61** _____(LC)   DDC: 320

Survey of Social Science, Government and Politics

Bessette, Joseph M. (ed). Salem, 1995. 5 vols. *Cloth:* $375.00/set.
Review Avg: 4.00   *OCLC:* 233   *Rating:* 4.47

Reviews
4 ARBA, 96:741

JA 64 _____(LC)   DDC: 947.084

Encyclopedia of Soviet Life

Zemtsov, Ilya. Transaction, 1991. 376p. *Cloth:* $59.95.
Review Avg: 3.00   *OCLC:* 267   *Rating:* 3.53

Reviews
3 ARBA, 92:721
4 Choice, Jul/Aug 1991, p1768
3 GSED, 1997, p376
2 LJ, Sep 1 1990, p216

JC 311 _____(LC)   DDC: 320.5

Encyclopedia of Nationalism

Snyder, Louis L. Paragon, 1990. 445p.
Review Avg: 3.40   *OCLC:* 820   *Rating:* 7.04

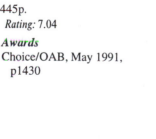

Reviews	*Awards*
3 ARBA, 91:766	Choice/OAB, May 1991,
4 Choice, Oct 1990, p288	p1430
3 LJ, Mar 1 1990, p90	
4 RBB, Jun 1 1990,	
p1922-1923	
3 WLB/R, Sep 1990,	
p128-130	

JC 319 _____(LC)   DDC: 327.1

Dictionary of Geopolitics

O'Loughlin, John (ed). Greenwood, 1994. 281p. *Cloth:* $75.00.
Review Avg: 3.25   *OCLC:* 359   *Rating:* 3.97

Reviews
3 ARBA, 95:708
4 Choice, May 1994, p1410
3 GSED, 1997, p349
3 LJ, Apr 1 1994, p88

◆**JC 423** _____(LC)   DDC: 321.8

The Encyclopedia of Democracy

Lipset, Seymour Martin (ed). Routledge, 1995. 4 vols. *Cloth:* $395.00/set.
Review Avg: 4.00   *OCLC:* 1046   *Rating:* 8.09

Reviews	*Awards*
4 ARBA, 97:612	LJ/BRS, Apr 15 1996,
4 Choice, Apr 1996, p1282	p40
4 LJ, Feb 15 1996,	
p142,144	
4 RBB, Mar 1 1996, p1205	
4 WLB/R, 1996	

JC 571 _____(LC)   DDC: 323.4

Encyclopedia of Human Rights

Lawson, Edward (ed). Taylor & Francis, 1996. 2nd ed. 1715p. *Cloth:* $250.00/set.
Review Avg: 3.67   *OCLC:* 564   *Rating:* 8.80

Reviews	*Awards*
3 ARBA, 92:563	LJ/BRS, Apr 15 1992,
5 ARBA, 97:517	p43
2 Choice, Dec 1991, p572	
4 GSED, 1997, p296	
3 RBB, Nov 15 1991,	
p642,644	
5 WLB/R, Nov 1991,	
p110,112	

JC 571 _____(LC)   DDC: 323

Historical Dictionary of Human Rights and Humanitarian Organizations

Gorman, Robert F. and Edward S. Mihalkanin. Scarecrow, 1997. 296p. *Cloth:* $44.00.
Note: Series—Historical Dictionaries of International Organizations, vol. 12.
Review Avg: 3.00   *OCLC:* 178   *Rating:* 3.36

Reviews
3 Choice, Dec 1997, p621

JC 573 _____(LC)   DDC: 320.5

The Concise Conservative Encyclopedia

Miner, Brad. Free, 1996. 303p. *Paper:* $15.00.
Review Avg: 4.00   *OCLC:* 383   *Rating:* 4.77

Reviews
4 ARBA, 98:691
4 RBB, Dec 15 1996, p746

JF 51 _____(LC)   DDC: 320

The Illustrated Encyclopedia of World Geography

Williams, Michael (ed). Oxford Un, 1993. 11 vols. *Cloth:* $45.00/vol.
Review Avg: 4.20   *OCLC:* 1007   *Rating:* 8.21

Reviews	*Awards*
3 ARBA, 92:674	LJ/BRS, Apr 15 1991,
4 GSED, 1997, p176	p44
5 LJ, Jan 1991, p90,94	
5 LJ, May 1 1993, p82	
4 LJ, Dec 1991, p134,136	

JF 51 _____(LC)   DDC: 320

The International Encyclopedia of World Geography: Comparative Government

Taylor, Peter J. Oxford Un, 1990. 256p. *Cloth:* $45.00.
Review Avg: 4.00   *OCLC:* 0   *Rating:* 4.00

Reviews
4 ARBA, 92:674

JF 51 _____(LC)   DDC: 423.1

Isms: A Compendium of Concepts, Doctrines, Traits and Beliefs from Ableism to Zygodactylism

Von Altendorf, Alan and Theresa von Altendorf. National Book Network, 1991. 335p. *Cloth:* $16.95.
Review Avg: 2.67   *OCLC:* 539   *Rating:* 3.75

Reviews
3 LJ, Nov 15 1991, p76
3 RBB, Jan 1 1992, p850
2 RQ, Sum 1992, p573

JF 501 _____(LC)   DDC: 328.73

Encyclopedia of the American Legislative System: Studies of the Principal Structures, Processes, and Policies of Congress and State Legislatures Since the Colonial Era

Silbey, Joel H. (ed). Scribner's, 1994. 3 vols. *Cloth:* $330.00/set.
Review Avg: 3.80   *OCLC:* 840   *Rating:* 11.48

Reviews	**Awards**
3 ARBA, 95:742	Choice/OAB, Jan 1995,
3 Choice, Nov 1994, p424	p719
4 GSED, 1997, p368	LJ/BRS, Apr 15 1995,
5 LJ, Jun 1 1994, p94,96	p39
4 RBB, Jul 1994,	RBB/ORS, May 1 1995,
p1973-1974	p1603

JF 1525 _____(LC)   DDC: 327.12

Spies: A Narrative Encyclopedia of Dirty Deeds and Double Dealing from Biblical Times to Today

Nash, Jay Robert. M. Evans, 1997. 624p. *Paper:* $24.95.
Review Avg: 2.00   *OCLC:* 219   *Rating:* 2.44

Reviews
2 ARBA, 98:701

JF 1525 _____(LC)   DDC: 327.12

Spy Book: The Encyclopedia of Espionage

Palomar, Norman and Thomas B. Allen. Random House, 1997. 633p.
Cloth: $35.00.
Review Avg: 3.33   *OCLC:* 444   *Rating:* 4.22

Reviews
3 Choice, May 1997, p1479
4 LJ, Apr 15 1997, p72
3 RBB, Apr 15 1997, p1453-1454

JK 9 _____(LC)   DDC: 320.973

The American Political Dictionary

Plano, Jack C. and Milton Greenberg. Holt, 1993. 9th ed. 672p. *Paper:* $21.95.
Review Avg: 3.00   *OCLC:* 382   *Rating:* 5.76

Reviews
3 GSED, 1997, p361

JK 9 _____(LC)   DDC: 328.73

Congressional Quarterly's American Congressional Dictionary

Kravitz, Walter. Congressional Quarterly, 1993. 305p. *Cloth:* $32.95.
Paper: $22.95.
Review Avg: 3.50   *OCLC:* 963   *Rating:* 5.43

Reviews
3 ARBA, 94:729
4 GSED, 1997, p357
3 RBB, Dec 1 1993, p709
4 WLB/R, Dec 1993, p76

JK 9 _____(LC)   DDC: 328.73

The Encyclopedic Dictionary of American Government

Wellek, Alex (ed). Dushkin, 1991. 4th ed. 352p. *Cloth:* $17.95. *Paper:* $12.95.
Note: Series—Encyclopedic Dictionary Reference Set, vol. 1.
Review Avg: 3.00   *OCLC:* 261   *Rating:* 5.52

Reviews
3 ARBA, 93:737
3 GSED, 1997, p371
3 RBB, Apr 15 1992, p1549

JK 9 _____(LC)   DDC: 320.973

The HarperCollins Dictionary of American Government and Politics

Shafritz, Jay M. HarperCollins, 1992. 656p. *Cloth:* $50.00.
Review Avg: 4.00   *OCLC:* 1078   *Rating:* 6.16

Reviews
5 ARBA, 93:736
3 Choice, Jul/Aug 1992, p1661
4 GSED, 1997, p362
5 LJ, Jun 1 1992, p118
4 RBB, May 1 1992, p1623
3 WLB/R, Apr 1992, p124-125

JK 9 _____(LC)   DDC: 320

Safire's New Political Dictionary: The Definitiive Guide to the New Language of Politics

Safire, William. Random House, 1993. 3rd ed. 930p. *Cloth:* $35.00.
Note: Originally entitled *Safire's Political Dictionary.*
Review Avg: 4.50   *OCLC:* 1125   *Rating:* 8.75

Reviews
5 GSED, 1997, p352
5 LJ, Nov 15 1993, p73
4 RBB, Jan 15 1994, p971-972
4 WLB/R, Mar 1994, p95-96

JK 468 _____(LC)   DDC: 327.1

United States Intelligence: An Encyclopedia

Watson, Bruce W. and others (eds). Garland, 1990. 792p. *Cloth:* $95.00.
Note: Series—Garland Reference Library of Social Science, vol. 589.
Review Avg: 3.50   *OCLC:* 730   *Rating:* 8.96

Reviews	**Awards**
3 ARBA, 91:734	Choice/OAB, May 1991,
4 Choice, Sep 1990, p84	p1430
4 GSED, 1997, p370	RBB/ORS, May 1 1991,
3 LJ, Jul 1990, p91	p1735

◆ The article titles in this encyclopedia are indexed by keyword in Part II.

3 RBB, Jul 1990,
  p2117-2118
4 WLB/R, Jun 1990,
  p150,154

◆**JK 511** _____(LC)   DDC: 353

Encyclopedia of the American Presidency
Levy, Leonard W. and Louis Fisher (eds). Macmillan, 1994. 4 vols.
(1827p.) _Cloth:_ $400.00/set.
Review Avg: 4.67   _OCLC:_ 1347   _Rating:_ 15.36

Reviews	Awards
5 ARBA, 95:542	Choice/OAB, Jan 1995,
4 Choice, Feb 1994, p913	p719
5 GSED, 1997, p207	Dartmouth, 1995
5 LJ, Jan 1994, p104	NYPL, 1994
4 RBB, Jan 15 1994, p956	RBB/ORS, May 1 1995,
5 WLB/R, Feb 1994, p80	p1603

JK 511 _____(LC)   DDC: 973.927

Encyclopedia of the Reagan-Bush Years
Levy, Peter B. Greenwood, 1996. 442p. _Cloth:_ $49.95.
Review Avg: 3.50   _OCLC:_ 378   _Rating:_ 4.26

Reviews
4 ARBA, 97:593
3 Choice, Oct 1996, p254
4 LJ, Jun 15 1996, p58
3 RBB, Jul 1996, p1843

JK 511 _____(LC)   DDC: 353

The Presidency A to Z: A Ready Reference Encyclopedia
Nelson, Michael (ed). Congressional Quarterly, 1994. Revised edi-
tion. 574p. _Cloth:_ $100.00.
Note: Series—CQ's Encyclopedia of American Government, vol. 2.
Review Avg: 3.00   _OCLC:_ 1089   _Rating:_ 9.18

Reviews	Awards
3 ARBA, 94:508	LJ/BRS, Apr 15 1993,
3 Choice, May 1993, p1448	p63
1 GSED, 1997, p210	
5 LJ, Mar 1 1993, p72	
3 RBB, Mar 15 1993, p1378	
3 WLB/R, Mar 1993, p113	

JK 1067 _____(LC)   DDC: 328.73

The Encyclopedia of the United States Congress
Bacon, Donald C. and others. Macmillan, 1995. 4 vols. (2360p.)
Cloth: $400.00/set.
Review Avg: 4.25   _OCLC:_ 1220   _Rating:_ 12.69

Reviews	Awards
3 ARBA, 96:720	Choice/OAB, Jan 1996,
5 Choice, Sep 1995, p80	p724
5 RBB, Aug 1995, p1536	LJ/BRS, Apr 15 1996,
4 WLB/R, Jun 1995, p84,86	p40
	NYPL, 1995

JK 1226 _____(LC)   DDC: 327

International Relations: A Political Dictionary
Plano, Jack C. and Roy Olton (writers). ABC-CLIO, 1995. 5th ed.
458p. _Cloth:_ $60.00. _Paper:_ $25.95.
Note: Originally entitled _The International Relations Dictionary._
Review Avg: 3.00   _OCLC:_ 598   _Rating:_ 6.20

Reviews
3 RBB, Apr 1 1996, p1390

JK 1991 _____(LC)   DDC: 324.7

Open Secrets: The Encyclopedia of Congressional Money Politics
Makinson, Larry and Joshua Goldstein. Congressional Quarterly,
1996. 4th ed. 1348p. _Cloth:_ $179.95.
Review Avg: 3.50   _OCLC:_ 367   _Rating:_ 6.23

Reviews
4 ARBA, 98:675, 4th ed.
3 ARBA, 95:736, 3rd ed.
3 Choice, Feb 1993, p939, 2nd ed.
4 GSED, 1997, p367
4 LJ, Dec 1992, p122,124, 2nd ed.
3 RBB, Nov 1 1992, p547-548, 2nd ed.

JK 2261 _____(LC)   DDC: 324.27

Encyclopedia of Third Parties in the United States
Kruschke, Earl R. ABC-CLIO, 1991. 223p. _Cloth:_ $65.00.
Review Avg: 3.43   _OCLC:_ 764   _Rating:_ 4.96

Reviews
3 ARBA, 92:683
4 Choice, Feb 1992, p876
4 GSED, 1997, p363
3 LJ, Aug 1991, p86
3 RBB, Nov 1 1991, p564
4 RQ, Sum 1992, p569-570
3 WLB/R, Dec 1991, p120

JK 2261 _____(LC)   DDC: 324.27

Political Parties and Elections in the United States: An Encyclopedia
Maisel, L. Sandy and Charles Bassett. Garland, 1991. 2 vols. _Cloth:_
$150.00/set.
Review Avg: 3.57   _OCLC:_ 949   _Rating:_ 11.47

Reviews	Awards
3 ARBA, 92:685	Choice/OAB, May 1992,
4 Choice, Dec 1991, p577	p1342
3 GSED, 1997, p366	LJ/BRS, Apr 15 1992,
3 LJ, Aug 1991, p88-90	p46
4 RBB, Nov 15 1991, p648	RBB/ORS, May 1 1992,
4 RQ, Spr 1992, p425	p1625
4 WLB/R, Nov 1991, p115	

JK 2352 _____(LC)   DDC: 324.27

The Encyclopedia of the Republican Party/The Encyclopedia of the Democratic Party
Kurian, George Thomas. Sharpe, 1997. 4 vols. (1864p.) _Cloth:_
$399.00/set.
Review Avg: 4.00   _OCLC:_ 64   _Rating:_ 4.13

Reviews	Awards
4 ARBA, 98:659	Choice/OAB, Jan 1998,
4 Choice, Apr 1997, p1310	p760
4 GSED, 1997, p364	
4 LJ, Nov 1 1996, p58,60	
4 RBB, Nov 15 1996,	
p605-606	

JL 195 _____(LC)   DDC: 324.27
Political Parties of the Americas, 1980s to 1990s: Canada, Latin America, and the West Indies
Ameringer, Charles D. (ed). Greenwood, 1992. 697p. *Cloth:* $99.50.
Review Avg: 3.25   *OCLC:* 184   *Rating:* 3.62

Reviews
3 ARBA, 94:720
3 Choice, May 1993, p1446,1448
4 LJ, Mar 15 1993, p72,74
3 WLB/R, May 1993, p121

JL 599.5 _____(LC)   DDC: 324.2
Political Parties of the Americas and the Caribbean: A Reference Guide
Alexander, Robert J. Greenwood, 1992. 341p. *Cloth:* $145.00.
Review Avg: 3.60   *OCLC:* 183   *Rating:* 3.97

Reviews
4 ARBA, 94:783
5 Choice, May 1993, p1446
3 LJ, Apr 1 1993, p92
2 RBB, Oct 15 1993, p474-475
4 WLB/R, May 1993, p121

JN 15 _____(LC)   DDC: 341.24
Historical Dictionary of the European Community
Dinan, Desmond. Scarecrow, 1993. 291p. *Paper:* $37.50.
Note: Series—International Organizations Series, no. 1.
Review Avg: 4.00   *OCLC:* 533   *Rating:* 5.07

Reviews
5 ARBA, 94:767
3 Choice, Jan 1994, p750
4 GSED, 1997, p373
4 LJ, Jun 1 1993, p102
4 RBB, Sep 1 1993, p88

JN 94 _____(LC)   DDC: 320.94
Political and Economic Encyclopaedia of Western Europe
Nicholson, Frances (ed). St James, 1990. 411p. *Cloth:* $85.00.
Review Avg: 3.00   *OCLC:* 224   *Rating:* 3.45

Reviews
3 ARBA, 92:714
3 Choice, Jun 1991, p1622

JN 96 _____(LC)   DDC: 947
Political and Economic Encyclopaedia of the Soviet Union and Eastern Europe
White, Stephen (ed). St James, 1990. 328p. *Cloth:* $85.00.
Review Avg: 3.00   *OCLC:* 179   *Rating:* 3.36

Reviews
3 ARBA, 92:104
3 Choice, Jun 1991, p1622

JN 6699 _____(LC)   DDC: 324.247
Dictionary of Political Parties and Organizations in Russia
Pribylovskii, Vladimir. Center for Strategic & International Studies, 1992. 129p. *Cloth:* $21.00. *Paper:* $14.95.
Note: Series—Significant Issues Series, vol. 14, no. 7.
Review Avg: 3.00   *OCLC:* 203   *Rating:* 3.41

Reviews
3 ARBA, 94:779

JQ 39 _____(LC)   DDC: 324.25
Political Parties of Asia and the Pacific: A Reference Guide
Fukui, Haruhiro (ed). Greenwood, 1992. 2nd ed. 369p. *Cloth:* $145.00.
Review Avg: 2.67   *OCLC:* 358   *Rating:* 5.39

Reviews
3 ARBA, 94:765
3 Choice, May 1993, p1446
2 RBB, May 1 1993, p1632-1634

JV 6450 _____(LC)   DDC: 325.73
Dictionary of American Immigration History
Cordasco, Francesco (ed). Scarecrow, 1990. 784p. *Cloth:* $97.50.
Review Avg: 3.50   *OCLC:* 949   *Rating:* 7.40

Reviews   **Awards**
4 ARBA, 91:777   RBB/ORS, May 1 1991,
3 Choice, Oct 1990, p280   p1734
3 LJ, Jul 1990, p84
4 RBB, Jun 1 1990, p1922

JX 1961 _____(LC)   DDC: 327.172
The ABC-CLIO Companion to the American Peace Movement in the Twentieth Century
Lunardini, Christine A. ABC-CLIO, 1994. 269p. *Cloth:* $55.00.
Note: Series—ABC-CLIO Companions to Key Issues in American History and Life.
Review Avg: 3.50   *OCLC:* 420   *Rating:* 4.34

Reviews
4 LJ, Jan 1995, p89
3 RBB, May 15 1995, p1673

JX 1974 _____(LC)   DDC: 327.174
Encyclopedia of Arms Control and Disarmament
Burns, Richard Dean (ed). Scribner's, 1993. 3 vols. *Cloth:* $280.00/set.
Review Avg: 4.00   *OCLC:* 573   *Rating:* 9.15

Reviews   **Awards**
3 ARBA, 94:797   Choice/OAB, Jan 1994,
4 Choice, Sep 1993, p80   p712
4 GSED, 1997, p386   RBB/ORS, May 1 1994,
5 LJ, Jul 1993, p68   p1627
4 RBB, Sep 15 1993, p187
4 WLB/R, Sep 1993, p116

JX 1977 _____(LC)   DDC: 341.23
Encyclopedia of the United Nations and International Agreements
Osmanczyk, Edmund Jan. Taylor & Francis, 1990. 2nd ed. 1220p. *Cloth:* $160.00.
Review Avg: 3.33   *OCLC:* 944   *Rating:* 7.22

Reviews
4 Choice, Mar 1991, p1102,1104
3 RBB, Feb 15 1991, p1248
3 WLB/R, Mar 1991, p129

◆ The article titles in this encyclopedia are indexed by keyword in Part II.

JX 4111_____(LC)   DDC: 911

The Encyclopedia of International Boundaries
Biger, Gideon. Facts On File, 1995. 543p. *Cloth:* $125.00.
Review Avg: 2.75   *OCLC:* 345   *Rating:* 5.44

Reviews   **Awards**
4 ARBA, 96:455   LJ/BRS, Apr 15 1996,
1 Choice, Apr 1996, p1282   p39
3 LJ, Apr 1 1995
3 RBB, Feb 15 1996,
  p1042,1044

K 487_____(LC)   DDC: 340

Law and Politics: A Cross-cultural Encyclopedia
Strouthes, Daniel P. ABC-CLIO, 1995. 301p. *Cloth:* $49.50.
Review Avg: 2.33   *OCLC:* 344   *Rating:* 3.02

Reviews
2 ARBA, 97:490
3 Choice, Jun 1996, p1624
2 LJ, Jul 1996, p106

K 540_____(LC)   DDC: 347

Great World Trials
Knappman, Edward W. (ed). Gale Research, 1997. 536p. *Cloth:* $50.00.
Review Avg: 4.00   *OCLC:* 332   *Rating:* 4.66

Reviews
4 ARBA, 98:532

K 3240_____(LC)   DDC: 341.4

Great Events from History II: Human Rights Series
Magill, Frank N. (ed). Salem, 1992. 5 vols. (2624p.) *Cloth:* $375.00/set.
Review Avg: 3.25   *OCLC:* 669   *Rating:* 4.59

Reviews
3 ARBA, 93:617
3 Choice, Apr 1993, p1296
4 LJ, Jan 1993, p96
3 WLB/R, Feb 1993, p104

◆**KF 154**_____(LC)   DDC: 349.73

American Justice
Bessette, Joseph M. (ed). Salem, 1996. 3 vols. (932p.) *Cloth:* $270.00/set.
Review Avg: 3.25   *OCLC:* 364   *Rating:* 5.98

Reviews   **Awards**
3 ARBA, 97:489   RBB/ORS, May 1 1997,
3 Choice, Nov 1996, p425   p1524
3 LJ, Jul 1996, p100
4 RBB, Oct 1 1996, p366

KF 154_____(LC)   DDC: 349.73

Encyclopedia of the American Judicial System: Studies of the Principal Institutions and Processes of Law
Janosik, Robert J. (ed). Scribner's, 1996. 3 vols. (1420p.) *Cloth:* $305.00/set.
Review Avg: 3.00   *OCLC:* 1431   *Rating:* 5.86

Reviews
3 GSED, 1997, p207n

KF 220_____(LC)   DDC: 347.737

Great American Trials
Knappman, Edward W. (ed). Gale Research, 1994. 872p. *Cloth:* $44.95. *Paper:* $17.95.
Review Avg: 4.00   *OCLC:* 993   *Rating:* 9.99

Reviews   **Awards**
5 ARBA, 95:613   NYPL, 1994
4 LJ, Feb 15 1994, p148   RBB/ORS, May 1 1995,
3 RBB, Feb 1 1994,   p1603
  p1024,1026
4 RQ, Sum 1994, p551-552
4 WLB/R, Mar 1994, p92

KF 385_____(LC)   DDC: 349.73

Historic U.S. Court Cases, 1690-1990: An Encyclopedia
Johnson, John W. Garland, 1992. 754p. *Cloth:* $125.00.
Note: Series—Garland Reference Library of the Social Sciences, vol. 497.
Review Avg: 3.50   *OCLC:* 1793   *Rating:* 7.09

Reviews
4 Choice, Sep 1992, p82
3 GSED, 1997, p269
4 LJ, Jun 15 1992, p70
3 RBB, Jun 1 1992, p1776

KF 2976.4_____(LC)   DDC: 346.7304

McCarthy's Desk Encyclopedia of Intellectual Property
McCarthy, J. Thomas. BNA, 1995. 556p. *Paper:* $75.00.
Review Avg: 3.67   *OCLC:* 157   *Rating:* 3.98

Reviews
3 ARBA, 92:533
4 Choice, Mar 1992, p1052
4 GSED, 1997, p272

KF 3317_____(LC)   DDC: 344.7301

Labor, Employment, and the Law: A Dictionary
Anglim, Christopher Thomas. ABC-CLIO, 1997. 549p. *Cloth:* $39.50.
Note: Series—Contemporary Legal Issues.
Review Avg: 3.50   *OCLC:* 153   *Rating:* 3.81

Reviews
3 ARBA, 98:515
4 Choice, Dec 1997, p620

KF 3775_____(LC)   DDC: 344.73

Environment and the Law: A Dictionary
Patton-Hulce, Vicki R. ABC-CLIO, 1995. 361p. *Cloth:* $39.50.
Review Avg: 4.00   *OCLC:* 215   *Rating:* 4.43

Reviews
4 Choice, May 1996, p1455
4 LJ, Apr 15 1996, p74
4 RBB, May 1 1996, p1520-1521

KF 4117_____(LC)   DDC: 344.73

Education and the Law: A Dictionary
Taylor, Bonnie B. ABC-CLIO, 1996. 288p. *Cloth:* $39.50.
Note: Series—Contemporary Legal Issues.
Review Avg: 3.00   *OCLC:* 442   *Rating:* 3.88

Reviews
3 ARBA, 97:491

KF 4290 _____ (LC)   DDC: 344.73
The Performing Arts Business Encyclopedia
DuBoff, Leonard. Allworth, 1996. 255p. *Paper:* $19.95.
Review Avg: 3.50   *OCLC:* 154   *Rating:* 3.81

Reviews
3 ARBA, 98:1265
4 Choice, Dec 1997, p614

◆**KF 4548** _____ (LC)   DDC: 342.73
Encyclopedia of the American Constitution
Levy, Leonard W. and others (eds). Scribner's, 1992. 4 vols.+ suppl.
(1992) *Cloth:* $350.00/set.
Note: Available on CD-ROM, 1996, $275.00.
Review Avg: 3.40   *OCLC:* 2527   *Rating:* 8.45

Reviews   *Awards*
3 ARBA, 93:576   Dartmouth, 1987
4 ARBA, 98:518, Review of
  CD-ROM
2 Choice, Apr 1991, p1296
4 Choice, Apr 1997, p1320,
  Review of CD-ROM
4 GSED, 1997, p264
1 LJ, Mar 15 1997, p97,
  Review of CD-ROM
4 RBB, Jun 1 1992,
  p1774-1775, supp.
4 RBB, Nov 15 1996, p610,
  Review of CD-ROM
4 RBB, Dec 15 1990, p880
4 WLB/R, May 1992,
  p123-124

KF 4557 _____ (LC)   DDC: 342.73
Encyclopedia of Constitutional Amendments, Proposed Amendments, and Amending Issues, 1789-1995
Vile, John R. ABC-CLIO, 1996. 427p. *Cloth:* $75.00.
Review Avg: 4.25   *OCLC:* 683   *Rating:* 9.62

Reviews   *Awards*
4 ARBA, 97:596   LJ/BRS, Apr 15 1997,
4 Choice, Mar 1997, p1144   p40
5 LJ, Nov 15 1996, p56   RBB/ORS, May 1 1997,
4 RBB, Dec 1 1996, p684   p1524

KF 8203.36 _____ (LC)   DDC: 342.73
The ABC-CLIO Companion to the Native American Rights Movement
Grossman, Mark. ABC-CLIO, 1996. 498p. *Cloth:* $60.00.
Review Avg: 4.00   *OCLC:* 551   *Rating:* 5.10

Reviews   *Awards*
4 Choice, Jul 1997, p1780   RBB/ORS, May 1 1998,
4 LJ, Jan 1997, p86   p1538

KF 8210 _____ (LC)   DDC: 323.1
Encyclopedia of American Indian Civil Rights
Olson, James S. (ed). Greenwood, 1997. 417p. *Cloth:* $65.00.
Review Avg: 3.50   *OCLC:* 224   *Rating:* 3.95

Reviews
3 ARBA, 98:562
4 RBB, Oct 15 1997, p427

◆**KF 8742** _____ (LC)   DDC: 347.73
The Oxford Companion to the Supreme Court of the United States
Hall, Kermit L. and others (eds). Oxford Un, 1992. 1032p. *Cloth:* $49.95.
Review Avg: 4.40   *OCLC:* 2367   *Rating:* 15.13

Reviews   *Awards*
3 ARBA, 94:554   LJ/BRS, Apr 15 1993,
5 Choice, Mar 1993, p1243   p62-63
5 LJ, Sep 1 1992, p170   NYPL, 1994
5 RBB, Dec 1 1992,   RBB/ORS, May 1 1993,
  p688,690   p1620
4 WLB/R, Feb 1993, p106

◆**KF 8742** _____ (LC)   DDC: 347.73
The Supreme Court A to Z: A Ready Reference Encyclopedia
Witt, Elder (ed). Congressional Quarterly, 1994. Revised edition.
528p. *Cloth:* $110.00.
Note: Series—CQ's Encyclopedia of American Government, vol. 3.
Review Avg: 4.20   *OCLC:* 910   *Rating:* 12.02

Reviews   *Awards*
5 ARBA, 94:556   Choice/OAB, Jan 1994,
5 Choice, Dec 1993, p591   p714
3 GSED, 1997, p281   RBB/ORS, May 1 1994,
5 LJ, Sep 1 1993, p177   p1627
3 RBB, Nov 1 1993, p570

KF 9325 _____ (LC)   DDC: 349.73
Sexuality and the Law: An Encyclopedia of Major Legal Cases
Leonard, Arthur S. (ed). Garland, 1993. 729p. *Cloth:* $95.00.
Note: Series— Garland Reference Library of Social Science, vol. 1272.
Review Avg: 3.60   *OCLC:* 813   *Rating:* 5.23

Reviews
3 ARBA, 94:570
3 Choice, Oct 1993, p268
4 GSED, 1997, p270
4 LJ, Jun 1 1993, p106
4 RBB, Oct 1 1993, p387

KH 926 _____ (LC)   DDC: 349.4
The Oxford Encyclopedia of European Community Law
Toth, A. G. Oxford Un, 1990. 550p. *Cloth:* $165.00.
Review Avg: 3.00   *OCLC:* 182   *Rating:* 3.36

Reviews
3 ARBA, 92:534
3 GSED, 1997, p276

LA 669.62 _____ (LC)   DDC: 370.9417
An Encyclopedia of Irish Schools, 1500-1800
Ward, Robert E. Mellen, 1995. 251p. *Cloth:* $89.95.
Review Avg: 3.00   *OCLC:* 32   *Rating:* 3.06

Reviews
3 ARBA, 96:315

◆ The article titles in this encyclopedia are indexed by keyword in Part II.

LB 15 _____(LC)　　　　DDC: 370
American Educators' Encyclopedia
Kapel, David E. and others. Greenwood, 1991. Revised edition. 716p.
Cloth: $95.00.
Review Avg: 3.25　*OCLC:* 730　*Rating:* 6.71

Reviews
3 ARBA, 93:330
4 GSED, 1997, p99
3 RBB, Jan 1 1992, p846
3 WLB/R, Apr 1992, p119-120

◆**LB 15** _____(LC)　　　　DDC: 370.7
Encyclopedia of Educational Research
Alkin, Marvin C. and others. Macmillan, 1992. 6th ed. 4 vols. *Cloth:*
$400.00/set.
Review Avg: 4.14　*OCLC:* 1555　*Rating:* 9.25

Reviews
3 ARBA, 93:331, 6th ed.
4 CRL, Mar 1993, p162, 6th ed.
5 Choice, Nov 1992, p440, 6th ed.
4 GSED, 1997, p100,120, 6th ed.
4 LJ, Jul 1992, p74, 6th ed.
4 RBB, Aug 1992, p2037, 6th ed.
5 WLB/R, Dec 1992, p109

LB 15 _____(LC)　　　　DDC: 378
Encyclopedia of Higher Education
Clark, Burton R. Pergamon, 1992. 4 vols. *Cloth:* $1500.00/set.
Review Avg: 4.00　*OCLC:* 520　*Rating:* 7.04

Reviews　　　　　　　**Awards**
3 ARBA, 93:358　　　　　Choice/OAB, Jan 1994,
5 Choice, Feb 1993, p938　　p712
4 GSED, 1997, p113

LB 15 _____(LC)　　　　DDC: 370
International Encyclopedia of Education: Research and Studies
Husen, Torsten and T. Neville Poslethwaite. Pergamon, 1994. 2nd ed.
12 vols. *Cloth:* $3795.00/set.
Note: Available on CD-ROM.
Review Avg: 4.67　*OCLC:* 520　*Rating:* 7.71

Reviews　　　　　　　**Awards**
5 ARBA, 95:337　　　　　Dartmouth, 1986
4 Choice, Oct 1994, p262
5 GSED, 1997, p104,405n

LB 15 _____(LC)　　　　DDC: 378
International Higher Education: An Encyclopedia
Altbach, Philip G. (ed). Garland, 1991. 2 vols. *Cloth:* $150.00/set.
Review Avg: 3.50　*OCLC:* 628　*Rating:* 6.76

Reviews　　　　　　　**Awards**
3 ARBA, 93:381　　　　　Choice/OAB, May 1992,
4 Choice, Sep 1991, p62　　p1342
3 GSED, 1997, p112
4 WLB/R, Jun 1991, p136

LB 17 _____(LC)　　　　DDC: 370
Encyclopedia of American Education
Unger, Harlow G. Facts On File, 1996. 3 vols. (1161p.) *Cloth:*
$175.00/set.
Review Avg: 4.33　*OCLC:* 1130　*Rating:* 8.59

Reviews　　　　　　　**Awards**
4 ARBA, 97:288　　　　　RBB/ORS, May 1 1997,
4 LJ, Sep 15 1996, p60　　　p1524
5 RBB, Nov 15 1996,
　p609-610

◆**LB 17** _____(LC)　　　　DDC: 370
Philosophy of Education: An Encyclopedia
Chambliss, J. J. (ed). Garland, 1996. 720p. *Cloth:* $95.00.
Note: Series— Garland Reference Library of the Humanities, vol.
1671.
Review Avg: 3.67　*OCLC:* 219　*Rating:* 4.11

Reviews
3 ARBA, 97:287
4 Choice, Jan 1997, p773-774
4 RBB, Nov 1 1996, p539-540

LB 43 _____(LC)　　　　DDC: 370.19
International Encyclopedia of National Systems of Education
Postlethwaite, T. Neville (ed). Pergamon, 1995. 1105p. *Cloth:*
$215.00.
Review Avg: 4.00　*OCLC:* 207　*Rating:* 4.41

Reviews
4 Choice, Sep 1997, p106

LB 1025.3 _____(LC)　　　　DDC: 371.1
International Encyclopedia of Teaching and Teacher Education
Anderson, Lorin W. Pergamon, 1995. 2nd ed. 878p. *Cloth:* $150.00.
Note: Based on *International Encyclopedia of Education*.
Review Avg: 4.00　*OCLC:* 267　*Rating:* 6.53

Reviews
4 ARBA, 97:298

LB 1027.55 _____(LC)　　　　DDC: 370.15
Historical Encyclopedia of School Psychology
Fagan, Thomas K. and Paul G. Warden (eds). Greenwood, 1996. 448p.
Cloth: $95.00.
Review Avg: 3.00　*OCLC:* 407　*Rating:* 3.81

Reviews
3 ARBA, 97:286
3 Choice, Sep 1996, p99-100

LB 1028.3 _____(LC)　　　　DDC: 371.3
The International Encyclopedia of Educational Technology
Plomp, Tjeerd and Donald P. Ely (eds). Pergamon, 1996. 2nd ed. 692p.
Review Avg: 3.50　*OCLC:* 158　*Rating:* 5.82

Reviews
4 ARBA, 91:359
3 Choice, May 1990, p1114

◆**LB 1139** _____(LC)   **DDC: 372.21**
Encyclopedia of Early Childhood Education
Williams, Leslie R. and Doris Pronin (eds). Garland, 1992. 518p.
Cloth: $95.00.
Review Avg: 4.75   *OCLC:* 1364   *Rating:* 9.48

Reviews   **Awards**
5 ARBA, 93:332   LJ/BRS, Apr 15 1993,
5 Choice, Nov 1992, p518   p58
5 GSED, 1997, p108
4 RBB, Sep 1 1992, p85

LB 1570 _____(LC)   **DDC: 375**
The International Encyclopedia of Curriculum
Lewy, Arieh (ed). Pergamon, 1991. 1064p. *Cloth:* $150.00.
Review Avg: 2.50   *OCLC:* 240   *Rating:* 2.98

Reviews
2 ARBA, 92:274
3 GSED, 1997, p103

LB 2822.75 _____(LC)   **DDC: 370**
International Encyclopedia of Educational Evaluation
Walberg, Herbert J. and Geneva D. Haertel (eds). Pergamon, 1990.
796p. *Cloth:* $175.00.
Note: Series—Advances in Education.
Review Avg: 4.00   *OCLC:* 511   *Rating:* 5.02

Reviews
4 ARBA, 91:300
4 GSED, 1997, p107

LC 191 _____(LC)   **DDC: 306.43**
International Encyclopedia of the Sociology of Education
Saha, Lawrence (ed). Pergamon, 1997. 961p. *Cloth:* $432.00.
Note: Resources in Education Series.
Review Avg: 4.00   *OCLC:* 75   *Rating:* 4.15

Reviews
4 ARBA, 98:268

LC 1099 _____(LC)   **DDC: 370.117**
Dictionary of Multicultural Education
Grant, Carl A. and Gloria Ladson-Billings (eds). Oryx, 1997. 308p.
Cloth: $49.95.
Review Avg: 3.50   *OCLC:* 356   *Rating:* 4.21

Reviews
4 ARBA, 98:267
3 RBB, Nov 1 1997, p508

◆**LC 2717** _____(LC)   **DDC: 371.97**
Encyclopedia of African-American Education
Jones-Wilson, Faustine C. and others (eds). Greenwood, 1996. 575p.
Cloth: $95.00.
Review Avg: 3.33   *OCLC:* 178   *Rating:* 3.69

Reviews
3 ARBA, 97:285
4 Choice, Feb 1997, p942
3 RBB, Dec 15 1996, p746-747

LC 4007 _____(LC)   **DDC: 371.9**
Concise Encyclopedia of Special Education
Reynolds, Cecil R. and Elaine Fletcher-Janzen. Wiley, 1990. 1215p.
Cloth: $99.95.
Note: Condensed version of *Encyclopedia of Special Education.*
Review Avg: 3.00   *OCLC:* 327   *Rating:* 3.65

Reviews
3 ARBA, 92:320
3 GSED, 1997, p115
3 RBB, May 1 1991, p1729-1732

ML 100 _____(LC)   **DDC: 780**
Concise Oxford Dictionary of Music
Kennedy, Michael (ed). Oxford Un, 1996. 4th ed. 815p *Cloth:* $15.95.
Review Avg: 4.00   *OCLC:* 184   *Rating:* 6.37

Reviews
4 GSED, 1997, p647

ML 100 _____(LC)   **DDC: 780**
Garland Encyclopedia of World Music
Stone, Ruth M. (ed). Garland, 1996. 10 vols. *Cloth:* $125.00.
Review Avg: 5.00   *OCLC:* 370   *Rating:* 5.74

Reviews
5 RBB, Nov 15 1997, p578, v. Africa

ML 100 _____(LC)   **DDC: 780**
The HarperCollins Dictionary of Music
Ammer, Christine. Harper Perennial, 1995. 3rd 512p. *Paper:* $18.00.
Note: Originally entitled *The Harper Dictionary of Music,* 1986.
Review Avg: 3.00   *OCLC:* 163   *Rating:* 5.33

Reviews
3 RBB, May 15 1991, p1833-1834

ML 100 _____(LC)   **DDC: 780**
The Oxford Dictionary of Music
Kennedy, Michael (ed). Oxford Un, 1994. 2nd ed. 960p. *Cloth:*
$35.00.
Review Avg: 4.00   *OCLC:* 1071   *Rating:* 8.14

Reviews
3 ARBA, 96:1270
4 Choice, Jun 1995, p1574
5 RBB, Mar 1 1995, p1274

ML 102 _____(LC)   **DDC: 782**
A-Z of Opera
Hamilton, Mary. Facts On File, 1990. 223p. *Cloth:* $27.95.
Review Avg: 2.67   *OCLC:* 326   *Rating:* 3.32

Reviews
3 ARBA, 92:1290
2 Choice, Apr 1991, p1290
3 RBB, Mar 1 1991, p1418

ML 102 _____(LC)   **DDC: 782.1**
The Concise Oxford Dictionary of Opera
Warrack, John. Oxford Un, 1996. 3rd ed. 561p. *Cloth:* $15.95.
Review Avg: 4.00   *OCLC:* 938   *Rating:* 7.88

◆ The article titles in this encyclopedia are indexed by keyword in Part II.

Reviews
4 GSED, 1997, p661

ML 102_____(LC)   **DDC: 782.32**

Dictionary of Western Church Music
Poultney, David. ALA, 1991. 234p. *Cloth:* $40.00.
Review Avg: 3.20   *OCLC:* 645   *Rating:* 4.49

Reviews
3 ARBA, 93:1269
3 Choice, May 1992, p1374
3 GSED, 1997, p673
4 LJ, Sep 1 1991, p182-183
3 RBB, Feb 15 1992, p1128

ML 102_____(LC)   **DDC: 786**

Encyclopedia of Keyboard Instruments
Palmieri, Robert. Garland, 1994. 2 vols. *Cloth:* $95.00/ vol. *Paper:* $22.95.
Note: Paperback entitled *Encyclopedia of the Piano*.
Review Avg: 4.50   *OCLC:* 434   *Rating:* 7.37

Reviews   *Awards*
5 Choice, May 1994,   Choice/OAB, Jan 1995,
  p1410,1412   p719
4 GSED, 1997, p657

ML 102_____(LC)   **DDC: 786.8**

Encyclopedia of Percussion
Beck, John H. (ed). Garland, 1995. 436p. *Cloth:* $75.00.
Review Avg: 3.50   *OCLC:* 489   *Rating:* 4.48

Reviews
3 ARBA, 96:1291
4 Choice, Apr 1995, p1312

ML 102_____(LC)   **DDC: 789.91**

Encyclopedia of Recorded Sound in the United States
Marco, Guy A. (ed). Garland, 1993. 910p. *Cloth:* $125.00.
Review Avg: 3.67   *OCLC:* 411   *Rating:* 4.49

Reviews
3 ARBA, 94:1313
3 Choice, Nov 1993, p430-432
5 LJ, Jul 1993, p68

ML 102_____(LC)   **DDC: 781.64**

Encyclopedia of the Blues
Herzhaft, Gerard. Un of Arkansas, 1992. 2nd ed. 513p. *Cloth:* $32.00. *Paper:* $16.95.
Review Avg: 2.83   *OCLC:* 473   *Rating:* 5.78

Reviews
3 ARBA, 94:1370
3 Choice, May 1993, p1442
3 GSED, 1997, p667
2 LJ, Sep 1 1992, p168
3 LJ, Jul 1997, p76, 2nd ed.
3 RBB, Jan 1 1993, p825

ML 102_____(LC)   **DDC: 782**

Encyclopedia of the Musical Theatre
Ganzl, Kurt. Schirmer, 1994. 2 vols. *Cloth:* $175.00/set.
Review Avg: 4.57   *OCLC:* 932   *Rating:* 12.43

Reviews   *Awards*
5 ARBA, 95:1415   Choice/OAB, Jan 1995,
5 Choice, Oct 1994, p260   p719
5 GSED, 1997, p720   Dartmouth, 1995
4 LJ, Jun 1 1994, p98   NYPL, 1994
5 RBB, Sep 1 1994, p68
4 RQ, Win 1994, p240-241
4 WLB/R, Sep 1994, p78

ML 102_____(LC)   **DDC: 784**

The Guinness Encyclopedia of Popular Music
Larkin, Colin (ed). Stockton, 1995. 2nd ed. 6 vols. *Cloth:* $295.00/set.
Review Avg: 4.56   *OCLC:* 1308   *Rating:* 17.18

Reviews   *Awards*
5 ARBA, 94:1363   Choice/OAB, Jan 1997,
5 ARBA, 96:1310, 2nd ed.   p740
5 Choice, Mar 1993, p1113   LJ/BRS, Apr 15 1996,
4 Choice, Mar 1996,   p40
  p98-99, 2nd ed.   NYPL, 1994
5 GSED, 1997, p663   RBB/ORS, May 1 1993,
4 LJ, Jan 1993, p98   p1620
5 LJ, Dec 1995, p92, 2nd
  ed.
4 RBB, Feb 15 1993,
  p1080,1082
4 WLB/R, Jan 1993, p108

ML 102_____(LC)   **DDC: 781.66**

Harmony Illustrated Encyclopedia of Country Music
Foege, Alec. Crown, 1994. 3rd ed. 208p. *Paper:* $19.00.
Review Avg: 3.00   *OCLC:* 262   *Rating:* 5.52

Reviews
3 GSED, 1997, p668

ML 102_____(LC)   **DDC: 781.66**

Harmony Illustrated Encyclopedia of Rock
Clifford, Mike. Harmony, 1992. 7th ed. 208p. *Paper:* $19.00.
Review Avg: 3.50   *OCLC:* 420   *Rating:* 6.34

Reviews
3 ARBA, 94:1378
4 GSED, 1997, p671

ML 102_____(LC)   **DDC: 782**

Harper Dictionary of Opera and Operetta
Anderson, James. HarperCollins, 1990. 691p. *Cloth:* $35.00.
Note: Revision of *Bloomsbury Dictionary of Opera and Operetta*.
Review Avg: 2.67   *OCLC:* 383   *Rating:* 3.44

Reviews
3 ARBA, 91:1296
2 Choice, Feb 1991, p909
3 RBB, Jan 15 1991, p1085-1086

ML 102_____(LC)   **DDC: 784.19**

The Illustrated Encyclopedia of Musical Instruments
Dearling, Robert (ed). Schirmer, 1996. 240p. *Cloth:* $75.00.
Review Avg: 3.75   *OCLC:* 555   *Rating:* 4.86

Reviews
5 ARBA, 97:1052
3 Choice, Apr 1997, p1310

4 LJ, Feb 1 1997, p72
3 RBB, Jan 1 1997, p892,894

ML 102   (LC)   **DDC: 782**

International Dictionary of Opera
LaRue, C. Steven (ed). St James, 1993. 2 vols. (1543p.) *Cloth:*
$250.00/set.
Review Avg: 4.17   *OCLC:* 328   *Rating:* 4.83

Reviews
5 ARBA, 94:1355
3 Choice, Oct 1993, p267
5 GSED, 1997, p659
5 LJ, May 1 1993, p82-83
3 RBB, Aug 1993, p2092
4 RQ, Win 1993, p288-289

ML 102   (LC)   **DDC: 785.42**

The New Grove Dictionary of Jazz
Kernfeld, Barry. Grove's, 1994. 1358p. *Cloth:* $350.00.
Review Avg: 3.50   *OCLC:* 261   *Rating:* 4.02

Reviews
4 ARBA, 90:1288
3 GSED, 1997, p669

ML 102   (LC)   **DDC: 782**

The New Grove Dictionary of Opera
Sadie, Stanley (ed). Grove's, 1992. 4 vols. *Cloth:* $850.00/set.
Review Avg: 5.00   *OCLC:* 997   *Rating:* 10.99

Reviews   *Awards*
5 ARBA, 94:1356   Choice/OAB, Jan 1994,
5 Choice, Jul/Aug 1993,   p712
  p1752-1753   LJ/BRS, Apr 15 1993,
5 GSED, 1997, p660   p61-62
5 LJ, Feb 15 1993,
  p160,162
5 RBB, Apr 1 1993, p1452

ML 102   (LC)   **DDC: 781.66**

New Rolling Stone Encyclopedia of Rock and Roll
Romanowski, Patricia and Holly George-Warren (eds). Fireside,
1995. 1120p. *Cloth:* $22.50.
Note: Revision of *The Rolling Stone Encyclopedia of Rock and Roll.*
Review Avg: 3.00   *OCLC:* 1063   *Rating:* 5.13

Reviews
3 RBB, Dec 15 1995, p726

ML 102   (LC)   **DDC: 784.19**

The Oxford Companion to Musical Instruments
Baines, Anthony C. Oxford Un, 1992. 404p. *Cloth:* $35.00.
Review Avg: 4.00   *OCLC:* 935   *Rating:* 5.87

Reviews
5 ARBA, 94:1338
3 Choice, Apr 1993, p1298
5 GSED, 1997, p656
3 RBB, Mar 15 1993, p1378
4 WLB/R, Mar 1993, p112

ML 102   (LC)   **DDC: 781.64**

The Oxford Companion to Popular Music
Gammond, Peter. Oxford Un, 1991. 739p. *Cloth:* $39.95.
Review Avg: 3.67   *OCLC:* 1500   *Rating:* 8.67

Reviews   *Awards*
4 ARBA, 92:1297   Choice/OAB, May 1992,
4 Choice, Oct 1991, p258   p1342
4 GSED, 1997, p664
2 LJ, Feb 15 1991,
  p184,186
3 RBB, Apr 1 1991,
  p1590-1591
5 WLB/R, Sep 1991,
  p124-126

ML 102   (LC)   **DDC: 782**

The Oxford Dictionary of Opera
Warrack, John and Ewan West. Oxford Un, 1992. 782p. *Cloth:*
$40.00.
Review Avg: 4.00   *OCLC:* 803   *Rating:* 5.61

Reviews
3 ARBA, 94:1357
5 Choice, Apr 1993, p1302
4 RBB, Feb 15 1993, p1082,1084

ML 102   (LC)   **DDC: 792.6**

*Stage It with Music: An Encyclopedic Guide to the American
Musical Theatre*
Hischak, Thomas S. Greenwood, 1993. 341p. *Cloth:* $45.00.
Review Avg: 3.60   *OCLC:* 586   *Rating:* 4.77

Reviews
3 ARBA, 94:1473
4 Choice, Dec 1993, p586
4 LJ, Jun 15 1993, p62
3 RBB, Aug 1993, p2095
4 RQ, Spr 1994, p427=428

ML 106   (LC)   **DDC: 780.971**

Encyclopedia of Music in Canada
Kallman, Helmut and others. Un of Toronto, 1992. 2nd ed. 1524p.
Cloth: $95.00.
Review Avg: 3.50   *OCLC:* 218   *Rating:* 5.94

Reviews
3 ARBA, 94:1312
4 GSED, 1997, p653

ML 128   (LC)   **DDC: 781.64**

Lissauer's Encyclopedia of Popular Music in America
Lissauer, Robert. Facts On File, 1996. 3 vols. (1530p.)
Note: Originally published by Paragon House.
Review Avg: 3.60   *OCLC:* 619   *Rating:* 4.84

Reviews
5 ARBA, 92:1296
3 ARBA, 97:1065
4 GSED, 1997, p662
3 LJ, Jun 1 1991, p126
3 RBB, Nov 1 1991, p568

◆ The article titles in this encyclopedia are indexed by keyword in Part II.

ML 410 _____ (LC)   DDC: **780**

The Beethoven Encyclopedia: His Life and Art from A to Z
Nettl, Paul. Carol, 1994. 325p. *Paper:* $12.95.
Note: Series—Midcentury Reference Library.
Review Avg: 5.00   *OCLC:* 71   *Rating:* 5.14

Reviews
5 ARBA, 96:1281

ML 410 _____ (LC)   DDC: **782.42166**

Rocket Man: The Encyclopedia of Elton John
Bernadin, Claude and Tom Stanton. Greenwood, 1995. 252p. *Cloth:*
$39.95.
Review Avg: 3.00   *OCLC:* 138   *Rating:* 3.28

Reviews
3 ARBA, 96:1331
3 LJ, Nov 1 1996, p58

ML 420 _____ (LC)   DDC: **782.42166**

The Elvis Encyclopedia: The Complete and Definitive Reference Book on the King of Rock and Roll
Stanley, David E. and Frank Coffey. General, 1994. 287p. *Cloth:*
$29.99.
Review Avg: 3.00   *OCLC:* 168   *Rating:* 3.34

Reviews
3 ARBA, 96:1335

ML 421 _____ (LC)   DDC: **782.42166**

The Ultimate Beatles Encyclopedia
Harry, Bill. Hyperion, 1992. 720p. *Cloth:* $40.00. *Paper:* $20.00.
Review Avg: 3.00   *OCLC:* 248   *Rating:* 3.50

Reviews
3 WLB/R, May 1994, p75-76

ML 1711 _____ (LC)   DDC: **782**

The American Musical Theatre: A Chronicle
Bordman, Gerald. Oxford Un, 1992. 2nd ed. 821p. *Cloth:* $49.95.
Paper: $21.95.
Review Avg: 3.50   *OCLC:* 1091   *Rating:* 7.68

Reviews
4 ARBA, 93:1385
3 RBB, Jul 1992, p1956

ML 3545 _____ (LC)   DDC: **784**

World Music: The Rough Guide
Broughton, Simon and others. Penguin, 1994. 697p. *Paper:* $19.95.
Review Avg: 5.00   *OCLC:* 797   *Rating:* 6.59

Reviews
5 LJ, Jan 1995, p92

N 3 _____ (LC)   DDC: **703**

The Concise Oxford Dictionary of Art and Artists
Chilvers, Ian (ed). Oxford Un, 1990. 517p. *Paper:* $10.95.
Review Avg: 2.50   *OCLC:* 204   *Rating:* 2.91

Reviews
3 ARBA, 92:981
2 GSED, 1997, p569

N 31 _____ (LC)   DDC: **703**

The Dictionary of Art
Turner, Jane (ed). Grove's, 1996. 34 vols. *Cloth:* $8800.00/set.
Review Avg: 5.00   *OCLC:* 1357   *Rating:* 13.71

Reviews	**Awards**
5 ARBA, 98:947	Choice/OAB, Jan 1998,
5 CRL, Mar 1997, p178-179	p759
5 Choice, Jan 1997,	Dartmouth, 1997
p761-762	LJ/BRS, Apr 15 1997,
5 LJ, Sep 15 1996, p54	p37
5 RBB, Dec 15 1996, p742	RBB/ORS, May 1 1997,
	p1524

N 31 _____ (LC)   DDC: **703**

The Thames and Hudson Dictionary of Art and Artists
Read, Herbert. Thames & Hudson, 1994. Revised edition. 384p.
Cloth: $19.95.
Review Avg: 3.00   *OCLC:* 214   *Rating:* 5.43

Reviews
3 GSED, 1997, p582

N 6465 _____ (LC)   DDC: **709.0344**

The Thames and Hudson Encyclopaedia of Impressionism
Denvir, Bernard. Thames & Hudson, 1990. 240p. *Cloth:* $11.95.
Review Avg: 3.00   *OCLC:* 566   *Rating:* 3.13

Reviews	**Awards**
3 GSED, 1997, p582	RBB/ORS, May 1 1991,
	p1735

N 6941 _____ (LC)   DDC: **759.9492**

Dutch Art: An Encyclopedia
Muller, Sheila D. (ed). Garland, 1997. 489p. + 140p. of plates. *Cloth:*
$125.00.
Note: Series— Garland Reference Library of the Humanities, vol.
1021.
Review Avg: 4.00   *OCLC:* 281   *Rating:* 4.56

Reviews
4 ARBA, 98:949
5 Choice, Sep 1997, p99
3 LJ, Jul 1997, p74,76

N 7400 _____ (LC)   DDC: **709.94**

Encyclopedia of Australian Art
McCulloch, Susan. Un of Hawaii, 1994. Rev. and updated 879p.
Cloth: $115.00.
Review Avg: 4.00   *OCLC:* 150   *Rating:* 6.30

Reviews
4 ARBA, 96:1032

N 7793 _____ (LC)   DDC: **704.9**

Encyclopedia of Women in Religious Art
Apostolos-Cappadona, Diane. Continuum, 1996. 442p. *Cloth:*
$39.50.
Review Avg: 3.33   *OCLC:* 310   *Rating:* 3.95

Reviews
3 ARBA, 97:797
4 LJ, Nov 15 1996, p54
3 RBB, Sep 15 1997, p266

N 7830 _____(LC)   **DDC: 704.9**
The Oxford Companion to Christian Art and Architecture
Murray, Peter. Oxford Un, 1997. 596p. *Cloth:* $45.00.
Review Avg: 3.67   *OCLC:* 808   *Rating:* 5.29

Reviews	*Awards*
4 Choice, Jul 1997, p1782	Choice/OAB, Jan 1998,
3 LJ, Jan 1997, p89	p760
4 RBB, Feb 15 1997, p1043	

N 7943 _____(LC)   **DDC: 704.9**
Encyclopedia of Medieval Church Art
Tasker, Edward G. Trafalgar Square, 1993. 320p. *Cloth:* $75.00.
Paper: $45.00/O.P.
Review Avg: 2.00   *OCLC:* 194   *Rating:* 2.39

Reviews
1 LJ, Jan 1995, p92
3 RBB, Mar 1 1994, p1288-1289

N 8600 _____(LC)   **DDC: 707.88**
The Art Business Encyclopedia
DuBoff, Leonard. Allworth, 1994. 320p. *Cloth:* $29.95. *Paper:*
$18.95.
Review Avg: 3.00   *OCLC:* 416   *Rating:* 3.83

Reviews
3 ARBA, 95:1004
2 ARBA, 96:1039
3 GSED, 1997, p571
4 LJ, Sep 1 1994, p172-173

NA 31 _____(LC)   **DDC: 720**
Dictionary of Architecture and Construction
Harris, Cyril M. (ed). McGraw-Hill, 1993. 2nd ed. 924p. *Cloth:*
$59.50.
Review Avg: 4.00   *OCLC:* 807   *Rating:* 9.61

Reviews	*Awards*
4 ARBA, 94:1051, 2nd ed.	Choice/OAB, Jan 1994,
4 Choice, Sep 1993, p78,	p712
2nd ed.	
4 GSED, 1997, p589	
4 RBB, Oct 1 1993, p380,	
2nd ed.	

NA 31 _____(LC)   **DDC: 720**
Encyclopedia of Architecture: Design, Engineering and Construction
Wilkes, Joseph A. (ed). Wiley, 1990. 5 vols. *Cloth:* $950.00/set.
Review Avg: 3.20   *OCLC:* 653   *Rating:* 4.51

Reviews
3 ARBA, 90:972, vol. 2
3 ARBA, 90:973, vol. 3
3 CRL, Sep 1991, p445
4 GSED, 1997, p587
3 RBB, Aug 1990, p2196

NA 31 _____(LC)   **DDC: 720**
The Penguin Dictionary of Architecture
Fleming, John and others (eds). Penguin, 1991. 4th ed. 512p. *Paper:*
$13.95.
Review Avg: 3.00   *OCLC:* 242   *Rating:* 5.48

Reviews
3 ARBA, 93:1038
3 GSED, 1997, p589

NA 40 _____(LC)   **DDC: 720**
Illustrated Encyclopedia of Architects and Architecture
Sharp, Dennis (eds). Watson-Guptill, 1991. 256p. *Cloth:* $39.95.
Review Avg: 3.00   *OCLC:* 342   *Rating:* 3.68

Reviews
3 ARBA, 93:1040

NA 40 _____(LC)   **DDC: 720**
International Dictionary of Architects and Architecture
Van Vynckt, Randall J. (ed). St James, 1993. 2 vols. *Cloth:* $250.00/
set.
Review Avg: 3.71   *OCLC:* 506   *Rating:* 4.72

Reviews
3 ARBA, 94:1055
4 Choice, Feb 1994, p916
4 GSED, 1997, p594
3 JAL, Nov 1993, p346-347
5 LJ, Sep 15 1993, p68
3 RQ, Sum 1994, p555
4 WLB/R, Nov 1993, p103-105

NA 380 _____(LC)   **DDC: 720**
Dictionary of Islamic Architecture
Peterson, Andrew. Routledge, 1996. 342p. *Cloth:* $89.95.
Review Avg: 3.67   *OCLC:* 223   *Rating:* 4.12

Reviews
3 CRL, Mar 1997, p179
3 Choice, Dec 1996, p593
5 LJ, Dec 1995, p94

NA 705 _____(LC)   **DDC: 720**
Encyclopedia of American Architecture
Packard, Robert T. and Balthazar Korab. McGraw-Hill, 1995. 2nd ed.
724p. *Cloth:* $89.50.
Review Avg: 3.33   *OCLC:* 910   *Rating:* 7.15

Reviews
3 ARBA, 96:1045
3 Choice, May 1995, p1433
4 GSED, 1997, p592
3 LJ, Mar 1 1995, p66
3 RBB, May 15 1995, p1676-1677
4 WLB/R, Apr 1995, p85-86

NA 2850 _____(LC)   **DDC: 721**
Elements of Style: A Practical Encyclopedia of Interior Architectural Details from 1485 to the Present
Calloway, Stephen (ed). Simon & Schuster, 1991. 544p. *Cloth:*
$65.00.
Review Avg: 4.00   *OCLC:* 751   *Rating:* 5.50

Reviews
4 LJ, Mar 15 1992, p76
4 RBB, Mar 15 1997, p1256, Rev. ed.

◆ The article titles in this encyclopedia are indexed by keyword in Part II.

NB 1170 _____(LC)   DDC: 730.4

The Encyclopedia of Sculpture Techniques

Mills, John. Watson-Guptill, 1990. 239p. *Cloth:* $32.50.
Review Avg: 3.50   *OCLC:* 257   *Rating:* 4.01

Reviews
3 ARBA, 91:1041
4 GSED, 1997, p598

NC 1766 _____(LC)   DDC: 791.43

The Encyclopedia of Animated Cartoons

Lenburg, Jeff. Facts On File, 1991. Revised edition. 466p. *Cloth:* $40.00.
Review Avg: 3.25   *OCLC:* 732   *Rating:* 6.71

Reviews
3 ARBA, 93:1347
4 Choice, May 1992, p1370
3 GSED, 1997, p713
3 RBB, Jan 1 1992, p847-848

NK 28 _____(LC)   DDC: 745.1

The David and Charles Encyclopedia of Everyday Antiques

Pearsall, Ronald. David & Charles, 1992. 256p. *Cloth:* $34.95.
Review Avg: 3.00   *OCLC:* 24   *Rating:* 3.05

Reviews
3 ARBA, 94:1023
3 GSED, 1997, p540

NK 30 _____(LC)   DDC: 745.1

Bulfinch Illustrated Encyclopedia of Antiques

Atterbury, Peter and Lars Tharp (eds). Little, Brown, 1994. 332p. *Cloth:* $50.00.
Review Avg: 3.67   *OCLC:* 392 ' *Rating:* 4.45

Reviews
3 ARBA, 95:968
4 GSED, 1997, p539
4 LJ, Feb 1 1995, p66

NK 1165 _____(LC)   DDC: 747

Encyclopedia of Interior Design

Banham, Joanna (ed). Fitzroy, 1997. 2 vols. (1450p.) *Cloth:* $250.00.
Review Avg: 4.50   *OCLC:* 207   *Rating:* 4.91

Reviews	**Awards**
4 ARBA, 98:935	Choice/OAB, Jan 1998,
5 Choice, Nov 1997, p452	p759
4 LJ, Sep 15 1997, p60	LJ/BRS, Apr 15 1998,
5 RBB, Nov 1 1997,	p47
p510,512	RBB/ORS, May 1 1998,
	p1538

NK 1370 _____(LC)   DDC: 745.4

The Design Encyclopedia

Byars, Mel. Wiley, 1994. 612p. *Cloth:* $60.00.
Review Avg: 4.50   *OCLC:* 379   *Rating:* 5.26

Reviews
5 ARBA, 95:982
4 GSED, 1997, p561

NK 1390 _____(LC)   DDC: 745.4442

Dictionary of Twentieth-Century Design

Pile, John. Da Capo, 1994. New ed. 312p. *Cloth:* $35.00. *Paper:* $18.95.
Review Avg: 3.40   *OCLC:* 740   *Rating:* 6.88

Reviews
3 ARBA, 92:922
3 Choice, Apr 1991, p1292-1293
4 GSED, 1997, p537
4 RBB, Dec 15 1990, p878
3 RQ, Fall 1991, p94-95

NK 1390 _____(LC)   DDC: 709.04

The Thames and Hudson Encyclopaedia of Twentieth Century Design and Designers

Julier, Guy. Norton, 1993. Revised edition. 216p. *Paper:* $12.95.
Review Avg: 3.50   *OCLC:* 377   *Rating:* 6.25

Reviews
3 ARBA, 95:984
4 Choice, Feb 1994, p916

NK 2115.5 _____(LC)   DDC: 745

The Illustrated Encyclopedia of Victoriana: A Comprehensive Guide to the Designs, Customs, and Inventions of the Victorian Era

Ruhling, Nancy and John Crosby Freeman. Running, 1994. 208p. *Cloth:* $24.95.
Review Avg: 3.50   *OCLC:* 5   *Rating:* 3.51

Reviews
4 LJ, Apr 15 1995, p66,68
3 RBB, May 1 1995, p1598

NX 70 _____(LC)   DDC: 700.3

The Oxford Illustrated Encyclopedia of the Arts

Norwich, John Julius. Oxford Un, 1990. 499p. *Cloth:* $49.95.
Note: Series—Oxford Illustrated Encyclopedia, vol. 5.
Review Avg: 2.83   *OCLC:* 533   *Rating:* 3.90

Reviews
3 ARBA, 91:932
1 Choice, Jul/Aug 1991, p1763
3 GSED, 1997, p518
3 LJ, Feb 15 1991, p188
4 RBB, Apr 1 1991, p1591-1592
3 WLB/R, Apr 1991, p120

NX 456 _____(LC)   DDC: 700.9

Great Events from History II: Arts and Culture Series

Magill, Frank N. (ed). Salem, 1993. 5 vols. (2678p.) *Cloth:* $375.00/set.
Review Avg: 3.20   *OCLC:* 403   *Rating:* 4.01

Reviews
3 ARBA, 94:984
3 LJ, Jan 1993, p96
3 LJ, Jan 1994, p106
3 RBB, Apr 15 1993, p1534-1535
4 WLB/R, Mar 1994, p92,94

NX 650_____(LC)   **DDC: 700**
The Oxford Guide to Classical Mythology in the Arts, 1300-1990s
Reid, Jane Davidson and Chris Rohmann. Oxford Un, 1993. 2 vols.
Cloth: $195.00/set.
Review Avg: 4.80   *OCLC:* 1362   *Rating:* 9.52

Reviews	Awards
5 ARBA, 94:1397	Choice/OAB, Jan 1994,
5 Choice, Dec 1993,	p714
p589-590	
5 LJ, Sep 1 1993, p176	
5 RBB, Nov 15 1993, p652	
4 WLB/R, Oct 1993, p95	

P 24_____(LC)   **DDC: 850.3**
Dictionary of Italian Literature
Bondanella, Peter and Julia Conaway Bondanella (eds). Greenwood, 1996. 716p. *Cloth:* $99.50.
Review Avg: 4.00   *OCLC:* 374   *Rating:* 4.75

Reviews	Awards
4 ARBA, 97:1010	Choice/OAB, Jan 1998,
4 Choice, Jan 1997, p768	p759
4 GSED, 1997, p637	

P 29_____(LC)   **DDC: 410**
The Encyclopedia of Language and Linguistics
Asher, R. E. (ed). Pergamon, 1993. 10 vols. *Cloth:* $2975.00/set.
Review Avg: 5.00   *OCLC:* 345   *Rating:* 9.69

Reviews	Awards
5 ARBA, 95:1024	Choice/OAB, Jan 1995,
5 Choice, Jun 1994, p1552	p719
5 GSED, 1997, p599	LJ/BRS, Apr 15 1995,
5 WLB/R, Jun 1994, p94	p39

P 29_____(LC)   **DDC: 410**
Encyclopedic Dictionary of Language and Languages
Crystal, David. Blackwell, 1992. 428p. *Cloth:* $12.50/Reprint.
Review Avg: 4.00   *OCLC:* 752   *Rating:* 5.50

Reviews
4 Choice, Sep 1993, p76
4 LJ, Feb 1 1993, p72
4 RBB, Apr 1 1993, p1456
4 WLB/R, Jun 1993, p123-124

P 29_____(LC)   **DDC: 410**
International Encyclopedia of Linguistics
Bright, William (ed). Oxford Un, 1992. 4 vols. *Cloth:* $395.00/set.
Review Avg: 4.33   *OCLC:* 914   *Rating:* 10.16

Reviews	Awards
3 ARBA, 93:1050	Choice/OAB, Jan 1993,
5 Choice, Sep 1992, p80	p734
5 GSED, 1997, p601	LJ/BRS, Apr 15 1992,
3 LJ, Apr 1 1992, p112	p44-45
5 RBB, Feb 1 1992, p1057	
5 WLB/R, Mar 1992,	
p115-116	

P 29_____(LC)   **DDC: 410**
Linguistics Encyclopedia
Malmkjaer, Kirsten (ed). Routledge, 1991. 575p. *Cloth:* $99.00.
Review Avg: 4.25   *OCLC:* 478   *Rating:* 5.21

Reviews
3 ARBA, 93:1052
5 Choice, Sep 1992, p80
4 GSED, 1997, p604
5 WLB/R, Jun 1992, p114

P 29_____(LC)   **DDC: 410**
Routledge Dictionary of Language and Linguistics
Bussmann, Hadumod. Routledge, 1996. 530p. *Cloth:* $99.00.
Review Avg: 4.00   *OCLC:* 320   *Rating:* 4.64

Reviews
4 Choice, Dec 1996, p587

P 87.5_____(LC)   **DDC: 302.23**
The Encyclopedia of Television, Cable, and Video
Reed, Robert M. and Maxine K. Reed. Van Nostrand Reinhold, 1992. 622p. *Cloth:* $64.95.
Review Avg: 3.00   *OCLC:* 233   *Rating:* 3.47

Reviews
3 GSED, 1997, p532n

P 87.5_____(LC)   **DDC: 302.23**
Webster's New World Dictionary of Media and Communications
Weiner, Richard. Prentice-Hall, 1996. Rev. and updated 676p. *Cloth:* $29.95.
Review Avg: 4.33   *OCLC:* 673   *Rating:* 7.68

Reviews
5 GSED, 1997, p524, 1997 ed.
5 LJ, Jun 15 1990, p110
3 RBB, Sep 1 1990, p91, 1990 ed.

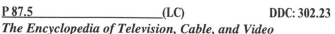◆**P 92**_____(LC)   **DDC: 302.23**
The ABC-CLIO Companion to the Media in America
Hollis, Daniel Webster. ABC-CLIO, 1995. 352p. *Cloth:* $55.00.
Note: Series—ABC-CLIO Companions to Key Issues in American History and Life.
Review Avg: 3.25   *OCLC:* 399   *Rating:* 4.05

Reviews
4 ARBA, 96:964
3 Choice, Jan 1996, p756
3 LJ, Nov 1 1995, p60
3 RBB, Dec 1 1995, p650

P 96_____(LC)   **DDC: 302.2**
From Talking Drums to the Internet: An Encyclopedia of Communications Technology
Gardner, Robert and Dennis Shortelle. ABC-CLIO, 1997. 355p. *Cloth:* $60.00.
Review Avg: 3.00   *OCLC:* 199   *Rating:* 3.40

Reviews
3 ARBA, 98:854

◆ The article titles in this encyclopedia are indexed by keyword in Part II.

P 106 _____(LC)   DDC: 410

An Encyclopaedia of Language
Collinge, N. E. (ed). Routledge, 1990. 1011p. *Cloth:* $79.95.
Review Avg: 4.00   *OCLC:* 772   *Rating:* 5.54

Reviews
3 ARBA, 91:1042
5 GSED, 1997, p600

P 371 _____(LC)   DDC: 401

Compendium of the World's Languages
Campbell, George L. (compiler). Routledge, 1991. 2 vols. (1574p.)
Cloth: $250.00/set.
Review Avg: 3.67   *OCLC:* 427   *Rating:* 4.52

Reviews
4 ARBA, 92:1012
4 Choice, Mar 1992, p1040
3 WLB/R, Dec 1991, p118

PA 31 _____(LC)   DDC: 880.9

The Concise Oxford Companion to Classical Literature
Howatson, M. C. and Ian Chilvers. Oxford Un, 1993. 575p. *Paper:*
$18.95.
Review Avg: 3.00   *OCLC:* 165   *Rating:* 3.33

Reviews
3 ARBA, 94:1198

PA 31 _____(LC)   DDC: 880.9

The Oxford Companion to Classical Literature
Howatson, M. C. Oxford Un, 1991. 2nd ed. 627p. *Cloth:* $45.00.
Review Avg: 3.00   *OCLC:* 1965   *Rating:* 8.93

Reviews
3 ARBA, 90:1099

PE 31 _____(LC)   DDC: 420

The Oxford Companion to the English Language
McArthur, Tom (ed). Oxford Un, 1992. 1184p. *Cloth:* $45.00.
Review Avg: 4.20   *OCLC:* 2055   *Rating:* 18.31

Reviews	**Awards**
3 ARBA, 93:1054	Choice/OAB, Jan 1994,
5 Choice, Jan 1993, p774	p714
4 LJ, Nov 1 1992, p81	Dartmouth, 1993
4 RBB, Oct 15 1992, p457	LJ/BRS, Apr 15 1993,
5 WLB/R, Nov 1992, p94-95	p62
	NYPL, 1994
	RBB/ORS, May 1 1993,
	p1620

PE 65 _____(LC)   DDC: 428.007

Encyclopedia of English Studies and Language Arts
Purves, Alan C. (ed). Scholastic, 1994. 2 vols. (1338p.) *Cloth:*
$150.00/set.
Review Avg: 3.50   *OCLC:* 426   *Rating:* 4.35

Reviews
3 ARBA, 95:929
3 Choice, Apr 1995, p1272
5 GSED, 1997, p515
3 LJ, Feb 1 1995, p68
3 RBB, Jan 15 1995, p958,960
4 WLB/R, Jan 1995, p78,80

PG 2940 _____(LC)   DDC: 891.7

The Modern Encyclopedia of East Slavic, Baltic, and Eurasian Literature
Rollberg, Peter. Academic International, 1996. 246p. *Cloth:* $38.50.
Review Avg: 4.00   *OCLC:* 268   *Rating:* 4.54

Reviews
4 ARBA, 98:1170, vol. 10

PG 7007 _____(LC)   DDC: 891.8

Dictionary of Polish Literature
Czerwinski, E. J. (ed). Greenwood, 1994. 488p. *Cloth:* $85.00.
Review Avg: 4.00   *OCLC:* 330   *Rating:* 4.66

Reviews
4 GSED, 1997, p640

PK 2902 _____(LC)   DDC: 891.1

Encyclopedia of Indian Literature
Datta, Amaresh. Humanities, 1993. 6 vols. *Cloth:* $52.00/vol.
Review Avg: 5.00   *OCLC:* 59   *Rating:* 7.12

Reviews	**Awards**
5 Choice, Oct 1993, p265	Choice/OAB, Jan 1994,
5 Choice, Feb 1996, p927	p712

PM 155 _____(LC)   DDC: 897

Dictionary of Native American Literature
Wiget, Andrew (ed). Garland, 1994. 598p. *Cloth:* $95.00. *Paper:*
$22.95.
Note: The paperback is entitled *Handbook of Native American Literature.*
Review Avg: 3.86   *OCLC:* 1093   *Rating:* 12.05

Reviews	**Awards**
4 Choice, Jun 1995,	Choice/OAB, Jan 1996,
p1566,1568	p724
4 GSED, 1997, p628	LJ/BRS, Apr 15 1995,
3 JAL, May 1993, p130-131	p38
4 LJ, Jan 1995, p82	RBB/ORS, May 1 1995,
5 RBB, Apr 1 1995, p1442	p1603
3 RQ, Sum 1993, p564-565	
4 WLB/R, May 1993,	
p114-115	

PN 41 _____(LC)   DDC: 810.9

Benet's Reader's Encyclopedia of American Literature
Murphy, Bruce. HarperCollins, 1996. 4th ed. 1144p. *Cloth:* $50.00.
Review Avg: 3.71   *OCLC:* 1659   *Rating:* 11.03

Reviews	**Awards**
5 ARBA, 92:1155	RBB/ORS, May 1 1992,
3 ARBA, 98:843, 4th ed.	p1625
4 CRL, Sep 1992, p421-422	
4 GSED, 1997, p626	
3 LJ, Jan 1992, p104	
4 RBB, Dec 15 1991, p781	
3 WLB/R, Dec 1991,	
p116-117	

PN 41 _____(LC)   DDC: 801

Dictionary of Concepts in Literary Criticism
Harris, Wendell V. Greenwood, 1992. 444p. *Cloth:* $75.00.

Note: Series—Reference Sources for the Social Sciences and Humanities, no. 12.
Review Avg: 3.80   *OCLC:* 510   *Rating:* 4.82

Reviews
5 ARBA, 93:1111
3 Choice, Oct 1992, p272-274
4 GSED, 1997, p613
3 LJ, Mar 15 1992, p76
4 RBB, May 15 1992, p1714

PN 41_____(LC)   **DDC: 803**
Merriam-Webster's Encyclopedia of Literature
Merriam-Webster, 1995. 1236p. *Cloth:* $39.95.
Review Avg: 4.33   *OCLC:* 1347   *Rating:* 7.02

Reviews
4 ARBA, 96:1146
5 LJ, Jul 1995, p74
4 RBB, Jul 1995, p1901

PN **44.5**_____(LC)   **DDC: 801.95**
A Glossary of Contemporary Literary Theory
Hawthorn, Jeremy. Routledge, 1994. 2nd ed. 329p. *Cloth:* $49.95.
Review Avg: 4.00   *OCLC:* 449   *Rating:* 6.90

Reviews
3 ARBA, 93:1113
5 Choice, Oct 1992, p272,274

PN 56_____(LC)   **DDC: 398.2**
Companion to Literary Myths, Heroes and Archetypes
Brunel, Pierre (ed). Routledge, 1992. 1223p. *Cloth:* $99.95.
Review Avg: 4.00   *OCLC:* 49   *Rating:* 4.10

Reviews
5 ARBA, 94:1155
4 GSED, 1997, p610
3 RBB, Nov 15 1994, p625-626
4 WLB/R, May 1993, p113-114

PN 56_____(LC)   **DDC: 809.915**
Encyclopedia of Allegorical Literature
Leeming, David Adams and Kathleeen Morgan Drowne. ABC-CLIO, 1996. 326p. *Cloth:* $65.00.
Note: Series—ABC-CLIO Literary Companion.
Review Avg: 3.67   *OCLC:* 195   *Rating:* 4.06

Reviews
4 Choice, Apr 1997, p1310,1312
4 LJ, Nov 15 1996, p56
3 RBB, Feb 1 1997, p964

PN 56_____(LC)   **DDC: 809**
Encyclopedia of Apocalyptic Literature
Zimbaro, Valerie P. ABC-CLIO, 1996. 400p. *Cloth:* $65.00.
Note: Series—ABC-CLIO Literary Companion.
Review Avg: 2.50   *OCLC:* 253   *Rating:* 3.01

Reviews
3 ARBA, 97:893
2 Choice, Jun 1997, p1647

PN 56_____(LC)   **DDC: 809.1**
Encyclopedia of Literary Epics
Jackson, Guida M. ABC-CLIO, 1996. 660p. *Cloth:* $65.00.
Note: Series—ABC-CLIO Literary Companion.
Review Avg: 3.00   *OCLC:* 355   *Rating:* 3.71

Reviews
3 Choice, Jul 1997, p1780

PN 56_____(LC)   **DDC: 398.22**
Encyclopedia of Traditional Epics
Jackson, Guida M. ABC-CLIO, 1994. 640p. *Cloth:* $65.00.
Review Avg: 3.67   *OCLC:* 1057   *Rating:* 7.78

Reviews   **Awards**
3 ARBA, 95:1322   RBB/ORS, May 1 1995,
4 Choice, Apr 1995, p1277   p1603
3 LJ, Sep 1 1994, p173-174
5 RBB, Nov 1 1994,
   p538,540
3 RQ, Sum 1995, p517
4 WLB/R, Mar 1995, p78

◆PN 56_____(LC)   **DDC: 809**
Encyclopedia of Utopian Literature
Snodgrass, Mary Ellen. ABC-CLIO, 1995. 644p. *Cloth:* $65.00.
Review Avg: 3.33   *OCLC:* 627   *Rating:* 8.58

Reviews   **Awards**
3 ARBA, 96:1147   LJ/BRS, Apr 15 1996,
3 LJ, Sep 15 1995, p62   p40
4 RBB, Oct 15 1995, p426   RBB/ORS, May 1 1996,
                               p1536

◆PN 81_____(LC)   **DDC: 801.95**
Encyclopedia of Contemporary Literary Theory: Approaches, Scholars, Terms
Makaryk, Irena R. (ed). Un of Toronto, 1993. 656p. *Cloth:* $150.00.
Paper: $39.95.
Note: Articles in Part 1 of this encyclopedia are indexed.
Review Avg: 3.75   *OCLC:* 588   *Rating:* 6.93

Reviews   **Awards**
3 ARBA, 94:1150   Choice/OAB, Jan 1994,
4 CRL, Mar 1995, p136   p712
4 Choice, Nov 1993, p430
4 GSED, 1997, p617

PN 81_____(LC)   **DDC: 820.9**
Encyclopedia of Literature and Criticism
Coyle, Martin and others (eds). Gale Research, 1991. 1299p. *Cloth:* $125.00.
Review Avg: 3.00   *OCLC:* 230   *Rating:* 3.46

Reviews
3 ARBA, 93:1116

PN 98_____(LC)   **DDC: 801.95**
A Dictionary of Critical Theory
Orr, Leonard. Greenwood, 1991. 464p. *Cloth:* $75.00.
Review Avg: 2.67   *OCLC:* 248   *Rating:* 3.17

Reviews
3 ARBA, 93:1114

◆ The article titles in this encyclopedia are indexed by keyword in Part II.

2 Choice, May 1992, p1372
3 GSED, 1997, p617n

◆**PN 98**_____(LC)   **DDC: 801**

Encyclopedia of Feminist Literary Theory
Kowaleski-Wallace, Elizabeth (ed). Garland, 1997. 449p. *Cloth:* $75.00.
Note: Series— Garland Reference Library of the Humanities; vol. 1582.
Review Avg: 3.00   *OCLC:* 414   *Rating:* 3.83

Reviews
3 Choice, Apr 1997, p1306-1307

PN 141_____(LC)   **DDC: 808.02**

Writer's Encyclopedia
Editors of Writer's Digest. Writer's Digest, 1996. 3rd ed. 499p. *Cloth:* $22.99.
Note: Revision of *Writing, A to Z.*
Review Avg: 3.43   *OCLC:* 368   *Rating:* 6.17

Reviews
3 ARBA, 91:952
4 ARBA, 97:750
3 Choice, Mar 1991, p1112
4 GSED, 1997, p528
3 LJ, Oct 1 1990, p87
3 RBB, Nov 15 1990, p683
4 WLB/R, Jan 1991, p127

PN 172_____(LC)   **DDC: 808**

Encyclopedia of Rhetoric and Composition: Communication from Ancient Times to the Information Age
Enos, Theresa. Garland, 1996. 803p. *Cloth:* $95.00.
Review Avg: 3.00   *OCLC:* 424   *Rating:* 3.85

Reviews
3 ARBA, 97:840
3 Choice, Jun 1996, p1614

PN 849_____(LC)   **DDC: 860**

Dictionary of the Literature of the Iberian Peninsula
Bleiberg, German and others (eds). Greenwood, 1993. 2 vols. *Cloth:* $195.00/vol.
Review Avg: 3.80   *OCLC:* 442   *Rating:* 6.68

Reviews   **Awards**
4 ARBA, 94:1289   LJ/BRS, Apr 15 1994,
3 Choice, Nov 1993, p428   p39
4 GSED, 1997, p636
4 RBB, Dec 15 1993,
 p775-776
4 RQ, Spr 1994, p412-414

PN 849_____(LC)   **DDC: 809**

Reader's Encyclopedia of Eastern European Literature
Pynsent, Robert B. (ed). HarperCollins, 1993. 605p. *Cloth:* $50.00.
Review Avg: 4.00   *OCLC:* 730   *Rating:* 5.46

Reviews
3 ARBA, 94:1281
4 Choice, Oct 1993, p272
3 GSED, 1997, p634
4 LJ, Jul 1993, p72

---

5 RBB, Oct 15 1993, p475
5 WLB/R, Sep 1993, p122,124

PN 1008.5_____(LC)   **DDC: 809**

International Companion Encyclopedia of Children's Literature
Hunt, Peter (ed). Routledge, 1996. 923p. *Cloth:* $125.00.
Review Avg: 4.00   *OCLC:* 410   *Rating:* 4.82

Reviews
4 Choice, Feb 1997, p944,946

◆**PN 1021**_____(LC)   **DDC: 808.1**

The New Princeton Encyclopedia of Poetry and Poetics
Preminger, Alex and T.V.F. Brogan. Princeton Un, 1993. 3rd ed. 1434p. *Cloth:* $125.00. *Paper:* $29.95.
Note: Revision of *Princeton Encyclopedia of Poetry and Poetics.*
Review Avg: 4.71   *OCLC:* 1373   *Rating:* 11.46

Reviews   **Awards**
5 ARBA, 94:1302, 3rd ed.   Choice/OAB, Jan 1994,
5 Choice, Oct 1993, p271,   p714
 3rd ed.
4 GSED, 1997, p644, 3rd
 ed.
5 JAL, Sep 1993, p275, 3rd
 ed.
5 LJ, Sep 1 1993, p174,
 3rd ed.
5 RBB, Dec 15 1993, p779,
 3rd ed.
4 WLB/R, Oct 1993, p93,95

PN 1861_____(LC)   **DDC: 792**

The World Encyclopedia of Contemporary Theatre
Rubin, Don (ed). Routledge, 1994. vol. 1, vol. 3 *Cloth:* $149.95.
Review Avg: 3.83   *OCLC:* 597   *Rating:* 5.02

Reviews
4 Choice, Jun 1995, p1581
4 Choice, Oct 1996, p260, vol. 3
4 LJ, Feb 15 1995, p152
4 LJ, Jun 1 1997, p94,96, vol. 3
3 RBB, May 15 1995, p1678
4 RBB, Dec 15 1997, p718, vol. 3

PN 1968_____(LC)   **DDC: 792.7**

The Encyclopedia of Vaudeville
Slide, Anthony. Greenwood, 1994. 605p. *Cloth:* $75.00.
Review Avg: 3.83   *OCLC:* 626   *Rating:* 11.08

Reviews   **Awards**
4 ARBA, 95:1417   Choice/OAB, Jan 1995,
4 CRL, Mar 1995, p137-138   p721
4 Choice, Oct 1994, p265   LJ/BRS, Apr 15 1995,
4 LJ, Jul 1994, p86   p41
3 RBB, May 1 1994, p1620   RBB/ORS, May 1 1995,
4 WLB/R, Sep 1994, p78   p1603

PN 1991.3_____(LC)   **DDC: 791.44**

Same Time... Same Station: An A-Z Guide to Radio from Jack Benny to Howard Stern
Lackmann, Ron. Facts On File, 1996. 370p. *Cloth:* $45.00.

Review Avg: 3.25   *OCLC:* 351   *Rating:* 3.95

Reviews
3 ARBA, 97:765
3 Choice, Apr 1996, p1288
4 LJ, Nov 1 1995, p60
3 RBB, Feb 15 1996, p1044

PN 1992_____(LC)   **DDC: 658.85**
Encyclopedia of Television
Newcomb, Horace (ed). Fitzroy, 1997. 3 vols. (1948p.) *Cloth:* $300.00.
Review Avg: 4.50   *OCLC:* 174   *Rating:* 4.85

Reviews   *Awards*
5 ARBA, 98:888   Choice/OAB, Jan 1998,
5 Choice, Oct 1997, p270   p760
4 LJ, Nov 1 1997, p70   LJ/BRS, Apr 15 1998,
4 RBB, Aug 1997, p1928   p49

PN 1992_____(LC)   **DDC: 791.45**
Les Brown's Encyclopedia of Television
Brown, Les (ed). Gale Research, 1992. 3rd ed. 723p. *Cloth:* $55.00. *Paper:* $22.95.
Review Avg: 3.25   *OCLC:* 1184   *Rating:* 7.62

Reviews
3 ARBA, 93:986
3 Choice, Oct 1992, p268
3 GSED, 1997, p529
4 RBB, Sep 1 1992, p86

PN 1992.3_____(LC)   **DDC: 384.55**
The Television Industry: A Historical Dictionary
Slide, Anthony. Greenwood, 1991. 374p. *Cloth:* $59.50.
Review Avg: 4.00   *OCLC:* 467   *Rating:* 4.93

Reviews
3 ARBA, 92:914
5 GSED, 1997, p535

PN 1992.8_____(LC)   **DDC: 791.45**
The Encyclopedia of TV Game Shows
Schwartz, David and others. Facts On File, 1995. 2nd ed. 587p. *Cloth:* $45.00.
Review Avg: 3.67   *OCLC:* 315   *Rating:* 6.30

Reviews
4 ARBA, 97:1113
3 RBB, Feb 15 1996, p1044
4 RQ, Sum 1996, p555-556

PN 1992.8_____(LC)   **DDC: 791.45**
The Encyclopedia of TV Science Fiction
Fulton, Roger. Trafalgar Square, 1997. New ed. 697p. *Paper:* $19.95.
Review Avg: 4.00   *OCLC:* 50   *Rating:* 6.10

Reviews
4 ARBA, 98:1283

PN 1993.45_____(LC)   **DDC: 791.43**
The Film Encyclopedia
Katz, Ephraim. HarperCollins, 1994. 2nd ed. 1496p. *Paper:* $25.00.
Review Avg: 4.50   *OCLC:* 1303   *Rating:* 9.11

Reviews
5 ARBA, 95:1371
4 Choice, Jan 1995, p752
5 GSED, 1997, p711
4 RBB, Oct 15 1994, p449

PN 1993.5_____(LC)   **DDC: 791.43**
Encyclopaedia of Indian Cinema
Rajadhyaksha, Ashish. British Film Institute, 1995. 568p. *Cloth:* $49.95.
Review Avg: 4.50   *OCLC:* 63   *Rating:* 4.63

Reviews
4 ARBA, 96:1381
5 Choice, Dec 1995, p599

PN 1993.5_____(LC)   **DDC: 791.43**
Encyclopedia of European Cinema
Vincendeau, Ginette. Facts On File, 1995. 524p. *Cloth:* $55.00.
Review Avg: 4.00   *OCLC:* 360   *Rating:* 4.72

Reviews
5 ARBA, 97:1111
3 Choice, Jul 1996, p1771
4 RBB, May 1 1996, p1520

PN 1993.5_____(LC)   **DDC: 384.8**
The Encyclopedia of Hollywood
Siegel, Scott and Barbara Siegel. Facts On File, 1990. 499p. *Cloth:* $45.00.
Review Avg: 3.75   *OCLC:* 519   *Rating:* 4.79

Reviews
5 ARBA, 91:1370
3 Choice, Sep 1990, p82
4 GSED, 1997, p718
3 RBB, May 1 1990, p1736

PN 1995.9_____(LC)   **DDC: 791.43**
Broadcasting It: An Encyclopaedia of Homosexuality on Film, Radio and TV in the UK, 1923-1993
Howes, Keith. Cassell, 1993. 960p. *Cloth:* $64.95. *Paper:* $27.95.
Review Avg: 3.50   *OCLC:* 146   *Rating:* 3.79

Reviews
3 ARBA, 95:858
4 GSED, 1997, p470
4 LJ, Apr 1 1994, p90
3 WLB/R, Jun 1994, p97

PN 1997.8_____(LC)   **DDC: 791.43**
The International Dictionary of Films and Filmmakers
Thomas, Nicholas and James Vinson (eds). St James, 1997. 3rd ed. 4 vols. *Cloth:* $495.00/set.
Review Avg: 3.71   *OCLC:* 649   *Rating:* 7.01

Reviews
3 ARBA, 94:1430
3 Choice, May 1991, p1458
3 Choice, Mar 1992, p1048
5 GSED, 1997, p710
4 LJ, Sep 1 1990, p214
3 RBB, Oct 15 1990, p470,472
5 WLB/R, Oct 1990, p127

◆ The article titles in this encyclopedia are indexed by keyword in Part II.

PN 1999 _____(LC)   DDC: 384

Disney A to Z: The Official Encyclopedia
Smith, Dave. Hyperion, 1996. 564p. _Paper:_ $29.45.
Review Avg: 2.50   _OCLC:_ 380   _Rating:_ 3.26

Reviews
3 Choice, Jan 1997, p775
2 LJ, Nov 15 1996, p56

PN 2035 _____(LC)   DDC: 792

The Concise Oxford Companion to the Theatre
Hartnoll, Phyllis and Peter Found. Oxford Un, 1992. 2nd ed. 568p.
Cloth: $35.00.
Review Avg: 4.25   _OCLC:_ 594   _Rating:_ 7.44

Reviews
5 ARBA, 94:1472
4 Choice, Apr 1993, p1292
5 GSED, 1997, p719
3 RBB, Mar 1 1993, p1251

PN 2035 _____(LC)   DDC: 792

International Dictionary of Theatre
Hawkins-Dady, Mark (ed). St James, 1992. 3 vols. _Cloth:_ $345.00/
set.
Review Avg: 3.57   _OCLC:_ 641   _Rating:_ 6.85

Reviews   **Awards**
3 ARBA, 93:1391   Choice/OAB, Jan 1994,
4 ARBA, 95:1421, vol. 2   p712
4 Choice, Dec 1993,
   p586-587
3 Choice, May 1996, p1450,
   vol. 2
4 GSED, 1997, p723
4 RBB, Sep 1 1994, p72
3 RBB, Mar 15 1996, p1315

PN 2035 _____(LC)   DDC: 792

The Oxford Companion to the Theatre
Hartnoll, Phyllis (ed). Oxford Un, 1992. 2nd ed. 568p. _Cloth:_ $49.95.
Review Avg: 5.00   _OCLC:_ 594   _Rating:_ 8.19

Reviews
5 GSED, 1997, p721

PN 2220 _____(LC)   DDC: 792.0973

The Oxford Companion to American Theatre
Bordman, Gerald. Oxford Un, 1992. 2nd ed. 735p. _Cloth:_ $49.95.
Review Avg: 4.00   _OCLC:_ 836   _Rating:_ 7.67

Reviews
3 ARBA, 90:1367
3 ARBA, 94:1480, 2nd ed.
5 Choice, May 1993, p1444
5 GSED, 1997, p727

PN 2287 _____(LC)   DDC: 791.43

The Laurel and Hardy Encyclopedia
Mitchell, Glenn. Batsford, 1995. 302p. _Cloth:_ $22.95.
Review Avg: 4.00   _OCLC:_ 124   _Rating:_ 4.25

Reviews
4 Choice, Oct 1995, p270

PN 2297 _____(LC)   DDC: 796.43092

The Marx Brothers Encyclopedia
Mitchell, Glenn. Batsford, 1996. 256p. _Paper:_ $19.95.
Review Avg: 4.00   _OCLC:_ 113   _Rating:_ 4.23

Reviews
4 Choice, Sep 1997, p100,102

PN 2924.5 _____(LC)   DDC: 792

New Kabuki Encyclopedia: An English-Language Adapta-
tion of Kabuki Jiten
Leiter, Samuel L. Greenwood, 1997. 823p. _Cloth:_ $115.00.
Review Avg: 4.00   _OCLC:_ 117   _Rating:_ 4.23

Reviews
4 ARBA, 98:1324

PN 3433.4 _____(LC)   DDC: 809.3

Science Fiction: The Illustrated Encyclopedia
Clute, John. Dorling, 1995. 312p. _Cloth:_ $39.95.
Review Avg: 4.00   _OCLC:_ 640   _Rating:_ 9.28

Reviews   **Awards**
3 ARBA, 96:1192   Choice/OAB, Jan 1997,
5 Choice, Jan 1996, p752   p739
                                    NYPL, 1995

PN 3448 _____(LC)   DDC: 809.3

Encyclopedia Mysteriosa: A Comprehensive Guide to the Art
of Detection in Print, Film, Radio, and Television
DeAndrea, William. Prentice-Hall, 1994. 405p. _Cloth:_ $27.50.
Review Avg: 3.25   _OCLC:_ 379   _Rating:_ 4.01

Reviews
3 ARBA, 95:932
3 GSED, 1997, p511
3 RBB, Feb 15 1995, p1109
4 WLB/R, Feb 1995, p66-67

PN 4784 _____(LC)   DDC: 070.4

Historical Dictionary of War Journalism
Roth, Michael P. Greenwood, 1997. 482p. _Cloth:_ $85.00.
Review Avg: 4.00   _OCLC:_ 122   _Rating:_ 4.24

Reviews
4 ARBA, 98:881
4 Choice, Nov 1997, p462

PN 6141 _____(LC)   DDC: 809.4

Encyclopedia of the Essay
Chevalier, Chevy. Fitzroy, 1997. 1002p. _Cloth:_ $125.00.
Review Avg: 4.00   _OCLC:_ 109   _Rating:_ 4.22

Reviews
4 ARBA, 98:1107

PN 6149 _____(LC)   DDC: 809.7

Encyclopedia of Satirical Literature
Snodgrass, Mary Ellen. ABC-CLIO, 1996. 559p. _Cloth:_ $65.00.
Review Avg: 2.00   _OCLC:_ 248   _Rating:_ 2.50

Reviews
3 ARBA, 97:892
1 Choice, Jun 1997, p1646

PQ 41_____(LC)   **DDC: 840.9**
The New Oxford Companion to Literature in French
France, Peter (ed). Oxford Un, 1995. 865p. *Cloth:* $49.95.
Review Avg: 4.25   *OCLC:* 1098   *Rating:* 6.45

Reviews
4 ARBA, 96:1252
4 Choice, Nov 1995, p442
5 LJ, Jul 1995, p74
4 RBB, Sep 1 1995, p109

PQ 226_____(LC)   **DDC: 840.3**
Guide to French Literature: 1789 to Present
Levi, Anthony. St James, 1992. 884p. *Cloth:* $115.00.
Review Avg: 3.00   *OCLC:* 431   *Rating:* 3.86

Reviews
3 ARBA, 93:1221

PQ 2042_____(LC)   **DDC: 848.509**
A Rousseau Dictionary
Dent, N. J. H. Blackwell, 1992. 279p. *Cloth:* $49.95.
Review Avg: 3.00   *OCLC:* 342   *Rating:* 3.68

Reviews
3 ARBA, 93:1396

PQ 2469_____(LC)   **DDC: 843**
The Jules Verne Encyclopedia
Taves, Brian and Stephen Michaluk, Jr. Scarecrow, 1996. 257p. *Cloth:* $54.50.
Review Avg: 2.00   *OCLC:* 152   *Rating:* 2.30

Reviews
2 Choice, Feb 1997, p951

PQ 4063_____(LC)   **DDC: 850.9**
Feminist Encyclopedia of Italian Literature
Russell, Rinaldina (ed). Greenwood, 1997. 402p. *Cloth:* $79.50.
Review Avg: 4.00   *OCLC:* 106   *Rating:* 4.21

Reviews
4 ARBA, 98:1177

PQ 7081_____(LC)   **DDC: 860.09**
Encyclopedia of Latin American Literature
Smith, Verity (ed). Dearborn, 1997. 926p. *Cloth:* $125.00.
Review Avg: 3.33   *OCLC:* 423   *Rating:* 4.18

Reviews   **Awards**
4 ARBA, 98:1178   RBB/ORS, May 1 1998,
3 Choice, Oct 1997, p270   p1538
3 LJ, Jun 1 1997, p90

PQ 7081_____(LC)   **DDC: 809**
Handbook of Latin American Literature
Foster, David William (compiler). Garland, 1992. 2nd ed. 608p. *Cloth:* $95.00. *Paper:* $18.95.
Review Avg: 5.00   *OCLC:* 679   *Rating:* 8.36

Reviews
5 ARBA, 94:1298

PQ 7106_____(LC)   **DDC: 860.9**
Dictionary of Mexican Literature
Cortes, Eladio (ed). Greenwood, 1992. 768p. *Cloth:* $95.00.
Review Avg: 4.67   *OCLC:* 748   *Rating:* 6.17

Reviews
5 ARBA, 94:1296
4 Choice, May 1993, p1438
5 GSED, 1997, p639
5 LJ, Apr 15 1993, p58
5 RBB, Apr 1 1993, p1455-1456
4 WLB/R, Apr 1993, p124

PQ 7378_____(LC)   **DDC: 860.9**
Dictionary of Twentieth-Century Cuban Literature
Martinez, Julio A. Greenwood, 1990. 537p. *Cloth:* $75.00.
Review Avg: 4.67   *OCLC:* 386   *Rating:* 5.44

Reviews
5 ARBA, 91:1230
4 Choice, Jun 1990, p1648
5 GSED, 1997, p633

PR 19_____(LC)   **DDC: 820.9**
The Oxford Companion to English Literature
Drabble, Margaret (ed). Oxford Un, 1995. Revised edition. 1171p. *Cloth:* $49.95.
Review Avg: 4.33   *OCLC:* 873   *Rating:* 8.08

Reviews
5 ARBA, 96:1231
4 Choice, Mar 1996, p1102
4 RBB, Jan 1 1996, p890

PR 109_____(LC)   **DDC: 820.9**
The Oxford Illustrated Literary Guide to Great Britain and Ireland
Eagle, Dorothy and Meic Stephens (eds). Oxford Un, 1992. 2nd ed. 322p. *Cloth:* $45.00.
Review Avg: 3.67   *OCLC:* 591   *Rating:* 6.85

Reviews
4 ARBA, 94:480
4 LJ, Oct 1 1992, p80
3 RBB, Nov 1 1992, p554

PR 149_____(LC)   **DDC: 820.9**
A Dictionary of Biblical Tradition in English Literature
Jeffrey, David Lyle (ed). Eerdmans, 1992. 960p. *Cloth:* $79.99.
Review Avg: 3.86   *OCLC:* 1091   *Rating:* 8.04

Reviews   **Awards**
3 ARBA, 94:1149   Choice/OAB, Jan 1994,
4 Choice, Jul/Aug 1993,   p712
  p1748
4 GSED, 1997, p614
3 JAL, Jul 1993, p200
4 RBB, Mar 1 1993,
  p1251,1263
5 RQ, Sum 1993, p563-564
4 WLB/R, Mar 1993, p108

♦ The article titles in this encyclopedia are indexed by keyword in Part II.

PR 149   **(LC)**   **DDC: 820.9**

An Encyclopedia of Flora and Fauna in English and American Literature

Milward, Peter. Mellen, 1992. 224p. *Cloth:* $69.95.
Review Avg: 3.00   *OCLC:* 64   *Rating:* 3.13

Reviews
3 ARBA, 94:1151
3 GSED, 1997, p618

PR 471   **(LC)**   **DDC: 820**

The Oxford Companion to Twentieth-Century Literature in English

Stringer, Jenny (ed). Oxford Un, 1996. 751p. *Cloth:* $45.00.
Review Avg: 3.50   *OCLC:* 237   *Rating:* 3.97

Reviews
3 Choice, Apr 1997, p1312,1314
4 RBB, Nov 15 1996, p612,614

PR 601   **(LC)**   **DDC: 821**

The Oxford Companion to Twentieth-Century Poetry in English

Hamilton, Ian (ed). Oxford Un, 1994. 602p. *Cloth:* $35.00.
Review Avg: 4.00   *OCLC:* 1457   *Rating:* 8.91

Reviews   **Awards**
4 Choice, Sep 1994, p74   Choice/OAB, Jan 1995,
4 GSED, 1997, p643   p721
4 LJ, Apr 15 1994, p68

PR 2362   **(LC)**   **DDC: 821**

The Spenser Encyclopedia

Hamilton, A. C. and others (eds). Un of Toronto, 1990. 858p. *Cloth:* $250.00.
Review Avg: 5.00   *OCLC:* 391   *Rating:* 7.78

Reviews   **Awards**
5 ARBA, 92:1211   Choice/OAB, May 1992,
5 Choice, Jul/Aug 1991,   p1343
  p1766

PR 2892   **(LC)**   **DDC: 822.3**

Shakespeare A to Z: The Essential Reference to His Plays, His Poems, His Life and Times, and More

Boyce, Charles. Facts On File, 1990. 742p. *Cloth:* $55.00. *Paper:* $16.00.
Review Avg: 4.20   *OCLC:* 1512   *Rating:* 9.22

Reviews   **Awards**
5 ARBA, 92:1209   RBB/ORS, May 1 1992,
3 Choice, Jul/Aug 1991,   p1625
  p1286
4 LJ, Aug 1990, p100
4 RBB, Mar 15 1991, p1524
5 RQ, Fall 1991, p109

PR 3532   **(LC)**   **DDC: 828**

The Samuel Johnson Encyclopedia

Rogers, Pat. Greenwood, 1996. 483p. *Cloth:* $85.00.
Review Avg: 4.00   *OCLC:* 165   *Rating:* 4.33

Reviews
4 ARBA, 97:994

4 Choice, Dec 1996, p594
4 LJ, Oct 15 1996, p53

PR 4623   **(LC)**   **DDC: 823.8**

Encyclopedia Sherlockiana: An A-to-Z Guide to the World of the Great Detective

Bunson, Matthew. Macmillan, 1994. 326p. *Cloth:* $25.00.
Review Avg: 3.50   *OCLC:* 202   *Rating:* 3.90

Reviews
4 GSED, 1997, p629
3 WLB/R, Feb 1995, p66-67

PR 5906   **(LC)**   **DDC: 821**

A William Butler Yeats Encyclopedia

McCready, Sam. Greenwood, 1997. 484p. *Cloth:* $95.00.
Review Avg: 4.00   *OCLC:* 172   *Rating:* 4.34

Reviews
4 ARBA, 98:1166

PR 6005   **(LC)**   **DDC: 823**

Agatha Christie A to Z: The Essential Reference to Her Life and Writings

Sova, Dawn B. Facts On File, 1996. 375p. *Cloth:* $40.00.
Review Avg: 4.00   *OCLC:* 94   *Rating:* 4.19

Reviews
4 LJ, Aug 1996, p66

PR 6019   **(LC)**   **DDC: 823**

James Joyce A to Z: The Essential Reference to the Life and Work

Fargnoli, A. Nicholas and Michael Patrick Gillespie. Facts On File, 1995. 304p. *Cloth:* $45.00.
Review Avg: 4.00   *OCLC:* 481   *Rating:* 4.96

Reviews
3 ARBA, 97:1009
5 Choice, Feb 1996, p927-928
4 LJ, Jun 15 1995, p60

PR 6025   **(LC)**   **DDC: 823**

A William Somerset Maugham Encyclopedia

Rogal, Samuel J. Greenwood, 1997. 376p. *Cloth:* $79.50.
Review Avg: 3.50   *OCLC:* 95   *Rating:* 3.69

Reviews
3 ARBA, 98:1160
4 Choice, Nov 1997, p456

PR 6045   **(LC)**   **DDC: 823**

Virginia Woolf A to Z: A Comprehensive Reference for Students, Teachers and Common Readers to Her Life, Work and Critical Reception

Hussey, Mark. Facts On File, 1995. 452p. *Cloth:* $50.00.
Note: Also published by Oxford University Press.
Review Avg: 3.00   *OCLC:* 372   *Rating:* 3.74

Reviews
3 ARBA, 96:1221
3 Choice, Jan 1996, p758

PR 8706_____(LC)   DDC: 820.9
The Oxford Companion to Irish Literature
Welch, Robert (ed). Oxford Un, 1996. 614p. *Cloth:* $49.95.
Review Avg: 4.00   *OCLC:* 624   *Rating:* 7.25

Reviews   **Awards**
4 Choice, Sep 1996, p104   Choice/OAB, Jan 1997,
4 RBB, Apr 15 1996, p1463   p740

PR 9080_____(LC)   DDC: 820.9
Encyclopedia of Post-Colonial Literatures in English
Benson, Eugene and L. W. Conolly (eds). Routledge, 1994. 2 vols.
(1874p.) *Cloth:* $225.00/set.
Review Avg: 4.25   *OCLC:* 479   *Rating:* 7.21

Reviews   **Awards**
5 ARBA, 95:1102   Choice/OAB, Jan 1996,
4 Choice, Feb 1995,   p724
  p915,917
4 GSED, 1997, p609
4 LJ, Oct 15 1994, p50

PR 9600.2_____(LC)   DDC: 820.9
The Oxford Companion to Australian Literature
Wilde, William H. and others. Oxford Un, 1995. 2nd ed. 833p. *Cloth:*
$79.00.
Review Avg: 3.67   *OCLC:* 348   *Rating:* 6.37

Reviews
4 ARBA, 96:1248
3 Choice, Jul/Aug 1995, p1714
4 LJ, May 15 1995, p66

PS 21_____(LC)   DDC: 810.9
The Oxford Companion to American Literature
Hart, James D. Oxford Un, 1995. 6th ed. 779p. *Cloth:* $49.95.
Review Avg: 3.67   *OCLC:* 1383   *Rating:* 8.44

Reviews
3 ARBA, 97:966
5 Choice, Mar 1996, p1096
3 RBB, Oct 1 1995, p353

PS 147_____(LC)   DDC: 810.9
*The Oxford Companion to Women's Writing in the United
States*
Davidson, Cathy N. and Linda Wagner-Martin (eds). Oxford Un,
1995. 1021p. *Cloth:* $45.00.
Review Avg: 4.50   *OCLC:* 1617   *Rating:* 7.73

Reviews
5 ARBA, 96:1200
4 LJ, Nov 15 1994, p62

PS 153_____(LC)   DDC: 810.8
The Oxford Companion to African American Literature
Andrews, William L. and others (eds). Oxford Un, 1997. 866p. *Cloth:*
$55.00.
Review Avg: 5.00   *OCLC:* 1316   *Rating:* 7.63

Reviews   **Awards**
5 ARBA, 98:1129   LJ/BRS, Apr 15 1998,
5 LJ, Apr 1 1997   p49
                                 RBB/ORS, May 1 1998,
                                   p1538

PS 169_____(LC)   DDC: 810
Encyclopedia of Frontier Literature
Snodgrass, Mary Ellen. ABC-CLIO, 1997. 540p. *Cloth:* $65.00.
Note: Series—ABC-CLIO Literary Companion.
Review Avg: 4.00   *OCLC:* 151   *Rating:* 4.30

Reviews
4 ARBA, 98:1130
4 RBB, Nov 15 1997, p576

PS 217_____(LC)   DDC: 810.9
Encyclopedia of Transcendentalism
Mott, Wesley T. (ed). Greenwood, 1996. 280p. *Cloth:* $75.00.
Review Avg: 4.00   *OCLC:* 332   *Rating:* 4.66

Reviews
4 ARBA, 97:964
4 Choice, Feb 1997, p943

PS 1330_____(LC)   DDC: 818
The Mark Twain Encyclopedia
LeMaster, J. R. and James D. Wilson (eds). Garland, 1993. 848p.
Cloth: $95.00.
Review Avg: 4.20   *OCLC:* 873   *Rating:* 7.95

Reviews   **Awards**
3 ARBA, 94:1240   RBB/ORS, May 1 1994,
5 Choice, Sep 1993, p84   p1627
5 LJ, May 1 1993, p83
4 RBB, Oct 15 1993, p474
4 WLB/R, May 1993, p119

PS 1331_____(LC)   DDC: 818
*Mark Twain A to Z: The Essential Reference to His Life and
Writings*
Rasmussen, R. Kent. Facts On File, 1995. 552p. *Cloth:* $45.00.
Review Avg: 4.50   *OCLC:* 671   *Rating:* 5.84

Reviews
5 ARBA, 96:1217
4 RBB, Oct 1 1995, p351

PS 1449_____(LC)   DDC: 813
A Stephen Crane Encyclopedia
Wertheim, Stanley. Greenwood, 1997. 413p. *Cloth:* $85.00.
Review Avg: 4.00   *OCLC:* 113   *Rating:* 4.23

Reviews
4 ARBA, 98:1134

PS 1880_____(LC)   DDC: 813
A Nathaniel Hawthorne Encyclopedia
Gale, Robert L. Greenwood, 1991. 583p. *Cloth:* $75.00.
Review Avg: 4.50   *OCLC:* 514   *Rating:* 5.53

Reviews
5 ARBA, 92:1171
4 Choice, Sep 1991, p58-60

◆ The article titles in this encyclopedia are indexed by keyword in Part II.

PS 2386_____(LC)   DDC: 813

A Herman Melville Encyclopedia
Gale, Robert L. Greenwood, 1995. 536p. *Cloth:* $79.50.
Review Avg: 3.00   *OCLC:* 381   *Rating:* 3.76

Reviews
3 ARBA, 96:1212

PS 2386_____(LC)   DDC: 813

A Melville Encyclopedia: The Novels
Kier, Kathleen E. (compiler). Whitston, 1994. 2nd ed. 1220p. *Cloth:*
$90.00.
Review Avg: 3.67   *OCLC:* 76   *Rating:* 5.82

Reviews
3 ARBA, 95:1194
4 Choice, Feb 1991, p916
4 WLB/R, Nov 1990, p152,154

PS 2630_____(LC)   DDC: 818

The Poe Encyclopedia
Frank, Frederick S. and Anthony Magistrale. Greenwood, 1997. 453p.
Cloth: $89.50.
Review Avg: 4.00   *OCLC:* 327   *Rating:* 4.65

Reviews
4 ARBA, 98:1137

PS 3572_____(LC)   DDC: 813

The Vonnegut Encyclopedia: An Authorized Compendium
Leeds, Marc. Greenwood, 1994. 693p. *Cloth:* $75.00.
Review Avg: 2.00   *OCLC:* 251   *Rating:* 2.50

Reviews
2 ARBA, 96:1219

PT 41_____(LC)   DDC: 830.9

The Feminist Encyclopedia of German Literature
Eigler, Friederike and Susanne Kord (eds). Greenwood, 1997. 676p.
Cloth: $89.50.
Review Avg: 5.00   *OCLC:* 162   *Rating:* 5.32

Reviews
5 Choice, Sep 1997, p99

PT 41_____(LC)   DDC: 830.3

The Oxford Companion to German Literature
Garland, Henry and Mary Garland. Oxford Un, 1997. 3rd ed. 951p.
Cloth: $75.00.
Review Avg: 4.50   *OCLC:* 4   *Rating:* 6.51

Reviews
4 ARBA, 98:1173
5 RBB, Dec 15 1997, p714

Q 121_____(LC)   DDC: 503

Gale Encyclopedia of Science
Travers, Bridget. Gale Research, 1996. 6 vols. (4136p.) *Cloth:*
$399.00/set.
Review Avg: 3.20   *OCLC:* 251   *Rating:* 5.70

Reviews   **Awards**
2 ARBA, 97:1238   NYPL, 1996
3 Choice, Jan 1997, p769

4 LJ, Sep 15 1996, p54
4 RBB, Oct 1 1996,
   p368,370
3 RQ, Spr 1997, p453-455

Q 121_____(LC)   DDC: 503

Macmillan Encyclopedia of Science
Kerrod, Robin and others. Macmillan, 1997. Revised edition. 12 vols.
Cloth: $360.00/set.
Review Avg: 3.00   *OCLC:* 437   *Rating:* 5.87

Reviews
3 ARBA, 92:1456
3 GSED, 1997, p797
3 RBB, Oct 15 1991, p466
3 RBB, Aug 1997, p1926-1927

Q 121_____(LC)   DDC: 503

McGraw-Hill Concise Encyclopedia of Science and Technology
Parker, Sybil P. (ed). McGraw-Hill, 1994. 3rd ed. 2241p. *Cloth:*
$115.00.
Note: Available on CD-ROM, McGraw-Hill Science and Technology
Reference Set.
Review Avg: 3.33   *OCLC:* 494   *Rating:* 6.32

Reviews
4 ARBA, 90:1427, 2nd ed.
3 ARBA, 95:1492, 3rd ed.
3 Choice, Jan 1995, p756, 3rd ed.

Q 121_____(LC)   DDC: 503

McGraw-Hill Encyclopedia of Science and Technology
Parker, Sybil P. (ed). McGraw-Hill, 1997. 8th ed. 20 vols. *Cloth:*
$1900.00/set.
Note: Available on CD-ROM, Multimedia Encyclopedia of Science
and Technology, 1995, $1300.00.
Review Avg: 4.55   *OCLC:* 1250   *Rating:* 9.05

Reviews
5 ARBA, 93:1446
3 ARBA, 95:1494, Review of CD-Rom
4 Choice, Oct 1995, p275-276, CD-ROM
5 Choice, Dec 1997, p617-618, 8th ed.
5 GSED, 1997, p798
3 GSED, 1997, p799, CD-ROM
5 LJ, Apr 15 1993, p84, 7th ed.
5 LJ, Sep 1 1997, p175-176, 8th ed.
5 RBB, Sep 1 1992, p80-81, 7th ed.
5 RBB, Sep 15 1997, p266,268, 8th ed.
5 WLB/R, Sep 1992, p116

Q 121_____(LC)   DDC: 503

The Raintree Illustrated Science Encyclopedia
Raintree, 1996. 4th ed. 18 vols. *Cloth:* $379.00/set.
Note: Available on CD-ROM, $429.00 (Windows and Mac).
Review Avg: 4.00   *OCLC:* 434   *Rating:* 6.87

Reviews
5 ARBA, 94:1569
4 GSED, 1997, p805
3 RBB, Jun 1 1992, p1778

Q 121 _____(LC)   **DDC: 503**

Van Nostrand's Scientific Encyclopedia: Animal Life, Biosciences, Chemistry, Earth and Atmospheric Sciences, Energy Sources and Power Technology

Considine, Douglas M. and Glenn D. Considine. Van Nostrand Reinhold, 1995. 8th ed. 2 vols. _Cloth:_ $195.00/set.
Review Avg: 3.25   _OCLC:_ 1229   _Rating:_ 7.71

Reviews
4 ARBA, 90:1430
3 ARBA, 96:1502
3 GSED, 1997, p787
3 RBB, May 1 1995, p1603,1604

Q 123 _____(LC)   **DDC: 503**

Academic Press Dictionary of Science and Technology

Morris, Christopher (ed). Academic, 1992. 2432p. _Cloth:_ $115.00.
Note: Available on CD-ROM.
Review Avg: 3.40   _OCLC:_ 1349   _Rating:_ 8.10

Reviews   **Awards**
3 ARBA, 93:1444   RBB/ORS, May 1 1993,
4 Choice, Feb 1993, p935   p1620
4 GSED, 1997, p783
1 LJ, May 1 1997, p147,
  Review of CD-ROM
5 RBB, Jan 15 1993, p934

Q 123 _____(LC)   **DDC: 503**

Dictionary of Science

Lafferty, Peter and Julian Rowe. Simon & Schuster, 1994. 678p. _Cloth:_ $45.00.
Review Avg: 3.80   _OCLC:_ 336   _Rating:_ 4.47

Reviews
4 Choice, Jul/Aug 1994, p1700
5 GSED, 1997, p794
4 LJ, May 1 1994, p94
3 RBB, Jul 1994, p1973
3 WLB/R, Jun 1994, p99-100

Q 123 _____(LC)   **DDC: 231.7**

Dictionary of Science and Creationism

Ecker, Ronald L. Prometheus, 1990. 263p. _Cloth:_ $41.95.
Review Avg: 4.00   _OCLC:_ 831   _Rating:_ 7.66

Reviews   **Awards**
5 ARBA, 91:1513   Choice/OAB, May 1991,
3 Choice, Jul/Aug 1990,   p1429
  p1804
4 RBB, May 1 1990, p1736

Q 123 _____(LC)   **DDC: 503**

Dictionary of Scientific Literacy

Brennan, Richard P. Wiley, 1992. 334p. _Cloth:_ $22.95.
Review Avg: 3.00   _OCLC:_ 1018   _Rating:_ 5.04

Reviews
3 ARBA, 93:1445
3 LJ, Mar 1 1992, p42
3 LJ, Dec 1991, p132
3 RBB, Feb 1 1992, p1053

Q 123 _____(LC)   **DDC: 503**

Encyclopedia of Physical Science and Technology

Meyers, Robert A. (ed). Academic, 1992. 2nd ed. 18 vols. (1480p.)
Cloth: $2757.00/set.
Note: Available on CD-ROM, 1995.
Review Avg: 4.50   _OCLC:_ 292   _Rating:_ 7.08

Reviews
5 ARBA, 94:1566
3 Choice, Oct 1997, p274-275, Review of CD-ROM
5 GSED, 1997, p790
5 LJ, Apr 15 1993, p84

Q 125 _____(LC)   **DDC: 509**

Great Events from History II: Science and Technology Series

Magill, Frank N. (ed). Salem, 1991. 5 vols. _Cloth:_ $375.00/set.
Review Avg: 3.00   _OCLC:_ 582   _Rating:_ 4.16

Reviews
3 ARBA, 92:1465
3 Choice, Mar 1992, p1044,1046
3 RBB, Dec 15 1991, p785-786
3 RQ, Spr 1992, p417-418

Q 126 _____(LC)   **DDC: 503**

World of Scientific Discovery

Travers, Bridget (ed). Gale Research, 1994. 776p. _Cloth:_ $75.00.
Review Avg: 3.75   _OCLC:_ 243   _Rating:_ 4.24

Reviews
4 ARBA, 95:1497
4 LJ, Apr 15 1994, p68
3 RBB, Jul 1994, p1980
4 WLB/R, May 1994, p76-77

Q 127 _____(LC)   **DDC: 509.174927**

Encyclopedia of the History of Arabic Science

Rashed, Roshdi and Regis Morelon. Routledge, 1996. 3 vols. (1105p.)
Cloth: $250.00/set.
Review Avg: 4.00   _OCLC:_ 97   _Rating:_ 4.19

Reviews
4 Choice, Dec 1996, p589
4 LJ, Apr 15 1997, p64

Q 158.5 _____(LC)   **DDC: 500**

The Holt Handbook of Current Science and Technology: A Sourcebook of Facts and Analysis Covering the Most Important Events in Science and Technology

Bunch, Bryan. Gale Research, 1996. 834p. _Cloth:_ $50.00.
Review Avg: 4.50   _OCLC:_ 82   _Rating:_ 4.66

Reviews
5 ARBA, 93:1455
4 RBB, Dec 15 1992, p762-763

Q 158.5 _____(LC)   **DDC: 500.2**

Magill's Survey of Science: Physical Science Series

Magill, Frank N. (ed). Salem, 1992. 6 vols. (2918p.) _Cloth:_ $475.00/set.
Review Avg: 4.00   _OCLC:_ 572   _Rating:_ 5.14

Reviews
3 ARBA, 93:1699

◆ The article titles in this encyclopedia are indexed by keyword in Part II.

4 Choice, Jul/Aug 1992, p1658-1659
4 LJ, Sep 15 1992, p62
5 WLB/R, May 1992, p128

Q 162 _____(LC) DDC: 500

The New Book of Popular Science
Holland, Lisa (ed). Grolier, 1996. Revised edition. 6 vols. *Cloth:* $219.00/set.
Review Avg: 4.40   *OCLC:* 281   *Rating:* 6.96

Reviews
5 ARBA, 92:1457, Rev. ed.
5 ARBA, 90:1437
5 ARBA, 93:1450
4 RBB, Oct 1 1992, p370, Rev. ed.
3 RBB, Sep 1 1990, p88-89

Q 173 _____(LC) DDC: 001.9

Encyclopedia of Strange and Unexplained Physical Phenomena
Clark, Jerome. Gale Research, 1993. 395p. *Cloth:* $49.95.
Review Avg: 3.60   *OCLC:* 628   *Rating:* 4.86

Reviews
3 ARBA, 94:813
3 GSED, 1997, p409
5 LJ, Jun 1 1994, p96
4 RBB, Oct 15 1993, p472
3 RQ, Win 1993, p284

QA 5 _____(LC) DDC: 510.3

Encyclopaedia of Mathematics
Hazewinkel, M. (ed). Kluwer, 1994. 10 vols. *Cloth:* $2490.00/set.
Paper: $699.006 vols.
Note: Available on CD-ROM, 1998.
Review Avg: 4.00   *OCLC:* 50   *Rating:* 4.10

Reviews
4 ARBA, 90:1771, Vol. 1
3 ARBA, 96:1827, vol. 10
5 GSED, 1997, p1020

QA 21 _____(LC) DDC: 510.9

Companion Encyclopedia of the History and Philosophy of the Mathematical Sciences
Grattan-Guinness, I. (ed). Routledge, 1994. 2 vols. *Cloth:* $175.00/set.
Review Avg: 3.67   *OCLC:* 568   *Rating:* 4.81

Reviews
3 ARBA, 95:1740
5 Choice, Sep 1994, p156-157
3 GSED, 1997, p1021

QA 76.15 _____(LC) DDC: 004

Concise Encyclopedia of Information Processing in Systems and Organizations
Sage, Andrew P. (ed). Pergamon, 1990. 548p. *Cloth:* $225.00.
Review Avg: 4.00   *OCLC:* 160   *Rating:* 4.32

Reviews
5 ARBA, 91:1727
3 Choice, Oct 1990, p280

QA 76.15 _____(LC) DDC: 004

Encyclopedia of Computer Science
Ralston, Anthony and Edwin D. Reilly (eds). Van Nostrand Reinhold, 1993. 3rd ed. 1664p. *Cloth:* $125.00.
Review Avg: 3.67   *OCLC:* 1317   *Rating:* 8.30

Reviews
3 ARBA, 94:1903
4 Choice, May 1993, p1438
4 GSED, 1997, p975

◆QA 76.15 _____(LC) DDC: 004

Macmillan Encyclopedia of Computers
Bitter, Gary G. (ed). Macmillan, 1992. 2 vols. *Cloth:* $200.00/set.
Review Avg: 3.33   *OCLC:* 1126   *Rating:* 9.58

Reviews
3 ARBA, 93:1678
5 Choice, Oct 1992, p276
3 GSED, 1997, p970
1 LJ, Jun 1 1992, p112
4 RBB, Sep 1 1992, p86
4 WLB/R, Jun 1992, p114

Awards
Choice/OAB, Jan 1993, p735
RBB/ORS, May 1 1993, p1620

QA 76.15 _____(LC) DDC: 004.16

McGraw-Hill Encyclopedia of Personal Computing
Gibilisco, Stan (ed). McGraw-Hill, 1995. 2nd ed. 1216p. *Cloth:* $89.95.
Review Avg: 4.00   *OCLC:* 365   *Rating:* 6.73

Reviews
4 RBB, May 15 1996, p1620

QA 76.575 _____(LC) DDC: 006.6

Multimedia Technology from A to Z
Dillon, Patrick M. and David C. Leonard. Oryx, 1995. 225p. *Paper:* $25.00.
Review Avg: 4.00   *OCLC:* 856   *Rating:* 5.71

Reviews
4 LJ, Jun 1 1995, p100

QA 76.758 _____(LC) DDC: 005

Concise Encyclopedia of Software Engineering
Morris, Derrick and Boris Tamm. Pergamon, 1993. 400p. *Cloth:* $345.00.
Review Avg: 3.00   *OCLC:* 103   *Rating:* 3.21

Reviews
3 ARBA, 94:1775
3 Choice, Feb 1994, p912

QA 76.758 _____(LC) DDC: 005.1

Encyclopedia of Software Engineering
Marciniak, John J. (ed). Wiley, 1994. 2 vols. *Cloth:* $249.00/set.
Note: Condensed in *Concise Encyclopedia of Software Engineering.*
Review Avg: 3.25   *OCLC:* 466   *Rating:* 4.18

Reviews
3 ARBA, 95:1607
3 Choice, Oct 1994, p258
3 GSED, 1997, p885
4 RBB, Jul 1994, p1974

QA 76.9 _____(LC)   DDC: 003
Concise Encyclopedia of Modelling and Simulation
Atherton, Derek P. and Pierre Borne (eds). Pergamon, 1992. 539p.
Cloth: $240.00.
Review Avg: 3.50   *OCLC:* 79   *Rating:* 3.66

Reviews
3 ARBA, 93:1674
4 GSED, 1997, p963

QA 76.9 _____(LC)   DDC: 004.6
Information Security: Dictionary of Concepts, Standards and Terms
Longley, Dennis and others. Macmillan, 1992. 620p. *Cloth:* $130.00.
Review Avg: 4.00   *OCLC:* 63   *Rating:* 4.13

Reviews
4 Choice, Jul/Aug 1993, p1752
4 GSED, 1997, p980

QA 76.9 _____(LC)   DDC: 004.6
The Online User's Encyclopedia: Bulletin Boards and Beyond
Aboba, Bernard. Addison-Wesley, 1993. 806p. *Paper:* $34.95.
Review Avg: 5.00   *OCLC:* 513   *Rating:* 6.03

Reviews
5 ARBA, 95:1701
5 GSED, 1997, p981

QA 276.14 _____(LC)   DDC: 519.5
The HarperCollins Dictionary of Statistics
Porkess, Roger. Harper Perennial, 1991. 267p. *Cloth:* $25.00. *Paper:* $12.95.
Review Avg: 3.00   *OCLC:* 319   *Rating:* 3.64

Reviews
3 ARBA, 93:904

QA 402 _____(LC)   DDC: 003
Systems and Control Encyclopedia: Theory, Technology, Applications
Singh, Maadan G. (ed). Pergamon, 1990. 8 vols. *Cloth:* $2300.00/set.
Note: Supplements—$390.00/vol.
Review Avg: 3.00   *OCLC:* 67   *Rating:* 3.13

Reviews
3 ARBA, 94:1570

QB 14 _____(LC)   DDC: 520
The Astronomy and Astrophysics Encyclopedia
Maran, Stephen P. (ed). Van Nostrand Reinhold, 1992. 1002p. *Cloth:* $89.95.
Review Avg: 4.67   *OCLC:* 907   *Rating:* 8.48

Reviews   **Awards**
5 ARBA, 93:1704   Choice/OAB, Jan 1993,
5 Choice, Mar 1992, p1037   p734
4 RBB, Mar 15 1992,
   p1399-1400

QB 14 _____(LC)   DDC: 520
Astronomy from A to Z: A Dictionary of Celestial Objects and Ideas
Schweighauser, Charles A. Un of Ill, 1991. 192p. *Paper:* $14.95.
Review Avg: 3.00   *OCLC:* 629   *Rating:* 4.26

Reviews
3 Choice, Jul/Aug 1991, p1765
3 LJ, Sep 1 1991, p184
3 RBB, Jun 1 1991, p1894

QB 14 _____(LC)   DDC: 520
Companion to the Cosmos
Gribbin, John. Little, Brown, 1996. 504p. *Cloth:* $29.95.
Review Avg: 3.50   *OCLC:* 460   *Rating:* 4.42

Reviews
3 Choice, May 1997, p1521
4 LJ, Feb 1 1997, p72

QB 14 _____(LC)   DDC: 520
The Facts On File Dictionary of Astronomy
Illingworth, Valerie. Facts On File, 1994. 3rd ed. 520p. *Cloth:* $29.95.
Paper: $14.95.
Review Avg: 3.50   *OCLC:* 345   *Rating:* 6.19

Reviews
3 ARBA, 95:1721
4 Choice, Feb 1995, p916

QB 14 _____(LC)   DDC: 520
The HarperCollins Dictionary of Astronomy and Space Science
Moore, Dianne F. HarperCollins, 1992. 338p. *Cloth:* $25.00. *Paper:* $13.00.
Review Avg: 3.00   *OCLC:* 205   *Rating:* 3.41

Reviews
3 ARBA, 93:1702
3 GSED, 1997, p1000

QB 14 _____(LC)   DDC: 520
McGraw-Hill Encyclopedia of Astronomy
Parker, Sybil P. and Jay M. Pasachoff (eds). McGraw-Hill, 1993. 2nd ed. 531p. *Cloth:* $75.50.
Note: From *McGraw-Hill Encyclopedia of Science and Technology.*
Review Avg: 3.00   *OCLC:* 362   *Rating:* 5.72

Reviews
3 ARBA, 94:1927, 2nd ed.
3 Choice, Oct 1993, p268, 2nd ed.
3 GSED, 1997, p1002, 2nd ed.
3 JAL, Sep 1993, p275, 2nd ed.
3 WLB/R, Sep 1993, p119-121, 2nd ed.

QB 15 _____(LC)   DDC: 520
History of Astronomy: An Encyclopedia
Lankford, John. Garland, 1997. 594p. *Cloth:* $95.00.
Note: Series— Garland Encyclopedias in the History of Science; Garland Reference Library of Social Science.
Review Avg: 3.75   *OCLC:* 63   *Rating:* 3.88

Reviews
3 ARBA, 98:1606

◆ The article titles in this encyclopedia are indexed by keyword in Part II.

3 Choice, Apr 1997, p1309-1310
4 LJ, Jan 1997, p86,88
5 RBB, Apr 15 1997, p1450

QB 54 _____(LC)   DDC: **574.5999**

The Extraterrestrial Encyclopedia: Our Search for Life in Outer Space

Angelo, Jr., Joseph A. Facts On File, 1991. Revised edition. 240p. *Cloth:* $40.00.
Review Avg: 4.00   *OCLC:* 416   *Rating:* 6.83

Reviews
5 ARBA, 93:805
4 GSED, 1997, p407
3 RBB, Jan 1 1992, p849

QB 209 _____(LC)   DDC: **529**

Encyclopedia of Time

Macey, Samuel L. (ed). Garland, 1994. 699p. *Cloth:* $95.00.
Note: Series—Garland Reference Library of Social Science, vol. 810.
Review Avg: 4.00   *OCLC:* 512   *Rating:* 5.02

Reviews
4 ARBA, 95:58
4 Choice, Sep 1994, p68
4 RBB, Sep 1 1994, p68
4 WLB/R, Sep 1994, p78

QB 401 _____(LC)   DDC: **523.9**

Moons of the Solar System: An Illustrated Encyclopedia

Stewart, John. McFarland, 1991. 244p. *Cloth:* $45.00.
Review Avg: 3.33   *OCLC:* 443   *Rating:* 4.22

Reviews
3 ARBA, 93:1707
3 Choice, May 1992, p1376
4 WLB/R, Apr 1992, p125-126

QB 980.5 _____(LC)   DDC: **523.1**

Encyclopedia of Cosmology: Historical, Philosophical, and Scientific Foundations of Modern Cosmology

Hetherington, Norriss S. (ed). Garland, 1993. 686p. *Cloth:* $125.00.
Review Avg: 4.25   *OCLC:* 402   *Rating:* 5.05

Reviews
5 ARBA, 94:1926
4 Choice, Nov 1993, p430
4 GSED, 1997, p999
4 WLB/R, Oct 1993, p86,88

QC 5 _____(LC)   DDC: **530**

Encyclopedia of Applied Physics

Trigg, George L. (ed). VCH, 1992. 20 vols. (in progress) *Cloth:* $5950.00/set.
Review Avg: 3.17   *OCLC:* 222   *Rating:* 3.61

Reviews
3 ARBA, 92:1750, vol. 1
3 ARBA, 97:1407-8, vol. 4
3 ARBA, 93:1734, vol. 3
3 ARBA, 93:1733, vol. 2
3 Choice, Mar 1992, p1042,1044
4 GSED, 1997, p1015

QC 5 _____(LC)   DDC: **530**

Encyclopedia of Modern Physics

Meyers, Robert A. (ed). Academic, 1990. 773p. *Cloth:* $116.00.
Review Avg: 3.00   *OCLC:* 442   *Rating:* 3.88

Reviews
3 ARBA, 92:1749
3 Choice, Jun 1990, p1650

QC 5 _____(LC)   DDC: **530**

Encyclopedia of Physics

Lerner, Rita G. and George L. Trigg. VCH, 1991. 2nd ed. 1408p. *Cloth:* $175.00.
Review Avg: 4.00   *OCLC:* 1201   *Rating:* 8.40

Reviews
5 ARBA, 92:1747
3 RBB, Aug 1991, p2171

QC 5 _____(LC)   DDC: **530**

Macmillan Encyclopedia of Physics

Rigden, John S. (ed). Macmillan, 1996. 4 vols. (1881p.) *Cloth:* $400.00/set.
Review Avg: 4.00   *OCLC:* 291   *Rating:* 4.58

Reviews   *Awards*
4 Choice, Jul 1997, p1780   Choice/OAB, Jan 1998,
4 LJ, Mar 15 1997, p56-67   p760
4 RBB, Apr 15 1997,
  p1451,1454

QC 5 _____(LC)   DDC: **530**

McGraw-Hill Encyclopedia of Physics

Parker, Sybil P. (ed). McGraw-Hill, 1993. 2nd ed. 1624p. *Cloth:* $95.50.
Review Avg: 3.40   *OCLC:* 389   *Rating:* 6.18

Reviews
4 ARBA, 94:1965
3 Choice, Oct 1993, p268
4 GSED, 1997, p1016
3 JAL, Sep 1993, p275
3 WLB/R, Sep 1993, p119-120

QC 82 _____(LC)   DDC: **530.8**

Sizes: The Illustrated Encyclopedia

Lord, John. HarperCollins, 1995. 374p. *Paper:* $15.00.
Review Avg: 3.50   *OCLC:* 509   *Rating:* 6.52

Reviews   *Awards*
4 ARBA, 96:1787   NYPL, 1995
3 Choice, Oct 1995, p268

QC 221.5 _____(LC)   DDC: **534**

Encyclopedia of Acoustics

Crocker, Malcolm J. (ed). Wiley, 1997. 4 vols. *Cloth:* $475.00.
Review Avg: 5.00   *OCLC:* 184   *Rating:* 5.37

Reviews
5 ARBA, 98:1619

QC 494.2 _____(LC)   DDC: 701.8
The Color Compendium
Hope, Augustine and Margaret Walch. Van Nostrand Reinhold, 1990. 360p. *Cloth:* $49.95.
Review Avg: 3.00   *OCLC:* 608   *Rating:* 4.22

Reviews
4 ARBA, 91:1011
2 Choice, Apr 1990, p1300

QC 762 _____(LC)   DDC: 538
Encyclopedia of Nuclear Magnetic Resonance
Grant, David M. and Robin K. Harris (eds). Wiley, 1996. 8 vols. (5323p.) *Cloth:* $3600.00.
Review Avg: 4.00   *OCLC:* 170   *Rating:* 4.34

Reviews
4 Choice, Jun 1997, p1638

QC 854 _____(LC)   DDC: 551.5
Encyclopedia of Climate and Weather
Schneider, Stephen H. (ed). Oxford Un, 1996. 2 vols. (929p.) *Cloth:* $195.00/set.
Review Avg: 3.20   *OCLC:* 1401   *Rating:* 10.00

Reviews   **Awards**
3 ARBA, 97:1396   Choice/OAB, Jan 1997,
4 Choice, Oct 1996, p250   p740
3 GSED, 1997, p1007   RBB/ORS, May 1 1997,
3 LJ, Jun 1 1996, p94   p1524
3 RBB, Aug 1996, p1924

QC 981.8 _____(LC)   DDC: 551.6
Dictionary of Global Climate Change
Maunder, W. John. Routledge, 1994. 2nd ed. 257p. *Cloth:* $45.00.
Review Avg: 3.67   *OCLC:* 517   *Rating:* 8.70

Reviews   **Awards**
3 ARBA, 94:1949   Choice/OAB, Jan 1994,
5 Choice, May 1993, p1445   p712
3 GSED, 1997, p1006

QD 4 _____(LC)   DDC: 540
Concise Encyclopedia Chemistry
Eagleson, Mary. Gruyter, 1994. 1201p. *Cloth:* $99.95.
Review Avg: 3.00   *OCLC:* 627   *Rating:* 4.25

Reviews
3 ARBA, 95:1713
3 Choice, Oct 1994, p257
3 GSED, 1997, p986
3 LJ, Apr 15 1994, p64
3 RBB, Sep 1 1994, p66

QD 4 _____(LC)   DDC: 540
Macmillan Encyclopedia of Chemistry
Lagowski, Joseph J. (ed). Macmillan, 1997. 4 vols. (1696p.) *Cloth:* $400.00.
Review Avg: 3.50   *OCLC:* 436   *Rating:* 4.37

Reviews
3 ARBA, 98:1601
4 LJ, Dec 1997, p92

QD 5 _____(LC)   DDC: 540
McGraw-Hill Encyclopedia of Chemistry
Parker, Sybil P. (ed). McGraw-Hill, 1993. 2nd ed. 1249p. *Cloth:* $95.50.
Note: From McGraw-Hill Encyclopedia of Science and Technology.
Review Avg: 3.33   *OCLC:* 505   *Rating:* 6.34

Reviews
5 ARBA, 94:1935
3 Choice, Oct 1993, p268
3 GSED, 1997, p991
3 JAL, Sep 1993, p275
3 RQ, Win 1993, p290
3 WLB/R, Sep 1993, p119-121

QD 65 _____(LC)   DDC: 540
Lange's Handbook of Chemistry
Dean, John Aurie. McGraw-Hill, 1992. 14th ed. 1485p. *Cloth:* $79.50.
Review Avg: 3.00   *OCLC:* 1032   *Rating:* 7.06

Reviews
3 ARBA, 93:1716

QD 71.5 _____(LC)   DDC: 543
Encyclopedia of Analytical Science
Townshend, Alan (ed). Academic, 1995. 10 vols. (6059p.) *Cloth:* $1950.00/set.
Review Avg: 3.00   *OCLC:* 165   *Rating:* 3.33

Reviews
3 ARBA, 96:1495
3 Choice, Mar 1996, p1092

QD 415 _____(LC)   DDC: 574.19
Concise Encyclopedia of Biochemistry and Molecular Biology
Scott, Thomas A. and E. Ian Mercer. Gruyter, 1997. 3rd ed. 737p. *Cloth:* $99.95.
Review Avg: 3.75   *OCLC:* 649   *Rating:* 7.05

Reviews
3 ARBA, 90:1481
4 ARBA, 98:1599, 3rd ed.
4 Choice, Sep 1997, p103
4 LJ, Jul 1997, p74, 3rd ed.

QD 415 _____(LC)   DDC: 660
Encyclopedia of Common Natural Ingredients Used in Food, Drugs, and Cosmetics
Leung, Albert Y. and Steven Foster. Wiley, 1996. 2nd ed. 649p. *Cloth:* $120.00.
Review Avg: 4.00   *OCLC:* 385   *Rating:* 6.77

Reviews
4 GSED, 1997, p954

QE 5 _____(LC)   DDC: 550
The Concise Oxford Dictionary of Earth Sciences
Allaby, Ailsa and Michael Allaby. Oxford Un, 1990. 410p. *Cloth:* $39.95.
Review Avg: 3.50   *OCLC:* 435   *Rating:* 4.37

◆ The article titles in this encyclopedia are indexed by keyword in Part II.

Reviews
3 ARBA, 92:1730
4 Choice, Nov 1990, p452

QE 5 _____ (LC)   DDC: 550
Encyclopedia of Earth Sciences
Dasch, E. Julius (ed). Macmillan, 1996. 2 vols. (1273p.) *Cloth:* $190.00.
Review Avg: 4.00   *OCLC:* 904   *Rating:* 5.81

Reviews
4 Choice, Jan 1997, p768
4 RBB, Nov 1 1996, p538

QE 5 _____ (LC)   DDC: 550
Encyclopedia of Earth System Science
Nierenberg, William A. Academic, 1992. 4 vols. *Cloth:* $950.00/set.
Review Avg: 3.80   *OCLC:* 435   *Rating:* 6.67

Reviews
3 ARBA, 93:1721
4 Choice, Jul/Aug 1992, p1654
4 GSED, 1997, p997
4 LJ, Feb 15 1992, p156
4 RBB, Mar 15 1992, p1400-1401

Awards
RBB/ORS, May 1 1997, p1524

QE 5 _____ (LC)   DDC: 550
Macmillan Encyclopedia of Earth Sciences
Dasch, E. Julius (ed). Macmillan, 1996. 2 vols. (1273p.) *Cloth:* $200.00/set.
Review Avg: 3.75   *OCLC:* 296   *Rating:* 4.34

Reviews
4 ARBA, 97:1391
4 LJ, Oct 15 1996, p52
4 RBB, Nov 1 1996, p538
3 RQ, Spr 1997, p456-457

◆**QE 28** _____ (LC)   DDC: 550
Magill's Survey of Science: Earth Science Series
Magill, Frank N. (ed). Salem, 1990. 5 vols. (2804p.) *Cloth:* $425.00/set.
Review Avg: 3.60   *OCLC:* 899   *Rating:* 7.40

Reviews
3 ARBA, 91:1778
4 Choice, Oct 1990, p286
4 LJ, Sep 15 1990, p74
4 RBB, Sep 1 1990, p87
3 RQ, Win 1990, p296

Awards
Choice/OAB, May 1991, p1430

QE 355 _____ (LC)   DDC: 549
Encyclopedia of Minerals
Roberts, Willard L. and others. Van Nostrand Reinhold, 1990. 2nd ed. 979p. *Cloth:* $99.95.
Note: Also published by Chapman & Hall, 1995.
Review Avg: 4.33   *OCLC:* 695   *Rating:* 7.72

Reviews
5 ARBA, 91:1790
3 Choice, Jun 1990, p1662
5 GSED, 1997, p1012

QE 392 _____ (LC)   DDC: 553.8
The Encyclopedia of Gemstones and Minerals
Holden, Martin. Facts On File, 1991. 303p. *Cloth:* $45.00.
Review Avg: 3.50   *OCLC:* 747   *Rating:* 4.99

Reviews
3 Choice, Sep 1992, p72
4 GSED, 1997, p1009
4 LJ, Feb 15 1992, p160
3 RBB, Mar 15 1992, p1402

QE 521 _____ (LC)   DDC: 551.2
The Encyclopedia of Earthquakes and Volcanoes
Ritchie, David. Facts On File, 1994. 232p. *Cloth:* $40.00.
Review Avg: 4.00   *OCLC:* 1156   *Rating:* 8.31

Reviews
4 ARBA, 95:496
5 Choice, Jul/Aug 1994, p1753
3 GSED, 1997, p182
3 RBB, Apr 15 1994, p1551-1552
5 WLB/R, Jun 1994, p97

Awards
NYPL, 1994

QE 862 _____ (LC)   DDC: 567.9
The Dinosaur Society's Dinosaur Encyclopedia
Lessem, Don and Donald F. Glut. Random House, 1993. 533p. *Cloth:* $25.00.
Review Avg: 3.75   *OCLC:* 587   *Rating:* 4.92

Reviews
3 ARBA, 95:1734
3 GSED, 1997, p1013
4 RBB, Apr 15 1994, p1551
5 WLB/R, Apr 1994, p88-89

QE 862 _____ (LC)   DDC: 567.9
Dinosaurs, The Encyclopedia
Glut, Donald F. McFarland, 1996. 1076p. *Cloth:* $145.00.
Review Avg: 4.33   *OCLC:* 154   *Rating:* 4.64

Reviews
4 ARBA, 98:1618
5 LJ, Nov 1 1997, p68
4 RBB, Nov 1 1997, p508

Awards
RBB/ORS, May 1 1998, p1538

QE 862 _____ (LC)   DDC: 567.9
Encyclopedia of Dinosaurs
Currie, Philip J. and Kevin Padian. Academic, 1997. 869p. *Cloth:* $9.95.
Review Avg: 4.00   *OCLC:* 374   *Rating:* 4.75

Reviews
4 LJ, Nov 1 1997, p68
4 RBB, Nov 1 1997, p508

Awards
LJ/BRS, Apr 15 1998, p47

QH 75 _____ (LC)   DDC: 574.5
Encyclopedia of Endangered Species
Emanoil, Mary (ed). Gale Research, 1994. 1230p. *Cloth:* $95.00.
Review Avg: 3.29   *OCLC:* 355   *Rating:* 6.00

Reviews
3 ARBA, 95:1564
4 Choice, Mar 1995, p1080

Awards
Choice/OAB, Jan 1996, p724

3 GSED, 1997, p861
3 LJ, Jan 1995, p84
3 RBB, Feb 1 1995, p1026
3 RQ, Sum 1995, p516
4 WLB/R, Jan 1995, p78

QH 302.5 _____(LC)   DDC: 574
Concise Encyclopedia Biology
Scott, Thomas A. Gruyter, 1996. 1287p. *Cloth:* $99.95.
Review Avg: 4.20   *OCLC:* 699   *Rating:* 5.60

Reviews
5 ARBA, 97:1266
4 Choice, Oct 1996, p249
4 GSED, 1997, p837
4 LJ, May 15 1996, p53
4 RBB, Oct 1 1996, p1921-1922

◆QH 302.5 _____(LC)   DDC: 574
Encyclopedia of Life Sciences
O'Daly, Anne. Cavendish, 1996. 9 vols. *Cloth:* $459.95/set.
Review Avg: 4.00   *OCLC:* 193   *Rating:* 4.39

Reviews
4 ARBA, 97:1268
4 GSED, 1997, p840
4 RBB, Jul 1996, p1843

QH 302.5 _____(LC)   DDC: 574
The HarperCollins Dictionary of Biology
Hale, W. G. and J. P. Margham. Harper Perennial, 1991. 569p. *Cloth:* $25.00. *Paper:* $12.95.
Review Avg: 3.00   *OCLC:* 395   *Rating:* 3.79

Reviews
3 ARBA, 92:1518
3 RBB, May 15 1991, p1833-1834

QH 307.2 _____(LC)   DDC: 574
Magill's Survey of Science: Life Science Series
Magill, Frank N. (ed). Salem, 1991. 6 vols. (2763p.) *Cloth:* $475.00/set.
Review Avg: 3.75   *OCLC:* 811   *Rating:* 5.37

Reviews
3 ARBA, 92:1522
4 Choice, Jun 1991, p1619
4 LJ, May 15 1991, p77-78
4 WLB/R, Apr 1991, p119

◆QH 332 _____(LC)   DDC: 174.2
Encyclopedia of Bioethics
Reich, Warren T. Macmillan, 1995. 2nd ed. 5 vols. *Cloth:* $475.00/set.
Note: Available on CD-ROM, 1995, $450.00 (Single-user), $550.00 (Network).
Review Avg: 4.88   *OCLC:* 1975   *Rating:* 18.83

Reviews
5 ARBA, 96:1429
4 ARBA, 98:1333, Review of CD-ROM

Awards
Choice/OAB, Jan 1996, p724
Dartmouth, 1996

5 Choice, Oct 1995, p262
5 Choice, Apr 1995, p1320, Review of CD-ROM
5 GSED, 1997, p916
5 LJ, Jul 1995, p70
5 RBB, Aug 1995, p1967
5 RBB, Oct 15 1996, p447, Review of CD-ROM
LJ/BRS, Apr 15 1996, p40
RBB/ORS, May 1 1996, p1536

QH 506 _____(LC)   DDC: 574.8
Encyclopedia of Molecular Biology and Molecular Medicine
Meyers, Robert A. (ed). VCH, 1996. 6 vols. *Cloth:* $1650.00.
Note: Available on laser optical disk.
Review Avg: 4.00   *OCLC:* 475   *Rating:* 4.95

Reviews
3 ARBA, 97:1269
5 ARBA, 97:1271
4 Choice, Jan 1997, p768

QH 540 _____(LC)   DDC: 628
McGraw-Hill Encyclopedia of Environmental Sciences
Parker, Sybil P. and Robert A. Corbitt (eds). McGraw-Hill, 1993. 3rd ed. 749p. *Cloth:* $85.50.
Review Avg: 3.00   *OCLC:* 489   *Rating:* 5.98

Reviews
3 GSED, 1997, p1040

QH 540.4 _____(LC)   DDC: 574.5
The Concise Oxford Dictionary of Ecology
Allaby, Michael (ed). Oxford Un, 1994. 415p. *Cloth:* $13.95.
Review Avg: 3.50   *OCLC:* 602   *Rating:* 4.70

Reviews
3 ARBA, 96:1854
4 Choice, Jan 1995, p744

QH 540.4 _____(LC)   DDC: 574.5
Encyclopedia of Environmental Biology
Nierenberg, William A. (ed). Academic, 1995. 3 vols. (2168p.) *Cloth:* $475.00/set.
Review Avg: 4.00   *OCLC:* 604   *Rating:* 7.21

Reviews
4 ARBA, 96:1856
4 Choice, Jan 1996, p756

Awards
Choice/OAB, Jan 1997, p740

QL 7 _____(LC)   DDC: 591
The Illustrated Encyclopedia of Wildlife
Pearl, Mary Corliss. En Britannica, 1990. 15 vols. (3053p.) *Cloth:* $429.00/set.
Review Avg: 3.50   *OCLC:* 350   *Rating:* 4.20

Reviews
4 ARBA, 92:1559
4 GSED, 1997, p865
3 RBB, Aug 1991, p2172
3 RBB, Jun 15 1992, p1869-1870

QL 7 _____(LC)   DDC: 591
The International Wildlife Encyclopedia
Burton, Maurice and Robert Burton (eds). Cavendish, 1990. Revised edition. 25 vols. (2899p.) *Cloth:* $499.95/set.

◆ The article titles in this encyclopedia are indexed by keyword in Part II.

Note: Also called *Marshall Cavendish International Wildlife Encyclopedia.*
Review Avg: 3.75   *OCLC:* 426   *Rating:* 6.60

Reviews
5 ARBA, 91:1555, Rev. ed.
3 ARBA, 90:1515
4 RBB, Oct 15 1990, p472,474
3 RBB, Jun 15 1992, p1870, Rev. ed.

QL 9 _____ (LC)   **DDC: 591**
Concise Oxford Dictionary of Zoology
Allaby, Michael (ed). Oxford Un, 1991. 508p. *Cloth:* $39.95.
Review Avg: 3.33   *OCLC:* 391   *Rating:* 4.11

Reviews
3 ARBA, 93:1529
4 Choice, Jun 1992, p1516
3 GSED, 1997, p856

QL 49 _____ (LC)   **DDC: 591**
Wildlife of the World
Cavendish, 1994. 13 vols. *Cloth:* $299.95/set.
Review Avg: 4.00   *OCLC:* 364   *Rating:* 4.73

Reviews
5 ARBA, 95:1561
3 RBB, May 15 1994, p1717
4 WLB/R, Jun 1994, p100

QL 82 _____ (LC)   **DDC: 591.52**
The Grolier World Encyclopedia of Endangered Species
Grolier, 1993. 10 vols. *Cloth:* $319.00/set.
Review Avg: 4.00   *OCLC:* 348   *Rating:* 4.70

Reviews
3 ARBA, 94:1680
4 GSED, 1997, p863
5 RBB, Sep 1 1993, p86-87

QL 83 _____ (LC)   **DDC: 591.52**
Endangered Wildlife of the World
Cavendish, 1993. 11 vols. *Cloth:* $399.95/set.
Review Avg: 3.50   *OCLC:* 604   *Rating:* 4.71

Reviews
3 ARBA, 94:1676
4 LJ, May 1 1993, p80
3 RBB, May 1 1993, p1624-1626
4 WLB/R, Nov 1993, p101-102

QL 83 _____ (LC)   **DDC: 591.52**
The Grolier Student Encyclopedia of Endangered Species
Grolier, 1995. 10 vols. *Cloth:* $199.00/set.
Review Avg: 3.00   *OCLC:* 293   *Rating:* 3.59

Reviews
3 ARBA, 96:1597

QL 100 _____ (LC)   **DDC: 591.6**
Dangerous Aquatic Animals of the World
Halstead, Bruce W. Darwin, 1992. 264p. *Cloth:* $60.00.
Review Avg: 3.50   *OCLC:* 369   *Rating:* 4.24

Reviews
3 ARBA, 94:1746
4 LJ, Dec 1992, p124,126

QL 364.2 _____ (LC)   **DDC: 595**
The Encyclopedia of Land Invertebrate Behaviour
Preston-Mafham, Rod and Ken Preston-Mafham. MIT, 1993. 320p.
Cloth: $47.50.
Review Avg: 4.00   *OCLC:* 542   *Rating:* 5.08

Reviews
3 ARBA, 95:1592
5 Choice, Feb 1994, p957
4 GSED, 1997, p870

QL 404 _____ (LC)   **DDC: 594**
The Encyclopedia of Shells
Wye, Kenneth R. (ed). Facts On File, 1991. 288p. *Cloth:* $45.00.
Review Avg: 3.25   *OCLC:* 410   *Rating:* 4.07

Reviews
5 ARBA, 95:1211
3 Choice, Jun 1992, p1531
2 LJ, Dec 1991, p136
3 RBB, Jan 15 1992, p972

QL 541.5 _____ (LC)   **DDC: 595.78**
The Encyclopedia of Butterflies
Feltwell, John. Prentice-Hall, 1993. 288p. *Cloth:* $40.00.
Review Avg: 3.67   *OCLC:* 620   *Rating:* 4.91

Reviews
3 Choice, Apr 1994, p1270
3 RBB, Apr 15 1994, p1551
5 WLB/R, Mar 1994, p91

QL 666 _____ (LC)   **DDC: 597.96**
The Encyclopedia of Snakes
Mattison, Chris. Facts On File, 1995. 256p. *Cloth:* $35.00.
Review Avg: 4.00   *OCLC:* 843   *Rating:* 5.69

Reviews
4 ARBA, 96:1637
4 Choice, Mar 1996, p1100
4 RBB, Aug 1995, p1919

QL 672.2 _____ (LC)   **DDC: 598**
The Illustrated Encyclopedia of Birds: The Definitive Reference to Birds of the World
Perrins, Christopher M. Prentice-Hall, 1991. 420p. *Cloth:* $50.00.
Review Avg: 3.60   *OCLC:* 558   *Rating:* 4.72

Reviews
4 Choice, Jul/Aug 1992, p1657
4 GSED, 1997, p869
3 LJ, Dec 1991, p134
4 RBB, Feb 1 1992, p1057
3 RBB, Jun 15 1992, p1872

QL 681 _____ (LC)   **DDC: 598**
Birds of North America: Life Histories for the 21st Century
Poole, Peter Stettenheim and Frank B. Gill. AOU, 1994. 18 vols.
Cloth: $195.00/vol.
Review Avg: 5.00   *OCLC:* 80   *Rating:* 7.16

Reviews	Awards
5 ARBA, 95:1565	Choice/OAB, Jan 1994,
5 Choice, Oct 1993, p262	p712
5 LJ, Jun 1 1994, p94	

QL 701 _____ (LC)   DDC: 599
Grzimek's Encyclopedia of Mammals
Grzimek, Bernhard (ed). McGraw-Hill, 1990. 2nd ed. 5 vols. *Cloth:* $500.00/set.
Note: Available on CD-ROM, The Multimedia Encyclopedia of Mammalian Biology.
Review Avg: 4.33   *OCLC:* 1613   *Rating:* 11.56

Reviews	Awards
5 ARBA, 91:1593	Choice/OAB, May 1991,
5 CRL, Sep 1990, p442	p1429
4 Choice, Jun 1990, p1654	
5 GSED, 1997, p864	
3 RBB, Jun 15 1992, p1872	
4 WLB/R, Mar 1990, p128	

QL 703 _____ (LC)   DDC: 599
Walker's Mammals of the World
Nowak, Ronald M. and John L. Paradiso (eds). Johns Hopkins Un, 1991. 5th ed. 2 vols. *Cloth:* $89.95/set.
Review Avg: 3.40   *OCLC:* 1208   *Rating:* 7.82

Reviews
3 ARBA, 93:1572
3 Choice, Apr 1992, p1211-1212
4 RBB, Mar 15 1992, p1404-1406
3 RBB, Jun 15 1992, p1872-1874
4 WLB/R, Mar 1992, p119-122

QL 706.2 _____ (LC)   DDC: 599
Encyclopedia of Mammals
MacDonald, David W. Cavendish, 1997. 17 vols. *Cloth:* $459.95.
Review Avg: 4.00   *OCLC:* 286   *Rating:* 4.57

Reviews
4 ARBA, 98:1469
4 LJ, May 15 1997, p70

QL 737 _____ (LC)   DDC: 599.73
The Whitehead Encyclopedia of Deer
Whitehead, G. Kenneth. Voyageur, 1993. 604p. *Cloth:* $140.00.
Review Avg: 3.50   *OCLC:* 77   *Rating:* 3.65

Reviews
3 ARBA, 94:1742
4 GSED, 1997, p874
3 LJ, Jun 1 1993, p110
4 RBB, Sep 1 1993, p91-92

◆QP 11 _____ (LC)   DDC: 612
Encyclopedia of Human Biology
Dulbecco, Renato (ed). Academic, 1997. 2nd ed. 8 vols. *Cloth:* $2299.00/set.
Review Avg: 5.00   *OCLC:* 831   *Rating:* 12.66

Reviews	Awards
5 ARBA, 92:1516	Choice/OAB, May 1992,
5 Choice, Oct 1991, p256	p1341

5 GSED, 1997, p839	LJ/BRS, Apr 15 1992,
5 LJ, Apr 15 1991, p82	p42
5 LJ, Dec 1997, p90, 2nd ed.	

QP 360 _____ (LC)   DDC: 612.8
The Blackwell Dictionary of Neuropsychology
Beaumont, J. Graham and others (eds). Blackwell, 1996. 788p. *Cloth:* $95.00.
Review Avg: 4.00   *OCLC:* 271   *Rating:* 4.54

Reviews
4 ARBA, 97:626

QP 376 _____ (LC)   DDC: 612.82
The Brain Encyclopedia
Turkington, Carol. Facts On File, 1996. 316p. *Cloth:* $40.00.
Review Avg: 3.00   *OCLC:* 449   *Rating:* 3.90

Reviews
4 ARBA, 97:1334
2 LJ, Jul 1996, p106
3 RBB, Sep 15 1996, p280

QP 771 _____ (LC)   DDC: 613.2
The Doctor's Vitamin and Mineral Encyclopedia
Hendler, Sheldon Saul. Simon & Schuster, 1990. 496p. *Cloth:* $24.95.
Review Avg: 4.00   *OCLC:* 953   *Rating:* 7.91

Reviews	Awards
4 ARBA, 91:1709	NYPL, 1991

QP 771 _____ (LC)   DDC: 612.3
The Encyclopedia of Vitamins, Minerals and Supplements
Navarra, Tova and Myron A. Lipkowitz. Facts On File, 1996. 288p. *Cloth:* $35.00. *Paper:* $17.95.
Review Avg: 3.00   *OCLC:* 617   *Rating:* 4.23

Reviews
3 ARBA, 97:1263
3 Choice, Sep 1996, p103-104
3 LJ, Jun 15 1996, p58
3 RBB, May 1 1996, p1524,1526

QR 9 _____ (LC)   DDC: 576
Encyclopedia of Microbiology
Lederberg, Joshua (ed). Academic, 1992. 4 vols. (2518p.) *Cloth:* $699.00/set.
Review Avg: 3.67   *OCLC:* 679   *Rating:* 7.03

Reviews	Awards
3 ARBA, 94:1636	Choice/OAB, Jan 1994,
4 Choice, Apr 1993, p1294	p712
4 GSED, 1997, p844	

QR 180.4 _____ (LC)   DDC: 616.07
Encyclopedia of Immunology
Roitt, Ivan M. Academic, 1992. 3 vols. (1578p.) *Cloth:* $499.00/set.
Review Avg: 4.00   *OCLC:* 461   *Rating:* 4.92

Reviews
4 Choice, Dec 1992, p600-601
4 GSED, 1997, p923

◆ The article titles in this encyclopedia are indexed by keyword in Part II.

QR 358 _____(LC)   DDC: 576.64
Encyclopedia of Virology
Webster, Robert G. and Allan Granoff (eds). Academic, 1994. 3 vols.
(2128p.) *Cloth:* $499.00/set.
Note: Available on CD-ROM, Encyclopedia of Virology Plus, 1996,
$475.00.
Review Avg: 4.20   *OCLC:* 375   *Rating:* 4.95

Reviews
5 ARBA, 95:1680
4 ARBA, 98:1442, Review of CD-ROM
3 Choice, Jul/Aug 1994, p1702
5 GSED, 1997, p949
4 LJ, Jun 15 1994, p58

R 125 _____(LC)   DDC: 610
The World Book-Rush-Presbyterian-St. Luke's Medical Center Medical Encyclopedia: Your Guide to Good Health
World Book, 1995. 7th ed. 1072p. *Cloth:* $39.95.
Review Avg: 2.50   *OCLC:* 161   *Rating:* 4.82

Reviews
3 ARBA, 92:1664
2 ARBA, 97:1335, 7th ed.
3 LJ, Apr 1 1991, p118
2 RBB, May 1 1991, p1749

R 130.5 _____(LC)   DDC: 616
Diseases
Bunch, Bryan (ed). Grolier, 1997. 8 vols. *Cloth:* $269.00.
Review Avg: 4.00   *OCLC:* 328   *Rating:* 4.66

Reviews
4 ARBA, 98:1557
4 RBB, Apr 15 1997, p1448,1450

R 133 _____(LC)   DDC: 610
Companion Encyclopedia of the History of Medicine
Bynum, William F. and Roy Porter. Routledge, 1993. 2 vols. *Cloth:* $199.95/set.
Review Avg: 5.00   *OCLC:* 655   *Rating:* 6.31

Reviews
5 ARBA, 95:1654
5 GSED, 1997, p921,1021
5 LJ, Oct 15 1993, p58

R 733 _____(LC)   DDC: 615.5
The Alternative Advisor: The Complete Guide to Natural Therapies and Alternative Treatments
Editors of Time-Life Books. Time-Life, 1997. 400p. *Cloth:* $24.95.
Review Avg: 4.00   *OCLC:* 427   *Rating:* 4.85

Reviews
4 LJ, Aug 1997, p74

R 733 _____(LC)   DDC: 615.5
Alternative Healing: The Complete A-Z Guide to More than 150 Alternative Therapies
Kastner, Mark and Hugh Burroughs. Holt, 1996. 358p. *Cloth:* $16.95.
Review Avg: 3.60   *OCLC:* 74   *Rating:* 3.75

Reviews
3 ARBA, 95:1671

3 Choice, Oct 1995, p270
5 GSED, 1997, p936
4 LJ, Oct 15 1993, p60
3 RBB, Nov 15 1993, p644

R 733 _____(LC)   DDC: 615.5
The Alternative Health and Medicine Encyclopedia
Marti, James. Gale Research, 1995. 376p. *Cloth:* $49.95. *Paper:* $15.95.
Review Avg: 3.00   *OCLC:* 614   *Rating:* 4.23

Reviews
3 ARBA, 96:1716
3 Choice, Oct 1995, p270
3 LJ, Mar 1 1995, p64
3 RBB, Apr 15 1995, p1517

R 733 _____(LC)   DDC: 615.5
Alternative Health Care: The Encyclopedia of Choices in Healing
Olsen, Kristin Gottschalk. Pocket, 1994. Revised edition. 325p. *Paper:* $8.95.
Note: Originally entitled *The Encyclopedia of Alternative Health Care.*
Review Avg: 3.33   *OCLC:* 559   *Rating:* 6.45

Reviews
3 ARBA, 91:1662
4 LJ, Jan 1990, p102
3 RBB, Mar 15 1990, p1498

R 733 _____(LC)   DDC: 615.5
A Dictionary of Mind and Body: Therapies, Techniques and Ideas in Alternative Medicine, the Healing Arts and Psychology
Watson, Donald. Trafalgar Square, 1996. 423p. *Paper:* $16.95.
Review Avg: 4.00   *OCLC:* 202   *Rating:* 4.40

Reviews
4 Choice, Jan 1997, p776

R 733 _____(LC)   DDC: 615.5
The Encyclopedia of Alternative Medicine: A Complete Family Guide to Complementary Therapies
Jacobs, Jennifer. Journey Editions, 1996. 320p. *Paper:* $24.95.
Review Avg: 4.00   *OCLC:* 200   *Rating:* 4.40

Reviews
4 ARBA, 97:1345

R 733 _____(LC)   DDC: 610
Health and Illness: A Cross-Cultural Encyclopedia
Levinson, David and Laura Gaccione. ABC-CLIO, 1997. 253p. *Cloth:* $49.50.
Review Avg: 3.00   *OCLC:* 209   *Rating:* 3.42

Reviews
3 LJ, Oct 1 1997, p70,72

R 857 _____(LC)   DDC: 610
Concise Encyclopedia of Medical and Dental Materials
Williams, David (ed). Elsevier, 1990. 412p. *Cloth:* $210.00.
Note: From *Encyclopedia of Materials Science and Engineering.*

Review Avg: 3.00   *OCLC:* 164   *Rating:* 3.33

Reviews
3 ARBA, 92:1662
3 Choice, Sep 1991, p54

RA 395_____(LC)   **DDC: 362.1**
Encyclopedia of U.S. Biomedical Policy
Blank, Robert H. and Janna C. Merrick (eds). Greenwood, 1996. 363p.
Cloth: $89.50.
Review Avg: 3.50   *OCLC:* 354   *Rating:* 4.21

Reviews
3 ARBA, 97:1330
4 Choice, Jan 1997, p766

RA 418_____(LC)   **DDC: 306.4**
Dictionary of Medical Sociology
Cockerham, William C. Greenwood, 1997. 169p. *Cloth:* $69.50.
Review Avg: 2.00   *OCLC:* 205   *Rating:* 2.41

Reviews
2 ARBA, 98:1524

RA 649_____(LC)   **DDC: 614.4**
The Encyclopedia of Plague and Pestilence
Kohn, George C. (ed). Facts On File, 1995. 408p. *Cloth:* $40.00.
Review Avg: 3.00   *OCLC:* 833   *Rating:* 6.67

Reviews   **Awards**
2 ARBA, 96:1725   NYPL, 1995
4 RBB, Aug 1995, p1970

◆**RA 776**_____(LC)   **DDC: 613.2**
Macmillan Health Encyclopedia
Bohlander, Richard and others (eds). Macmillan, 1993. 9 vols. *Cloth:*
$360.00/set.
Review Avg: 4.00   *OCLC:* 482   *Rating:* 4.96

Reviews
3 ARBA, 94:1803
5 GSED, 1997, p913
4 RBB, Sep 15 1993, p188-189

RA 776_____(LC)   **DDC: 613.2**
*Wellness Encyclopedia: The Comprehensive Resource to
Safeguarding Health and Preventing Illness*
Houghton, 1991. 512p. *Cloth:* $29.45.
Review Avg: 3.75   *OCLC:* 1497   *Rating:* 6.74

Reviews
3 ARBA, 92:1642
4 GSED, 1997, p919
4 LJ, Feb 15 1991, p188
4 LJ, Feb 1 1993, p74

RA 776.9_____(LC)   **DDC: 613.2**
The Encyclopedia of Health
Sheehan, Angela (ed). Cavendish, 1994. Revised edition. 14 vols.
Cloth: $299.95/set.
Review Avg: 3.50   *OCLC:* 200   *Rating:* 5.90

Reviews
4 ARBA, 92:1633
3 RBB, May 1 1991, p1742

◆**RA 778**_____(LC)   **DDC: 616**
The Harvard Guide to Women's Health
Carlson, Karen J. and others. Harvard Un, 1996. 718p. *Cloth:* $39.95.
Paper: $24.95.
Note: Available on CD-ROM, $29.95; with paperback, $39.95.
Review Avg: 4.00   *OCLC:* 1554   *Rating:* 9.11

Reviews   **Awards**
4 LJ, Apr 15 1996, p72   NYPL, 1996
4 LJ, Apr 1 1997, p136,
  Review of CD-ROM
4 RBB, Jun 1 1996,
  p1772-1773

RA 778_____(LC)   **DDC: 613.0424**
The New A to Z of Women's Health: A Concise Encyclopedia
Ammer, Christine. Facts On File, 1995. 3rd ed. 562p. *Cloth:* $40.00.
Review Avg: 3.60   *OCLC:* 19   *Rating:* 5.64

Reviews
3 ARBA, 90:1675
3 ARBA, 96:1680, 3rd ed.
4 Choice, Apr 1996, p1344
4 RBB, Jan 15 1990, p1044-1045
4 RBB, Jan 1 1996, p886, 3rd ed.

RA 778_____(LC)   **DDC: 613.0424**
Planned Parenthood Women's Health Encyclopedia
Planned Parenthood Federation of America. Crown, 1996. 448p.
Paper: $22.00.
Review Avg: 2.50   *OCLC:* 378   *Rating:* 3.26

Reviews
2 LJ, Sep 15 1996, p58
3 RBB, Nov 1 1996, p532,534

◆**RA 778**_____(LC)   **DDC: 616**
Women's Encyclopedia of Health and Emotional Healing
Foley, Denise, Eileen Nechas and the editors of Prevention Magazine.
Rodale, 1993. 517p. *Cloth:* $27.95.
Review Avg: 3.50   *OCLC:* 20   *Rating:* 3.54

Reviews
5 ARBA, 94:1805
2 LJ, Feb 1 1993, p70,72

RA 784_____(LC)   **DDC: 613.2**
Encyclopedia of Nutrition and Good Health
Ronzio, Robert A. Facts On File, 1997. 486p. *Cloth:* $45.00. *Paper:*
$19.95.
Review Avg: 3.50   *OCLC:* 418   *Rating:* 4.34

Reviews
4 ARBA, 98:1521
3 RBB, Jun 1 1997, p1756,1758

RA 784_____(LC)   **DDC: 613.2**
*Foods That Harm, Foods That Heal: An A-Z Guide to Safe
and Healthy Eating*
Reader's Digest (eds.). Reader's Digest, 1997. 400p. *Cloth:* $30.00.
Review Avg: 4.00   *OCLC:* 10   *Rating:* 4.02

Reviews
4 LJ, Feb 1 1997, p72

◆ The article titles in this encyclopedia are indexed by keyword in Part II.

RA 788   (LC)   DDC: 613.9

The Practical Encyclopedia of Sex and Health: From Aphrodisiacs and Hormones to Potency, Stress and Yeast Infection
Bechtel, Stefan and the editors of Prevention and Men's Health magazines. Rodale, 1993. 352p. *Cloth:* $26.95.
Note: Also called *Sex Encyclopedia,* Simon & Schuster, $14.00/paper.
Review Avg: 2.75   *OCLC:* 32   *Rating:* 2.81

Reviews
3 ARBA, 95:1647
3 GSED, 1997, p930
2 RBB, Sep 1 1993, p90
3 WLB/R, Oct 1993, p96

RA 1213   (LC)   DDC: 615.9

Toxics A to Z: A Guide to Everyday Pollution Hazards
Harte, John and others. Un of California, 1991. 479p. *Cloth:* $75.00.
Paper: $20.00.
Review Avg: 3.50   *OCLC:* 1818   *Rating:* 11.14

Reviews	**Awards**
3 ARBA, 93:1769	LJ/BRS, Apr 15 1992,
3 Choice, Mar 1992, p1058	p44
4 LJ, Nov 1 1991, p88,90	NYPL, 1993
4 RBB, Dec 1 1991, p720	

RA 1224.5   (LC)   DDC: 615.9

Poisons and Antidotes
Turkington, Carol. Facts On File, 1994. 372p. *Cloth:* $27.95. *Paper:* $12.95.
Review Avg: 3.40   *OCLC:* 825   *Rating:* 5.05

Reviews
3 ARBA, 95:1686
4 Choice, Jun 1994, p1564
3 LJ, Feb 1 1994, p72
3 RBB, Feb 1 1994, p1027-1028
4 RQ, Sum 1994, p563-564

RB 155.5   (LC)   DDC: 616

The Encyclopedia of Genetic Disorders and Birth Defects
Wynbrandt, James and Mark D. Ludman. Facts On File, 1991. 426p.
Cloth: $50.00.
Review Avg: 3.33   *OCLC:* 1089   *Rating:* 5.51

Reviews
3 ARBA, 92:1681
3 Choice, Jul/Aug 1991, p1768
4 RBB, May 1 1991, p1732-1734

RC 41   (LC)   DDC: 610

Magill's Medical Guide: Health and Illness
Editors of Salem Press. Salem, 1995. 3 vols. + 3 vols. suppl. *Cloth:* $270.00/set.
Review Avg: 3.50   *OCLC:* 1020   *Rating:* 5.54

Reviews
3 ARBA, 96:1700
3 Choice, Oct 1995, p268-269
4 LJ, Jul 1995, p72,74
4 RBB, Oct 1 1995, p351

RC 41   (LC)   DDC: 610

The Oxford Medical Companion
Walton, John and others. Oxford Un, 1994. 1038p. *Cloth:* $50.00.
Note: Originally entitled *Oxford Companion to Medicine.*
Review Avg: 3.00   *OCLC:* 1095   *Rating:* 5.19

Reviews
3 Choice, May 1995, p1432-1433
4 LJ, Jan 1995, p90
2 RBB, Feb 1 1995, p1028-1029

RC 71   (LC)   DDC: 610.28

Concise Encyclopedia of Biological and Biomedical Measurement Systems
Payne, Peter A. (ed). Pergamon, 1991. 490p. *Cloth:* $280.00.
Review Avg: 3.00   *OCLC:* 77   *Rating:* 3.15

Reviews
3 ARBA, 93:1635

RC 81   (LC)   DDC: 616

The American Medical Association Family Medical Guide
Clayman, Charles B. Random House, 1994. 3rd ed. 880p. *Cloth:* $35.00.
Note: Available on CD-ROM, 1995, $49.95.
Review Avg: 4.00   *OCLC:* 1399   *Rating:* 8.80

Reviews
4 ARBA, 96:1707
4 RBB, Mar 15 1996, p1307-1308

RC 81   (LC)   DDC: 613

Columbia University College of Physicians and Surgeons Complete Home Medical Guide
Kass, Frederic and others (eds). Crown, 1995. 3rd Revised edition. 476p. *Cloth:* $39.95.
Review Avg: 4.00   *OCLC:* 551   *Rating:* 7.10

Reviews
4 WLB/R, Mar 1993, p107-108
4 WLB/R, 1995

RC 81   (LC)   DDC: 616.02

Home Encyclopedia of Symptoms, Ailments and Their Natural Remedies
Smythe, Angela and others. Harper/ San Francisco, 1994. 2nd ed. 446p. *Cloth:* $24.95. *Paper:* $9.95.
Review Avg: 3.00   *OCLC:* 106   *Rating:* 5.21

Reviews
3 ARBA, 93:1640

RC 81   (LC)   DDC: 613

Mayo Clinic Family Health Book: The Ultimate Home Medical Reference
Larson, David E. and others (ed). Morrow, 1990. 2nd ed. 1378p. *Cloth:* $40.00.
Note: Available on CD-ROM, 1995, $59.95.
Review Avg: 4.67   *OCLC:* 2011   *Rating:* 12.69

Reviews	**Awards**
5 LJ, Dec 1990, p120	LJ/BRS, Apr 15 1991,
4 RBB, Mar 15 1996, p1307	p45
5 WLB/R, Jan 1991, p125	

RC 81 _____(LC)   **DDC: 610**
The New Complete Medical and Health Encyclopedia
Wagman, Richard J. Ferguson, 1994. 4 vols. (1363p.) *Cloth:* $79.95/
set.
Review Avg: 3.00   *OCLC:* 49   *Rating:* 3.10

Reviews
3 ARBA, 95:1646
3 GSED, 1997, p929

RC 81 _____(LC)   **DDC: 613**
Prevention's Giant Book of Health Facts: The Ultimate Reference for Personal Health
Feltrian, John (ed). Rodale, 1991. 599p. *Cloth:* $26.95.
Review Avg: 3.50   *OCLC:* 627   *Rating:* 4.75

Reviews
4 ARBA, 92:1639
3 LJ, Dec 1990, p122

RC 81 _____(LC)   **DDC: 610**
The Visual Encyclopedia of Natural Healing: A Step-by-Step Pictorial Guide to Solving 100 Everyday Health Problems
Feinstein, Alice (ed). Rodale, 1991. 423p. *Cloth:* $26.95.
Review Avg: 3.00   *OCLC:* 651   *Rating:* 4.30

Reviews
3 ARBA, 92:1661
3 LJ, Mar 15 1991, p86

RC 262 _____(LC)   **DDC: 616.994**
The Cancer Dictionary
Altman, Roberta and Michael Sarg. Facts On File, 1992. 334p. *Cloth:* $40.00. *Paper:* $16.95.
Review Avg: 3.50   *OCLC:* 1364   *Rating:* 10.23

Reviews   *Awards*
4 ARBA, 94:1858   NYPL, 1993
4 Choice, May 1993, p1435 RBB/ORS, May 1 1993,
4 GSED, 1997, p942   p1620
3 LJ, Oct 1 1992, p78
3 RBB, Dec 1 1992, p686
3 WLB/R, Mar 1993,
  p105-106

RC 262 _____(LC)   **DDC: 616.994**
Encyclopedia of Cancer
Bertino, Joseph R. (ed). Academic, 1996. 2134p. *Cloth:* $550.00.
Review Avg: 4.00   *OCLC:* 471   *Rating:* 6.94

Reviews   *Awards*
4 Choice, Jun 1997, p1638 LJ/BRS, Apr 15 1997,
4 RBB, Jan 1 1997, p892   p38

RC 437 _____(LC)   **DDC: 616.89**
The Encyclopedia of Mental Health
Kahn, Ada P. and Jan Fawcett. Facts On File, 1993. 464p. *Cloth:* $50.00.
Review Avg: 3.40   *OCLC:* 1227   *Rating:* 5.85

Reviews
3 ARBA, 95:780
3 Choice, Mar 1994, p1098
3 GSED, 1997, p399

4 LJ, Oct 1 1993, p89
4 RBB, Dec 1 1993, p712

RC 437 _____(LC)   **DDC: 616.89**
The Encyclopedia of Psychiatry, Psychology and Psychoanalysis
Wolman, Benjamin B. (ed). Holt, 1996. 649p. *Cloth:* $135.00.
Note: Based on *International Encyclopedia.*
Review Avg: 3.67   *OCLC:* 592   *Rating:* 4.85

Reviews   *Awards*
5 Choice, Jul 1997,   Choice/OAB, Jan 1998,
  p1778-1779   p759
2 LJ, Jun 15 1997, p60
4 RBB, Jun 1 1997, p1758

RC 475.7 _____(LC)   **DDC: 616.89**
A Dictionary for Psychotherapists: Dynamic Concepts in Psychotherapy
Chessick, Richard D. Aronson, 1993. 405p. *Cloth:* $50.00.
Review Avg: 3.33   *OCLC:* 174   *Rating:* 3.68

Reviews
3 ARBA, 95:776
3 Choice, Nov 1993, p424
4 GSED, 1997, p392

RC 488.5 _____(LC)   **DDC: 616.89**
The Dictionary of Family Psychology and Family Therapy
Sauber, S. Richard and others. Sage, 1993. 2nd ed. 468p. *Cloth:* $65.00. *Paper:* $29.95.
Review Avg: 3.33   *OCLC:* 567   *Rating:* 6.46

Reviews
3 ARBA, 94:810
4 Choice, Mar 1994, p1092
3 GSED, 1997, p404

RC 501.4 _____(LC)   **DDC: 616.89**
The Encyclopedia of Evolving Techniques in Psychodynamic Therapy
Solomon, Irving. Aronson, 1992. 402p. *Cloth:* $50.00.
Review Avg: 3.00   *OCLC:* 148   *Rating:* 3.30

Reviews
3 Choice, Jun 1993, p1610

RC 501.4 _____(LC)   **DDC: 616.89**
Psychoanalytic Terms and Concepts
Moore, Burness E. and Bernard D. Fine. APA, 1990. 210p. *Cloth:* $35.00.
Review Avg: 3.50   *OCLC:* 360   *Rating:* 4.22

Reviews
3 ARBA, 91:791
4 Choice, Jul/Aug 1990, p1810

RC 514 _____(LC)   **DDC: 616.89**
The Encyclopedia of Schizophrenia and the Psychotic Disorders
Noll, Richard. Facts On File, 1992. 374p. *Cloth:* $50.00.
Review Avg: 3.25   *OCLC:* 1003   *Rating:* 5.26

◆ The article titles in this encyclopedia are indexed by keyword in Part II.

Reviews
3 ARBA, 93:799
3 Choice, Oct 1992, p277-278
3 GSED, 1997, p402
4 RBB, Apr 1 1992, p1472

RC 522 _____(LC)   **DDC: 616.97**

Allergies A-Z
Lipkowitz, Myron A. and Tova Navarra. Facts On File, 1994. 352p.
Cloth: $40.00.
Review Avg: 3.43   *OCLC:* 894   *Rating:* 5.22

Reviews
3 ARBA, 95:1677
3 Choice, Dec 1994, p577
4 GSED, 1997, p941
3 LJ, Oct 1 1994, p71
4 RBB, Nov 15 1994, p621-622
3 RQ, Spr 1995, p385-386
4 WLB/R, Dec 1994, p70

RC 537 _____(LC)   **DDC: 616.85**

The Encyclopedia of Depression
Roesch, Roberta. Facts On File, 1991. 263p. *Cloth:* $45.00.
Review Avg: 2.50   *OCLC:* 629   *Rating:* 3.76

Reviews
2 ARBA, 92:1683
1 Choice, Sep 1991, p68
4 LJ, Apr 15 1991, p86,88
3 RBB, Jul 1991, p2066

RC 547 _____(LC)   **DDC: 616.8**

The Encyclopedia of Sleep and Sleep Disorders
Thorpy, Michael J. and Jan Yager. Facts On File, 1991. 298p. *Cloth:*
$50.00.
Review Avg: 3.00   *OCLC:* 747   *Rating:* 4.49

Reviews
3 Choice, Apr 1991, p1295
3 GSED, 1997, p391n
2 LJ, Aug 1990, p108
4 RBB, Jan 1 1991, p950-952

RC 552 _____(LC)   **DDC: 616.85**

The Encyclopedia of Obesity and Eating Disorders
Cassell, Dana K. Facts On File, 1994. 259p. *Cloth:* $45.00.
Review Avg: 3.25   *OCLC:* 895   *Rating:* 5.04

Reviews
3 ARBA, 95:1678
3 Choice, Sep 1994, p64
3 GSED, 1997, p944
4 RBB, May 15 1994, p1714

RC 570 _____(LC)   **DDC: 616.85**

Encyclopedia of Mental and Physical Handicaps
Tver, David F. and Betty M. Tver. Pro-Ed, 1991. 267p. *Cloth:* $39.00.
Review Avg: 3.00   *OCLC:* 185   *Rating:* 3.37

Reviews
3 ARBA, 92:322
3 GSED, 1997, p116

RC 584 _____(LC)   **DDC: 616.97**

Encyclopedia of Allergy and Environmental Illness: A Self-Help Approach
Rothera, Ellen. David & Charles, 1991. 224p.
Review Avg: 3.00   *OCLC:* 171   *Rating:* 3.34

Reviews
3 LJ, Dec 1991, p136

◆**RC 952.5** _____(LC)   **DDC: 612.6**

Encyclopedia of Gerontology: Age, Aging and the Aged
Birren, James E. (ed). Academic, 1996. 2 vols. (1474p.) *Cloth:*
$300.00/set.
Review Avg: 3.67   *OCLC:* 405   *Rating:* 6.48

Reviews   *Awards*
4 ARBA, 97:667   LJ/BRS, Apr 15 1997,
3 Choice, Mar 1997, p1136   p38
4 RBB, Dec 1 1996, p682

RC 963 _____(LC)   **DDC: 613.6**

Encyclopaedia of Occupational Health and Safety
Parmeggiani, Luigi. International Labour Office, 1997. 4th ed. 4 vols.
Cloth: $240.00/set.
Review Avg: 3.00   *OCLC:* 7   *Rating:* 5.01

Reviews
3 Choice, June 1992, p502, 3rd ed.

RE 91 _____(LC)   **DDC: 362.4**

The Encyclopedia of Blindness and Vision Impairment
Sardegna, Jill and T. Otis Paul. Facts On File, 1991. 329p. *Cloth:*
$50.00.
Review Avg: 3.80   *OCLC:* 932   *Rating:* 7.66

Reviews   *Awards*
3 ARBA, 92:1685   RBB/ORS, May 1 1992,
4 Choice, Sep 1991, p68,70   p1625
5 GSED, 1997, p950
4 LJ, Feb 1 1991, p74
3 RBB, May 15 1991, p1833

RF 290 _____(LC)   **DDC: 617.8**

Encyclopedia of Deafness and Hearing Disorders
Turkington, Carol and Allen Sussman. Facts On File, 1992. 278p.
Cloth: $45.00.
Review Avg: 3.50   *OCLC:* 868   *Rating:* 5.24

Reviews
3 ARBA, 93:1656
4 Choice, Sep 1992, p94
4 GSED, 1997, p945
3 LJ, Feb 15 1992, p162
4 RBB, Apr 1 1992, p1470-1472
3 WLB/R, May 1992, p123

RG 525 _____(LC)   **DDC: 618.2**

The A-to-Z of Pregnancy and Childbirth: A Concise Encyclopedia
Evans, Nancy. Hunter House, 1994. 336p. *Cloth:* $29.95. *Paper:*
$16.95.
Review Avg: 3.00   *OCLC:* 375   *Rating:* 3.75

Reviews
3 ARBA, 95:1645
3 LJ, Nov 1 1993, p72

◆**RG 525** _____(LC)   **DDC: 618.2**
Encyclopedia of Childbearing: Critical Perspectives
Rothman, Barbara Katz. Holt, 1993. 446p.
Note: Owl Book edition.
Review Avg: 4.20   *OCLC:* 735   *Rating:* 7.67

Reviews	*Awards*
5 ARBA, 94:1831	RBB/ORS, May 1 1994,
5 Choice, Apr 1993,	p1627
p1293-1294	
5 GSED, 1997, p931	
3 RBB, Jun 1993, p1896	
3 RQ, Sum 1993, p566-567	

RJ 61 _____(LC)   **DDC: 618.92**
The Disney Encyclopedia of Baby and Child Care
Palfrey, Judith and others (eds). Hyperion, 1995. 2 vols. /set. *Paper:* $29.95.
Review Avg: 3.00   *OCLC:* 366   *Rating:* 3.73

Reviews
3 LJ, Mar 1 1995, p99
3 RBB, Mar 1 1995, p1168

RJ 61 _____(LC)   **DDC: 618.92**
The Practical Pediatrician: The A to Z Guide to Your Child's Health, Behavior and Safety
Markel, Howard and Frank A. Oski. Freeman, 1996. 364p. *Paper:* $16.95.
Review Avg: 4.00   *OCLC:* 473   *Rating:* 4.95

Reviews
4 ARBA, 97:1354
4 LJ, Nov 1 1996, p62
4 RBB, Sep 1 1996, p170

RJ 206 _____(LC)   **DDC: 613.2**
The Yale Guide to Children's Nutrition
Tamborlane, William V. Yale Un, 1997. 415p. *Paper:* $40.00.
Review Avg: 5.00   *OCLC:* 665   *Rating:* 6.33

Reviews
5 LJ, Feb 15 1997, p129

RL 41 _____(LC)   **DDC: 616.5**
Skin Deep: An A-Z of Skin Disorders, Treatments, and Health
Turkington, Carol and Jeffrey S. Dover. Facts On File, 1996. 404p. *Cloth:* $40.00.
Review Avg: 4.00   *OCLC:* 815   *Rating:* 5.63

Reviews
4 ARBA, 97:1333

RM 36 _____(LC)   **DDC: 615.5**
The Prevention How-to Dictionary of Healing Remedies and Techniques: From Acupressure and Aspirin to Yoga and Yogurt
Feltman, John (ed). Rodale, 1992. 499p. *Cloth:* $26.95.

Review Avg: 3.33   *OCLC:* 507   *Rating:* 4.34
Reviews
3 ARBA, 93:136
3 GSED, 1997, p938
4 LJ, Jul 1992, p78

RM 267 _____(LC)   **DDC: 615**
Encyclopedia of Antibiotics
Glasby, John S. Wiley, 1993. 3rd ed. 515p. *Cloth:* $259.95.
Review Avg: 4.00   *OCLC:* 129   *Rating:* 6.26
Reviews
4 ARBA, 94:1871
4 GSED, 1997, p953

RM 666 _____(LC)   **DDC: 615**
The Illustrated Encyclopedia of Essential Oils: The Complete Guide to the Use of Oils in Aromatherapy and Herbalism
Lawless, Julia. Element, 1995. 256p. *Paper:* $18.95.
Review Avg: 4.00   *OCLC:* 99   *Rating:* 4.20

Reviews
4 ARBA, 97:1346

RS 164 _____(LC)   **DDC: 615**
Encyclopedia of Medicinal Plants
Chevallier, Andrew. Dorling, 1996. 336p. *Cloth:* $39.95.
Review Avg: 4.00   *OCLC:* 1246   *Rating:* 10.49

Reviews	*Awards*
4 ARBA, 97:1343	LJ/BRS, Apr 15 1997,
4 Choice, Mar 1997, p1134	p37
4 LJ, Dec 1996, p82	RBB/ORS, May 1 1997,
4 RBB, Dec 1 1996, p629	p1524

RS 192 _____(LC)   **DDC: 615**
Encyclopedia of Pharmaceutical Technology
Swarbick, James and James C. Boyan (eds). Dekker, 1996. 14 vols. *Cloth:* $175.00.
Review Avg: 3.67   *OCLC:* 121   *Rating:* 3.91

Reviews
4 ARBA, 94:1870, vol. 7
3 ARBA, 91:1710, vol. 2
4 GSED, 1987, p957

RT 51 _____(LC)   **DDC: 610.73**
Nurse's Quick Reference: An A-to-Z Guide to 1,001 Professional Problems
Springhouse, 1990. 373p. *Cloth:* $29.95.
Review Avg: 3.00   *OCLC:* 347   *Rating:* 3.69

Reviews
3 ARBA, 91:1704

RX 76 _____(LC)   **DDC: 615.5**
An Encyclopedia of Homeopathy
Smith, Trevor. Atrium, 1994. 2nd ed. 317p. *Paper:* $19.95.
Review Avg: 3.00   *OCLC:* 38   *Rating:* 5.08

Reviews
3 ARBA, 95:1673
3 GSED, 1997, p939

◆ The article titles in this encyclopedia are indexed by keyword in Part II.

RX 461 _____(LC)   DDC: **613**

The Woman's Encyclopedia of Natural Healing: The New Healing Techniques of Over 100 Leading Alternative Practitioners

Null, Gary. Seven Stories, 1997. 411p. _Paper:_ $19.95.

Review Avg: 3.50   _OCLC:_ 340   _Rating:_ 4.18

Reviews
3 ARBA, 98:1550
4 LJ, Jan 1997, p90

♦**RZ 433** _____(LC)   DDC: **615.5**

An Encyclopedia of Natural Medicine

Murray, Michael T. and Joseph E. Pizzorno. Prima, 1991. 622p. _Cloth:_ $28.95. _Paper:_ $18.95.

Review Avg: 4.25   _OCLC:_ 1099   _Rating:_ 6.45

Reviews
5 ARBA, 93:1634
5 GSED, 1997, p937
4 LJ, May 1 1991, p72
3 RBB, Jun 1 1991, p1899

RZ 999 _____(LC)   DDC: **615.5**

The Encyclopedia of Bodywork: From Acupressure to Zane Therapy

Stillerman, Elaine. Facts On File, 1996. 320p. _Cloth:_ $35.00.

Review Avg: 3.00   _OCLC:_ 202   _Rating:_ 3.40

Reviews
3 ARBA, 97:1350

S 411 _____(LC)   DDC: **630**

Encyclopedia of Agricultural Science

Arntzen, Charles J. and Ellen M. Ritter (eds). Academic, 1994. 4 vols. (2744p.) _Cloth:_ $595.00/set.

Review Avg: 4.80   _OCLC:_ 382   _Rating:_ 9.56

Reviews	**Awards**
5 ARBA, 95:1507	Choice/OAB, Jan 1996,
4 Choice, Jun 1995, p1568	p724
5 GSED, 1997, p807	LJ/BRS, Apr 15 1995,
5 RBB, Jun 1 1995,	p38
p1815-1816	
5 WLB/R, Apr 1995, p85	

SB 351 _____(LC)   DDC: **581.6**

Encyclopedia of Herbs and Their Uses

Brown, Deni. Dorling, 1995. 424p. _Cloth:_ $39.95.

Review Avg: 4.00   _OCLC:_ 889   _Rating:_ 9.78

Reviews	**Awards**
4 ARBA, 96:1585	LJ/BRS, Apr 15 1996,
4 Choice, Mar 1996, p1160	p39
4 LJ, Dec 1995, p88	RBB/ORS, May 1 1996,
4 RBB, Feb 1 1996,	p1536
p953-954	

SB 403.2 _____(LC)   DDC: **635.9**

The Encyclopedia of Flowers

Fell, Derek. Smithmark, 1993. 208p. _Cloth:_ $19.98.

Review Avg: 3.00   _OCLC:_ 354   _Rating:_ 3.71

Reviews
3 ARBA, 94:1654
3 GSED, 1997, p846
3 RBB, Mar 1 1993, p1146

SB 434 _____(LC)   DDC: **635.9**

Rodale's Illustrated Encyclopedia of Perennials

Phillips, Ellen and C. Colson Burrell. Rodale, 1993. 533p. _Cloth:_ $27.95.

Review Avg: 4.33   _OCLC:_ 548   _Rating:_ 5.43

Reviews
5 ARBA, 94:1620
5 GSED, 1997, p828
3 RBB, May 1 1993, p1634

SB 450.95 _____(LC)   DDC: **635**

The American Horticultural Society Encyclopedia of Gardening

Brickell, Christopher (ed). Dorling, 1997. 2nd ed. 1092p. _Cloth:_ $79.95.

Review Avg: 4.50   _OCLC:_ 819   _Rating:_ 10.14

Reviews	**Awards**
4 ARBA, 94:1617	LJ/BRS, Apr 15 1994,
5 ARBA, 98:1432	p38
5 GSED, 1997, p822	LJ/BRS, Apr 15 1998,
4 LJ, Nov 15 1993, p68	p46
5 RBB, Mar 15 1990, p1496	RBB/ORS, May 1 1998,
4 RQ, Fall 1994, p97-98	p1538

SB 450.95 _____(LC)   DDC: **635.9**

The Wise Garden Encyclopedia

Seymour, E. L. D. HarperCollins, 1990. 1043p. _Cloth:_ $45.00.

Review Avg: 3.00   _OCLC:_ 443   _Rating:_ 3.89

Reviews
3 RBB, Jan 15 1991, p1089-1090

SB 453.5 _____(LC)   DDC: **635.0484**

Rodale's All-New Encyclopedia of Organic Gardening: The Indispensable Resource for Every Gardener

Bradley, Fern Marshall and Barbara W. Ellis (eds). Rodale, 1992. 690p. _Cloth:_ $29.95. _Paper:_ $17.95.

Review Avg: 5.00   _OCLC:_ 1066   _Rating:_ 7.13

Reviews
5 ARBA, 94:1619
5 GSED, 1997, p830
5 LJ, Mar 1 1992, p86

SF 285 _____(LC)   DDC: **636.1**

The Encyclopedia of the Horse

Edwards, Elwyn Hartley. Dorling, 1994. 400p. _Cloth:_ $39.95.

Review Avg: 4.50   _OCLC:_ 893   _Rating:_ 10.29

Reviews	**Awards**
5 ARBA, 95:1582	LJ/BRS, Apr 15 1995,
5 GSED, 1997, p835,860	p38
5 LJ, Nov 15 1994, p60	RBB/ORS, May 1 1995,
3 RBB, Dec 1 1994, p701	p1603
4 RQ, Sum 1995, p516-517	
5 WLB/R, Dec 1994, p72	

SF 291 _____(LC)   **DDC: 636.1**

International Encyclopedia of Horse Breeds

Hendricks, Bonnie L. Un of Oklahoma, 1995. 479p. *Cloth:* $65.00.
Paper: $14.95.
Review Avg: 4.00   *OCLC:* 504   *Rating:* 5.01

Reviews
4 ARBA, 97:1291
4 Choice, May 1996, p1450
4 LJ, Sep 1 1995, p162
4 RBB, Nov 1 1995, p505-504

SF 422 _____(LC)   **DDC: 636.7**

The Encyclopedia of the Dog

Fogle, Bruce. Dorling, 1995. 312p. *Cloth:* $39.95.
Review Avg: 4.00   *OCLC:* 865   *Rating:* 7.73

Reviews   *Awards*
4 ARBA, 96:1620   RBB/ORS, May 1 1996,
4 RBB, Oct 1 1995,   p1536
 p346-347

SF 442.2 _____(LC)   **DDC: 636.8**

The Cat Fanciers' Association Cat Encyclopedia

Thompson, Will. Simon & Schuster, 1995. 220p. *Cloth:* $30.00.
Review Avg: 5.00   *OCLC:* 172   *Rating:* 5.34

Reviews
5 LJ, Apr 1 1990, p106,108

SF 442.2 _____(LC)   **DDC: 599.74**

Cat World: A Feline Encyclopedia

Morris, Desmond. Penguin, 1997. 496p. *Cloth:* $29.95.
Review Avg: 3.67   *OCLC:* 263   *Rating:* 4.20

Reviews
4 ARBA, 98:1465
4 LJ, Dec 1996, p86
3 RBB, Feb 1 1997, p963

SF 442.2 _____(LC)   **DDC: 636.8**

The Encyclopedia of the Cat

Fogle, Bruce. Dorling, 1997. 240p. *Cloth:* $34.95.
Review Avg: 4.67   *OCLC:* 351   *Rating:* 5.37

Reviews   *Awards*
5 ARBA, 98:1463   LJ/BRS, Apr 15 1998,
5 LJ, Nov 1 1997, p68   p47
4 RBB, Nov 15 1997, p577   RBB/ORS, May 1 1998,
                             p1538

SF 447 _____(LC)   **DDC: 636.8**

Encyclopedia of Cat Health and Care

American Animal Hospital Assn. with Les Sussman. Hearst, 1994.
291p. *Cloth:* $25.00.
Review Avg: 3.00   *OCLC:* 361   *Rating:* 3.72

Reviews
3 LJ, Mar 15 1995, p58

SF 456.5 _____(LC)   **DDC: 639.3**

An Illustrated Encyclopedia of Aquarium Fish

Sandford, Gina. Howell, 1995. 256p. *Cloth:* $29.95.
Review Avg: 4.00   *OCLC:* 312   *Rating:* 4.62

Reviews
4 RBB, Mar 1 1996, p1211-1212

SF 457.1 _____(LC)   **DDC: 639.3**

Macmillan Book of the Marine Aquarium

Dakin, Nick. Macmillan, 1992. 400p. *Cloth:* $80.00.
Review Avg: 3.00   *OCLC:* 435   *Rating:* 3.87

Reviews
3 ARBA, 94:1717
3 Choice, Nov 1993, p428
3 LJ, Aug 1993, p92
3 RBB, Dec 1 1993, p710,712

SF 756.7 _____(LC)   **DDC: 599.051**

The Veterinarian's Encyclopedia of Animal Behavior

Beaver, Bonnie V. Iowa State Un, 1994. 307p. *Cloth:* $29.95.
Review Avg: 3.50   *OCLC:* 174   *Rating:* 3.85

Reviews
4 ARBA, 96:1554
3 Choice, May 1995, p1424

SH 411 _____(LC)   **DDC: 799.1**

The Dorling Kindersley Encyclopedia of Fishing

Wood, Ian (ed). Dorling, 1994. 288p. *Cloth:* $39.95.
Review Avg: 4.25   *OCLC:* 568   *Rating:* 9.39

Reviews   *Awards*
5 ARBA, 95:815   LJ/BRS, Apr 15 1995,
4 GSED, 1997, p442   p38
4 RBB, Jun 1 1994, p1874   RBB/ORS, May 1 1995,
4 WLB/R, Jun 1994, p93   p1603

T 9 _____(LC)   **DDC: 609**

The Oxford Illustrated Encyclopedia of Invention and Technology

Finniston, Monty and Christopher Bissell (eds). Oxford Un, 1992.
391p. *Cloth:* $49.95.
Note: Series—Oxford Illustrated Encyclopedia, vol. 1.
Review Avg: 3.17   *OCLC:* 594   *Rating:* 4.36

Reviews
3 ARBA, 91:932
3 ARBA, 93:1451, 6th vol.
3 ARBA, 90:535-6
3 Choice, Jan 1993, p774
3 LJ, Mar 1 1993, p70
4 RBB, Dec 1 1992, p690

T 15 _____(LC)   **DDC: 609**

An Encyclopaedia of the History of Technology

McNeil, Ian (ed). Routledge, 1990. 1062p. *Cloth:* $79.95.
Review Avg: 3.00   *OCLC:* 697   *Rating:* 3.72

Reviews
3 GSED, 1997, p800

T 15 _____(LC)   **DDC: 609**

World of Invention

Travers, Bridget (ed). Gale Research, 1994. 770p. *Cloth:* $75.00.
Review Avg: 3.00   *OCLC:* 587   *Rating:* 4.17

◆ The article titles in this encyclopedia are indexed by keyword in Part II.

Reviews
3 LJ, Feb 1 1994, p73
3 RBB, Jul 1994, p1980

T 37 _____(LC)   DDC: 609

The Blackwell Encyclopedia of Industrial Archaeology
Trinder, Barrie (ed). Blackwell, 1993. 964p. *Cloth:* $150.00.
Review Avg: 3.25   *OCLC:* 197   *Rating:* 3.64

Reviews
3 ARBA, 94:484
3 Choice, Sep 1993, p74
3 GSED, 1997, p188
4 LJ, Feb 1 1993, p70

T 58.5 _____(LC)   DDC: 004

Encyclopaedic Dictionary of Information Technology and Systems
Cawkell, A. E. Bowker, 1993. 339p. *Cloth:* $96.00.
Review Avg: 2.33   *OCLC:* 158   *Rating:* 2.65

Reviews
3 ARBA, 95:1689
1 Choice, Oct 1994, p257
3 GSED, 1997, p959

T 548 _____(LC)   DDC: 641.2

Larousse Encyclopedia of Wine
Foulkes, Christopher. Larousse, 1994. 608p. *Cloth:* $40.00.
Review Avg: 3.25   *OCLC:* 264   *Rating:* 3.78

Reviews
3 ARBA, 96:1527
3 Choice, Apr 1995, p1278
3 LJ, Jan 1995, p89
4 RBB, Dec 1 1994, p705

TA 9 _____(LC)   DDC: 620

McGraw-Hill Encyclopedia of Engineering
Parker, Sybil P. (ed). McGraw-Hill, 1993. 2nd ed. 1414p. *Cloth:* $95.50.
Note: From *McGraw Hill Encyclopedia of Science and Technology.*
Review Avg: 3.00   *OCLC:* 405   *Rating:* 5.81

Reviews
3 ARBA, 94:1785
3 Choice, Oct 1993, p268
3 GSED, 1997, p895
3 JAL, Sep 1993, p275
3 RQ, Win 1993, p290-291
3 WLB/R, Sep 1993, p119-121

TA 145 _____(LC)   DDC: 620

Magill's Survey of Science: Applied Science Series
Magill, Frank N. (ed). Salem, 1993. 6 vols. (2918p.) *Cloth:* $475.00/set.
Review Avg: 3.25   *OCLC:* 491   *Rating:* 4.23

Reviews
3 ARBA, 94:1583
4 Choice, Sep 1994, p72
3 LJ, Dec 1993, p114
3 WLB/R, Jun 1993, p126

TA 165 _____(LC)   DDC: 681

Concise Encyclopedia of Measurement and Instrumentation
Finklestein, L. and K.T.V. Grattan (eds). Pergamon, 1994. 434p. *Cloth:* $280.00.
Review Avg: 4.00   *OCLC:* 143   *Rating:* 4.29

Reviews
4 ARBA, 96:1641
4 Choice, Sep 1994, p64,66

TA 402 _____(LC)   DDC: 620.11

Concise Encyclopedia of Building and Construction Materials
Cahn, Robert W. Pergamon, 1990. 682p. *Cloth:* $230.00.
Note: From *Encyclopedia of Materials Science and Engineering.*
Review Avg: 3.00   *OCLC:* 165   *Rating:* 3.33

Reviews
3 ARBA, 91:1631

TA 402 _____(LC)   DDC: 620.1

Concise Encyclopedia of Materials Economics, Policy and Management
Bever, Michael B. and Robert W. Cahns (eds). Pergamon, 1993. 460p. *Paper:* $265.00.
Note: Series—Advances in Materials Science and Engineering.
Review Avg: 3.00   *OCLC:* 33   *Rating:* 3.07

Reviews
3 ARBA, 94:1794
3 GSED, 1997, p903

TA 402 _____(LC)   DDC: 620.11

Materials Handbook: An Encyclopedia for Purchasing Agents, Engineers, Executives, and Foremen
Brady, George S. and Henry R. Clauser. McGraw-Hill, 1996. 14th ed. 1136p. *Cloth:* $74.50.
Review Avg: 3.50   *OCLC:* 632   *Rating:* 6.76

Reviews
3 ARBA, 92:1617
4 RBB, Dec 1 1991, p722

TA 404.8 _____(LC)   DDC: 620.1

The Encyclopedia of Advanced Materials
Bloor, David and others (eds). Pergamon, 1994. 4 vols. *Cloth:* $1600.00/set.
Review Avg: 3.00   *OCLC:* 174   *Rating:* 3.35

Reviews
3 ARBA, 96:1664
3 Choice, Apr 1995, p1272
3 RBB, Jun 1 1995, p1821

TA 418.9 _____(LC)   DDC: 620.1

Concise Encyclopedia of Composite Materials
Kelly, Anthony (ed). Elsevier, 1994. Revised edition. 349p. *Paper:* $60.00.
Review Avg: 3.00   *OCLC:* 215   *Rating:* 5.43

Reviews
3 ARBA, 95:1632
3 Choice, Jan 1995, p744
3 GSED, 1997, p906

TA 418.9 _____(LC)   DDC: 620.1
International Encyclopedia of Composites
Lee, Stuart M. VCH, 1991. 6 vols. *Cloth:* $275.00.
Review Avg: 3.00   *OCLC:* 175   *Rating:* 3.35

Reviews
3 GSED, 1997, p906n

TA 1145 _____(LC)   DDC: 388
Concise Encyclopedia of Traffic and Transportation
Papageorgiou, Markos (ed). Pergamon, 1991. 658p. *Cloth:* $410.00/
set.
Review Avg: 3.00   *OCLC:* 110   *Rating:* 3.22

Reviews
3 ARBA, 93:1613
3 Choice, Mar 1992, p1111

TA 1509 _____(LC)   DDC: 621.36
Encyclopedia of Lasers and Optical Technology
Meyers, Robert A. (ed). Academic, 1991. 764p. *Cloth:* $102.00.
Review Avg: 3.00   *OCLC:* 340   *Rating:* 3.68

Reviews
3 ARBA, 92:1604

TD 9 _____(LC)   DDC: 333.7
The Encyclopedia of Environmental Studies
Ashworth, William. Facts On File, 1991. 470p. *Cloth:* $65.00.
Review Avg: 3.60   *OCLC:* 1062   *Rating:* 5.72

Reviews
3 ARBA, 92:1773
4 Choice, Jun 1992, p1513
4 GSED, 1997, p1029
3 RBB, Jan 15 1992, p972
4 WLB/R, Mar 1992, p118-119

TD 9 _____(LC)   DDC: 628
The Facts On File Dictionary of Environmental Science
Stevenson, L. Harold and Bruce Wyman. Facts On File, 1991. 294p.
Cloth: $27.95. *Paper:* $15.95.
Review Avg: 4.00   *OCLC:* 1299   *Rating:* 8.60

Reviews   **Awards**
5 ARBA, 92:1775   RBB/ORS, May 1 1993,
4 Choice, Mar 1992, p1056   p1620
4 GSED, 1997, p1035
4 LJ, Sep 1 1991, p184-186
3 RBB, Feb 1 1992, p1054

TD 223 _____(LC)   DDC: 333.91
Water Quality and Availability: A Reference Handbook
Miller, E. Willard and Ruby M. Miller. ABC-CLIO, 1992. 430p.
Cloth: $39.50.
Review Avg: 3.50   *OCLC:* 789   *Rating:* 5.08

Reviews
4 Choice, May 1993, p1445
3 RBB, Apr 1 1993, p1460

TD 351 _____(LC)   DDC: 553.7
The Water Encyclopedia: A Compendium of Useful Information on Water Resources
Van der Leeden, Frits and others. Lewis, 1990. 2nd ed. 808p. *Cloth:*
$125.00.
Review Avg: 4.50   *OCLC:* 1022   *Rating:* 8.54

Reviews
5 ARBA, 91:1785
4 Choice, Jun 1990, p1663-1664

TD 785.5 _____(LC)   DDC: 628.4
Encyclopedia of Garbage
Coffel, Steve. Facts On File, 1996. 311p. *Cloth:* $60.00.
Review Avg: 3.00   *OCLC:* 225   *Rating:* 3.45

Reviews
3 ARBA, 97:1425

TD 794.5 _____(LC)   DDC: 363.72
The McGraw-Hill Recycling Handbook
Lund, Herbert F. (ed). McGraw-Hill, 1993. 1 vol. *Cloth:* $84.50.
Review Avg: 4.50   *OCLC:* 935   *Rating:* 6.37

Reviews
5 ARBA, 95:1782
4 Choice, Jul/Aug 1993, p1800
5 RBB, Apr 1 1993, p1457-1458
4 WLB/R, Mar 1993, p111-112

TJ 163.235 _____(LC)   DDC: 333.79
Encyclopedia of Energy Technology and the Environment
Bisio, Attilio and Sharon Boots (eds). Wiley, 1995. 4 vols. *Cloth:*
$900.00/set.
Note: Series—Wiley Encyclopedia Series in Environmental Sciences.
Review Avg: 4.00   *OCLC:* 414   *Rating:* 6.83

Reviews   **Awards**
3 ARBA, 96:1830   Choice/OAB, Jan 1996,
5 Choice, Sep 1995, p80   p724

TJ 163.235 _____(LC)   DDC: 333.79
Wiley Encyclopedia of Energy and the Environment
Bisio, Attilio and Sharon Boots (eds). Wiley, 1996. 2 vols. (1562p.)
Cloth: $195.00.
Review Avg: 4.00   *OCLC:* 544   *Rating:* 5.09

Reviews
4 Choice, Mar 1997, p1144-1145

TJ 210.4 _____(LC)   DDC: 629.8
Concise International Encyclopedia of Robotics: Applications and Automation
Dorf, Richard C. (ed). Wiley, 1990. 1190p. *Cloth:* $99.95.
Review Avg: 5.00   *OCLC:* 256   *Rating:* 5.51

Reviews
5 ARBA, 91:1748

TJ 210.4 _____(LC)   DDC: 629.8
The McGraw-Hill Illustrated Encyclopedia of Robotics and Artificial Intelligence
Gibilisco, Stan (ed). McGraw-Hill, 1994. 420p. *Cloth:* $34.95.

Review Avg: 4.00   *OCLC:* 658   *Rating:* 5.32

Reviews
4 ARBA, 96:1753
4 RBB, Jan 1 1995, p843-844

TJ 1075 _____(LC)   DDC: **621.89**

Encyclopedia of Tribology
Kajdas, C. and others. Elsevier, 1990. 478p. *Cloth:* $156.50.
Review Avg: 3.00   *OCLC:* 107   *Rating:* 3.21

Reviews
3 ARBA, 92:1625

TK 7804 _____(LC)   DDC: **621.381**

Encyclopedia of Electronics
Gibilisco, Stan and Neil Sclater (eds). TAB, 1990. 2nd ed. 960p.
Cloth: $69.50.
Review Avg: 4.00   *OCLC:* 1118   *Rating:* 8.24

Reviews
5 ARBA, 91:1616
3 Choice, Dec 1990, p607
4 RBB, Nov 1 1990, p564,567

TK 7871.85 _____(LC)   DDC: **621.381**

Concise Encyclopedia of Magnetic and Superconducting Materials
Evetts, Jan (ed). Pergamon, 1992. 582p. *Cloth:* $260.00.
Review Avg: 3.00   *OCLC:* 119   *Rating:* 3.24

Reviews
3 ARBA, 93:1592

TK 7874 _____(LC)   DDC: **621.381**

International Encyclopedia of Integrated Circuits
Gibilisco, Stan (ed). McGraw-Hill, 1992. 2nd ed. 1142p. *Cloth:*
$84.95.
Review Avg: 3.25   *OCLC:* 278   *Rating:* 5.81

Reviews
4 ARBA, 93:1594, 2nd ed.
3 ARBA, 90:1591
3 GSED, 1997, p890
3 RBB, May 1 1992, p1629, 2nd ed.

TK 9956 _____(LC)   DDC: **621.3841**

Amateur Radio Encyclopedia
Gibilisco, Stan (ed). TAB, 1994. 593p. *Cloth:* $50.00. *Paper:* $24.95.
Review Avg: 4.25   *OCLC:* 440   *Rating:* 5.13

Reviews
5 ARBA, 95:960
4 Choice, Mar 1994, p1160,1162
5 GSED, 1997, p533
3 RBB, Mar 1 1994, p1287-1288

TL 509 _____(LC)   DDC: **387.7097**

The Airline Industry
Leary, William M. (ed). Facts On File, 1992. 531p. *Cloth:* $99.00.
Note: Series—Encyclopedia of American Business History and Biography.
Review Avg: 3.67   *OCLC:* 675   *Rating:* 5.02

Reviews
3 ARBA, 93:248
4 Choice, Jan 1993, p759-760
4 LJ, Jan 1993, p96

TL 509 _____(LC)   DDC: **629.1**

The Illustrated Encyclopedia of General Aviation
Garrison, Paul. TAB, 1990. 2nd ed. 462p. *Cloth:* $34.95. *Paper:* $24.95.
Review Avg: 3.00   *OCLC:* 413   *Rating:* 5.83

Reviews
3 ARBA, 91:1818
3 RBB, Jun 15 1990, p2031

TL 788 _____(LC)   DDC: **629.4**

Dictionary of Space Technology
Williamson, Mark. Hilger, 1990. 401p. *Cloth:* $50.00.
Review Avg: 4.00   *OCLC:* 430   *Rating:* 6.86

Reviews   **Awards**
4 ARBA, 92:1595   Choice/OAB, May 1991,
4 Choice, Oct 1990, p290   p1430

TL 789 _____(LC)   DDC: **001.94**

The UFO Encyclopedia
Clark, Jerome. Omnigraphics, 1990. 3 vols. *Cloth:* $95.00/vol.
Note: Second edition available now.
Review Avg: 3.20   *OCLC:* 279   *Rating:* 3.76

Reviews
3 ARBA, 93:807
3 ARBA, 97:632
3 Choice, Oct 1992, p270
4 GSED, 1997, p410
3 RBB, Jul 1992, p1958

TP 9 _____(LC)   DDC: **660**

Encyclopedia of Chemical Technology
Kroschwitz, Jacqueline I. and Mary Howe-Grant (eds). Wiley, 1995.
5th ed. 25 vols. plus index and suppl. *Cloth:* $275.00/set.
Note: Now called *Kirk-Othmer Encyclopedia of Chemical Technology*.
Review Avg: 5.00   *OCLC:* 570   *Rating:* 8.14

Reviews
5 ARBA, 94:1768
5 Choice, Mar 1993, p1110
5 GSED, 1997, p880

TP 9 _____(LC)   DDC: **660**

Encyclopedic Dictionary of Chemical Technology
Noether, Dorit. VCH, 1993. 297p. *Cloth:* $59.50.
Review Avg: 3.50   *OCLC:* 396   *Rating:* 4.29

Reviews
4 ARBA, 94:1936
3 Choice, Apr 1994, p1278
4 GSED, 1997, p992
3 RBB, Apr 15 1994, p1552

TP 9　　　　　　　　　　(LC)　　　DDC: 660
Kirk-Othmer Concise Encyclopedia of Chemical Technology
Howe-Grant, Mary (ed). Wiley, 1993. 4th ed. 3 vols. (1117p.) *Cloth:* $275.00/set.
Review Avg: 5.00　*OCLC:* 1054　*Rating:* 9.11

Reviews
5 GSED, 1997, p990

TP 248.16　　　　　　　(LC)　　　DDC: 660
Biotechnology from A to Z
Bains, William. Oxford Un, 1993. 358p. *Cloth:* $19.95.
Review Avg: 3.00　*OCLC:* 471　*Rating:* 3.94

Reviews
3 ARBA, 94:1790
3 Choice, Jan 1994, p818
3 GSED, 1997, p898

TP 248.16　　　　　　　(LC)　　　DDC: 660
The Facts On File Dictionary of Biotechnology and Genetic Engineering
Steinberg, Mark L. and Sharon D. Cosloy. Facts On File, 1994. 197p. *Cloth:* $27.95.
Review Avg: 2.33　*OCLC:* 559　*Rating:* 3.45

Reviews
3 Choice, Dec 1994, p581,582
3 GSED, 1997, p899
1 LJ, Jun 15 1994, p62

TP 368.2　　　　　　　(LC)　　　DDC: 664
Encyclopedia of Food Science and Technology
Hui, Y. H. (ed). Wiley, 1992. 4 vols. *Cloth:* $695.00/set.
Review Avg: 3.86　*OCLC:* 436　*Rating:* 6.73

Reviews　　　　　　　　*Awards*
3 ARBA, 94:1600　　　Choice/OAB, Jan 1993,
3 ARBA, 93:1473　　　　p734
5 Choice, Dec 1993, p584
5 Choice, Sep 1992, p76
4 GSED, 1997, p813
3 RBB, Nov 15 1993, p650
4 WLB/R, Nov 1993, p101

TP 546　　　　　　　(LC)　　　DDC: 661.2
Oz Clarke's Encyclopedia of Wine: An Illustrated A-to-Z Guide to Wines of the World
Clarke, Oz. Simon & Schuster, 1993. 448p. *Cloth:* $35.00.
Review Avg: 3.00　*OCLC:* 127　*Rating:* 3.25

Reviews
3 RBB, Feb 15 1994, p1109

TP 548　　　　　　　(LC)　　　DDC: 641.2
Hugh Johnson's Modern Encyclopedia of Wine
Johnson, Hugh. Simon & Schuster, 1991. 3rd ed. 576p. *Cloth:* $35.00.
Review Avg: 3.00　*OCLC:* 167　*Rating:* 5.33

Reviews
3 ARBA, 92:1488

TP 548　　　　　　　(LC)　　　DDC: 641.2
The New Sotheby's Wine Encyclopedia: A Comprehensive Reference Guide to the Wines of the World
Stevenson, Tom. Dorling, 1997. 600p. *Cloth:* $50.00.
Note: Updated edition of *Sotheby's World Wine Encyclopedia*, 1988.
Review Avg: 4.00　*OCLC:* 95　*Rating:* 4.19

Reviews　　　　　　　*Awards*
3 ARBA, 98:1424　　　LJ/BRS, Apr 15 1998,
5 LJ, Dec 1997, p94　　　p49
4 RBB, Dec 1 1997, p658

TP 548　　　　　　　(LC)　　　DDC: 641.2
The Oxford Companion to Wine
Robinson, Jancis (ed). Oxford Un, 1994. 1088p. *Cloth:* $49.95.
Review Avg: 4.20　*OCLC:* 651　*Rating:* 5.50

Reviews
4 ARBA, 96:1528
4 Choice, Apr 1995, p1278
5 GSED, 1997, p818
4 LJ, Dec 1994, p84
4 RBB, Dec 1 1994, p705

TP 553　　　　　　　(LC)　　　DDC: 641.2
Oz Clarke's New Encyclopedia of French Wine
Clarke, Oz. Simon & Schuster, 1990. 240p. *Cloth:* $24.95.
Review Avg: 3.00　*OCLC:* 99　*Rating:* 3.20

Reviews
3 ARBA, 92:1484

TP 568　　　　　　　(LC)　　　DDC: 641.23
Encyclopedia of Beer
Rhodes, Christine and others (eds). Holt, 1995. 512p. *Cloth:* $35.00.
Review Avg: 4.00　*OCLC:* 257　*Rating:* 8.51

Reviews　　　　　　　*Awards*
4 ARBA, 96:1525　　　LJ/BRS, Apr 15 1996,
4 LJ, Mar 1 1996, p72　　　p40
4 RBB, Dec 15 1995, p725　RBB/ORS, May 1 1996,
　　　　　　　　　　　p1536

TP 1087　　　　　　　(LC)　　　DDC: 668.9
Concise Encyclopedia of Polymer Processing and Applications
Cornish, Patrick J. (ed). Pergamon, 1992. 771p. *Cloth:* $280.00.
Review Avg: 3.00　*OCLC:* 68　*Rating:* 3.14

Reviews
3 ARBA, 93:1582

TP 1087　　　　　　　(LC)　　　DDC: 668.9
Concise Encyclopedia of Polymer Science and Engineering
Kroschwitz, Jacqueline I. (ed). Wiley, 1990. 1341p. *Cloth:* $135.00.
Review Avg: 3.00　*OCLC:* 331　*Rating:* 3.66

Reviews
3 ARBA, 92:1596
3 Choice, Feb 1991, p910

◆ The article titles in this encyclopedia are indexed by keyword in Part II.

TR 9 _____(LC)   DDC: 770
The Focal Encyclopedia of Photography
Stroebel, Leslie and Richard D. Zakia. Butterworth, 1993. 3rd ed. 914p. *Cloth:* $125.00. *Paper:* $49.95.
Review Avg: 4.25   *OCLC:* 914   *Rating:* 10.08

Reviews
3 ARBA, 94:1036
5 Choice, Dec 1993, p58
4 GSED, 1997, p568
5 WLB/R, Nov 1993, p10

Awards
Choice/OAB, Jan 1994, p712

TR 848 _____(LC)   DDC: 778
Pre-Cinema History: An Encyclopedia and Annotated Bibliography of the Moving Image Before 1896
Hecht, Hermann. Saur, 1993. 476p. *Cloth:* $165.00.
Review Avg: 3.00   *OCLC:* 137   *Rating:* 3.27

Reviews
3 Choice, Nov 1993, p432,434

TS 195 _____(LC)   DDC: 688.8
Wiley Encyclopedia of Packaging Technology
Brody, Aaron L. and Kenneth S. Marsh (eds). Wiley, 1997. 2nd ed. 1023p. *Cloth:* $225.00.
Review Avg: 3.50   *OCLC:* 176   *Rating:* 5.85

Reviews
3 ARBA, 98:1493
4 Choice, Nov 1997, p458

TS 532.15 _____(LC)   DDC: 683.4
The Encyclopedia of Sporting Firearms
Petzal, David E. Facts On File, 1991. 448p. *Cloth:* $50.00.
Review Avg: 4.25   *OCLC:* 560   *Rating:* 7.37

Reviews
5 ARBA, 92:932
5 GSED, 1997, p543
4 LJ, Apr 1 1991, p118
3 RBB, Jul 1991, p2066,2068

Awards
LJ/BRS, Apr 15 1992, p43

TS 722 _____(LC)   DDC: 553.8
The Larousse Encyclopedia of Precious Gems
Bariaud, Pierre and Jean-Paul Poirot. Van Nostrand Reinhold, 1992. 248p. *Cloth:* $60.00.
Review Avg: 3.33   *OCLC:* 135   *Rating:* 3.60

Reviews
3 ARBA, 93:1725
4 Choice, Sep 1992, p72
3 GSED, 1997, p1010

TS 1309 _____(LC)   DDC: 677
The Encyclopedia of Textiles
Jerde, Judith. Facts On File, 1992. 260p. *Cloth:* $45.00.
Review Avg: 3.00   *OCLC:* 774   *Rating:* 4.55

Reviews
3 ARBA, 93:1007
3 Choice, Dec 1992, p602
3 GSED, 1997, p556

3 LJ, Mar 15 1992, p76
3 RBB, Jun 1 1992, p1774

TT 186 _____(LC)   DDC: 684.082
Illustrated Encyclopedia of Woodworking Handtools, Instruments and Devices
Blackburn, Graham. Globe, 1992. 147p. *Paper:* $14.95.
Review Avg: 3.00   *OCLC:* 204   *Rating:* 3.41

Reviews
3 ARBA, 93:1610
3 GSED, 1997, p910
3 LJ, Mar 1 1992, p80
3 RBB, May 1 1992, p1623

TT 505 _____(LC)   DDC: 746.9
Contemporary Fashion
Martin, Richard (ed). St James, 1995. 575p. *Cloth:* $135.00.
Note: Revision of *St. James Fashion Encyclopedia,* 1997.
Review Avg: 3.00   *OCLC:* 699   *Rating:* 4.40

Reviews
3 RBB, Dec 1 1995, p654
3 WLB/R, 1995

TT 919.5 _____(LC)   DDC: 738.1
Potter's Dictionary of Materials and Techniques
Hamer, Frank and Janet Hamer. Un of Pennsylvania, 1991. 3rd ed. 384p. *Cloth:* $49.95.
Review Avg: 3.00   *OCLC:* 429   *Rating:* 5.86

Reviews
3 ARBA, 92:950
3 RBB, Jan 1 1992, p851

TX 349 _____(LC)   DDC: 641
The Concise Encyclopedia of Foods and Nutrition
Ensminger, Audrey H. and others. CRC, 1995. 1178p. *Cloth:* $125.95.
Note: Condensed version of *Foods and Nutrition Encyclopedia,* 1994.
Review Avg: 4.00   *OCLC:* 323   *Rating:* 4.65

Reviews
4 ARBA, 96:1524

TX 349 _____(LC)   DDC: 641
The Dictionary of American Food and Drink
Mariani, John F. Hearst, 1994. 2nd ed. 475p. *Paper:* $19.95.
Review Avg: 3.00   *OCLC:* 550   *Rating:* 6.10

Reviews
3 GSED, 1997, p817

TX 349 _____(LC)   DDC: 641
Dictionary of Nutrition and Food Technology
Bender, Arnold E. Butterworth, 1990. 6th ed. 336p. *Cloth:* $74.95.
Review Avg: 5.00   *OCLC:* 238   *Rating:* 7.48

Reviews
5 ARBA, 92:1481

TX 349 _____(LC)   **DDC: 641**

Encyclopaedia of Food Science, Food Technology and Nutrition

Macrae, Robert and others (eds). Academic, 1993. 8 vols. (5500p.) *Cloth:* $2100.00/set.

Review Avg: 4.00   *OCLC:* 278   *Rating:* 4.56

Reviews
4 Choice, Dec 1993, p584
4 GSED, 1997, p811
4 RBB, Nov 15 1993, p650
4 WLB/R, Nov 1993, p101

◆**TX 349** _____(LC)   **DDC: 641**

Foods and Nutrition Encyclopedia

Ensminger, Audrey H. and others. CRC, 1994. 2nd ed. 2 vols. (2415p.) *Cloth:* $125.00/set.

Review Avg: 4.00   *OCLC:* 741   *Rating:* 7.48

Reviews
5 ARBA, 95:1515
3 Choice, Jul/Aug 1994, p1702
4 GSED, 1997, p812

TX 349 _____(LC)   **DDC: 641**

The Visual Food Encyclopedia: The Definitive Practical Guide to Food and Cooking

D'Amico, Serge and Francois Fortin (eds). Macmillan, 1996. 685p. *Cloth:* $49.95.

Note: From *Dictionnaire Encyclopedique des Aliments.*

Review Avg: 4.00   *OCLC:* 241   *Rating:* 4.48

Reviews   **Awards**
4 RBB, Mar 15 1997, p1261   NYPL, 1997

TX 406 _____(LC)   **DDC: 641.3**

The Encyclopedia of Herbs, Spices, and Flavorings

Ortiz, Elisabeth Lambert. Dorling, 1992. 288p. *Cloth:* $34.95.

Review Avg: 3.00   *OCLC:* 695   *Rating:* 8.39

Reviews   **Awards**
3 WLB/R, Feb 1993,   LJ/BRS, Apr 15 1993,
   p103-104   p59-60
                            NYPL, 1993

TX 743 _____(LC)   **DDC: 641**

Edible Plants and Animals: Unusual Foods from Aardvark to Zambia

Livingston, A. D. and Helen Livingston. Facts On File, 1993. 292p. *Cloth:* $27.95.

Review Avg: 3.50   *OCLC:* 370   *Rating:* 4.24

Reviews
3 ARBA, 95:1516
4 WLB/R, Nov 1993, p105

◆**U 21.75** _____(LC)   **DDC: 355**

Women and the Military: An Encyclopedia

Sherrow, Victoria. ABC-CLIO, 1996. 381p. *Cloth:* $65.00.

Review Avg: 3.50   *OCLC:* 638   *Rating:* 6.78

Reviews   **Awards**
4 ARBA, 97:563   RBB/ORS, May 1 1997,
3 Choice, Jun 1997,   p1524
   p1644,1646

U 24 _____(LC)   **DDC: 355**

Brassey's Encyclopedia of Military History and Biography

Margiotta, Franklin D. Brassey's, 1994. 1197p. *Cloth:* $44.95.

Note: Articles previously published in *International and Military Defense Encyclopedia.*

Review Avg: 4.00   *OCLC:* 363   *Rating:* 4.73

Reviews
4 ARBA, 96:682
4 Choice, Apr 1995, p1268

U 24 _____(LC)   **DDC: 355**

A Dictionary of Military History and the Art of War

Corvisier, Andre. Blackwell, 1994. Revised edition. 916p. *Cloth:* $64.95.

Review Avg: 3.80   *OCLC:* 428   *Rating:* 6.66

Reviews
4 ARBA, 95:687
4 Choice, Jan 1995, p748
4 GSED, 1997, p321
3 LJ, Feb 15 1994, p148
4 RBB, Mar 1 1995, p1268

U 24 _____(LC)   **DDC: 355**

The Dictionary of Modern War

Luttwak, Edward and Stuart Koehl. HarperCollins, 1991. 680p. *Cloth:* $45.00.

Review Avg: 3.00   *OCLC:* 426   *Rating:* 5.85

Reviews   **Awards**
3 ARBA, 92:648   NYPL, 1992
2 Choice, Oct 1991,
   p262-263
4 GSED, 1997, p328
3 RBB, Sep 15 1991, p192

U 24 _____(LC)   **DDC: 355**

International Military and Defense Encyclopedia

Dupuy, Trevor N. Brassey's, 1993. 6 vols. (3132p.) *Cloth:* $1250.00/set.

Review Avg: 4.14   *OCLC:* 314   *Rating:* 6.77

Reviews   **Awards**
3 ARBA, 94:688   Choice/OAB, Jan 1994,
5 Choice, May 1993   p712
3 JAL, Jul 1993, p201
5 LJ, Mar 15 1993, p70
3 RBB, Aug 1993,
   p2084-2085
5 RQ, Fall 1993, p129-130
5 WLB/R, Apr 1993,
   p121-122

U 24 _____(LC)   **DDC: 355**

International Military Encyclopedia

Tobias, Norman (ed). Academic International, 1992. 3 vols. *Cloth:* $37.00.

Review Avg: 3.33   *OCLC:* 44   *Rating:* 3.42

◆ The article titles in this encyclopedia are indexed by keyword in Part II.

Reviews
3 ARBA, 93:702
3 Choice, Mar 1993, p1114,1116
4 WLB/R, Feb 1993, p105

U 24 _____(LC)   DDC: 355
The Soviet Military Encyclopedia
Green, William C. and W. Robert Reeves (eds). Westview, 1993. 4 vols. *Cloth:* $375.00/set.
Review Avg: 4.50   *OCLC:* 89   *Rating:* 4.68

Reviews
5 ARBA, 94:686
4 Choice, Jan 1994, p762

U 27 _____(LC)   DDC: 355
The Reader's Companion to Military History
Cowley, Robert and Geoffrey Parker (eds). Houghton, 1996. 573p. *Cloth:* $45.00.
Review Avg: 3.33   *OCLC:* 480   *Rating:* 4.29

Reviews
3 ARBA, 98:616
3 Choice, May 1997, p1480
4 RBB, Feb 1 1997, p966

U 51 _____(LC)   DDC: 355
The Encyclopedia of Amazons: Women Warriors from Antiquity to the Modern Era
Salmonson, Jessica Amanda. Paragon, 1991. 290p. *Cloth:* $21.95.
Review Avg: 2.60   *OCLC:* 602   *Rating:* 3.80

Reviews
3 ARBA, 92:862
1 Choice, Dec 1991, p578
3 GSED, 1997, p504
3 LJ, Jul 1991, p90-92
3 WLB/R, Oct 1991, p118

U 815 _____(LC)   DDC: 623
The Penguin Encyclopedia of Weapons and Military Technology
Macksey, Kenneth. Viking Penguin, 1993. 391p. *Cloth:* $29.95.
Review Avg: 4.00   *OCLC:* 7   *Rating:* 4.01

Reviews
3 ARBA, 93:774
5 WLB/R, Dec 1994, p74

UA 23 _____(LC)   DDC: 355
Encyclopedia of the American Military: Studies of the History, Traditions, Policies, Institutions, and Roles
Jessup, John E. (ed). Scribner's, 1994. 3 vols. *Cloth:* $330.00/set.
Review Avg: 4.33   *OCLC:* 621   *Rating:* 11.57

Reviews	*Awards*
5 ARBA, 95:688	Choice/OAB, Jan 1995, p719
4 Choice, Nov 1994, p424,426	LJ/BRS, Apr 15 1995, p39
5 GSED, 1997, p326	RBB/ORS, May 1 1995, p1603
3 RBB, Nov 15 1994, p626-627	
5 RQ, Win 1994, p238-240	
4 WLB/R, Oct 1994, p78-79	

UA 770 _____(LC)   DDC: 355
The Military Encyclopedia of Russia and Eurasia
Jones, David R. (ed). Academic International, 1994. 242p. *Cloth:* $37.00.
Note: Vols. 1-7 in print, vol. 8 scheduled for Spring 1996.
Review Avg: 1.00   *OCLC:* 11   *Rating:* 1.02

Reviews
1 ARBA, 96:146

UB 270 _____(LC)   DDC: 327.12
The Spycatcher's Encyclopedia of Espionage
Wright, Peter. Stoddart, 1991. 265p. *Paper:* $14.95.
Review Avg: 1.00   *OCLC:* 5   *Rating:* 1.01

Reviews
1 ARBA, 93:787

UC 533 _____(LC)   DDC: 355.1
Encyclopedia of United States Army Insignia and Uniforms
Emerson, William K. Un of Oklahoma, 1996. 674p. *Cloth:* $125.00.
Review Avg: 4.00   *OCLC:* 341   *Rating:* 4.68

Reviews
4 ARBA, 98:624
4 RBB, Mar 1 1997, p1186,1188

UC 533 _____(LC)   DDC: 355.1
U.S. Army Patches: An Illustrated Encyclopedia of Cloth Unit Insignia
Stein, Barry Jason. Un South Carolina, 1997. 222p. *Cloth:* $39.95.
Review Avg: 4.00   *OCLC:* 116   *Rating:* 4.23

Reviews
4 ARBA, 98:625

UF 500 _____(LC)   DDC: 956.7044
Encyclopedia of the Persian Gulf War
Grossman, Mark. ABC-CLIO, 1995. 522p. *Cloth:* $75.00.
Review Avg: 3.75   *OCLC:* 804   *Rating:* 9.36

Reviews	*Awards*
4 ARBA, 97:454	Choice/OAB, Jan 1997, p740
4 Choice, May 1996, p1448	LJ/BRS, Apr 15 1996, p40
4 LJ, May 1 1996, p88	
3 RBB, Apr 15 1996, p1458	

UG 633 _____(LC)   DDC: 358.4
Historical Dictionary of the U.S. Air Force
Bright, Charles D. (ed). Greenwood, 1992. 713p. *Cloth:* $85.00.
Review Avg: 3.33   *OCLC:* 406   *Rating:* 4.14

Reviews
3 ARBA, 94:698
3 Choice, Nov 1992, p444
4 LJ, Apr 1 1992, p112

V 23 _____(LC)   DDC: 623.8
Ships of the World: An Historical Encyclopedia
Paine, Lincoln P. Houghton, 1997. 680p. *Cloth:* $50.00.
Review Avg: 4.00   *OCLC:* 217   *Rating:* 4.43

Reviews
4 ARBA, 98:1651

V 23   (LC)   DDC: 359
United States Navy: A Dictionary
Watson, Bruce W. and Susan M. Watson. Garland, 1991. 948p. *Cloth:* $110.00.
Review Avg: 3.00   *OCLC:* 188   *Rating:* 3.38

Reviews
3 LJ, Jun 1 1991, p128,130

VK 1250   (LC)   DDC: 910.45
Shipwrecks: An Encyclopedia of the World's Worst Disasters at Sea
Ritchie, David. Facts On File, 1996. 292p. *Cloth:* $40.00.
Review Avg: 3.00   *OCLC:* 362   *Rating:* 3.72

Reviews
3 ARBA, 97:1448

Z 40   (LC)   DDC: 411
The Blackwell Encyclopedia of Writing Systems
Coulmas, Florian. Blackwell, 1996. 603p. *Cloth:* $74.95.
Review Avg: 3.00   *OCLC:* 275   *Rating:* 3.55

Reviews
3 ARBA, 97:811
3 Choice, Feb 1997, p942
3 LJ, Feb 1 1996, p68

Z 118   (LC)   DDC: 686.2
Graphic Arts Encyclopedia
Stevenson, George A. and revised by William A. Pakan. Design, 1992. 3rd ed. 582p. *Cloth:* $57.95.
Review Avg: 3.50   *OCLC:* 356   *Rating:* 6.21

Reviews
3 ARBA, 93:1042
4 GSED, 1997, p596

Z 282.5   (LC)   DDC: 070.5
International Book Publishing: An Encyclopedia
Altbach, Philip G. (ed). Garland, 1995. 736p. *Cloth:* $40.00.
Note: Series— Garland Reference Library of the Humanities, vol. 1562.
Review Avg: 4.00   *OCLC:* 282   *Rating:* 4.56

Reviews
4 LJ, Jun 1 1995, p106

Z 657   (LC)   DDC: 098
The Encyclopedia of Censorship
Green, Jonathan. Facts On File, 1990. 388p.
Review Avg: 3.40   *OCLC:* 1467   *Rating:* 8.33

Reviews   *Awards*
4 ARBA, 91:635   NYPL, 1991
4 Choice, Jun 1990, p1654
3 GSED, 1997, p309
3 RBB, Mar 15 1990, p1498
3 WLB/R, Mar 1990, p126,128

Z 658   (LC)   DDC: 363.3
Free Expression and Censorship in America: An Encyclopedia
Foerstel, Herbert N. (ed). Greenwood, 1997. 260p. *Cloth:* $65.00.
Review Avg: 3.33   *OCLC:* 359   *Rating:* 4.05

Reviews
4 ARBA, 98:584
3 Choice, Oct 1997, p276
3 RBB, Jul 1997, p1834

Z 721   (LC)   DDC: 020.3
Encyclopedia of Library History
Wiegand, Wayne A. and Donald G. Davis (eds). Garland, 1994. 707p. *Cloth:* $95.00.
Review Avg: 3.80   *OCLC:* 533   *Rating:* 4.87

Reviews
3 ARBA, 95:637
5 Choice, Jun 1994, p1552
3 GSED, 1997, p314
3 RBB, May 1 1994, p1618
5 WLB/R, May 1994, p80

Z 1006   (LC)   DDC: 020.3
International Encyclopedia of Information and Library Science
Feather, John and Paul Sturges (eds). Routledge, 1996. 492p. *Cloth:* $130.00.
Review Avg: 3.00   *OCLC:* 203   *Rating:* 3.41

Reviews
3 Choice, May 1997, p1476

Z 1006   (LC)   DDC: 020.3
World Encyclopedia of Library and Information Services
Wedgeworth, Robert (ed). ALA, 1993. 3rd ed. 905p. *Cloth:* $200.00.
Review Avg: 3.60   *OCLC:* 538   *Rating:* 6.68

Reviews
4 ARBA, 94:609
3 Choice, Feb 1994, p923
4 GSED, 1997, p315
3 JAL, Nov 1993, p337-338
4 RBB, Jan 1 1994, p853

Z 6514   (LC)   DDC: 016.809
The Johns Hopkins Guide to Literary Theory and Criticism
Groden, Michael and Martin Kreiswirth. Johns Hopkins Un, 1994. 775p. *Cloth:* $65.00.
Review Avg: 4.00   *OCLC:* 1061   *Rating:* 6.12

Reviews
5 ARBA, 95:1104
4 CRL, Mar 1995, p136
3 Choice, Jul/Aug 1994, p1703
3 LJ, Mar 1 1994, p81
4 RBB, Jul 1994, p1975
5 WLB/R, Jun 1994, p99

Z 6514.P7   (LC)   DDC: 809.3
Beacham's Encyclopedia of Popular Fiction
Beetz, Kirk H. (ed). Beacham, 1996. 11 vols. *Cloth:* $550.00.
Review Avg: 4.00   *OCLC:* 182   *Rating:* 4.36

Reviews
4 LJ, Mar 1 1997, p68
4 RBB, Mar 1 1997, p1183

◆ The article titles in this encyclopedia are indexed by keyword in Part II.

Title Index

◆ The article titles in this encyclopedia are indexed by keyword in Part II.

♦ The article titles in this encyclopedia are indexed by keyword in Part II.

Encyclopedia of American Political Reform, E 839.5

◆ Encyclopedia of American Prisons, HV 9471

Encyclopedia of American Religions, BL 2530

The Encyclopedia of American Religious History, BL 2525

◆ Encyclopedia of American Social History, HN 57

Encyclopedia of American Wrestling, GV 1198.12

Encyclopedia of Analytical Science, QD 71.5

The Encyclopedia of Ancient Egypt, DT 58

Encyclopedia of Ancient Mesoamerica, F 1219

Encyclopedia of Angels, BL 477

The Encyclopedia of Animated Cartoons, NC 1766

Encyclopedia of Antibiotics, RM 267

Encyclopedia of Apocalyptic Literature, PN 56

Encyclopedia of Applied Physics, QC 5

An Encyclopedia of Archetypal Symbolism, BL 603

Encyclopedia of Architecture: Design, Engineering and Construction, NA 31

Encyclopedia of Arms Control and Disarmament, JX 1974

Encyclopedia of Assassinations, HV 6278

Encyclopedia of Australian Art, N 7400

The Encyclopedia of Bad Taste, E 169.12

Encyclopedia of Banking and Finance, HG 151

Encyclopedia of Beer, TP 568

Encyclopedia of Biblical and Christian Ethics, BJ 1199

The Encyclopedia of Biblical Errancy, BS 533

◆ Encyclopedia of Bioethics, QH 332

The Encyclopedia of Blindness and Vision Impairment, RE 91

The Encyclopedia of Bodywork: From Acupressure to Zane Therapy, RZ 999

The Encyclopedia of Britain, DA 27.5

Encyclopedia of Business, HF 1001

The Encyclopedia of Butterflies, QL 541.5

Encyclopedia of Cancer, RC 262

Encyclopedia of Career Change and Work Issues, HF 5381

The Encyclopedia of Career Choices for the 1990s: A Guide to Entry Level Jobs, HF 5383

The Encyclopedia of Careers and Vocational Guidance, HF 5381

Encyclopedia of Cat Health and Care, SF 447

The Encyclopedia of Celtic Wisdom, BL 900

The Encyclopedia of Censorship, Z 657

Encyclopedia of Chemical Technology, TP 9

◆ Encyclopedia of Childbearing: Critical Perspectives, RG 525

◆ Encyclopedia of Classical Philosophy, B 163

Encyclopedia of Climate and Weather, QC 854

The Encyclopedia of College Basketball, GV 885.7

Encyclopedia of Common Natural Ingredients Used in Food, Drugs, and Cosmetics, QD 415

Encyclopedia of Computer Science, QA 76.15

Encyclopedia of Constitutional Amendments, Proposed Amendments, and Amending Issues, 1789-1995, KF 4557

Encyclopedia of Consumer Brands, HF 5415.3

◆ Encyclopedia of Contemporary Literary Theory: Approaches, Scholars, Terms, PN 81

Encyclopedia of Cosmology: Historical, Philosophical, and Scientific Foundations of Modern Cosmology, QB 980.5

Encyclopedia of Creation Myths, BL 325

Encyclopedia of Cultural Anthropology, GN 307

Encyclopedia of Deafness and Hearing Disorders, RF 290

◆ The Encyclopedia of Democracy, JC 423

The Encyclopedia of Depression, RC 537

Encyclopedia of Dinosaurs, QE 862

◆ Encyclopedia of Disability and Rehabilitation, HV 1568

The Encyclopedia of Drug Abuse, HV 5804

◆ Encyclopedia of Drugs and Alcohol, HV 5804

◆ Encyclopedia of Early Childhood Education, LB 1139

Encyclopedia of Early Christianity, BR 162.2

Encyclopedia of Earth Sciences, QE 5

Encyclopedia of Earth System Science, QE 5

The Encyclopedia of Earthquakes and Volcanoes, QE 521

The Encyclopedia of Eastern Philosophy and Religion: Buddhism, Hinduism, Taoism, Zen, BL 1005

◆ Encyclopedia of Educational Research, LB 15

Encyclopedia of Electronics, TK 7804

Encyclopedia of Endangered Species, QH 75

Encyclopedia of Energy Technology and the Environment, TJ 163.235

Encyclopedia of English Studies and Language Arts, PE 65

Encyclopedia of Environmental Biology, QH 540.4

The Encyclopedia of Environmental Studies, TD 9

The Encyclopedia of Erotic Wisdom: A Reference Guide to the Symbolism, Techniques, Rituals, Sacred Texts, Psychology, Anatomy, and History of Sexuality, HQ 12

◆ Encyclopedia of Ethics, BJ 63

Encyclopedia of European Cinema, PN 1993.5

◆ The Encyclopedia of Evolution: Humanity's Search for Its Origins, GN 281

The Encyclopedia of Evolving Techniques in Psychodynamic Therapy, RC 501.4

An Encyclopedia of Famous Suicides, HV 6545

◆ Encyclopedia of Feminist Literary Theory, PN 98

Encyclopedia of Financial Gerontology, HQ 1061

An Encyclopedia of Flora and Fauna in English and American Literature, PR 149

The Encyclopedia of Flowers, SB 403.2

Encyclopedia of Food Science and Technology, TP 368.2

Encyclopedia of Frontier Literature, PS 169

The Encyclopedia of Gambling, HV 6710

Encyclopedia of Garbage, TD 785.5

The Encyclopedia of Gemstones and Minerals, QE 392

The Encyclopedia of Genetic Disorders and Birth Defects, RB 155.5

♦ The article titles in this encyclopedia are indexed by keyword in Part II.

◆ The article titles in this encyclopedia are indexed by keyword in Part II.

◆ The article titles in this encyclopedia are indexed by keyword in Part II.

♦ The article titles in this encyclopedia are indexed by keyword in Part II.

◆ The article titles in this encyclopedia are indexed by keyword in Part II.

Subject Headings Index

Abnormalities, Human

The Encyclopedia of Genetic Disorders and Birth Defects, RB 155.5

Accounting

The History of Accounting: An International Encyclopedia, HF 5605

Acoustics

Encyclopedia of Acoustics, QC 221.5

Adolescence

◆ Encyclopedia of Adolescence, HQ 796

Adoption

◆ The Encyclopedia of Adoption, HV 875.55

Adulthood

◆ Encyclopedia of Adult Development, BF 724.5

Aeronautics

The Airline Industry, TL 509

The Illustrated Encyclopedia of General Aviation, TL 509

Aesthetics

A Companion to Aesthetics, BH 56

Africa

The Encyclopedia of African-American Heritage, E 185

Africa, North

The Encyclopedia of the Modern Middle East, 1800-1994, DS 43

Africa, North—Antiquities

The Oxford Encyclopedia of Archaeology in the Near East, DS 56

Afro-American churches

Encyclopedia of African American Religions, BR 563

Afro-American women

◆ Black Women in America: An Historical Encyclopedia, E 185.86

The Facts On File Encyclopedia of Black Women, E 185.96

Afro-Americans

The African American Encyclopedia, E 185

◆ Dictionary of Afro-American Slavery, E 441

◆ The Encyclopedia of African-American Culture and History, E 185

The Encyclopedia of African-American Heritage, E 185

Afro-Americans—Civil rights

The ABC-CLIO Companion to the Civil Rights Movement, E 185.61

Encyclopedia of African-American Civil Rights: From Emancipation to the Present, E 185

Historical Dictionary of the Civil Rights Movement, E 185.61

Afro-Americans—Education

◆ Encyclopedia of African-American Education, LC 2717

Afro-Americans—History

The ABC-CLIO Companion to the Civil Rights Movement, E 185.61

Afro-Americans in literature

The Oxford Companion to African American Literature, PS 153

Afro-Americans—Religion

Encyclopedia of African American Religions, BR 563

Aged

◆ Encyclopedia of Aging: A Comprehensive Resource in Gerontology and Geriatrics, HQ 1061

Encyclopedia of Financial Gerontology, HQ 1061

◆ Encyclopedia of Home Care for the Elderly, HV 1461

The Graying of America: An Encyclopedia of Aging, Health, Mind, and Behavior, HQ 1064

Older Americans Almanac: A Reference Work on Seniors in the United States, HQ 1064

Aggressiveness (Psychology)

Aggression and Conflict: A Cross-Cultural Encyclopedia, HM 136

Aging

The Encyclopedia of Aging and the Elderly, HQ 1061

Agriculture

Encyclopedia of Agricultural Science, S 411

◆ Foods and Nutrition Encyclopedia, TX 349

Aircraft industry

The Airline Industry, TL 509

Airlines

The Airline Industry, TL 509

Alaska

The Encyclopedia of the Far West, F 591

Alcoholism

The Encyclopedia of Alcoholism, HV 5017

◆ Encyclopedia of Drugs and Alcohol, HV 5804

Allegory

Encyclopedia of Allegorical Literature, PN 56

Allergy

Allergies A-Z, RC 522

Encyclopedia of Allergy and Environmental Illness: A Self-Help Approach, RC 584

Alternative medicine

The Alternative Advisor: The Complete Guide to Natural Therapies and Alternative Treatments, R 733

Alternative Healing: The Complete A-Z Guide to More than 150 Alternative Therapies, R 733

The Alternative Health and Medicine Encyclopedia, R 733

Alternative Health Care: The Encyclopedia of Choices in Healing, R 733

A Dictionary of Mind and Body: Therapies, Techniques and Ideas in Alternative Medicine, the Healing Arts and Psychology, R 733

The Encyclopedia of Alternative Medicine: A Complete Family Guide to Complementary Therapies, R 733

Health and Illness: A Cross-Cultural Encyclopedia, R 733

The Woman's Encyclopedia of Natural Healing: The New Healing Techniques of Over 100 Leading Alternative Practitioners, RX 461

Amateur radio stations

Amateur Radio Encyclopedia, TK 9956

America—Discovery and exploration

◆ The Christopher Columbus Encyclopedia, E 111

Columbus Dictionary, E 111

Legend and Lore of the Americas Before 1492: An Encyclopedia of Visitors, Explorers and Immigrants, E 61

America—Foreign relations

Encyclopedia of the Inter-American System, F 1410

America—Social life and customs

The Cowboy Encyclopedia, E 20

American literature

Dictionary of Native American Literature, PM 155

Encyclopedia of Frontier Literature, PS 169

Encyclopedia of Transcendentalism, PS 217

A Herman Melville Encyclopedia, PS 2386

Mark Twain A to Z: The Essential Reference to His Life and Writings, PS 1331

The Mark Twain Encyclopedia, PS 1330

A Melville Encyclopedia: The Novels, PS 2386

A Nathaniel Hawthorne Encyclopedia, PS 1880

The Oxford Companion to African American Literature, PS 153

The Oxford Companion to American Literature, PS 21

The Oxford Companion to English Literature, PR 19

The Oxford Companion to Twentieth-Century Literature in English, PR 471

The Oxford Companion to Women's Writing in the United States, PS 147

The Vonnegut Encyclopedia: An Authorized Compendium, PS 3572

American poetry

The Oxford Companion to Twentieth-Century Poetry in English, PR 601

Americans—Latin America

The United States in Latin America: A Historical Dictionary, F 1418

Angels

Angels A to Z, BL 477

Encyclopedia of Angels, BL 477

Animal behavior

The Veterinarian's Encyclopedia of Animal Behavior, SF 756.7

Animals

An Encyclopedia of Flora and Fauna in English and American Literature, PR 149

The Illustrated Encyclopedia of Wildlife, QL 7

Wildlife of the World, QL 49

Antarctic region

Antarctica: An Encyclopedia, G 855

Anthropology

Companion Encyclopedia of Anthropology, GN 25

Anti-communist movements

Encyclopedia of the McCarthy Era, E 743.5

Anti-Nazi movement

Encyclopedia of German Resistance to the Nazi Movement, DD 256.5

Antibiotics

Encyclopedia of Antibiotics, RM 267

Antidotes

Poisons and Antidotes, RA 1224.5

Antiques

Bulfinch Illustrated Encyclopedia of Antiques, NK 30

The David and Charles Encyclopedia of Everyday Antiques, NK 28

Apocalyptic literature

Encyclopedia of Apocalyptic Literature, PN 56

Apparitions

The Encyclopedia of Ghosts and Spirits, BF 1461

Aquarium animals

An Illustrated Encyclopedia of Aquarium Fish, SF 456.5

Aquatic animals

Dangerous Aquatic Animals of the World, QL 100

Arabs

Encyclopedia of the History of Arabic Science, Q 127

Archaeology

Dictionary of Concepts in Archaeology, CC 70

The Oxford Companion to Archaeology, CC 78

Archetype (Psychology)

An Encyclopedia of Archetypal Symbolism, BL 603

Architects

Illustrated Encyclopedia of Architects and Architecture, NA 40

International Dictionary of Architects and Architecture, NA 40

Architecture

Dictionary of Architecture and Construction, NA 31

Encyclopedia of American Architecture, NA 705

Encyclopedia of Architecture: Design, Engineering and Construction, NA 31

Illustrated Encyclopedia of Architects and Architecture, NA 40

International Dictionary of Architects and Architecture, NA 40

The Penguin Dictionary of Architecture, NA 31

Architecture, Classical

An Encyclopedia of the History of Classical Archaeology, DE 5

Architecture—Details

Elements of Style: A Practical Encyclopedia of Interior Architectural Details from 1485 to the Present, NA 2850

Architecture, Islamic

Dictionary of Islamic Architecture, NA 380

Arms control

Encyclopedia of Arms Control and Disarmament, JX 1974

Art

Benet's Reader's Encyclopedia of American Literature, PN 41

The Concise Oxford Dictionary of Art and Artists, N 3

The Dictionary of Art, N 31

The Thames and Hudson Dictionary of Art and Artists, N 31

Art and religion

Encyclopedia of Women in Religious Art, N 7793

Art, Australian

Encyclopedia of Australian Art, N 7400

Art, British

The 1890s: An Encyclopedia of British Literature, Art, and Culture, DA 560

Art, Classical

An Encyclopedia of the History of Classical Archaeology, DE 5

Art—Collectors and collecting

The Art Business Encyclopedia, N 8600

Art, Dutch

Dutch Art: An Encyclopedia, N 6941

Art—Economic aspects

The Art Business Encyclopedia, N 8600

Art—Marketing

The Art Business Encyclopedia, N 8600

Art, Medieval

Encyclopedia of Medieval Church Art, N 7943

Arthurian romances

The Encyclopaedia of Arthurian Legends, DA 152.5

The New Arthurian Encyclopedia, DA 152

Artificial intelligence

The McGraw-Hill Illustrated Encyclopedia of Robotics and Artificial Intelligence, TJ 210.4

Artists

The Concise Oxford Dictionary of Art and Artists, N 3

The Thames and Hudson Dictionary of Art and Artists, N 31

Arts

The Oxford Illustrated Encyclopedia of the Arts, NX 70

Arts, American

The Encyclopedia of Bad Taste, E 169.12

Arts and society

Great Events from History II: Arts and Culture Series, NX 456

Arts, Modern

The Encyclopedia of Bad Taste, E 169.12

Great Events from History II: Arts and Culture Series, NX 456

♦ The article titles in this encyclopedia are indexed by keyword in Part II.

Biological diversity—Measurement

Concise Encyclopedia of Biological and Biomedical Measurement Systems, RC 71

Biology

Concise Encyclopedia Biology, QH 302.5

♦ Encyclopedia of Human Biology, QP 11

The HarperCollins Dictionary of Biology, QH 302.5

Biomedical materials

Concise Encyclopedia of Medical and Dental Materials, R 857

Biotechnology

Biotechnology from A to Z, TP 248.16

Encyclopedia of Molecular Biology and Molecular Medicine, QH 506

The Facts On File Dictionary of Biotechnology and Genetic Engineering, TP 248.16

Birds

Birds of North America: Life Histories for the 21st Century, QL 681

The Illustrated Encyclopedia of Birds: The Definitive Reference to Birds of the World, QL 672.2

Blindness

The Encyclopedia of Blindness and Vision Impairment, RE 91

Blues (Music)

Encyclopedia of the Blues, ML 102

Boundaries

The Encyclopedia of International Boundaries, JX 4111

Brain

The Brain Encyclopedia, QP 376

Brand choice

Encyclopedia of Consumer Brands, HF 5415.3

Brand name products

Encyclopedia of Consumer Brands, HF 5415.3

Brewing

Encyclopedia of Beer, TP 568

Britons—Kings and rulers

The Encyclopaedia of Arthurian Legends, DA 152.5

The New Arthurian Encyclopedia, DA 152

Broadcasting

Broadcasting It: An Encyclopaedia of Homosexuality on Film, Radio and TV in the UK, 1923-1993, PN 1995.9

Broadway

Broadway: An Encyclopedic Guide to the History, People and Places of Times Square, F 128.65

Buddhism

Historical Dictionary of Buddhism, BQ 130

Building

Dictionary of Architecture and Construction, NA 31

Building materials

Concise Encyclopedia of Building and Construction Materials, TA 402

Business

Encyclopedia of Business, HF 1001

Great Events from History II: Business and Commerce, HC 55

♦ International Encyclopedia of Business and Management, HF 1001

Business cycles

♦ Business Cycles and Depressions: An Encyclopedia, HB 3711

Butterflies

The Encyclopedia of Butterflies, QL 541.5

Byzantine Empire

The Oxford Dictionary of Byzantium, DF 521

Calendars

Religious Holidays and Calendars: An Encyclopedic Handbook, CE 6

Campaign funds

Open Secrets: The Encyclopedia of Congressional Money Politics, JK 1991

Canada

Encyclopedia of Music in Canada, ML 106

Cancer

The Cancer Dictionary, RC 262

Encyclopedia of Cancer, RC 262

Career changes

Encyclopedia of Career Change and Work Issues, HF 5381

Caribbean Area

The Dictionary of Contemporary Politics of Central America and Caribbean, F 2183

Political and Economic Encyclopaedia of South America and the Caribbean, F 1410

Political Parties of the Americas and the Caribbean: A Reference Guide, JL 599.5

Cartoon characters

The Encyclopedia of Animated Cartoons, NC 1766

Catholic Church

The HarperCollins Encyclopedia of Catholicism, BC 841

The Modern Catholic Encyclopedia, BX 841

The New Dictionary of Catholic Social Thought, BX 1753

Our Sunday Visitor's Catholic Encyclopedia, BX 841

Cats

The Cat Fanciers' Association Cat Encyclopedia, SF 442.2

Cat World: A Feline Encyclopedia, SF 442.2

Encyclopedia of Cat Health and Care, SF 447

The Encyclopedia of the Cat, SF 442.2

Celts

Dictionary of Celtic Religion and Culture, BL 900

The Encyclopedia of Celtic Wisdom, BL 900

Censorship

The Encyclopedia of Censorship, Z 657

Free Expression and Censorship in America: An Encyclopedia, Z 658

Central America

The Dictionary of Contemporary Politics of Central America and Caribbean, F 2183

Encyclopedia of Ancient Mesoamerica, F 1219

Ceramic materials

Potter's Dictionary of Materials and Techniques, TT 919.5

Chemical engineering

Encyclopedic Dictionary of Chemical Technology, TP 9

Chemistry

Concise Encyclopedia Chemistry, QD 4

Lange's Handbook of Chemistry, QD 65

Macmillan Encyclopedia of Chemistry, QD 4

McGraw-Hill Encyclopedia of Chemistry, QD 5

Chemistry, Analytic

Encyclopedia of Analytical Science, QD 71.5

Chemistry, Technical

Encyclopedia of Chemical Technology, TP 9

Encyclopedic Dictionary of Chemical Technology, TP 9

Kirk-Othmer Concise Encyclopedia of Chemical Technology, TP 9

Chess

The Chess Encyclopedia, GV 1314.5

The Oxford Companion to Chess, GV 1445

Child care

The Disney Encyclopedia of Baby and Child Care, RJ 61

Child development

The Disney Encyclopedia of Baby and Child Care, RJ 61

The Family Encyclopedia of Child Psychology and Development, BF 721

Growing Up: A Cross-Cultural Encyclopedia, HQ 767.84

The Parent's Desk Reference: The Ultimate Family Encyclopedia from Conception to College, HQ 769

Child psychology

The Family Encyclopedia of Child Psychology and Development, BF 721

♦ The article titles in this encyclopedia are indexed by keyword in Part II.

♦ The article titles in this encyclopedia are indexed by keyword in Part II.

◆ The article titles in this encyclopedia are indexed by keyword in Part II.

Europe—Colonies

◆ Encyclopedia of the North American Colonies, E 45

Europe, Eastern

Dictionary of East European History Since 1945, DJK 50

Political and Economic Encyclopaedia of the Soviet Union and Eastern Europe, JN 96

Europe—History

The Columbia Dictionary of European Political History Since 1914, D 424

Dictionary of European History and Politics Since 1945, D 1051

Europe—Politics and government

Political and Economic Encyclopaedia of Western Europe, JN 94

European communities

European Communities Encyclopedia and Directory, HC 241.2

Historical Dictionary of the European Community, JN 15

Evolution

Dictionary of Science and Creationism, Q 123

Excavations (Archaeology)

Archaeological Encyclopedia of the Holy Land, BS 622

An Encyclopedia of the History of Classical Archaeology, DE 5

The New Encyclopedia of Archaeological Excavations in the Holy Land, DS 111

Export marketing

The International Business Dictionary and Reference, HF 1359

Facts and feasts

Religious Holidays and Calendars: An Encyclopedic Handbook, CE 6

Fairies

American Elves: An Encyclopedia of Little People from the Lore of 300 Ethnic Groups of the Western Hemisphere, GR 549

Spirits, Fairies, Gnomes, and Goblins: An Encyclopedia of the Little People, GR 549

Family

The Dictionary of Family Psychology and Family Therapy, RC 488.5

◆ Encyclopedia of Marriage and the Family: The Definitive Guide to the Challenges and Realities Facing the Modern Family, HQ 9

◆ Marriage, Family, and Relationships: A Cross-Cultural Encyclopedia, GN 480

Family psychotherapy

The Dictionary of Family Psychology and Family Therapy, RC 488.5

Family therapy

The Dictionary of Family Psychology and Family Therapy, RC 488.5

Fantastic literature

The Poe Encyclopedia, PS 2630

Fashion

Contemporary Fashion, TT 505

The Illustrated Encyclopaedia of Costume and Fashion: From 1066 to the Present, GT 580

Fashion designers

Contemporary Fashion, TT 505

Feminism

American Women's History: An A to Z of People, Organizations, Issues, and Events, HQ 1115

Dictionary of Feminist Theologies, BT 83.55

The Dictionary of Feminist Theory, HQ 1115

The Encyclopedia of Women's History in America, HQ 1410

Feminist literary criticism

◆ Encyclopedia of Feminist Literary Theory, PN 98

Fencing

The Encyclopedia of the Sword, GV 1143.2

Finance

Banking and Finance, 1913-1989, HG 2481

Encyclopedia of Banking and Finance, HG 151

Encyclopedia of Business, HF 1001

The Fitzroy Dearborn Encyclopedia of Banking and Finance, HG 151

The New Palgrave Dictionary of Money and Finance, HG 151

Financial security

Encyclopedia of Financial Gerontology, HQ 1061

Firearms

The Encyclopedia of Sporting Firearms, TS 532.15

Fishing

The Dorling Kindersley Encyclopedia of Fishing, SH 411

Flowers

The Encyclopedia of Flowers, SB 403.2

Folk music

Garland Encyclopedia of World Music, ML 100

World Music: The Rough Guide, ML 3545

Folklore

◆ American Folklore: An Encyclopedia, GR 101

The Oxford Companion to Australian Folklore, GR 365

Food

The Concise Encyclopedia of Foods and Nutrition, TX 349

The Dictionary of American Food and Drink, TX 349

Encyclopaedia of Food Science, Food Technology and Nutrition, TX 349

Foods and Nutrition Encyclopedia, TX 349

◆ Foods and Nutrition Encyclopedia, TX 349

The Visual Food Encyclopedia: The Definitive Practical Guide to Food and Cooking, TX 349

Food animals

Edible Plants and Animals: Unusual Foods from Aardvark to Zambia, TX 743

Food habits

Encyclopedia of North American Eating and Drinking Traditions, Customs, and Rituals, GT 2853

Food industry and trade

Dictionary of Nutrition and Food Technology, TX 349

Encyclopaedia of Food Science, Food Technology and Nutrition, TX 349

Encyclopedia of Food Science and Technology, TP 368.2

Food of animal origin

Edible Plants and Animals: Unusual Foods from Aardvark to Zambia, TX 743

Football

College Football Encyclopedia: The Authoritative Guide to 124 Years of College Football, GV 956.8

The Sports Encyclopedia: Pro Football, The Modern Era 1972-1996, GV 955

Total Football: The Official Encyclopedia of the National Football League, GV 955.5

Forecasting

◆ Encyclopedia of the Future, CB 158

Foreign trade regulation

Encyclopedia of the North American Free Trade Agreement, the New American Community, and Latin-American Trade, HC 94

Fortune-telling

Divining the Future: Prognostication from Astrology to Zoomancy, BF 1751

France

Dictionary of the Napoleonic Wars, DC 147

Dictionary of Twentieth Century Culture: French Culture 1900-1975, GN 307

Historical Dictionary of the French Fourth and Fifth Republics, 1946-1990, DC 401

Medieval France: An Encyclopedia, DC 33.2

Free trade

Encyclopedia of the North American Free Trade Agreement, the New American Community, and Latin-American Trade, HC 94

Freedom of speech

Free Expression and Censorship in America: An Encyclopedia, Z 658

French literature

Guide to French Literature: 1789 to Present, PQ 226

The New Oxford Companion to Literature in French, PQ 41

◆ The article titles in this encyclopedia are indexed by keyword in Part II.

Health policy

Encyclopedia of U.S. Biomedical Policy, RA 395

Herbs

Encyclopedia of Herbs and Their Uses, SB 351

The Encyclopedia of Herbs, Spices, and Flavorings, TX 406

Heresies, Christian

Crimes of Perception: An Encyclopedia of Heresies and Heretics, BT 1315.2

Encyclopedia of Heresies and Heretics, BT 1315.2

Heresies, Jewish

Crimes of Perception: An Encyclopedia of Heresies and Heretics, BT 1315.2

Heresy

Crimes of Perception: An Encyclopedia of Heresies and Heretics, BT 1315.2

Hinduism

Encyclopaedia of the Hindu World, BL 1105

Historical Dictionary of Hinduism, BL 1105

Popular Dictionary of Hinduism, BL 2003

Hispanic Americans

The Hispanic-American Almanac: A Reference Work on Hispanics in the United States, E 184

Latino Encyclopedia, E 184

Historical geography

Encyclopedia of Geographical Features in World History: Europe and the Americas, G 141

History

Dictionary of Historical Terms, D 9

The Hutchinson Dictionary of Ideas, B 105

The Hutchinson Dictionary of World History, D 9

The Illustrated Encyclopedia of World History, D 9

Larousse Dictionary of World History, D 9

World History: A Dictionary of Important People, Places, and Events from Ancient Times to the Present, D 9

Worldmark Encyclopedia of the Nations, G 63

History, Ancient

A Dictionary of Ancient History, DE 5

History, Local

The Oxford Companion to Local and Family History, CS 9

History, Modern

The ABC-CLIO World History Companion to the Industrial Revolution, D 359.7

A Dictionary of Nineteenth-Century World History, D 356

Dictionary of Twentieth-Century History, D 419

Dictionary of Twentieth Century History: 1914-1990, D 419

The Facts On File Encyclopedia of the Twentieth Century, D 419

The Global Village Companion: An A-to-Z Guide to Understanding Current World Affairs, D 419

Great Events from History: Worldwide Twentieth Century Series, D 421

A History of the World in the Twentieth Century, D 421

Larousse Dictionary of Twentieth Century History, D 419

The New Penguin Dictionary of Modern History, 1789-1945, D 205

History, Modern—18th century

A Dictionary of Eighteenth-Century World History, D 286

Hobbes, Thomas

A Hobbes Dictionary, B 1246

Hockey

Complete Encyclopedia of Hockey, GV 847.8

Holistic medicine

Alternative Healing: The Complete A-Z Guide to More than 150 Alternative Therapies, R 733

The Alternative Health and Medicine Encyclopedia, R 733

Alternative Health Care: The Encyclopedia of Choices in Healing, R 733

Holmes, Sherlock

Encyclopedia Sherlockiana: An A-to-Z Guide to the World of the Great Detective, PR 4623

Holocaust, Jewish (1939-1945)

The Encyclopedia of the Holocaust, D 804

The Holocaust: A Grolier Student Library, D 804.25

Home care

◆ Encyclopedia of Home Care for the Elderly, HV 1461

Homeopathy

An Encyclopedia of Homeopathy, RX 76

Homosexuality

Broadcasting It: An Encyclopaedia of Homosexuality on Film, Radio and TV in the UK, 1923-1993, PN 1995.9

Cassell's Encyclopedia of Queer Myth, Symbol, and Spirit: Gay, Lesbian, Bisexual, and Transgender Lore, BL 795

◆ Encyclopedia of Homosexuality, HQ 76

Horses

The Encyclopedia of the Horse, SF 285

International Encyclopedia of Horse Breeds, SF 291

Human behavior

◆ Encyclopedia of Human Behavior, BF 31

Human biology

◆ Encyclopedia of Human Biology, QP 11

Human ecology

◆ Human Environments: A Cross-Cultural Encyclopedia, GF 4

The Illustrated Encyclopedia of World Geography, JF 51

Human evolution

◆ The Encyclopedia of Evolution: Humanity's Search for Its Origins, GN 281

Human geography

Dictionary of Human Geography, GF 4

The Oxford Illustrated Encyclopedia of Peoples and Cultures, GN 11

Human reproduction

◆ Encyclopedia of Childbearing: Critical Perspectives, RG 525

Language of Sex: An A to Z Guide, HQ 9

Human rights

Encyclopedia of Human Rights, JC 571

Great Events from History II: Human Rights Series, K 3240

Historical Dictionary of Human Rights and Humanitarian Organizations, JC 571

Humanitarian assistance

Historical Dictionary of Human Rights and Humanitarian Organizations, JC 571

Humanities

The Columbia Dictionary of Modern Literary and Cultural Criticism, BH 39

The Hutchinson Dictionary of Ideas, B 105

Key Ideas in Human Thought, B 41

Hydrology

The Water Encyclopedia: A Compendium of Useful Information on Water Resources, TD 351

Hygiene

The Encyclopedia of Health, RA 776.9

Hygiene, Sexual

The A-to-Z of Women's Sexuality: A Concise Encyclopedia, HQ 30

Language of Sex: An A to Z Guide, HQ 9

The Practical Encyclopedia of Sex and Health: From Aphrodisiacs and Hormones to Potency, Stress and Yeast Infection, RA 788

Hypersensitivity

Allergies A-Z, RC 522

Immunology

Encyclopedia of Immunology, QR 180.4

Imposters and imposture

Encyclopedia of Hoaxes, AG 6

Impressionism (Art)

The Thames and Hudson Encyclopaedia of Impressionism, N 6465

◆ The article titles in this encyclopedia are indexed by keyword in Part II.

♦ The article titles in this encyclopedia are indexed by keyword in Part II.

Medicine

Magill's Medical Guide: Health and Illness, RC 41

The Oxford Medical Companion, RC 41

Medicine—History

Companion Encyclopedia of the History of Medicine, R 133

Medicine, Industrial

Encyclopaedia of Occupational Health and Safety, RC 963

Medicine, Popular

The American Medical Association Family Medical Guide, RC 81

Columbia University College of Physicians and Surgeons Complete Home Medical Guide, RC 81

A Dictionary of Mind and Body: Therapies, Techniques and Ideas in Alternative Medicine, the Healing Arts and Psychology, R 733

The Encyclopedia of Alternative Medicine: A Complete Family Guide to Complementary Therapies, R 733

Home Encyclopedia of Symptoms, Ailments and Their Natural Remedies, RC 81

Mayo Clinic Family Health Book: The Ultimate Home Medical Reference, RC 81

The New Complete Medical and Health Encyclopedia, RC 81

Prevention's Giant Book of Health Facts: The Ultimate Reference for Personal Health, RC 81

The Visual Encyclopedia of Natural Healing: A Step-by-Step Pictorial Guide to Solving 100 Everyday Health Problems, RC 81

The Woman's Encyclopedia of Natural Healing: The New Healing Techniques of Over 100 Leading Alternative Practitioners, RX 461

The World Book-Rush-Presbyterian-St. Luke's Medical Center Medical Encyclopedia: Your Guide to Good Health, R 125

Medicine, Preventive

Wellness Encyclopedia: The Comprehensive Resource to Safeguarding Health and Preventing Illness, RA 776

Melville, Herman

A Herman Melville Encyclopedia, PS 2386

A Melville Encyclopedia: The Novels, PS 2386

Memory

◆ Encyclopedia of Learning and Memory, BF 318

The Encyclopedia of Memory and Memory Disorders, BF 371

Memory disorders

The Encyclopedia of Memory and Memory Disorders, BF 371

Mental health

The Encyclopedia of Mental Health, RC 437

Mentally handicapped

Encyclopedia of Mental and Physical Handicaps, RC 570

Metaphysics

Handbook of Metaphysics and Ontology, BD 111

Methodism

Historical Dictionary of Methodism, BX 8211

Mexican literature

Dictionary of Mexican Literature, PQ 7106

Mexico

Encyclopedia of Ancient Mesoamerica, F 1219

Encyclopedia of Mexico: History, Society and Culture, F 1210

Microbiology

Encyclopedia of Microbiology, QR 9

Microcomputers

McGraw-Hill Encyclopedia of Personal Computing, QA 76.15

Middle Ages

The Encyclopedia of the Middle Ages, D 114

The Middle Ages: An Encyclopedia for Students, D 114

Middle East

An A to Z of the Middle East, DS 43

Civilizations of the Ancient Near East, DS 557

The Encyclopedia of the Modern Middle East, 1800-1994, DS 43

The Middle East, DS 63.1

The Middle East: A Political Dictionary, DS 61

Middle East—Antiquities

The Oxford Encyclopedia of Archaeology in the Near East, DS 56

Middle East—Mythology

The Encyclopaedia of Middle Eastern Mythology and Religion, BL 1060

Middle West

The Encyclopedia of the Central West, F 351

Military art and science

Brassey's Encyclopedia of Military History and Biography, U 24

A Dictionary of Military History and the Art of War, U 24

The Dictionary of Modern War, U 24

Encyclopedia of the American Military: Studies of the History, Traditions, Policies, Institutions, and Roles, UA 23

Encyclopedia of Twentieth Century Conflict: Land Warfare, D 25

The Harper Encyclopedia of Military History: From 3500 B.C. to the Present, D 25

International Military and Defense Encyclopedia, U 24

International Military Encyclopedia, U 24

The Military Encyclopedia of Russia and Eurasia, UA 770

The Penguin Encyclopedia of Modern Warfare: 1850 to the Present Day, D 431

The Penguin Encyclopedia of Weapons and Military Technology, U 815

Reference Guide to United States Military History, E 181

The Soviet Military Encyclopedia, U 24

Military history

The Battle Book: Crucial Conflicts in History from 1469 BC to the Present, D 25

Encyclopedia of Invasions and Conquests from Ancient Times to the Present, D 25

The Harper Encyclopedia of Military History: From 3500 B.C. to the Present, D 25

The Reader's Companion to Military History, U 27

Warfare and Armed Conflicts: A Statistical Reference to Casualty and Other Figures, 1618-1991, D 214

Military history, Modern

Encyclopedia of Twentieth Century Conflict: Land Warfare, D 25

Mind and body therapies

The Encyclopedia of Bodywork: From Acupressure to Zane Therapy, RZ 999

Mineralogy

The Encyclopedia of Gemstones and Minerals, QE 392

Encyclopedia of Minerals, QE 355

Minerals

The Encyclopedia of Vitamins, Minerals and Supplements, QP 771

Minerals in human nutrition

The Doctor's Vitamin and Mineral Encyclopedia, QP 771

Minor league baseball

The Encyclopedia of Minor League Baseball: The Official Record of Minor League Baseball, GV 875

Molecular biology

Concise Encyclopedia of Biochemistry and Molecular Biology, QD 415

Encyclopedia of Molecular Biology and Molecular Medicine, QH 506

Molecular genetics

Encyclopedia of Molecular Biology and Molecular Medicine, QH 506

Moon

Moons of the Solar System: An Illustrated Encyclopedia, QB 401

Mormon Church

Encyclopedia of Mormonism: The History, Scripture, Doctrine, and Procedure of the Church of Jesus Christ of Latter-Day Saints, BX 8605.5

◆ The article titles in this encyclopedia are indexed by keyword in Part II.

Historical Dictionary of Mormonism,
   BX 8605.5

Motion picture actors and actresses

The International Dictionary of Films and Filmmakers, PN 1997.8

The Marx Brothers Encyclopedia, PN 2297

Motion picture industry

The Encyclopedia of Hollywood, PN 1993.5

Motion pictures

Broadcasting It: An Encyclopaedia of Homosexuality on Film, Radio and TV in the UK,
   1923-1993, PN 1995.9

The Film Encyclopedia, PN 1993.45

Motion pictures—Europe

Encyclopedia of European Cinema, PN 1993.5

Motion pictures—India

Encyclopaedia of Indian Cinema, PN 1993.5

Motion pictures—Plots, themes, etc.

The International Dictionary of Films and Filmmakers, PN 1997.8

Mountaineering

Climbing: The Complete Reference, GV 200

Encyclopaedia of Mountaineering, GV 199.85

Multicultural education

Dictionary of Multicultural Education, LC 1099

Multiculturalism

Encyclopedia of Multiculturalism, E 184

Multimedia systems

Multimedia Technology from A to Z,
   QA 76.575

Murder

Encyclopedia of Assassinations, HV 6278

World Encyclopedia of Twentieth Century
   Murder, HV 6515

Music

Benet's Reader's Encyclopedia of American
   Literature, PN 41

Concise Oxford Dictionary of Music, ML 100

Encyclopedia of Music in Canada, ML 106

Garland Encyclopedia of World Music,
   ML 100

The Guinness Encyclopedia of Popular Music,
   ML 102

The HarperCollins Dictionary of Music,
   ML 100

The Oxford Dictionary of Music, ML 100

World Music: The Rough Guide, ML 3545

Musical instruments

The Illustrated Encyclopedia of Musical Instruments, ML 102

The Oxford Companion to Musical Instruments, ML 102

Musicals

The American Musical Theatre: A Chronicle,
   ML 1711

Encyclopedia of the Musical Theatre, ML 102

Stage It with Music: An Encyclopedic Guide
   to the American Musical Theatre, ML 102

Musicians

The Beethoven Encyclopedia: His Life and Art
   from A to Z, ML 410

The Elvis Encyclopedia: The Complete and Definitive Reference Book on the King of
   Rock and Roll, ML 420

Rocket Man: The Encyclopedia of Elton John,
   ML 410

The Ultimate Beatles Encyclopedia, ML 421

Mutual funds

The Mutual Fund Encyclopedia, HG 4530

Mythology

The Encyclopedia of Mythology, BL 715

♦ Man, Myth, and Magic: The Illustrated Encyclopedia of Mythology, Religion, and the
   Unknown, BF 1411

World Mythology, BL 311

Mythology, Assyro-Babylonian

Dictionary of Ancient Near Eastern Mythology, BL 1060

Mythology, Celtic

Dictionary of Celtic Religion and Culture,
   BL 900

Mythology, Classical

The Encyclopedia of Mythology: Gods, Heroes, and Legends of the Greeks and Romans, BL 715

The Oxford Guide to Classical Mythology in
   the Arts, 1300-1990s, NX 650

Mythology in literature

Companion to Literary Myths, Heroes and Archetypes, PN 56

Mythology, Oriental

Dictionary of Ancient Near Eastern Mythology, BL 1060

Napoleonic Wars

Dictionary of the Napoleonic Wars, DC 147

Natal astrology

The Astrology Encyclopedia, BF 1655

National socialism

Encyclopedia of German Resistance to the
   Nazi Movement, DD 256.5

Nationalism

Encyclopedia of Nationalism, JC 311

Natural history

The New Book of Popular Science, Q 162

Natural products

Encyclopedia of Common Natural Ingredients
   Used in Food, Drugs, and Cosmetics,
   QD 415

Nature conservation

The Green Encyclopedia, GE 10

Naturopathy

♦ An Encyclopedia of Natural Medicine, RZ 433

Naval art and science

United States Navy: A Dictionary, V 23

Neurology

The Brain Encyclopedia, QP 376

Neuropsychology

The Blackwell Dictionary of Neuropsychology, QP 360

New Age movement

♦ New Age Encyclopedia, BP 605

New left

♦ Encyclopedia of the American Left, HX 86

New York (N.Y.)

Broadway: An Encyclopedic Guide to the History, People and Places of Times Square,
   F 128.65

The Encyclopedia of New York City, F 128.3

Newfoundland

Encyclopedia of Newfoundland and Labrador,
   FC 2154

Nonviolence

♦ Protest, Power and Change: Encyclopedia of
   Nonviolent Action from ACT-UP to
   Woman's Suffrage, HM 278

Normandy (France)

D-Day Encyclopedia, D 756.5

North America

Colonial Wars of North America, 1512-1763:
   An Encyclopedia, E 46.5

♦ Encyclopedia of the North American Colonies,
   E 45

Great Events from History: North American
   Series, E 45

**North America—Social life and
customs**

♦ American Folklore: An Encyclopedia, GR 101

Northmen

Medieval Scandinavia: An Encyclopedia,
   DL 30

Nuclear magnetic resonance

Encyclopedia of Nuclear Magnetic Resonance,
   QC 762

Numismatics

The International Encyclopaedic Dictionary of
   Numismatics, CJ 67

Nursing

Nurse's Quick Reference: An A-to-Z Guide to 1,001 Professional Problems, RT 51

Nutrition

The Concise Encyclopedia of Foods and Nutrition, TX 349

Dictionary of Nutrition and Food Technology, TX 349

Encyclopaedia of Food Science, Food Technology and Nutrition, TX 349

Encyclopedia of Nutrition and Good Health, RA 784

◆ Foods and Nutrition Encyclopedia, TX 349

Foods That Harm, Foods That Heal: An A-Z Guide to Safe and Healthy Eating, RA 784

Obesity

The Encyclopedia of Obesity and Eating Disorders, RC 552

Occultism

Encyclopedia of Afterlife Beliefs and Phenomena, BF 1311

Encyclopedia of Occultism and Parapsychology: A Compendium of Information on the Occult Sciences, Magic, Demonology, Superstitions, Spiritualism, Mysticism, Metaphysics, Psychical Science, and Parapsychology, BF 1407

Harper's Encyclopedia of Mystical and Paranormal Experience, BF 1407

◆ Man, Myth, and Magic: The Illustrated Encyclopedia of Mythology, Religion, and the Unknown, BF 1411

Occupational medicine

Encyclopaedia of Occupational Health and Safety, RC 963

Occupations

The Encyclopedia of Career Choices for the 1990s: A Guide to Entry Level Jobs, HF 5383

VGM's Careers Encyclopedia, HF 5382.5

Old age

The Graying of America: An Encyclopedia of Aging, Health, Mind, and Behavior, HQ 1064

Older Americans Almanac: A Reference Work on Seniors in the United States, HQ 1064

Ontology

Handbook of Metaphysics and Ontology, BD 111

Opera

A-Z of Opera, ML 102

The Concise Oxford Dictionary of Opera, ML 102

Harper Dictionary of Opera and Operetta, ML 102

International Dictionary of Opera, ML 102

The New Grove Dictionary of Opera, ML 102

The Oxford Dictionary of Opera, ML 102

Optics

Encyclopedia of Lasers and Optical Technology, TA 1509

Oral tradition

◆ Storytelling Encyclopedia: Historical, Cultural, and Multiethnic Approaches to Oral Traditions Around the World, GR 72

Organic gardening

Rodale's All-New Encyclopedia of Organic Gardening: The Indispensable Resource for Every Gardener, SB 453.5

Organic wastes

Encyclopedia of Garbage, TD 785.5

Orthodox Eastern Church

Historical Dictionary of the Orthodox Church, BX 230

Pacific Islands

Political Parties of Asia and the Pacific: A Reference Guide, JQ 39

Packaging

Wiley Encyclopedia of Packaging Technology, TS 195

Palestine

Archaeological Encyclopedia of the Holy Land, BS 622

The New Encyclopedia of Archaeological Excavations in the Holy Land, DS 111

Pan-Americanism

Encyclopedia of the Inter-American System, F 1410

Parapsychology

◆ Alternative Realities: The Paranormal, the Mystic and Transcendent in Human Experience, BF 1031

Encyclopedia of Occultism and Parapsychology: A Compendium of Information on the Occult Sciences, Magic, Demonology, Superstitions, Spiritualism, Mysticism, Metaphysics, Psychical Science, and Parapsychology, BF 1407

The Encyclopedia of Parapsychology and Psychical Research, BF 1025

The Encyclopedia of the Paranormal, BF 1025

Harper's Encyclopedia of Mystical and Paranormal Experience, BF 1407

The Paranormal: An Illustrated Encyclopedia, B 1031

Parenting

Parenting A to Z: A Guide to Everything from Conception to College, HQ 769

The Parent's Desk Reference: The Ultimate Family Encyclopedia from Conception to College, HQ 769

Peace movements

The ABC-CLIO Companion to the American Peace Movement in the Twentieth Century, JX 1961

Pediatrics

The Practical Pediatrician: The A to Z Guide to Your Child's Health, Behavior and Safety, RJ 61

Percussion instruments

Encyclopedia of Percussion, ML 102

Perennials

Rodale's Illustrated Encyclopedia of Perennials, SB 434

Performing arts

The Performing Arts Business Encyclopedia, KF 4290

Persian Gulf War, 1991

Encyclopedia of the Persian Gulf War, UF 500

Petroleum industry and trade

International Petroleum Encyclopedia, HD 9560.1

Pets

The Encyclopedia of the Dog, SF 422

An Illustrated Encyclopedia of Aquarium Fish, SF 456.5

Macmillan Book of the Marine Aquarium, SF 457.1

Pharmacy

Encyclopedia of Pharmaceutical Technology, RS 192

Philosophers

A Hobbes Dictionary, B 1246

A Kant Dictionary, B 2751

A Rousseau Dictionary, PQ 2042

Philosophy

The Blackwell Companion to Philosophy, B 21

◆ The Blackwell Dictionary of Twentieth-Century Social Thought, H 41

A Dictionary of Philosophy, B 41

Dictionary of Philosophy and Religion: Eastern and Western Thought, B 41

◆ Encyclopedia of Philosophy, B 41

Encyclopedia of the Enlightenment, B 802

The Hutchinson Dictionary of Ideas, B 105

Key Ideas in Human Thought, B 41

The Oxford Companion to Philosophy, B 51

The Oxford Dictionary of Philosophy, B 41

A Wittgenstein Dictionary, B 3376

Philosophy, Ancient

◆ Encyclopedia of Classical Philosophy, B 163

Philosophy of mind

◆ A Companion to the Philosophy of Mind, BD 418.3

Philosophy, Oriental

The Encyclopedia of Eastern Philosophy and Religion: Buddhism, Hinduism, Taoism, Zen, BL 1005

◆ The article titles in this encyclopedia are indexed by keyword in Part II.

Photography

The Focal Encyclopedia of Photography, TR 9

Physical anthropology

Dictionary of Concepts in Physical Anthropology, GN 50.3

History of Physical Anthropology: An Encyclopedia, GN 50.3

Physical fitness

The Encyclopedia of Health, RA 776.9

Physical measurements

Sizes: The Illustrated Encyclopedia, QC 82

Physical sciences

Encyclopedia of Physical Science and Technology, Q 123

Magill's Survey of Science: Physical Science Series, Q 158.5

Physically handicapped

Encyclopedia of Mental and Physical Handicaps, RC 570

Physics

Encyclopedia of Applied Physics, QC 5

Encyclopedia of Modern Physics, QC 5

Encyclopedia of Physics, QC 5

Macmillan Encyclopedia of Physics, QC 5

McGraw-Hill Encyclopedia of Physics, QC 5

Physiology

◆ Encyclopedia of Human Biology, QP 11

Plantagenet, House of

The Plantagenet Encyclopedia: An Alphabetical Guide to 400 Years of English History, DA 225

Plants

An Encyclopedia of Flora and Fauna in English and American Literature, PR 149

Plants, Edible

Edible Plants and Animals: Unusual Foods from Aardvark to Zambia, TX 743

Pluralism (Social sciences)

Encyclopedia of Multiculturalism, E 184

◆ Gale Encyclopedia of Multicultural America, E 184

Poe, Edgar Allan

The Poe Encyclopedia, PS 2630

Poetry

◆ The New Princeton Encyclopedia of Poetry and Poetics, PN 1021

Poets

The Oxford Companion to Twentieth-Century Poetry in English, PR 601

Poets, Irish

A William Butler Yeats Encyclopedia, PR 5906

Poisoning

Poisons and Antidotes, RA 1224.5

Police

◆ The Encyclopedia of Police Science, HV 7901

Polish literature

Dictionary of Polish Literature, PG 7007

Political action committees

Open Secrets: The Encyclopedia of Congressional Money Politics, JK 1991

Political parties

Dictionary of Political Parties and Organizations in Russia, JN 6699

Political Parties and Elections in the United States: An Encyclopedia, JK 2261

Political Parties of Asia and the Pacific: A Reference Guide, JQ 39

Political Parties of the Americas, 1980s to 1990s: Canada, Latin America, and the West Indies, JL 195

Political Parties of the Americas and the Caribbean: A Reference Guide, JL 599.5

Political science

The Columbia Dictionary of European Political History Since 1914, D 424

The Dictionary of Contemporary Politics of Central America and Caribbean, F 2183

The Dictionary of Twentieth-Century World Politics, JA 61

Dictionary of World Politics: A Reference Guide to Concepts, Ideas and Institutions, JA 61

◆ Encyclopedia of Government and Politics, JA 61

The Encyclopedia of International Boundaries, JX 4111

Illustrated Dictionary of Constitutional Concepts, JA 61

◆ The Oxford Companion to Politics of the World, JA 61

Political and Economic Encyclopaedia of South America and the Caribbean, F 1410

Political and Economic Encyclopaedia of the Soviet Union and Eastern Europe, JN 96

Political and Economic Encyclopaedia of Western Europe, JN 94

Political Dictionary of the State of Israel, DS 126.5

◆ Survey of Social Science, Government and Politics, JA 61

Worldmark Encyclopedia of the Nations, G 63

Politicians

The Encyclopedia of Revolutions and Revolutionaries: From Anarchism to Zhou Enlai, D 21.3

Pollution

The Encyclopedia of Environmental Studies, TD 9

Encyclopedia of Garbage, TD 785.5

Environment and the Law: A Dictionary, KF 3775

Polymers

Concise Encyclopedia of Polymer Processing and Applications, TP 1087

Concise Encyclopedia of Polymer Science and Engineering, TP 1087

Popes

The Pope Encyclopedia: An A to Z of the Holy See, BX 955.2

Popular culture

The Encyclopedia of Bad Taste, E 169.12

Jane and Michael Stern's Encyclopedia of Pop Culture, E 169.12

Popular literature

Beacham's Encyclopedia of Popular Fiction, Z 6514.P7

Popular music

Lissauer's Encyclopedia of Popular Music in America, ML 128

The Oxford Companion to Popular Music, ML 102

Portugal

Dictionary of the Literature of the Iberian Peninsula, PN 849

Pottery craft

Potter's Dictionary of Materials and Techniques, TT 919.5

Power resources

Encyclopedia of Energy Technology and the Environment, TJ 163.235

Wiley Encyclopedia of Energy and the Environment, TJ 163.235

Prayer

The Encyclopedia of Jewish Prayer: Ashkenazic and Sephardic Rites, BM 660

Precious stones

The Larousse Encyclopedia of Precious Gems, TS 722

Pregnancy

The A-to-Z of Pregnancy and Childbirth: A Concise Encyclopedia, RG 525

◆ Encyclopedia of Childbearing: Critical Perspectives, RG 525

Presbyterian Church

Encyclopedia of the Reformed Faith, BX 9406

Presidents

American Presidents, E 176.1

◆ Encyclopedia of the American Presidency, JK 511

Encyclopedia of the Reagan-Bush Years, JK 511

James Madison and the American Nation, 1751-1836: An Encyclopedia, E 342

The Presidency A to Z: A Ready Reference Encyclopedia, JK 511

Presley, Elvis

The Elvis Encyclopedia: The Complete and Definitive Reference Book on the King of Rock and Roll, ML 420

Printing

Graphic Arts Encyclopedia, Z 118

Prisons

Dictionary of American Penology: An Introductory Guide, HV 9304

◆ Encyclopedia of American Prisons, HV 9471

Propaganda, Communist

Encyclopedia of Soviet Life, JA 64

Psychiatry

The Encyclopedia of Mental Health, RC 437

The Encyclopedia of Psychiatry, Psychology and Psychoanalysis, RC 437

Psychical research

The Encyclopedia of Parapsychology and Psychical Research, BF 1025

Psychoanalysis

The Encyclopedia of Evolving Techniques in Psychodynamic Therapy, RC 501.4

The Encyclopedia of Psychiatry, Psychology and Psychoanalysis, RC 437

Psychoanalytic Terms and Concepts, RC 501.4

Psychoanalysis and feminism

Feminism and Psychoanalysis: A Critical Dictionary, BF 175.4

Psychoanalytic therapy

The Encyclopedia of Evolving Techniques in Psychodynamic Therapy, RC 501.4

Psychology

Companion Encyclopedia of Psychology, BF 31

Concise Encyclopedia of Psychology, BF 31

A Dictionary of Mind and Body: Therapies, Techniques and Ideas in Alternative Medicine, the Healing Arts and Psychology, R 733

◆ Encyclopedia of Human Behavior, BF 31

The Encyclopedia of Psychiatry, Psychology and Psychoanalysis, RC 437

◆ Encyclopedia of Psychology, BF 31

The Encyclopedic Dictionary of Psychology, BF 31

Gale Encyclopedia of Psychology, BF 31

The International Dictionary of Psychology, BF 31

A Student's Dictionary of Psychology, BF 31

Survey of Social Science: Psychology Series, BF 31

Psychotherapy

A Dictionary for Psychotherapists: Dynamic Concepts in Psychotherapy, RC 475.7

The Encyclopedia of Evolving Techniques in Psychodynamic Therapy, RC 501.4

Psychotic disorders

The Encyclopedia of Schizophrenia and the Psychotic Disorders, RC 514

Publishers and publishing

International Book Publishing: An Encyclopedia, Z 282.5

Quacks and quackery

Encyclopedia of Hoaxes, AG 6

Quality control

The McGraw-Hill Encyclopedia of Quality Terms and Concepts, HD 62.15

Rabbinical literature

Dictionary of Judaism in the Biblical Period: 450 B.C.E. to 600 C.E., BM 50

Race relations

Dictionary of Race and Ethnic Relations, GN 496

Radio

Broadcasting It: An Encyclopaedia of Homosexuality on Film, Radio and TV in the UK, 1923-1993, PN 1995.9

Radio programs

Same Time… Same Station: An A-Z Guide to Radio from Jack Benny to Howard Stern, PN 1991.3

Rare animals

Endangered Wildlife of the World, QL 83

The Grolier Student Encyclopedia of Endangered Species, QL 83

The Grolier World Encyclopedia of Endangered Species, QL 82

Real estate

Arnold Encyclopedia of Real Estate, HD 1365

Reconstruction

The ABC-CLIO Companion to American Reconstruction, 1863-1877, E 668

Historical Dictionary of Reconstruction, E 668

Recreation

Dictionary of Concepts in Recreation and Leisure Studies, GV 11

Recycling

The McGraw-Hill Recycling Handbook, TD 794.5

Reformation

The Oxford Encyclopedia of the Reformation, BR 302.8

Reformed Church

Encyclopedia of the Reformed Faith, BX 9406

Refuse and refuse disposal

Encyclopedia of Garbage, TD 785.5

Religion

Concise Dictionary of Religion, BL 31

Contemporary Religions: A World Guide, BL 31

Continuum Dictionary of Religion, BL 31

Dictionary of Cults, Sects, Religions and the Occult, BL 31

Dictionary of Philosophy and Religion: Eastern and Western Thought, B 41

Eliade Guide to World Religions, BL 80.2

The Encyclopaedia of Middle Eastern Mythology and Religion, BL 1060

Encyclopedia of American Religions, BL 2530

The Encyclopedia of American Religious History, BL 2525

The Encyclopedia of Eastern Philosophy and Religion: Buddhism, Hinduism, Taoism, Zen, BL 1005

Encyclopedia of Religions in the United States: One Hundred Religious Groups Speak for Themselves, BL 2520

Handbook of Denominations in the United States, BL 2525

The HarperCollins Dictionary of Religion, BL 31

The Illustrated Encyclopedia of Active New Religions, Sects, and Cults, BL 80.2

Larousse Dictionary of Beliefs and Religions, BL 31

Longman Guide to Living Religions, BL 80.2

◆ Man, Myth, and Magic: The Illustrated Encyclopedia of Mythology, Religion, and the Unknown, BF 1411

A New Dictionary of Religions, BL 31

The Oxford Dictionary of World Religions, BJ 31

Religion: A Cross-Cultural Encyclopedia, BL 80.2

Religions of the World: The Illustrated Guide to Origins, Beliefs, Traditions and Festivals, BS 80.2

Religion and literature

A Dictionary of Biblical Tradition in English Literature, PR 149

Religious broadcasting

Prime-Time Religion: An Encyclopedia of Religious Broadcasting, BV 656

Religious thought

Encyclopedia of Religious Controversies in the United States, BR 515

Renaissance

The Thames and Hudson Encyclopaedia of Impressionism, N 6465

Republican Party

The Encyclopedia of the Republican Party/The Encyclopedia of the Democratic Party, JK 2352

Retirement income

Encyclopedia of Financial Gerontology, HQ 1061

◆ The article titles in this encyclopedia are indexed by keyword in Part II.

Revolutions

The Encyclopedia of Revolutions and Revolutionaries: From Anarchism to Zhou Enlai, D 21.3

Historical Dictionary of Revolutionary China, 1839-1976, DS 740.2

Rhetoric

Encyclopedia of Rhetoric and Composition: Communication from Ancient Times to the Information Age, PN 172

Robotics

Concise International Encyclopedia of Robotics: Applications and Automation, TJ 210.4

The McGraw-Hill Illustrated Encyclopedia of Robotics and Artificial Intelligence, TJ 210.4

Rock music

Harmony Illustrated Encyclopedia of Rock, ML 102

New Rolling Stone Encyclopedia of Rock and Roll, ML 102

Rocket Man: The Encyclopedia of Elton John, ML 410

Rocketry

Dictionary of Space Technology, TL 788

Romanticism

Encyclopedia of Romanticism: Culture in Britain, 1780-1830, DA 529

Rome—History

Encyclopedia of the Roman Empire, DG 270

Rousseau, Jean-Jacques

A Rousseau Dictionary, PQ 2042

Running races

National Road Race Encyclopedia, GV 1061.2

Russia

Encyclopedia of Russian History: From the Christianization of Kiev to the Breakup of the USSR, DK 36

Russia (Federation)

Dictionary of Political Parties and Organizations in Russia, JN 6699

Russia and the Commonwealth A to Z, DK 286

Russian literature

The Modern Encyclopedia of East Slavic, Baltic, and Eurasian Literature, PG 2940

Satellites

Moons of the Solar System: An Illustrated Encyclopedia, QB 401

Satire

Encyclopedia of Satirical Literature, PN 6149

Scandinavia

Medieval Scandinavia: An Encyclopedia, DL 30

Schizophrenia

The Encyclopedia of Schizophrenia and the Psychotic Disorders, RC 514

School psychology

Historical Encyclopedia of School Psychology, LB 1027.55

Science

Academic Press Dictionary of Science and Technology, Q 123

Dictionary of Science, Q 123

Dictionary of Science and Creationism, Q 123

Dictionary of Scientific Literacy, Q 123

Encyclopedia of Strange and Unexplained Physical Phenomena, Q 173

Encyclopedia of the History of Arabic Science, Q 127

Gale Encyclopedia of Science, Q 121

The Holt Handbook of Current Science and Technology: A Sourcebook of Facts and Analysis Covering the Most Important Events in Science and Technology, Q 158.5

Key Ideas in Human Thought, B 41

Macmillan Encyclopedia of Science, Q 121

Magill's Survey of Science: Applied Science Series, TA 145

McGraw-Hill Concise Encyclopedia of Science and Technology, Q 121

McGraw-Hill Encyclopedia of Science and Technology, Q 121

The New Book of Popular Science, Q 162

The Raintree Illustrated Science Encyclopedia, Q 121

Van Nostrand's Scientific Encyclopedia: Animal Life, Biosciences, Chemistry, Earth and Atmospheric Sciences, Energy Sources and Power Technology, Q 121

World of Scientific Discovery, Q 126

Science fiction

Science Fiction: The Illustrated Encyclopedia, PN 3433.4

Science fiction television programs

The Encyclopedia of TV Science Fiction, PN 1992.8

Science—History

Great Events from History II: Science and Technology Series, Q 125

Scotland

Collins Encyclopaedia of Scotland, DA 772

A Companion to Scottish History: From the Reformation to the Present, DA 757.9

Scotland—Church history

Dictionary of Scottish Church History and Theology, BR 782

Sculpture—Techniques

The Encyclopedia of Sculpture Techniques, NB 1170

Secret service

Spy Book: The Encyclopedia of Espionage, JF 1525

Secret societies

The International Encyclopedia of Secret Societies and Fraternal Orders, HS 119

Sects

Contemporary Religions: A World Guide, BL 31

Dictionary of Cults, Sects, Religions and the Occult, BL 31

Encyclopedia of American Religions, BL 2530

Encyclopedic Handbook of Cults in America, BL 2525

Handbook of Denominations in the United States, BL 2525

Self-care, Health

The Alternative Advisor: The Complete Guide to Natural Therapies and Alternative Treatments, R 733

A Dictionary of Mind and Body: Therapies, Techniques and Ideas in Alternative Medicine, the Healing Arts and Psychology, R 733

The Woman's Encyclopedia of Natural Healing: The New Healing Techniques of Over 100 Leading Alternative Practitioners, RX 461

Sex

The A-to-Z of Women's Sexuality: A Concise Encyclopedia, HQ 30

♦ Dr. Ruth's Encyclopedia of Sex, HQ 9

The Encyclopedia of Erotic Wisdom: A Reference Guide to the Symbolism, Techniques, Rituals, Sacred Texts, Psychology, Anatomy, and History of Sexuality, HQ 12

♦ Human Sexuality: An Encyclopedia, HQ 9

The International Encyclopedia of Sexuality, HQ 21

Language of Sex: An A to Z Guide, HQ 9

The Practical Encyclopedia of Sex and Health: From Aphrodisiacs and Hormones to Potency, Stress and Yeast Infection, RA 788

Sex and law

Sexuality and the Law: An Encyclopedia of Major Legal Cases, KF 9325

Sex customs

The Encyclopedia of Erotic Wisdom: A Reference Guide to the Symbolism, Techniques, Rituals, Sacred Texts, Psychology, Anatomy, and History of Sexuality, HQ 12

The International Encyclopedia of Sexuality, HQ 21

Sex in the Bible

And Adam Knew Eve: A Dictionary of Sex in the Bible, BS 680

Shakespeare, William

Shakespeare A to Z: The Essential Reference to His Plays, His Poems, His Life and Times, and More, PR 2892

Shamanism

The Encyclopedia of Celtic Wisdom, BL 900

Shells

The Encyclopedia of Shells, QL 404

Shipping

A Historical Dictionary of the U.S. Merchant Marine and Shipping Industry Since the Introduction of Steam, HE 745

Ships

Ships of the World: An Historical Encyclopedia, V 23

Shipwrecks

Shipwrecks: An Encyclopedia of the World's Worst Disasters at Sea, VK 1250

Signs and symbols

The Continuum Encyclopedia of Symbols, AZ 108

Dictionary of Symbolism: Cultural Icons and the Meanings Behind Them, AZ 108

Sikhism

Encyclopaedia of Sikh Religion and Culture, BL 2017.3

A Popular Dictionary of Sikhism, BL 2017.3

Skin

Skin Deep: An A-Z of Skin Disorders, Treatments, and Health, RL 41

Slavery

◆ Dictionary of Afro-American Slavery, E 441

Sleep

◆ Encyclopedia of Sleep and Dreaming, BF 1078

The Encyclopedia of Sleep and Sleep Disorders, RC 547

Sleep disorders

◆ Encyclopedia of Sleep and Dreaming, BF 1078

The Encyclopedia of Sleep and Sleep Disorders, RC 547

Small business

The Entrepreneur and Small Business Problem Solver: An Encyclopedic Reference and Guide, HD 62.7

Snakes

The Encyclopedia of Snakes, QL 666

Soccer

The Encyclopedia of World Cup Soccer, GV 943.49

The World Encyclopedia of Soccer, GV 943

Social change

◆ Encyclopedia of the Future, CB 158

Social conflict

Aggression and Conflict: A Cross-Cultural Encyclopedia, HM 136

Social ethics

Dictionary of Ethics, Theology and Society, BJ 63

Social history

◆ Encyclopedia of American Social History, HN 57

Encyclopedia of Social History, HN 28

Social interaction

◆ Encyclopedia of Relationships Across the Lifespan, HM 132

Social medicine

Dictionary of Medical Sociology, RA 418

Social problems

Encyclopedia of World Problems and Human Potential, HN 1

Social psychology

The Blackwell Encyclopedia of Social Psychology, HM 251

Social sciences

◆ The Blackwell Dictionary of Twentieth-Century Social Thought, H 41

The Columbia Dictionary of Modern Literary and Cultural Criticism, BH 39

The Hutchinson Dictionary of Ideas, B 105

Key Ideas in Human Thought, B 41

◆ The Social Science Encyclopedia, H 41

Social service

◆ Encyclopedia of Social Work, HV 35

Socialism

◆ Encyclopedia of the American Left, HX 86

Socialization

Growing Up: A Cross-Cultural Encyclopedia, HQ 767.84

Sociology

The Blackwell Dictionary of Sociology: A User's Guide to Sociological Language, HM 17

Companion Encyclopedia of Anthropology, GN 25

The Concise Oxford Dictionary of Sociology, HM 17

◆ Encyclopedia of Sociology, HM 17

The Encyclopedic Dictionary of Sociology, HM 17

The HarperCollins Dictionary of Sociology, HM 17

The Oxford Illustrated Encyclopedia of Peoples and Cultures, GN 11

Survey of Social Science: Sociology Series, HM 17

Sociology, Christian

The New Dictionary of Catholic Social Thought, BX 1753

Software engineering

Concise Encyclopedia of Software Engineering, QA 76.758

Encyclopedia of Software Engineering, QA 76.758

Sound recording industry

Encyclopedia of Recorded Sound in the United States, ML 102

Sound recordings

Encyclopedia of Recorded Sound in the United States, ML 102

Soviet literature

The Modern Encyclopedia of East Slavic, Baltic, and Eurasian Literature, PG 2940

Soviet Union

Dictionary of Political Parties and Organizations in Russia, JN 6699

Encyclopedia of Russian History: From the Christianization of Kiev to the Breakup of the USSR, DK 36

Encyclopedia of Soviet Life, JA 64

The Military Encyclopedia of Russia and Eurasia, UA 770

Political and Economic Encyclopaedia of the Soviet Union and Eastern Europe, JN 96

Russia and the Commonwealth A to Z, DK 286

The Soviet Military Encyclopedia, U 24

Space science

The HarperCollins Dictionary of Astronomy and Space Science, QB 14

Spain

Historical Dictionary of Modern Spain, 1700-1988, DP 192

Historical Dictionary of the Spanish Empire, 1402-1975, DP 56

Spain—Literature

Dictionary of the Literature of the Iberian Peninsula, PN 849

Spanish-American War, 1898

Historical Dictionary of the Spanish American War, E 715

The War of 1898 and U.S. Interventions 1898-1934: An Encyclopedia, E 745

Special education

Concise Encyclopedia of Special Education, LC 4007

Spenser, Edmund

The Spenser Encyclopedia, PR 2362

Spices

Encyclopedia of Herbs and Their Uses, SB 351

The Encyclopedia of Herbs, Spices, and Flavorings, TX 406

Spies

Spies: A Narrative Encyclopedia of Dirty Deeds and Double Dealing from Biblical Times to Today, JF 1525

Spirits

Spirits, Fairies, Gnomes, and Goblins: An Encyclopedia of the Little People, GR 549

◆ The article titles in this encyclopedia are indexed by keyword in Part II.

◆ The article titles in this encyclopedia are indexed by keyword in Part II.

◆ The article titles in this encyclopedia are indexed by keyword in Part II.

Dewey Decimal Index

♦ The article titles in this encyclopedia are indexed by keyword in Part II.

◆ The article titles in this encyclopedia are indexed by keyword in Part II.

◆ The article titles in this encyclopedia are indexed by keyword in Part II.

♦ The article titles in this encyclopedia are indexed by keyword in Part II.

A Dictionary of Mind and Body: Therapies, Techniques and Ideas in Alternative Medicine, the Healing Arts and Psychology, R 733

The Encyclopedia of Alternative Medicine: A Complete Family Guide to Complementary Therapies, R 733

The Encyclopedia of Bodywork: From Acupressure to Zane Therapy, RZ 999

An Encyclopedia of Homeopathy, RX 76

♦ An Encyclopedia of Natural Medicine, RZ 433

The Prevention How-to Dictionary of Healing Remedies and Techniques: From Acupressure and Aspirin to Yoga and Yogurt, RM 36

615.8

Encyclopedia of Native American Healing, E 98

615.9

Poisons and Antidotes, RA 1224.5

Toxics A to Z: A Guide to Everyday Pollution Hazards, RA 1213

616

The American Medical Association Family Medical Guide, RC 81

Diseases, R 130.5

The Encyclopedia of Genetic Disorders and Birth Defects, RB 155.5

♦ The Harvard Guide to Women's Health, RA 778

♦ Women's Encyclopedia of Health and Emotional Healing, RA 778

616.02

Home Encyclopedia of Symptoms, Ailments and Their Natural Remedies, RC 81

616.07

Encyclopedia of Immunology, QR 180.4

616.5

Skin Deep: An A-Z of Skin Disorders, Treatments, and Health, RL 41

616.8

The Encyclopedia of Sleep and Sleep Disorders, RC 547

616.85

The Encyclopedia of Depression, RC 537

Encyclopedia of Mental and Physical Handicaps, RC 570

The Encyclopedia of Obesity and Eating Disorders, RC 552

616.89

A Dictionary for Psychotherapists: Dynamic Concepts in Psychotherapy, RC 475.7

The Dictionary of Family Psychology and Family Therapy, RC 488.5

The Encyclopedia of Evolving Techniques in Psychodynamic Therapy, RC 501.4

The Encyclopedia of Mental Health, RC 437

The Encyclopedia of Psychiatry, Psychology and Psychoanalysis, RC 437

The Encyclopedia of Schizophrenia and the Psychotic Disorders, RC 514

Psychoanalytic Terms and Concepts, RC 501.4

616.97

Allergies A-Z, RC 522

Encyclopedia of Allergy and Environmental Illness: A Self-Help Approach, RC 584

616.994

The Cancer Dictionary, RC 262

Encyclopedia of Cancer, RC 262

617.8

Encyclopedia of Deafness and Hearing Disorders, RF 290

618.2

The A-to-Z of Pregnancy and Childbirth: A Concise Encyclopedia, RG 525

♦ Encyclopedia of Childbearing: Critical Perspectives, RG 525

618.92

The Disney Encyclopedia of Baby and Child Care, RJ 61

The Practical Pediatrician: The A to Z Guide to Your Child's Health, Behavior and Safety, RJ 61

620

Magill's Survey of Science: Applied Science Series, TA 145

McGraw-Hill Encyclopedia of Engineering, TA 9

620.1

Concise Encyclopedia of Composite Materials, TA 418.9

Concise Encyclopedia of Materials Economics, Policy and Management, TA 402

The Encyclopedia of Advanced Materials, TA 404.8

International Encyclopedia of Composites, TA 418.9

620.11

Concise Encyclopedia of Building and Construction Materials, TA 402

Materials Handbook: An Encyclopedia for Purchasing Agents, Engineers, Executives, and Foremen, TA 402

621.36

Encyclopedia of Lasers and Optical Technology, TA 1509

621.381

Concise Encyclopedia of Magnetic and Superconducting Materials, TK 7871.85

Encyclopedia of Electronics, TK 7804

International Encyclopedia of Integrated Circuits, TK 7874

621.3841

Amateur Radio Encyclopedia, TK 9956

621.89

Encyclopedia of Tribology, TJ 1075

623

The Penguin Encyclopedia of Weapons and Military Technology, U 815

623.8

Ships of the World: An Historical Encyclopedia, V 23

628

Concise Encyclopedia of Environmental Systems, GE 10

The Facts On File Dictionary of Environmental Science, TD 9

McGraw-Hill Encyclopedia of Environmental Science and Engineering, GE 10

McGraw-Hill Encyclopedia of Environmental Sciences, QH 540

628.4

Encyclopedia of Garbage, TD 785.5

629.1

The Illustrated Encyclopedia of General Aviation, TL 509

629.228

National Road Race Encyclopedia, GV 1061.2

629.4

Dictionary of Space Technology, TL 788

629.8

Concise International Encyclopedia of Robotics: Applications and Automation, TJ 210.4

The McGraw-Hill Illustrated Encyclopedia of Robotics and Artificial Intelligence, TJ 210.4

630

Encyclopedia of Agricultural Science, S 411

635

The American Horticultural Society Encyclopedia of Gardening, SB 450.95

635.0484

Rodale's All-New Encyclopedia of Organic Gardening: The Indispensable Resource for Every Gardener, SB 453.5

635.9

The Encyclopedia of Flowers, SB 403.2

Rodale's Illustrated Encyclopedia of Perennials, SB 434

The Wise Garden Encyclopedia, SB 450.95

636.1

The Encyclopedia of the Horse, SF 285

♦ The article titles in this encyclopedia are indexed by keyword in Part II.

◆ The article titles in this encyclopedia are indexed by keyword in Part II.

A Melville Encyclopedia: The Novels, PS 2386

A Nathaniel Hawthorne Encyclopedia, PS 1880

A Stephen Crane Encyclopedia, PS 1449

The Vonnegut Encyclopedia: An Authorized Compendium, PS 3572

818

Mark Twain A to Z: The Essential Reference to His Life and Writings, PS 1331

The Mark Twain Encyclopedia, PS 1330

The Poe Encyclopedia, PS 2630

820

The Oxford Companion to Twentieth-Century Literature in English, PR 471

820.9

A Dictionary of Biblical Tradition in English Literature, PR 149

An Encyclopedia of Flora and Fauna in English and American Literature, PR 149

Encyclopedia of Literature and Criticism, PN 81

Encyclopedia of Post-Colonial Literatures in English, PR 9080

The Oxford Companion to Australian Literature, PR 9600.2

The Oxford Companion to English Literature, PR 19

The Oxford Companion to Irish Literature, PR 8706

The Oxford Illustrated Literary Guide to Great Britain and Ireland, PR 109

821

The Oxford Companion to Twentieth-Century Poetry in English, PR 601

The Spenser Encyclopedia, PR 2362

A William Butler Yeats Encyclopedia, PR 5906

822.3

Shakespeare A to Z: The Essential Reference to His Plays, His Poems, His Life and Times, and More, PR 2892

823

Agatha Christie A to Z: The Essential Reference to Her Life and Writings, PR 6005

James Joyce A to Z: The Essential Reference to the Life and Work, PR 6019

Virginia Woolf A to Z: A Comprehensive Reference for Students, Teachers and Common Readers to Her Life, Work and Critical Reception, PR 6045

A William Somerset Maugham Encyclopedia, PR 6025

823.8

Encyclopedia Sherlockiana: An A-to-Z Guide to the World of the Great Detective, PR 4623

828

The Samuel Johnson Encyclopedia, PR 3532

830.3

The Oxford Companion to German Literature, PT 41

830.9

The Feminist Encyclopedia of German Literature, PT 41

840.3

Guide to French Literature: 1789 to Present, PQ 226

840.9

The New Oxford Companion to Literature in French, PQ 41

843

The Jules Verne Encyclopedia, PQ 2469

848.509

A Rousseau Dictionary, PQ 2042

850.3

Dictionary of Italian Literature, P 24

850.9

Feminist Encyclopedia of Italian Literature, PQ 4063

860

Dictionary of the Literature of the Iberian Peninsula, PN 849

860.09

Encyclopedia of Latin American Literature, PQ 7081

860.9

Dictionary of Mexican Literature, PQ 7106

Dictionary of Twentieth-Century Cuban Literature, PQ 7378

880.9

The Concise Oxford Companion to Classical Literature, PA 31

The Oxford Companion to Classical Literature, PA 31

891.1

Encyclopedia of Indian Literature, PK 2902

891.7

The Modern Encyclopedia of East Slavic, Baltic, and Eurasian Literature, PG 2940

891.8

Dictionary of Polish Literature, PG 7007

897

Dictionary of Native American Literature, PM 155

903

Dictionary of Historical Terms, D 9

The Hutchinson Dictionary of World History, D 9

The Illustrated Encyclopedia of World History, D 9

Larousse Dictionary of World History, D 9

The New Penguin Dictionary of Modern History, 1789-1945, D 205

World History: A Dictionary of Important People, Places, and Events from Ancient Times to the Present, D 9

Worldmark Encyclopedia of the Nations, G 63

904.7

Warfare and Armed Conflicts: A Statistical Reference to Casualty and Other Figures, 1618-1991, D 214

909

The New Standard Jewish Encyclopedia, DS 102.8

909.07

The Encyclopedia of the Middle Ages, D 114

The Middle Ages: An Encyclopedia for Students, D 114

909.08

The Encyclopedia of Revolutions and Revolutionaries: From Anarchism to Zhou Enlai, D 21.3

909.09

Encyclopedia of the Second World, D 847

909.097

Dictionary of the British Empire and Commonwealth, DA 16

909.0972

Dictionary of Third World Terms, HC 59.7

The Encyclopedia of the Third World, HC 59.7

909.7

A Dictionary of Eighteenth-Century World History, D 286

909.81

A Dictionary of Nineteenth-Century World History, D 356

909.8103

The ABC-CLIO World History Companion to the Industrial Revolution, D 359.7

909.82

Almanac of Modern Terrorism, HV 6431

Dictionary of Twentieth-Century History, D 419

Dictionary of Twentieth Century History: 1914-1990, D 419

Encyclopedia of the Cold War, D 843

The Facts On File Encyclopedia of the Twentieth Century, D 419

The Global Village Companion: An A-to-Z Guide to Understanding Current World Affairs, D 419

♦ The article titles in this encyclopedia are indexed by keyword in Part II.

The Encyclopedia of the Third Reich, DD 256.5

944

Medieval France: An Encyclopedia, DC 33.2

944.082

Historical Dictionary of the French Fourth and Fifth Republics, 1946-1990, DC 401

946

Historical Dictionary of Modern Spain, 1700-1988, DP 192

Historical Dictionary of the Spanish Empire, 1402-1975, DP 56

947

Encyclopedia of Russian History: From the Christianization of Kiev to the Breakup of the USSR, DK 36

Political and Economic Encyclopaedia of the Soviet Union and Eastern Europe, JN 96

947.08

Dictionary of East European History Since 1945, DJK 50

947.084

Encyclopedia of Soviet Life, JA 64

947.085

Russia and the Commonwealth A to Z, DK 286

948.02

Medieval Scandinavia: An Encyclopedia, DL 30

949.5

The Oxford Dictionary of Byzantium, DF 521

951

Historical Dictionary of Revolutionary China, 1839-1976, DS 740.2

951.9

Historical Dictionary of the Republic of Korea, DS 909

951.904

Historical Dictionary of the Korean War, DS 918

The Korean War: An Encyclopedia, DS 918

952

The Encyclopedia of Japan: Japanese History and Culture, from Abacus to Zori, DS 805

Japan: An Illustrated Encyclopedia, DS 805

Japan Encyclopedia, DS 805

956

An A to Z of the Middle East, DS 43

The Encyclopedia of the Modern Middle East, 1800-1994, DS 43

The Middle East, DS 63.1

The Middle East: A Political Dictionary, DS 61

956.7044

Encyclopedia of the Persian Gulf War, UF 500

956.94

Historical Dictionary of Israel, DS 126.5

Political Dictionary of the State of Israel, DS 126.5

959.05

Dictionary of the Modern Politics of South-East Asia, DS 518.1

959.704

Encyclopedia of the Vietnam War, DS 557.7

970

American Indians, E 76.2

Colonial Wars of North America, 1512-1763: An Encyclopedia, E 46.5

Great Events from History: North American Series, E 45

970.004

The Encyclopedia of North American Indians, E 76.2

Encyclopedia of North American Indians: Native American History, Culture, and Life from Paleo-Indians to the Present, E 76.2

◆ Native America in the Twentieth Century: An Encyclopedia, E 76.2

The Native North American Almanac, E 77

The Native Tribes of North America: A Concise Encyclopedia, E 76.2

Scholastic Encyclopedia of the North American Indian, E 76.2

World Dance: The Language of Native American Culture, E 76.2

970.01

Legend and Lore of the Americas Before 1492: An Encyclopedia of Visitors, Explorers and Immigrants, E 61

970.015

◆ The Christopher Columbus Encyclopedia, E 111

Columbus Dictionary, E 111

971.8

Encyclopedia of Newfoundland and Labrador, FC 2154

972

Encyclopedia of Ancient Mesoamerica, F 1219

Encyclopedia of Mexico: History, Society and Culture, F 1210

972.8

The Dictionary of Contemporary Politics of Central America and Caribbean, F 2183

Indians of Central and South America: An Ethnohistorical Dictionary, F 1434

973

◆ Dictionary of American History, E 174

Encyclopedia of American History, E 174.5

Encyclopedia of Rural America: The Land and People, E 169.12

The Encyclopedia of the Far West, F 591

◆ Encyclopedia of the United States in the Twentieth Century, E 740.7

The Encyclopedic Dictionary of American History, E 174

Facts About the States, E 180

Great Events from History: American Series, E 178

◆ The Reader's Companion to American History, E 174

Reference Guide to United States Military History, E 181

Worldmark Encyclopedia of the States, E 156

973.0468

The Hispanic-American Almanac: A Reference Work on Hispanics in the United States, E 184

Latino Encyclopedia, E 184

973.04924

Jewish-American History and Culture: An Encyclopedia, E 184

973.0495

The Asian American Encyclopedia, E 184

Japanese American History: An A-to-Z Reference from 1868 to the Present, E 184

973.0496

The African American Encyclopedia, E 185

◆ The Encyclopedia of African-American Culture and History, E 185

The Encyclopedia of African-American Heritage, E 185

973.3

The American Revolution, 1775-1783: An Encyclopedia, E 208

The Blackwell Encyclopedia of the American Revolution, E 208

Encyclopedia of the American Revolution, E 208

973.4

James Madison and the American Nation, 1751-1836: An Encyclopedia, E 342

973.5

Encyclopedia of the War of 1812, E 354

973.7

The American Civil War: A Multicultural Encyclopedia, E 456

973.713

Encyclopedia of the Confederacy, E 487

973.8

The ABC-CLIO Companion to American Reconstruction, 1863-1877, E 668

◆ The article titles in this encyclopedia are indexed by keyword in Part II.

Publishers Index

This index is arranged alphabetically by publisher code. (The code is a shortened form of the publisher's name.) The full name of the publisher appears under the publisher code if it is not identical to the code. Address, phone and fax numbers, URL, and e-mail address are given for each publisher, followed by an alphabetical list of publications.

ABC-CLIO
130 Cremona Drive
POB 1911
Santa Barbara, CA 93116-1911
805-968-1911; 800-368-6868; fax 805-685-9685
www.abc-clio.com
library@abc-clio.com

The ABC-CLIO Companion to American Reconstruction, 1863-1877, E 668

The ABC-CLIO Companion to the 1960s Counterculture in America, E 169.02

The ABC-CLIO Companion to the American Labor Movement, HD 6508

The ABC-CLIO Companion to the American Peace Movement in the Twentieth Century, JX 1961

The ABC-CLIO Companion to the Civil Rights Movement, E 185.61

The ABC-CLIO Companion to the Disability Rights Movement, HV 1553

The ABC-CLIO Companion to the Environmental Movement, GE 197

◆ The ABC-CLIO Companion to the Media in America, P 92

The ABC-CLIO Companion to the Native American Rights Movement, KF 8203.36

◆ The ABC-CLIO Companion to Transportation in America, HE 203

The ABC-CLIO Companion to Women in the Workplace, HD 6095

◆ The ABC-CLIO Companion to Women's Progress in America, HQ 1410

The ABC-CLIO World History Companion to the Industrial Revolution, D 359.7

Aggression and Conflict: A Cross-Cultural Encyclopedia, HM 136

The Cowboy Encyclopedia, E 20

Education and the Law: A Dictionary, KF 4117

Encyclopedia of Allegorical Literature, PN 56

Encyclopedia of American Indian Costume, E 98

Encyclopedia of American Political Reform, E 839.5

Encyclopedia of Apocalyptic Literature, PN 56

Encyclopedia of Constitutional Amendments, Proposed Amendments, and Amending Issues, 1789-1995, KF 4557

Encyclopedia of Creation Myths, BL 325

Encyclopedia of Frontier Literature, PS 169

Encyclopedia of Geographical Features in World History: Europe and the Americas, G 141

Encyclopedia of Heresies and Heretics, BT 1315.2

Encyclopedia of Invasions and Conquests from Ancient Times to the Present, D 25

Encyclopedia of Literary Epics, PN 56

Encyclopedia of Native American Healing, E 98

Encyclopedia of North American Eating and Drinking Traditions, Customs, and Rituals, GT 2853

Encyclopedia of Rural America: The Land and People, E 169.12

Encyclopedia of Russian History: From the Christianization of Kiev to the Breakup of the USSR, DK 36

Encyclopedia of Satirical Literature, PN 6149

Encyclopedia of the Persian Gulf War, UF 500

Encyclopedia of the War of 1812, E 354

Encyclopedia of Third Parties in the United States, JK 2261

Encyclopedia of Traditional Epics, PN 56

◆ Encyclopedia of Utopian Literature, PN 56

◆ Encyclopedia of Values and Ethics, BJ 63

Encyclopedia of Women and Sports, GV 709

◆ Encyclopedia of World Sport: From Ancient Times to the Present, GV 567

Environment and the Law: A Dictionary, KF 3775

◆ Ethnic Relations: A Cross-Cultural Encyclopedia, GN 496

From Talking Drums to the Internet: An Encyclopedia of Communications Technology, P 96

The Global Village Companion: An A-to-Z Guide to Understanding Current World Affairs, D 419

Growing Up: A Cross-Cultural Encyclopedia, HQ 767.84

Guide to the Gods, BL 473

Health and Illness: A Cross-Cultural Encyclopedia, R 733

◆ Human Environments: A Cross-Cultural Encyclopedia, GF 4

The Hutchinson Dictionary of Ideas, B 105

The Hutchinson Dictionary of World History, D 9

The International Development Dictionary, HF 1359

International Relations: A Political Dictionary, JK 1226

Labor, Employment, and the Law: A Dictionary, KF 3317

Law and Politics: A Cross-cultural Encyclopedia, K 487

Legend and Lore of the Americas Before 1492: An Encyclopedia of Visitors, Explorers and Immigrants, E 61

◆ Marriage, Family, and Relationships: A Cross-Cultural Encyclopedia, GN 480

The Middle East: A Political Dictionary, DS 61

The Oxford Companion to Australian Military History, DU 112.3

Religion: A Cross-Cultural Encyclopedia, BL 80.2

Spirits, Fairies, Gnomes, and Goblins: An Encyclopedia of the Little People, GR 549

Water Quality and Availability: A Reference Handbook, TD 223

◆ Women and the Military: An Encyclopedia, U 21.75

World Encyclopedia of Cities, HT 108.5

Abingdon
Abingdon Press
POB 801
Nashville, TN 37202-0801
615-749-6000; 800-251-3320; fax 615-749-6512

Handbook of Denominations in the United States, BL 2525

Academic
Academic Press Inc.
525 B Street
Suite 1900
San Diego, CA 92101-4495
619-699-6410/orders; 800-874-6418/fax; claims; fax 619-699-6380
www.academicpress.com
ap@acad.com

◆ The article titles in this encyclopedia are indexed by keyword in Part II.

Academic Press Dictionary of Science and Technology, Q 123

Encyclopaedia of Food Science, Food Technology and Nutrition, TX 349

Encyclopedia of Agricultural Science, S 411

Encyclopedia of Analytical Science, QD 71.5

Encyclopedia of Cancer, RC 262

Encyclopedia of Dinosaurs, QE 862

Encyclopedia of Earth System Science, QE 5

Encyclopedia of Environmental Biology, QH 540.4

◆ Encyclopedia of Gerontology: Age, Aging and the Aged, RC 952.5

◆ Encyclopedia of Human Behavior, BF 31

◆ Encyclopedia of Human Biology, QP 11

Encyclopedia of Immunology, QR 180.4

Encyclopedia of Lasers and Optical Technology, TA 1509

Encyclopedia of Microbiology, QR 9

Encyclopedia of Modern Physics, QC 5

Encyclopedia of Physical Science and Technology, Q 123

Encyclopedia of Virology, QR 358

Academic International
Academic International Press Inc.
POB 1111
Gulf Breeze, FL 32562
904-932-5479
www.gulf.net/~bevon
aipress@aol.com;bevon@gulf. net

International Military Encyclopedia, U 24

The Military Encyclopedia of Russia and Eurasia, UA 770

The Modern Encyclopedia of East Slavic, Baltic, and Eurasian Literature, PG 2940

Addison-Wesley
Addison-Wesley Longman Inc.
1 Jacob Way
Reading, MA 01867
617-944-3700; fax 617-944-9351
www.awl.com

Dictionary of European History and Politics Since 1945, D 1051

The Online User's Encyclopedia: Bulletin Boards and Beyond, QA 76.9

ALA
American Library Association
50 E Huron Street
Chicago, IL 60611
312-944-6780; 800-545-2433; fax 312-944-8741
www.ala.org
vhawkins@ala.org

Dictionary of Western Church Music, ML 102

World Encyclopedia of Library and Information Services, Z 1006

Allworth
Allworth Press
10 E 23rd Street
Suite 400
New York, NY 10010
212-777-8395; 800-992-7288; fax 212-777-8261
www.allworth.com
pub@allworth.com

The Art Business Encyclopedia, N 8600

The Performing Arts Business Encyclopedia, KF 4290

AOU
American Ornithologists Union
National Museum of Natural History
Tenth & Constitution Avenue
Washington, DC 20560
202-381-5286
www.birdsofna.org

Birds of North America: Life Histories for the 21st Century, QL 681

APA
American Psychoanalytic Association
309 East 49th Street
New York, NY 10017
212-752-0450; 800-937-8000/orders
apsa.org

Psychoanalytic Terms and Concepts, RC 501.4

Aronson
Jason Aronson Inc.
230 Livingston Street
Northvale, NJ 07647
201-767-4093; 800-782-0015; fax 201-767-4330
www.aronson.com

A Dictionary for Psychotherapists: Dynamic Concepts in Psychotherapy, RC 475.7

The Encyclopedia of Evolving Techniques in Psychodynamic Therapy, RC 501.4

The Encyclopedia of Jewish Genealogy, CS 21

The Encyclopedia of Jewish Prayer: Ashkenazic and Sephardic Rites, BM 660

Encyclopedia of Jewish Symbols, BM 5

The Jewish Encyclopedia of Moral and Ethical Issues, BJ 1285

Associated Un Presses
Associated University Presses
440 Forsgate Drive
Cranbury, NJ 08512
609-655-4770; fax 609-655-8366

New Encyclopedia of Zionism and Israel, DS 149

Atrium
Atrium Publishers Group
3356 Coffey Lane
Santa Rosa, CA 95403
707-542-5400; 800-275-2606

An Encyclopedia of Homeopathy, RX 76

Baker
Baker Books
POB 6287
Grand Rapids, MI 49516-6287
800-877-2665; 616-676-9185; fax 800-398-3111
www.bakerbooks.com
orders@bakerbooks.com

Concise Dictionary of Christian Theology, BR 95

Evangelical Dictionary of Theology, BR 95

New Twentieth-Century Encyclopedia of Religious Knowledge, BR 95

Baseball America
Baseball America, Inc.
600 S. Duke Street
Durham, NC 27701
919-682-0635; 800-845-2726; fax 919-682-2880
www.fanlink.com/ba/bookstore/index.html

The Encyclopedia of Minor League Baseball: The Official Record of Minor League Baseball, GV 875

Batsford
B. T. Batsford Ltd.
see Un of Pennsylvania

The Laurel and Hardy Encyclopedia, PN 2287

The Marx Brothers Encyclopedia, PN 2297

Beacham
Beacham Publishing Corp.
POB 830
Osprey, FL 34229-0830
941-480-9644; 800-466-9644; fax 941-485-5322
beachampub@aol.com

Beacham's Encyclopedia of Popular Fiction, Z 6514.P7

Bedrick
Peter Bedrick Books Inc.
2112 Broadway
Suite 318
New York, NY 10023
212-496-0751; 800-788-3123; fax 212-496-1158

Dictionary of Historical Terms, D 9

Dictionary of the Second World War, D 740

Belknap
Belknap Press of Harvard University Press
79 Garden Street
Cambridge, MA 02138
617-495-2480

A History of the World in the Twentieth Century,
D 421

Blackwell
Blackwell Publishers
350 Main Street
6th Floor
Malden, MA 02148-5018
781-388-8200; fax 802-878-1102
blackwellpub.com
Blackwell@world.std.com

The Blackwell Companion to Philosophy, B 21

The Blackwell Companion to the Enlightenment,
CB 411

The Blackwell Dictionary of Cognitive Psychology, BF 311

The Blackwell Dictionary of Judaica, BM 50

The Blackwell Dictionary of Neuropsychology,
QP 360

The Blackwell Dictionary of Sociology: A
User's Guide to Sociological Language,
HM 17

◆ The Blackwell Dictionary of Twentieth-Century
Social Thought, H 41

The Blackwell Encyclopedia of Industrial Archaeology, T 37

The Blackwell Encyclopedia of Modern Christian Thought, BR 95

The Blackwell Encyclopedia of Social Psychology, HM 251

The Blackwell Encyclopedia of the American
Revolution, E 208

The Blackwell Encyclopedia of Writing Systems, Z 40

A Companion to Aesthetics, BH 56

A Companion to American Thought, E 169.1

A Companion to Epistemology, BD 161

◆ A Companion to the Philosophy of Mind,
BD 418.3

A Dictionary of Ancient History, DE 5

A Dictionary of Cultural and Critical Theory,
HM 101

A Dictionary of Eighteenth-Century World History, D 286

Dictionary of Human Geography, GF 4

A Dictionary of Military History and the Art of
War, U 24

A Dictionary of Nineteenth-Century World History, D 356

A Dictionary of Philosophy, B 41

Encyclopedic Dictionary of Language and Languages, P 29

Feminism and Psychoanalysis: A Critical Dictionary, BF 175.4

A Hobbes Dictionary, B 1246

A Kant Dictionary, B 2751

A New Dictionary of Religions, BL 31

A Rousseau Dictionary, PQ 2042

A Wittgenstein Dictionary, B 3376

BNA
BNA Books
1250 23rd Street, NW
3rd Floor
Washington, DC 20037-1165
202-833-7470; 800-960-1220; fax 202-833-
7490
www.bna.com/bnabooks
bnaplus@bna.com

McCarthy's Desk Encyclopedia of Intellectual
Property, KF 2976.4

Books on Demand
UMI
300 North Zeeb Road
Ann Arbor, MI 48106-1346
313-761-4700; 800-521-0600; fax 313-665-
5022

Encyclopedia of American Wrestling,
GV 1198.12

Bowker
Reed Reference Publishing Co.
121 Chanlon Road
New Providence, NJ 07974
908-464-6800; 800-521-8110; fax 908-464-
3553
www.bowker.com
info@bowker.com

Encyclopaedic Dictionary of Information Technology and Systems, T 58.5

Boydell
Boydell & Brewer, Ltd.
P. O. Box 41026
Rochester, NY 14604-4126
716-275-0419; fax 716-271-8778
www.rochester.edu/research/URPress

Dictionary of Celtic Religion and Culture,
BL 900

Brassey's
Brassey's Inc.
22883 Quicksilver Drive
Suite 100
Dulles, VA 20166
800-775-2518; 703-260-0602; fax 703-260-
0701
www.brasseys.com
brasseys@aol.com

Brassey's Encyclopedia of Military History and
Biography, U 24

International Military and Defense Encyclopedia, U 24

British Film Institute
Indiana University Press
601 N Morton Street
Bloomington, IN 47404-3797
812-855-4203; 800-842-6796; fax 812-855-
7931

Encyclopaedia of Indian Cinema, PN 1993.5

Butterworth
Butterworth-Heinemann
225 Wildwood Avenue
Woburn, MA 01801
781-904-2500; 800-366-2665; fax 781-933-
6333
www.bh.com
orders@repp.com

Dictionary of Nutrition and Food Technology,
TX 349

The Focal Encyclopedia of Photography, TR 9

Carlson
Carlson Publishing Inc.
POB 023350
Brooklyn, NY 11202
718-875-7460; 800-336-7460
carlsol3@ix.netcom.com

◆ Black Women in America: An Historical Encyclopedia, E 185.86

Carol
Carol Publishing Group
120 Enterprise Avenue
Secaucus, NJ 07094
201-866-0490; fax 201-866-8159

The Beethoven Encyclopedia: His Life and Art
from A to Z, ML 410

The Encyclopedia of Popular Misconceptions,
AZ 999

Carroll & Graf
19 W 21st Street
Suite 601
New York, NY 10010-6806
212-889-8772

The Encyclopedia of Pro Basketball Team Histories, GV 885.515

Cassell
Cassell Academic
POB 605
Herndon, VA 20172
703-661-1500
www.continuum-books.com

Broadcasting It: An Encyclopaedia of Homosexuality on Film, Radio and TV in the UK,
1923-1993, PN 1995.9

◆ The article titles in this encyclopedia are indexed by keyword in Part II.

Cavendish
Marshall Cavendish Corp.
99 White Plains Road
POB 2001
Tarrytown, NY 10591-9001
914-332-8888; 800-821-9881; fax 914-366-9888
www.marshallcavendish. com
marshallcavendish@ compuserve.com

The African American Encyclopedia, E 185

The Asian American Encyclopedia, E 184

The Encyclopedia of Health, RA 776.9

◆ Encyclopedia of Life Sciences, QH 302.5

Encyclopedia of Mammals, QL 706.2

Encyclopedia of Multiculturalism, E 184

The Encyclopedia of North American Indians, E 76.2

◆ Encyclopedia of Social Issues, HN 57

Encyclopedia of World Geography, G 133

Endangered Wildlife of the World, QL 83

The International Wildlife Encyclopedia, QL 7

Latino Encyclopedia, E 184

◆ Man, Myth, and Magic: The Illustrated Encyclopedia of Mythology, Religion, and the Unknown, BF 1411

Marshall Cavendish Illustrated Encyclopedia of Discovery and Exploration, G 175

Wildlife of the World, QL 49

Center for Strategic & International Studies
1800 K Street, NW
Suite 400
Washington, DC 20006-2294
202-775-3119; fax 202-775-3199

Dictionary of Political Parties and Organizations in Russia, JN 6699

Columbia Un
Columbia University Press
562 W 113th Street
New York, NY 10025
212-666-1000; 800-944-8648; fax 212-316-9422
www.columbia.edu/cu/cup

The Columbia Companion to British History, DA 34

The Columbia Dictionary of European Political History Since 1914, D 424

The Columbia Dictionary of Modern Literary and Cultural Criticism, BH 39

Concept
Concept Publishing Co.
POB 500
New York, NY 14592
716-243-3148

Encyclopaedia of the Hindu World, BL 1105

Congressional Quarterly
Congressional Quarterly Inc.
1414 22nd Street, NW
Washington, DC 20037-1003
202-887-8500; 800-638-1710/orders only; fax 202-887-6706

Congressional Quarterly's American Congressional Dictionary, JK 9

Illustrated Dictionary of Constitutional Concepts, JA 61

International Conflict: A Chronological Encyclopedia of Conflicts and Their Management, D 842

The Middle East, DS 63.1

Open Secrets: The Encyclopedia of Congressional Money Politics, JK 1991

The Presidency A to Z: A Ready Reference Encyclopedia, JK 511

◆ The Supreme Court A to Z: A Ready Reference Encyclopedia, KF 8742

Continuum
Continuum Publishing Group
370 Lexington Avenue
Suite 1700
New York, NY 10017
212-953-5858; 800-937-5557; fax 212-953-5944
www.continuum-books.com
contin@tiac.net

Continuum Dictionary of Religion, BL 31

The Continuum Encyclopedia of Symbols, AZ 108

Dictionary of Christian Art, BV 150

◆ Dr. Ruth's Encyclopedia of Sex, HQ 9

Encyclopedia of German Resistance to the Nazi Movement, DD 256.5

Encyclopedia of Women in Religious Art, N 7793

The International Encyclopedia of Sexuality, HQ 21

Cooperative Alumni Assn
Cooperative Alumni Association
250 Rainbow Lane
Richmond, KY 40475
606-623-0695

Cooperative-Credit Union Dictionary and Reference (including Encyclopedic Materials), HD 2954

Courage
Courage Books
125 S 22nd Street
Philadelphia, PA 19103
215-567-5080; 800-345-5359; fax 215-568-2919

The Encyclopedia of Mythology: Gods, Heroes, and Legends of the Greeks and Romans, BL 715

CRC
CRC Press Inc.
2000 Corporate Blvd, NW
Boca Raton, FL 33431
561-994-0555; 800-272-7737; fax 800-374-3411
www.foodchem.crcpress.com

The Concise Encyclopedia of Foods and Nutrition, TX 349

◆ Foods and Nutrition Encyclopedia, TX 349

Crossroad
Distributed by Sterling Publishing Co.
387 Park Avenue, S
New York, NY 10016-8810
212-532-7160; 800-367-9692 (orders only); fax 212-532-4922
www.sterlingpub.com

Dictionary of Fundamental Theology, BT 1102

Encyclopedia of Religions in the United States: One Hundred Religious Groups Speak for Themselves, BL 2520

The International Dictionary of Psychology, BF 31

Crown
Crown Publishing Group
201 E 50th Street
New York, NY 10022
212-751-2600; 800-726-0600/customers only; fax 301-857-9460
www.randomhouse.com

Columbia University College of Physicians and Surgeons Complete Home Medical Guide, RC 81

Harmony Illustrated Encyclopedia of Country Music, ML 102

Planned Parenthood Women's Health Encyclopedia, RA 778

The Pope Encyclopedia: An A to Z of the Holy See, BX 955.2

Curzon
Humanities Press International
165 First Avenue
Atlantic Highlands, NJ 07716
732-872-1441; fax 732-872-0717

A Popular Dictionary of Judaism, BM 50

Da Capo
Da Capo Press Inc.
233 Spring Street
New York, NY 10013
212-620-8000; 800-221-9369; fax 212-463-0742
plenum.com
info@plenum.com

Dictionary of Twentieth-Century Design, NK 1390

Darwin
Darwin Press Inc.
POB 2202
Princeton, NJ 08543
609-737-1349; fax 609-737-0929
darwinpress@earthlink. net

Dangerous Aquatic Animals of the World,
QL 100

David & Charles
see Sterling Publishing Co.

The David and Charles Encyclopedia of Everyday Antiques, NK 28

Encyclopedia of Allergy and Environmental Illness: A Self-Help Approach, RC 584

Dearborn
Dearborn Financial Publishing
155 N Wacker Drive
Chicago, IL 60606-1719
312-836-4400; 800-621-9621; fax 312-836-
1021
www.dearborn.com

Encyclopedia of Latin American Literature,
PQ 7081

The Mutual Fund Encyclopedia, HG 4530

Dekker
Marcel Dekker
270 Madison Avenue
New York, NY 10016
212-696-9000; 800-228-1160; fax 212-685-
4540
www.dekker.com
bookorders@dekker.com

Encyclopedia of Pharmaceutical Technology,
RS 192

Design
150 Fifth Avenue
New York, NY 10011
212-627-7000; 800-592-6657; fax 212-627-
7028

Graphic Arts Encyclopedia, Z 118

Dorling
Dorling Kindersley
95 Madison Avenue
New York, NY 10016
212-213-4800; 888-342-5357/orders only;
fax 212-213-5240
www.dk.com

The American Horticultural Society Encyclopedia of Gardening, SB 450.95

The Dorling Kindersley Encyclopedia of Fishing, SH 411

Encyclopedia of Herbs and Their Uses, SB 351

The Encyclopedia of Herbs, Spices, and Flavorings, TX 406

Encyclopedia of Medicinal Plants, RS 164

The Encyclopedia of the Cat, SF 442.2

The Encyclopedia of the Dog, SF 422

The Encyclopedia of the Horse, SF 285

The New Sotheby's Wine Encyclopedia: A Comprehensive Reference Guide to the Wines of
the World, TP 548

Science Fiction: The Illustrated Encyclopedia,
PN 3433.4

Doubleday
Doubleday & Co. Inc.
1540 Broadway
New York, NY 10036
212-354-6500; 800-223-6834; fax 212-302-
7985
bdd.com

The Anchor Bible Dictionary, BS 440

Dushkin
Dushkin Publishing Group Inc.
Sluice Dock
Guilford, CT 06437
203-453-4351; 800-243-6532; fax 203-453-
6000
www.dushkin.com

The Encyclopedic Dictionary of American Government, JK 9

The Encyclopedic Dictionary of American History, E 174

The Encyclopedic Dictionary of Economics,
HB 61

The Encyclopedic Dictionary of Psychology,
BF 31

The Encyclopedic Dictionary of Sociology,
HM 17

Eerdmans
William B. Eerdmans Publishing Co.
255 Jefferson Avenue, SE
Grand Rapids, MI 49503-4554
616-459-4591; 800-253-7521/orders only;
fax 616-459-6540
sales@eerdmans.com

A Dictionary of Biblical Tradition in English
Literature, PR 149

Dictionary of the Ecumenical Movement,
BX 6.3

Element
Element Books
160 N Washington Street
Boston, MA 02114
617-248-9494; 800-528-0275/orders only;
fax 617-248-0909
element@cove.com

The Encyclopaedia of Middle Eastern Mythology and Religion, BL 1060

The Encyclopedia of Celtic Wisdom, BL 900

The Illustrated Encyclopedia of Essential Oils:
The Complete Guide to the Use of Oils in
Aromatherapy and Herbalism, RM 666

Elgar
Edward Elgar Publishing
6 Market Street
Northampton, MA 01060
413-584-5551; fax 413-584-9933
www.e-elgar.co.uk
rhenning@e-elgar.com

A Dictionary of Econometrics, HB 139

An Encyclopedia of Keynesian Economics,
HB 99.7

Elsevier
Elsevier Science Publishing Co.
POB 945
Madison Square Station
New York, NY 10159-0945
212-633-3730; 888-437-4636; fax 212-633-
3680
www.elsevier.com
usinfo-f@elsevier.com

Concise Encyclopedia of Composite Materials,
TA 418.9

Concise Encyclopedia of Medical and Dental
Materials, R 857

Encyclopedia of Tribology, TJ 1075

En Britannica
Encyclopaedia Britannica
310 S Michigan Avenue
Chicago, IL 60604
312-347-7966; 800-323-1229; fax 312-347-
7135
www.eb.com

The Illustrated Encyclopedia of Wildlife, QL 7

Facts On File
11 Penn Plaza
New York, NY 10001
212-967-8800; 800-678-3633; fax 212-967-
9196
www.factsonfile.com

A-Z of Opera, ML 102

Agatha Christie A to Z: The Essential Reference
to Her Life and Writings, PR 6005

The Airline Industry, TL 509

Allergies A-Z, RC 522

Almanac of Modern Terrorism, HV 6431

♦ Alternative Realities: The Paranormal, the Mystic and Transcendent in Human Experience,
BF 1031

Banking and Finance, 1913-1989, HG 2481

Banking and Finance to 1913, HG 2461

The Brain Encyclopedia, QP 376

Broadway: An Encyclopedic Guide to the History, People and Places of Times Square,
F 128.65

The Cancer Dictionary, RC 262

The Chess Encyclopedia, GV 1314.5

Climbing: The Complete Reference, GV 200

Companion to Irish History, 1603-1921: From the Submission of Tyrone to Partition, DA 912

A Companion to Scottish History: From the Reformation to the Present, DA 757.9

Companion to the Industrial Revolution, HC 254.5

Cowboys and the Wild West: An A-Z Guide from the Chisholm Trail to the Silver Screen, F 596

Dictionary of Symbolism: Cultural Icons and the Meanings Behind Them, AZ 108

Divining the Future: Prognostication from Astrology to Zoomancy, BF 1751

Edible Plants and Animals: Unusual Foods from Aardvark to Zambia, TX 743

♦ The Encyclopedia of Adoption, HV 875.55

The Encyclopedia of African-American Heritage, E 185

The Encyclopedia of Aging and the Elderly, HQ 1061

The Encyclopedia of Alcoholism, HV 5017

Encyclopedia of American Education, LB 17

The Encyclopedia of American Religious History, BL 2525

The Encyclopedia of Ancient Egypt, DT 58

Encyclopedia of Ancient Mesoamerica, F 1219

Encyclopedia of Angels, BL 477

The Encyclopedia of Animated Cartoons, NC 1766

Encyclopedia of Assassinations, HV 6278

The Encyclopedia of Blindness and Vision Impairment, RE 91

The Encyclopedia of Bodywork: From Acupressure to Zane Therapy, RZ 999

The Encyclopedia of Censorship, Z 657

Encyclopedia of Deafness and Hearing Disorders, RF 290

The Encyclopedia of Depression, RC 537

The Encyclopedia of Drug Abuse, HV 5804

The Encyclopedia of Earthquakes and Volcanoes, QE 521

The Encyclopedia of Environmental Studies, TD 9

Encyclopedia of European Cinema, PN 1993.5

The Encyclopedia of Gambling, HV 6710

Encyclopedia of Garbage, TD 785.5

The Encyclopedia of Gemstones and Minerals, QE 392

The Encyclopedia of Genetic Disorders and Birth Defects, RB 155.5

Encyclopedia of Gods: Over 2,500 Deities of the World, BL 473

The Encyclopedia of Hollywood, PN 1993.5

The Encyclopedia of International Boundaries, JX 4111

The Encyclopedia of Japan: Japanese History and Culture, from Abacus to Zori, DS 805

The Encyclopedia of Memory and Memory Disorders, BF 371

The Encyclopedia of Mental Health, RC 437

The Encyclopedia of Native American Religions: An Introduction, E 98

The Encyclopedia of North American Sports History, GV 567

Encyclopedia of Nutrition and Good Health, RA 784

The Encyclopedia of Obesity and Eating Disorders, RC 552

The Encyclopedia of Plague and Pestilence, RA 649

The Encyclopedia of Revolutions and Revolutionaries: From Anarchism to Zhou Enlai, D 21.3

The Encyclopedia of Schizophrenia and the Psychotic Disorders, RC 514

The Encyclopedia of Shells, QL 404

The Encyclopedia of Sleep and Sleep Disorders, RC 547

The Encyclopedia of Snakes, QL 666

The Encyclopedia of Sporting Firearms, TS 532.15

The Encyclopedia of TV Game Shows, PN 1992.8

The Encyclopedia of Textiles, TS 1309

The Encyclopedia of the Central West, F 351

Encyclopedia of the Cold War, D 843

Encyclopedia of the Enlightenment, B 802

The Encyclopedia of the Far West, F 591

Encyclopedia of the First World, G 63

Encyclopedia of the McCarthy Era, E 743.5

The Encyclopedia of the Middle Ages, D 114

Encyclopedia of the Roman Empire, DG 270

Encyclopedia of the Second World, D 847

The Encyclopedia of the Third World, HC 59.7

♦ The Encyclopedia of Violence: Origins, Attitudes, Consequences, HM 291

The Encyclopedia of Vitamins, Minerals and Supplements, QP 771

The Encyclopedia of Women's History in America, HQ 1410

The Extraterrestrial Encyclopedia: Our Search for Life in Outer Space, QB 54

The Facts On File Dictionary of Astronomy, QB 14

The Facts On File Dictionary of Biotechnology and Genetic Engineering, TP 248.16

The Facts On File Dictionary of Environmental Science, TD 9

The Facts On File Encyclopedia of Black Women, E 185.96

The Facts On File Encyclopedia of the Twentieth Century, D 419

The International Encyclopedia of Secret Societies and Fraternal Orders, HS 119

Iron and Steel in the Twentieth Century, HD 9515

James Joyce A to Z: The Essential Reference to the Life and Work, PR 6019

Japanese American History: An A-to-Z Reference from 1868 to the Present, E 184

Key Ideas in Human Thought, B 41

Language of Sex: An A to Z Guide, HQ 9

Lissauer's Encyclopedia of Popular Music in America, ML 128

Mark Twain A to Z: The Essential Reference to His Life and Writings, PS 1331

The New A to Z of Women's Health: A Concise Encyclopedia, RA 778

The New Standard Jewish Encyclopedia, DS 102.8

Poisons and Antidotes, RA 1224.5

Professional Baseball Franchises: From the Abbeville Athletics to the Zanesville Indians, GV 875

Reference Guide to United States Military History, E 181

Religions of the World: The Illustrated Guide to Origins, Beliefs, Traditions and Festivals, BS 80.2

Same Time… Same Station: An A-Z Guide to Radio from Jack Benny to Howard Stern, PN 1991.3

Shakespeare A to Z: The Essential Reference to His Plays, His Poems, His Life and Times, and More, PR 2892

Shipwrecks: An Encyclopedia of the World's Worst Disasters at Sea, VK 1250

Skin Deep: An A-Z of Skin Disorders, Treatments, and Health, RL 41

Two Hundred Years of the American Circus: From Aba-Daba to the Zoppe-Zavatta Troupe, GV 1815

Virginia Woolf A to Z: A Comprehensive Reference for Students, Teachers and Common Readers to Her Life, Work and Critical Reception, PR 6045

Wizards and Sorcerers: From Abracadabra to Zoroastrianism, BF 1588

World Dance: The Language of Native American Culture, E 76.2

Ferguson

Ferguson Educational Publishing
200 W Madison Street
Third Floor
Chicago, IL 60606
312-580-5480; 800-306-9941; fax 312-580-4948
www.fergpubco.com
fergpub@aol.com

Career Discovery Encyclopedia, HF 5381.2

The Encyclopedia of Careers and Vocational Guidance, HF 5381

The New Complete Medical and Health Encyclopedia, RC 81

Fine Communications
60 West 66th Street
Second Floor
New York, New York 10023
212-595-3500; fax 212-595-3779
mjfbooks@aol.com

The Historical Encyclopedia of World War II, D 740

Fireside
Fireside Books
8356 Olive Boulevard
St. Louis, MO 63132
314-991-1335

New Rolling Stone Encyclopedia of Rock and Roll, ML 102

Fitzroy
Fitzroy Dearborn
70 E Walton Street
Chicago, IL 60611
312-587-0131; 800-850-8102; fax 312-587-1049
www.fitzroydearborn.com

Encyclopedia of Interior Design, NK 1165

Encyclopedia of Mexico: History, Society and Culture, F 1210

Encyclopedia of Television, PN 1992

Encyclopedia of the Essay, PN 6141

The Fitzroy Dearborn Encyclopedia of Banking and Finance, HG 151

Fortress Press
426 S. Fifth Street
Box 1209
Minneapolis, MN 55440-1209
612-330-3300; 800-328-4648; fax 612-330-3455
www.augsburgfortress.org
afp_bookstore.topic@ecunet.org

Jesus and His World: An Archaeological and Cultural Dictionary, BR 130.5

Free
Free Press
1230 Avenue of the Americas
New York, NY 10020
212-698-7000; 800-223-2348/customer service; fax 800-445-6991
www.simonsays/com/thefreepress/

The Concise Conservative Encyclopedia, JC 573

Freeman
W. H. Freeman & Co.
41 Madison Avenue
35th Floor
New York, NY 10010
212-576-9400; 800-877-5351; fax 212-689-2383
www.whfreeman.com

The Practical Pediatrician: The A to Z Guide to Your Child's Health, Behavior and Safety, RJ 61

Gale Research
835 Penobscot Building
Detroit, MI 48226-4094
313-961-2242; 800-877-GALE; fax 313-961-6083
www.gale.com/gale.html

The Alternative Health and Medicine Encyclopedia, R 733

Angels A to Z, BL 477

The Astrology Encyclopedia, BF 1655

Complete Encyclopedia of Hockey, GV 847.8

Contemporary Religions: A World Guide, BL 31

Dictionary of Twentieth Century Culture: American Culture After World War II, E 169.12

Dictionary of Twentieth Century Culture: French Culture 1900-1975, GN 307

The Dream Encyclopedia, BF 1091

Encyclopedia of Afterlife Beliefs and Phenomena, BF 1311

Encyclopedia of American Industries, HC 102

Encyclopedia of American Religions, BL 2530

Encyclopedia of Business, HF 1001

The Encyclopedia of College Basketball, GV 885.7

Encyclopedia of Endangered Species, QH 75

Encyclopedia of Global Industries, HD 2324

Encyclopedia of Hoaxes, AG 6

Encyclopedia of Literature and Criticism, PN 81

Encyclopedia of Occultism and Parapsychology: A Compendium of Information on the Occult Sciences, Magic, Demonology, Superstitions, Spiritualism, Mysticism, Metaphysics, Psychical Science, and Parapsychology, BF 1407

Encyclopedia of Strange and Unexplained Physical Phenomena, Q 173

◆ Environmental Encyclopedia, GE 10

European Communities Encyclopedia and Directory, HC 241.2

◆ Gale Encyclopedia of Multicultural America, E 184

Gale Encyclopedia of Psychology, BF 31

Gale Encyclopedia of Science, Q 121

Great American Trials, KF 220

Great World Trials, K 540

The Hispanic-American Almanac: A Reference Work on Hispanics in the United States, E 184

The Holt Handbook of Current Science and Technology: A Sourcebook of Facts and Analysis Covering the Most Important Events in Science and Technology, Q 158.5

Islam and Islamic Groups: A Worldwide Reference Guide, BP 10

Les Brown's Encyclopedia of Television, PN 1992

◆ New Age Encyclopedia, BP 605

Older Americans Almanac: A Reference Work on Seniors in the United States, HQ 1064

Political and Economic Encyclopaedia of South America and the Caribbean, F 1410

The Vampire Book: The Encyclopedia of the Undead, GR 830

The World Encyclopedia of Soccer, GV 943

World of Invention, T 15

World of Scientific Discovery, Q 126

Worldmark Encyclopedia of the Nations, G 63

Worldmark Encyclopedia of the States, E 156

Garland
Garland Publishing
19 Union Square, W
8th Floor
New York, NY 10003-3382
212-414-0659; 800-627-6273; fax 212-308-9399
www.garlandpub.com
info@garland.com

◆ American Folklore: An Encyclopedia, GR 101

The American Revolution, 1775-1783: An Encyclopedia, E 208

◆ Business Cycles and Depressions: An Encyclopedia, HB 3711

Colonial Wars of North America, 1512-1763: An Encyclopedia, E 46.5

◆ Conservation and Environmentalism: An Encyclopedia, GE 10

Dictionary of Native American Literature, PM 155

Dutch Art: An Encyclopedia, N 6941

The 1890s: An Encyclopedia of British Literature, Art, and Culture, DA 560

◆ Encyclopedia of Adolescence, HQ 796

Encyclopedia of African American Religions, BR 563

◆ Encyclopedia of American Prisons, HV 9471

Encyclopedia of Cosmology: Historical, Philosophical, and Scientific Foundations of Modern Cosmology, QB 980.5

◆ Encyclopedia of Early Childhood Education, LB 1139

Encyclopedia of Early Christianity, BR 162.2

◆ Encyclopedia of Ethics, BJ 63

◆ Encyclopedia of Feminist Literary Theory, PN 98

◆ Encyclopedia of Homosexuality, HQ 76

Encyclopedia of Keyboard Instruments, ML 102

◆ The article titles in this encyclopedia are indexed by keyword in Part II.

General

General Publishing Group
2701 Ocean Park Boulevard
Suite 140
Santa Monica, CA 90405
310-314-4000; fax 310-399-9145

Globe

Globe Pequot Press
POB 833
Old Saybrook, CT 06475
860-395-0440; 800-243-0495; fax 860-395-1418
www.globe-pequot.com
info@globe/pequot.com

Greenwood

Greenwood Publishing Group
88 Post Road, W
POB 5007
Westport, CT 06881-5007
203-226-3571; 800-225-5800; fax 203-222-1502
www.greenwood.com
bookinfo@greenwood.com

Historical Dictionary of the Spanish American War, E 715

Historical Dictionary of the Spanish Empire, 1402-1975, DP 56

Historical Dictionary of the U.S. Air Force, UG 633

A Historical Dictionary of the U.S. Merchant Marine and Shipping Industry Since the Introduction of Steam, HE 745

Historical Dictionary of War Journalism, PN 4784

Historical Encyclopedia of School Psychology, LB 1027.55

An Historical Encyclopedia of the Arab-Israeli Conflict, DS 119.7

Indians of Central and South America: An Ethnohistorical Dictionary, F 1434

International Encyclopedia of Foundations, HV 12

A Nathaniel Hawthorne Encyclopedia, PS 1880

New Kabuki Encyclopedia: An English-Language Adaptation of Kabuki Jiten, PN 2924.5

The Poe Encyclopedia, PS 2630

Political Parties of Asia and the Pacific: A Reference Guide, JQ 39

Political Parties of the Americas, 1980s to 1990s: Canada, Latin America, and the West Indies, JL 195

Political Parties of the Americas and the Caribbean: A Reference Guide, JL 599.5

Rocket Man: The Encyclopedia of Elton John, ML 410

The Samuel Johnson Encyclopedia, PR 3532

Stage It with Music: An Encyclopedic Guide to the American Musical Theatre, ML 102

A Stephen Crane Encyclopedia, PS 1449

The Television Industry: A Historical Dictionary, PN 1992.3

United States in Asia: A Historical Dictionary, DS 33.4

The United States in Latin America: A Historical Dictionary, F 1418

The Vonnegut Encyclopedia: An Authorized Compendium, PS 3572

A William Butler Yeats Encyclopedia, PR 5906

A William Somerset Maugham Encyclopedia, PR 6025

Griffin
Griffin Publishing
544 W Colorado Street
Glendale, CA 91204
818-244-1470; fax 818-244-7408
www.griffinpublishing. com

National Road Race Encyclopedia, GV 1061.2

Grolier
Grolier Educational Corp.
6 Park Lawn Drive
Bethel, CT 06801
203-797-3500; 800-356-5590; fax 203-797-3285
publishing.grolier.com

The American Civil War: A Multicultural Encyclopedia, E 456

The American West: A Multicultural Encyclopedia, F 591

Diseases, R 130.5

The Grolier Library of World War I, D 522.7

The Grolier Student Encyclopedia of Endangered Species, QL 83

The Grolier World Encyclopedia of Endangered Species, QL 82

The Holocaust: A Grolier Student Library, D 804.25

The New Book of Popular Science, Q 162

The New Grolier Encyclopedia of World War II, D 743.5

Grove/Atlantic
Grove Weidenfeld
841 Broadway
4th Floor
New York, NY 10003-4793
212-614-7850; 800-638-6460; fax 212-614-7886

The Plantagenet Encyclopedia: An Alphabetical Guide to 400 Years of English History, DA 225

Grove's
Grove's Dictionaries of Music
345 Park Avenue, S
New York, NY 10010
212-689-9200; 800-221-2123; fax 212-689-9711
www.grovereference.com
grove@grovestocktn.com

The Dictionary of Art, N 31

The New Grove Dictionary of Jazz, ML 102

The New Grove Dictionary of Opera, ML 102

Gruyter
Walter de Gruyter
200 Saw Mill River Road
Hawthorne, NY 10532
914-747-0110
www.degruyter.de/

Concise Encyclopedia Biology, QH 302.5

Concise Encyclopedia Chemistry, QD 4

Concise Encyclopedia of Biochemistry and Molecular Biology, QD 415

Hall
G. K. Hall & Co.
see Macmillan

Encyclopedia of World Cultures, GN 307

Harmony
Harmony Books
see Crown

Harmony Illustrated Encyclopedia of Rock, ML 102

Harper Perennial
see HarperCollins

The Encyclopedia of Bad Taste, E 169.12

The HarperCollins Dictionary of Biology, QH 302.5

The HarperCollins Dictionary of Economics, HB 61

The HarperCollins Dictionary of Environmental Science, GF 11

The HarperCollins Dictionary of Music, ML 100

The HarperCollins Dictionary of Sociology, HM 17

The HarperCollins Dictionary of Statistics, QA 276.14

Jane and Michael Stern's Encyclopedia of Pop Culture, E 169.12

Harper/San Francisco
1160 Battery Street
San Francisco, CA 94111-1213
415-477-4400; 800-328-5125; fax 415-477-4444
www.harpercollins.com/imprints/harper-sanfrancisco/

The Concise Encyclopedia of Islam, BP 40

Eliade Guide to World Religions, BL 80.2

The HarperCollins Dictionary of Religion, BL 31

The HarperCollins Encyclopedia of Catholicism, BC 841

Harper's Encyclopedia of Mystical and Paranormal Experience, BF 1407

Home Encyclopedia of Symptoms, Ailments and Their Natural Remedies, RC 81

HarperCollins
HarperCollins Publishers
10 E 53rd Street
New York, NY 10022
212-207-7000; 800-242-7737; fax 212-207-7145
harpercollins.com

Benet's Reader's Encyclopedia of American Literature, PN 41

Collins Encyclopaedia of Scotland, DA 772

The Dictionary of Modern War, U 24

Encyclopedia of American History, E 174.5

Encyclopedia of Major League Baseball Teams, GV 875

The Film Encyclopedia, PN 1993.45

Golf Magazine's Encyclopedia of Golf, GV 965

Harper Dictionary of Opera and Operetta, ML 102

The Harper Encyclopedia of Military History: From 3500 B.C. to the Present, D 25

The HarperCollins Dictionary of American Government and Politics, JK 9

The HarperCollins Dictionary of Astronomy and Space Science, QB 14

Harper's Encyclopedia of Religious Education, BV 1461

Parenting A to Z: A Guide to Everything from Conception to College, HQ 769

Reader's Encyclopedia of Eastern European Literature, PN 849

Russia and the Commonwealth A to Z, DK 286

Sizes: The Illustrated Encyclopedia, QC 82

Total Football: The Official Encyclopedia of the National Football League, GV 955.5

The Wise Garden Encyclopedia, SB 450.95

Harvard Un
Harvard University Press
79 Garden Street
Cambridge, MA 02138
617-495-2600; 495-2480; fax 617-495-8924
www.hup.harvard,edu
cal@hup.harvard.edu

◆ The Harvard Guide to Women's Health, RA 778

Headline
Headline Book Publications
POB 52
Terra Alta, WV 26764
304-789-2508; 800-570-5951; fax 304-789-5951
www.headline.co.uk/
terraalta@aol.com

The Paranormal: An Illustrated Encyclopedia, B 1031

Hearst
Hearst Books
1350 Avenue of the Americas
New York, NY 10019
212-261-6770; 800-843-9389; fax 212-261-6599
www.hearstcorp.com/bpub.html

The Dictionary of American Food and Drink, TX 349

Encyclopedia of Cat Health and Care, SF 447

Hilger
A. Hilger
Redcliffe Way
Bristol BS1 6NX, England
297 481

Dictionary of Space Technology, TL 788

Hodge
Hodge & Braddock
POB 1894
Palatka, FL 32178
908-722-8000; 800-775-1500/customer service
www.hobrad.com
hobrad@hobrad.com

And Adam Knew Eve: A Dictionary of Sex in the Bible, BS 680

Holt
Henry Holt & Co.
115 W 18th Street
New York, NY 10011
212-387-9100; 800-672-2054/fax; fax 212-633-0748
www.hholt.com

Alternative Healing: The Complete A-Z Guide to More than 150 Alternative Therapies, R 733

The American Political Dictionary, JK 9

The Cold War Encyclopedia, D 840

Completely Queer: The Gay and Lesbian Encyclopedia, HQ 75

The Dictionary of Twentieth-Century World Politics, JA 61

Encyclopedia of Beer, TP 568

◆ Encyclopedia of Childbearing: Critical Perspectives, RG 525

Encyclopedia of Cultural Anthropology, GN 307

◆ The Encyclopedia of Evolution: Humanity's Search for Its Origins, GN 281

The Encyclopedia of Psychiatry, Psychology and Psychoanalysis, RC 437

The Encyclopedia of the Peoples of the World, GN 495.4

The Encyclopedia of the Victorian World: A Reader's Companion to the People, Places, Events, and Everyday Life of the Victorian Era, DA 550

World History: A Dictionary of Important People, Places, and Events from Ancient Times to the Present, D 9

World Mythology, BL 311

Houghton
Houghton Mifflin Co.
215 Park Avenue, S
New York, NY 10003
212-420-5800; fax 212-420-5855
www.hmco.com/trade/

Encyclopedia of North American Indians: Native American History, Culture, and Life from Paleo-Indians to the Present, E 76.2

◆ The Encyclopedia of the Environment, GE 10

◆ The Reader's Companion to American History, E 174

The Reader's Companion to Military History, U 27

Ships of the World: An Historical Encyclopedia, V 23

Visual Dictionary of Ancient Civilizations, CB 311

Wellness Encyclopedia: The Comprehensive Resource to Safeguarding Health and Preventing Illness, RA 776

Howell
Howell Book House
1633 Broadway
7th Floor
New York, NY 10019
212-654-8184; fax 212-654-4784
www.macmillanusa.com/mgr/ howell/

An Illustrated Encyclopedia of Aquarium Fish, SF 456.5

Human Kinetics
POB 5076
Champaign, IL 61820-5076
217-351-5076; 800-747-4457; fax 217-351-2674
www.humankinetics.com
maggie@hkusa.com

Sports Rules Encyclopedia, GV 731

Humanities
Humanities Press International
165 First Avenue
Atlantic Highlands, NJ 07716
732-872-1441; fax 732-872-0717
www.humanitiespress.com
hpmail@humanitiespress.com

An A to Z of the Middle East, DS 43

Dictionary of Philosophy and Religion: Eastern and Western Thought, B 41

Encyclopedia of Indian Literature, PK 2902

Popular Dictionary of Hinduism, BL 2003

Hunter House
Hunter House Inc.
POB 2914
Alameda, CA 94501-0914
510-865-5282; 800-266-5592; fax 510-865-4295
www.hunterhouse.com
hhi@hunterhouse.com

The A-to-Z of Pregnancy and Childbirth: A Concise Encyclopedia, RG 525

The A-to-Z of Women's Sexuality: A Concise Encyclopedia, HQ 30

Hyperion
114 Fifth Avenue
New York, NY 10011
212-633-4400; 800-343-9204; fax 212-633-4833

Disney A to Z: The Official Encyclopedia,
PN 1999

The Disney Encyclopedia of Baby and Child
Care, RJ 61

The Ultimate Beatles Encyclopedia, ML 421

Indiana Un
Indiana University Press
601 N Morton Street
Bloomington, IN 47404-3797
812-855-4203; 800-842-6796; fax 812-855-
7931
www.indiana.edu/-iupress
iupress@indiana.edu

The Encyclopedia of Indianapolis, F 534

Inner Traditions
Inner Traditions International Ltd.
1 Park Street
Rochester, VT 05767
802-767-3174; 800-246-8648; fax 802-767-
3726
www.gotoit.com
orders@gotoit.com

The Encyclopedia of Erotic Wisdom: A Reference Guide to the Symbolism, Techniques,
Rituals, Sacred Texts, Psychology, Anatomy,
and History of Sexuality, HQ 12

International Labour Office
1828 L Street, N.W.
Suite 801
Washington, DC 20036
202-653-7652; fax 202-653-7687
www.ilo.org/public/english/180publn/
books.htm
washilo@ilowbo

Encyclopaedia of Occupational Health and
Safety, RC 963

InterVarsity
InterVarsity Press
5206 Main Street
POB 1400
Downers Grove, IL 60515
630-734-4000; 800-843-9487; fax 630-734-
4200
www.gospelcom.net/ ivpress
mail@ipress.com

Concise Dictionary of Christianity in America,
BR 515

Concise Dictionary of Religion, BL 31

Dictionary of Christianity in America: A Comprehensive Resource on the Religious Impulse
That Shaped a Continent, BR 515

Dictionary of Jesus and the Gospels: A Compendium of Contemporary Biblical Scholarship,
BS 2555.2

Dictionary of Scottish Church History and Theology, BR 782

New Bible Dictionary, BS 440

New Dictionary of Christian Ethics and Pastoral
Theology, BJ 1199

Iowa State Un
Iowa State University Press
2121 S State Avenue
Ames, IA 50014-8300
515-292-0140; 800-862-6657/orders only;
fax 515-292-3348
www.isupress.edu
orders@isupress.edu

The Veterinarian's Encyclopedia of Animal Behavior, SF 756.7

Irwin
Irwin Professional Publishing
1333 Burr Ridge Parkway
Burr Ridge, IL 60521
708-789-4000; 800-634-3961; fax 800-926-
9495
www.mhhe.com/irwin/
ipro@irwin.com

Inside U.S. Business: A Concise Encyclopedia of
Leading Industries, HC 106.8

John Knox
John Knox Press
100 Witherspoon Street
Louisville, KY 40202-1396
502-569-5076

Encyclopedia of the Reformed Faith, BX 9406

Johns Hopkins Un
Johns Hopkins University Press
2715 N Charles Street
Baltimore, MD 21218-4319
410-516-6990; 800-537-5487; fax 410-516-
6998
www.press.jhu.edu/press/ ind.htm

The Johns Hopkins Guide to Literary Theory and
Criticism, Z 6514

Walker's Mammals of the World, QL 703

Journey Editions
153 Milk Street
5th Floor
Boston, MA 02109
617-951-4080; 800-526-2778; fax 617-951-
4045
www.tuttle-periplus.com

The Encyclopedia of Alternative Medicine: A
Complete Family Guide to Complementary
Therapies, R 733

Kluwer
Kluwer Academic Publications
101 Philip Drive, Assinippi Park
Norwell, MA 02061
617-871-6600; fax 617-871-6528
www.wkap.com
kluwer@wkap.com

Encyclopaedia of Mathematics, QA 5

Krause
Krause Publications
700 East State Street
Iola, WI 54990
715-445-2214; 888-457-2873; fax 715-445-
4087
www.krause.com
info@krause.com

The International Encyclopaedic Dictionary of
Numismatics, CJ 67

Larousse
Larousse Kingfisher Chambers
95 Madison Avenue
12th Floor
New York, NY 10016
212-686-1060; 800-497-1657; fax 212-686-
1082

Larousse Dictionary of Beliefs and Religions,
BL 31

Larousse Dictionary of Twentieth Century History, D 419

Larousse Dictionary of World History, D 9

Larousse Encyclopedia of Wine, T 548

Lewis
Lewis Publishers Inc.
121 S Main Street
POB 519
Chelsea, MI 48118
313-475-8619
www.crcpress.com

The Water Encyclopedia: A Compendium of
Useful Information on Water Resources,
TD 351

Little, Brown
Little, Brown & Co.
1271 Avenue of the Americas
New York, NY 10020
212-522-8700; 800-343-9204; fax 212-522-
2067

Bulfinch Illustrated Encyclopedia of Antiques,
NK 30

Companion to the Cosmos, QB 14

From Archetype to Zeitgeist: Powerful Ideas for
Powerful Thinking, AG 105

Liturgical
Liturgical Press
POB 7500
Saint John's Abbey
Collegeville, MN 56321-7500
612-363-2213; 800-858-5450; fax 612-363-
3299
www.litpress.org
sales@litpress.org

The Modern Catholic Encyclopedia, BX 841

◆ The article titles in this encyclopedia are indexed by keyword in Part II.

The New Dictionary of Catholic Social Thought, BX 1753

Lowell House
see NTC

The Reagan Years A to Z: An Alphabetical History of Ronald Reagan's Presidency, E 876

Lyons & Burford
31 W 21st Street
New York, NY 10010
212-620-9580; fax 212-929-1836

The Illustrated Encyclopedia of Billiards, GV 891

M. Evans
M. Evans & Co. Inc.
216 E 49th Street
New York, NY 10017
212-688-2810; fax 212-486-4544
Mevans@sprynet.com

Spies: A Narrative Encyclopedia of Dirty Deeds and Double Dealing from Biblical Times to Today, JF 1525

Macmillan
1633 Broadway
New York, NY 10019-6785
212-702-2000; 800-257-5755; fax 800-445-6991
www.simonsays.com

The Baseball Encyclopedia: The Complete and Official Record of Major League Baseball, GV 877

The Coptic Encyclopedia, BX 130.5

Dictionary of American Foreign Affairs, E 183.7

◆ Dictionary of American History, E 174

Dictionary of Judaism in the Biblical Period: 450 B.C.E. to 600 C.E., BM 50

◆ The Encyclopedia of African-American Culture and History, E 185

◆ Encyclopedia of Bioethics, QH 332

The Encyclopedia of Britain, DA 27.5

◆ Encyclopedia of Disability and Rehabilitation, HV 1568

◆ Encyclopedia of Drugs and Alcohol, HV 5804

Encyclopedia of Earth Sciences, QE 5

◆ Encyclopedia of Educational Research, LB 15

◆ Encyclopedia of Human Intelligence, BF 431

◆ Encyclopedia of Learning and Memory, BF 318

◆ Encyclopedia of Marriage and the Family: The Definitive Guide to the Challenges and Realities Facing the Modern Family, HQ 9

Encyclopedia of Mormonism: The History, Scripture, Doctrine, and Procedure of the Church of Jesus Christ of Latter-Day Saints, BX 8605.5

◆ Encyclopedia of Philosophy, B 41

◆ Encyclopedia of Sleep and Dreaming, BF 1078

◆ Encyclopedia of Sociology, HM 17

◆ Encyclopedia of Sports Science, GV 558

◆ Encyclopedia of the American Presidency, JK 511

Encyclopedia of the American West, F 591

◆ Encyclopedia of the Future, CB 158

The Encyclopedia of the Holocaust, D 804

The Encyclopedia of the Modern Middle East, 1800-1994, DS 43

The Encyclopedia of the Third Reich, DD 256.5

The Encyclopedia of the United States Congress, JK 1067

◆ Encyclopedia of the United States in the Twentieth Century, E 740.7

Encyclopedia Sherlockiana: An A-to-Z Guide to the World of the Great Detective, PR 4623

Information Security: Dictionary of Concepts, Standards and Terms, QA 76.9

Japan: An Illustrated Encyclopedia, DS 805

Macmillan Book of the Marine Aquarium, SF 457.1

Macmillan Encyclopedia of Chemistry, QD 4

◆ Macmillan Encyclopedia of Computers, QA 76.15

Macmillan Encyclopedia of Earth Sciences, QE 5

Macmillan Encyclopedia of Physics, QC 5

Macmillan Encyclopedia of Science, Q 121

Macmillan Encyclopedia of the Environment, GE 10

◆ Macmillan Health Encyclopedia, RA 776

The Native Tribes of North America: A Concise Encyclopedia, E 76.2

The New Encyclopedia of Archaeological Excavations in the Holy Land, DS 111

Political Dictionary of the State of Israel, DS 126.5

The Visual Food Encyclopedia: The Definitive Practical Guide to Food and Cooking, TX 349

Mansell
Mansell Publishing Ltd.
199 First Street
Room 204
Los Altos, CA 94022-2708
415-941-2037; fax 415-941-5338
www.mansell.com
mansell-r@mansell.com

Cassell Careers Encyclopedia, HF 5382.5

Marlow
Marlow & Co.
841 Broadway
4th Floor
New York, NY 10003
212-614-7880; 800-788-3123/orders only; fax 212-614-7887
LeahK6263@aol.com

World Encyclopedia of Twentieth Century Murder, HV 6515

McFarland
McFarland & Co. Inc. Publications
POB 611
Jefferson, NC 28640
910-246-4460; 800-253-2187; fax 910-246-5018
mcfarlandpub.com
mcfarland@skybest.com

American Elves: An Encyclopedia of Little People from the Lore of 300 Ethnic Groups of the Western Hemisphere, GR 549

Antarctica: An Encyclopedia, G 855

The British Empire: An Encyclopedia of the Crown's Holdings, 1493 through 1995, DA 16

The Cultural Encyclopedia of Baseball, GV 862.3

Custer and the Battle of the Little Bighorn: An Encyclopedia of the People, Places, Events, Indian Culture and Customs, Information Sources, Art and Films, E 83.876

Dinosaurs, The Encyclopedia, QE 862

Former Major League Teams: An Encyclopedia, GV 875

Greek and Roman Sport: A Dictionary of Athletes and Events from the Eighth Century B.C. to the Third Century, GV 17

Moons of the Solar System: An Illustrated Encyclopedia, QB 401

Warfare and Armed Conflicts: A Statistical Reference to Casualty and Other Figures, 1618-1991, D 214

McGraw-Hill
McGraw-Hill Companies
1211 Avenue of the Americas
New York, NY 10020
212-512-2000; 800-722-4726
mcgraw-hill.com

Dictionary of Architecture and Construction, NA 31

Encyclopedia of American Architecture, NA 705

The Encyclopedia of World Cup Soccer, GV 943.49

Grzimek's Encyclopedia of Mammals, QL 701

International Encyclopedia of Integrated Circuits, TK 7874

Lange's Handbook of Chemistry, QD 65

Materials Handbook: An Encyclopedia for Purchasing Agents, Engineers, Executives, and Foremen, TA 402

McGraw-Hill Concise Encyclopedia of Science and Technology, Q 121

McGraw-Hill Encyclopedia of Astronomy, QB 14

McGraw-Hill Encyclopedia of Chemistry, QD 5

◆ McGraw-Hill Encyclopedia of Economics, HB 61

McGraw-Hill Encyclopedia of Engineering, TA 9

McGraw-Hill Encyclopedia of Environmental Science and Engineering, GE 10

McGraw-Hill Encyclopedia of Environmental Sciences, QH 540

McGraw-Hill Encyclopedia of Personal Computing, QA 76.15

McGraw-Hill Encyclopedia of Physics, QC 5

The McGraw-Hill Encyclopedia of Quality Terms and Concepts, HD 62.15

McGraw-Hill Encyclopedia of Science and Technology, Q 121

The McGraw-Hill Illustrated Encyclopedia of Robotics and Artificial Intelligence, TJ 210.4

The McGraw-Hill Recycling Handbook, TD 794.5

World Geographical Encyclopedia, G 63

Mellen
Edwin Mellen Press
POB 450
Lewiston, NY 14092
716-754-2266; fax 716-754-4056
www.mellen.com
mellen@ag.net

An Encyclopedia of Flora and Fauna in English and American Literature, PR 149

An Encyclopedia of Irish Schools, 1500-1800, LA 669.62

Mercer Un
Mercer University Press
6316 Peake Road
Macon, GA 31207
912-752-2880; 800-637-2378; fax 912-752-2264
www.mupress.org
mupressorders@mercer.edu

Mercer Dictionary of the Bible, BS 440

Merriam-Webster
Merriam-Webster Inc.
47 Federal Street
Springfield, MA 01102
413-734-3134; 800-828-1880; fax 413-731-5979
www.m-w.com

Merriam-Webster's Encyclopedia of Literature, PN 41

MIT
MIT Press
5 Cambridge Center
Suite 4
Cambridge, MA 02142
617-625-8569; 800-356-0343

www.mitpr.mit.edu
MITPR-orders@MIT.edu

Dictionary of Environment and Development: People, Places, Ideas, and Organizations, GE 10

The Encyclopedia of Land Invertebrate Behaviour, QL 364.2

The MIT Dictionary of Modern Economics, HB 61

The MIT Encyclopedia of the Japanese Economy, HC 462.9

Morrow
William Morrow & Co.
1350 Avenue of the Americas
New York, NY 10019
212-261-6500; 800-237-0657; fax 212-779-0965
www.williammorrow.com
idavis@hearst.com

Mayo Clinic Family Health Book: The Ultimate Home Medical Reference, RC 81

Multiculture
Multiculture in Print
see Gale Research

The Native North American Almanac, E 77

NAL
NAL Books/Dutton
375 Hudson Street
New York, NY 10014-3657
212-366-2000; 800-331-4625/customer service; fax 212-366-2666

A Dictionary of Contemporary American History: 1945 to the Present, E 838.6

National Book Network
4720 Boston Way
Laudham, MD 20706
301-459-3366; 800-462-6420
litchman@unm.edu

Isms: A Compendium of Concepts, Doctrines, Traits and Beliefs from Ableism to Zygodactylism, JF 51

Natl Assn of Social Workers
National Association of Social Workers
750 First Street, NE
Suite 700
Washington, DC 20002-4241
202-408-8600; 800-638-8799; fax 202-336-8312
www.naswpress.org
press@naswdc.org

◆ Encyclopedia of Social Work, HV 35

Natl Book Network
National Book Network
see Element

The Encyclopaedia of Arthurian Legends, DA 152.5

Natl Geographic Society
National Geographic Society
1145 17th Street, NW
Washington, DC 20036
202-857-7000; 800-447-0647; fax 301-921-1575
www.nationalgeographic.com

Exploring Your World: The Adventure of Geography, G 63

Nelson
Thomas Nelson Inc.
POB 141000
Nelson Place at Elm Hill Pike
Nashville, TN 37214-1000
615-889-9000; 708-331-7172; 800-448-8403/fax; fax 615-391-5225
www.nelson.co.uk/

Encyclopedia of Biblical and Christian Ethics, BJ 1199

Norton
W. W. Norton & Co.
500 Fifth Avenue
New York, NY 10010
212-354-5500; 800-233-4830; fax 212-869-0856
www.wwnorton.com

The Thames and Hudson Encyclopaedia of Twentieth Century Design and Designers, NK 1390

Nova Science
Nova Science Publications Inc.
6080 Jericho Turnpike
Suite 207
Commack, NY 11725-2808
516-499-3103; fax 516-499-3146
novasci@aol.com

An Encyclopedia of Famous Suicides, HV 6545

NTC
NTC Publishing Group
4255 W Touhy Avenue
Lincolnwood, IL 60646-1975
847-679-5500; 800-323-4900; fax 847-679-2494
www.ntc-contemporary.com
NTCPUB@Tribune.com

A Popular Dictionary of Sikhism, BL 2017.3

◆ The article titles in this encyclopedia are indexed by keyword in Part II.

Ohio State Un
Ohio State University Press
1070 Carmack Road
Pressey Hall, Room 180
Columbus, OH 43210-1002
614-292-6930; fax 614-292-2065
www.ohiostatepress.org
mbucy@magnus.acs.ohio- state.edu
The Dictionary of Feminist Theory, HQ 1115

Omnigraphics
2400 Penobscot Building
Detroit, MI 48226
313-961-1340; 800-234-1340; fax 313-961-
** 1383**
Columbus Dictionary, E 111
Religious Holidays and Calendars: An Encyclopedic Handbook, CE 6
The UFO Encyclopedia, TL 789

Oryx
Oryx Press
4041 N Central Avenue
Suite 700
Phoenix, AZ 85012-3397
602-265-2651; 800-279-6799; fax 800-279-
** 4663**
www.oryxpress.com
info@oryxpress.com
Dictionary of Multicultural Education, LC 1099
◆ Encyclopedia of Adult Development, BF 724.5
Encyclopedia of Career Change and Work Issues, HF 5381
Multimedia Technology from A to Z, QA 76.575
Prime-Time Religion: An Encyclopedia of Religious Broadcasting, BV 656
◆ Storytelling Encyclopedia: Historical, Cultural, and Multiethnic Approaches to Oral Traditions Around the World, GR 72

Our Sunday Visitor
200 Noll Plaza
Huntington, IN 46750
219-356-8400; 800-348-2440; fax 219-356-
** 8472**
osvsales@aol.com
Our Sunday Visitor's Catholic Encyclopedia, BX 841

Oxford Un
Oxford University Press
198 Madison Avenue
New York, NY 10016-4314
212-726-6000; 800-451-7556; fax 212-726-
** 6455**
www.oup-usa.org
egr@oup.usa.org
The American Musical Theatre: A Chronicle, ML 1711
Biotechnology from A to Z, TP 248.16

The Concise Oxford Companion to Classical Literature, PA 31
The Concise Oxford Companion to the Theatre, PN 2035
The Concise Oxford Dictionary of Art and Artists, N 3
The Concise Oxford Dictionary of Earth Sciences, QE 5
The Concise Oxford Dictionary of Ecology, QH 540.4
The Concise Oxford Dictionary of Geography, G 63
Concise Oxford Dictionary of Music, ML 100
The Concise Oxford Dictionary of Opera, ML 102
The Concise Oxford Dictionary of Sociology, HM 17
Concise Oxford Dictionary of Zoology, QL 9
Dictionary of the Ancient Greek World, DF 16
Dictionary of Twentieth Century History: 1914-1990, D 419
Encyclopedia of Climate and Weather, QC 854
Encyclopedia of the Early Church, BR 66.5
Encyclopedia of U.S. Foreign Relations, E 183.7
The Illustrated Encyclopedia of World Geography, JF 51
International Encyclopedia of Linguistics, P 29
The International Encyclopedia of World Geography: Comparative Government, JF 51
The Jewish Religion: A Companion, BM 50
The New Oxford Companion to Literature in French, PQ 41
The Oxford Classical Dictionary, DE 5
The Oxford Companion to African American Literature, PS 153
The Oxford Companion to American Literature, PS 21
The Oxford Companion to American Theatre, PN 2220
The Oxford Companion to Archaeology, CC 78
The Oxford Companion to Australian Folklore, GR 365
The Oxford Companion to Australian Literature, PR 9600.2
The Oxford Companion to Australian Sport, GV 675
The Oxford Companion to Chess, GV 1445
The Oxford Companion to Christian Art and Architecture, N 7830
The Oxford Companion to Classical Literature, PA 31
The Oxford Companion to English Literature, PR 19
The Oxford Companion to German Literature, PT 41
The Oxford Companion to Irish Literature, PR 8706
The Oxford Companion to Local and Family History, CS 9

The Oxford Companion to Musical Instruments, ML 102
The Oxford Companion to Philosophy, B 51
◆ The Oxford Companion to Politics of the World, JA 61
The Oxford Companion to Popular Music, ML 102
The Oxford Companion to the Bible, BS 440
The Oxford Companion to the English Language, PE 31
◆ The Oxford Companion to the Supreme Court of the United States, KF 8742
The Oxford Companion to the Theatre, PN 2035
The Oxford Companion to Twentieth-Century Literature in English, PR 471
The Oxford Companion to Twentieth-Century Poetry in English, PR 601
The Oxford Companion to Wine, TP 548
The Oxford Companion to Women's Writing in the United States, PS 147
The Oxford Companion to World War II, D 740
The Oxford Dictionary of Byzantium, DF 521
The Oxford Dictionary of Music, ML 100
The Oxford Dictionary of Opera, ML 102
The Oxford Dictionary of Philosophy, B 41
The Oxford Dictionary of the Christian Church, BR 95
The Oxford Dictionary of the Jewish Religion, BM 50
The Oxford Dictionary of World Religions, BJ 31
The Oxford Encyclopedia of Archaeology in the Near East, DS 56
The Oxford Encyclopedia of European Community Law, KH 926
The Oxford Encyclopedia of the Modern Islamic World, DS 35.53
The Oxford Encyclopedia of the Reformation, BR 302.8
The Oxford Guide to Classical Mythology in the Arts, 1300-1990s, NX 650
The Oxford Illustrated Dictionary of Australian History, DU 90
The Oxford Illustrated Encyclopedia of Invention and Technology, T 9
The Oxford Illustrated Encyclopedia of Peoples and Cultures, GN 11
The Oxford Illustrated Encyclopedia of the Arts, NX 70
The Oxford Illustrated Encyclopedia of the Universe, AE 5
The Oxford Illustrated Literary Guide to Great Britain and Ireland, PR 109
The Oxford Medical Companion, RC 41

Paragon
Paragon House Publications
2700 University Avenue, W
Suite 47
Saint Paul, MN 55114-1016
612-644-3087; 877-747-2665; fax 612-644-
0997
www.paragonhouse.com
paragon@paragonhouse.com

Crimes of Perception: An Encyclopedia of Heresies and Heretics, BT 1315.2

The Encyclopedia of Amazons: Women Warriors from Antiquity to the Modern Era, U 51

Encyclopedia of Nationalism, JC 311

The Encyclopedia of Parapsychology and Psychical Research, BF 1025

World Encyclopedia of Organized Crime, HV 6017

Passport
Passport Books
4255 W Touhy Avenue
Lincolnwood, IL 60646-1975
847-679-5500; 800-323-4900; fax 847-674-
2494

Japan Encyclopedia, DS 805

Penguin
Penguin Books
see Viking Penguin

Cat World: A Feline Encyclopedia, SF 442.2

Encyclopaedia of Mountaineering, GV 199.85

The Illustrated Encyclopedia of Divination: A Practical Guide to the Systems That Can Reveal Your Destiny, BF 1751

The New Penguin Dictionary of Modern History, 1789-1945, D 205

The Penguin Dictionary of Architecture, NA 31

The Penguin Dictionary of Economics, HB 61

The Penguin Encyclopedia of Modern Warfare: 1850 to the Present Day, D 431

Total Baseball: The Ultimate Encyclopedia of Baseball, GV 863

World Music: The Rough Guide, ML 3545

PennWell
PennWell Books
1421 S Sheridan Road
Tulsa, OK 74112
918-835-3161; 800-752-9764/orders only;
fax 918-831-9555
www.energycatalog.com

International Petroleum Encyclopedia, HD 9560.1

Pergamon
Pergamon Press
660 White Plains Road
Tarrytown, NY 10591-5153
914-524-9200; fax 914-333-2444

Concise Encyclopedia of Biological and Biomedical Measurement Systems, RC 71

Concise Encyclopedia of Building and Construction Materials, TA 402

Concise Encyclopedia of Environmental Systems, GE 10

Concise Encyclopedia of Information Processing in Systems and Organizations, QA 76.15

Concise Encyclopedia of Magnetic and Superconducting Materials, TK 7871.85

Concise Encyclopedia of Materials Economics, Policy and Management, TA 402

Concise Encyclopedia of Measurement and Instrumentation, TA 165

Concise Encyclopedia of Modelling and Simulation, QA 76.9

Concise Encyclopedia of Polymer Processing and Applications, TP 1087

Concise Encyclopedia of Software Engineering, QA 76.758

Concise Encyclopedia of Traffic and Transportation, TA 1145

The Encyclopedia of Advanced Materials, TA 404.8

Encyclopedia of Higher Education, LB 15

The Encyclopedia of Human Development and Education: Theory, Research, and Studies, BF 713

The Encyclopedia of Language and Linguistics, P 29

The International Encyclopedia of Curriculum, LB 1570

International Encyclopedia of Education: Research and Studies, LB 15

International Encyclopedia of Educational Evaluation, LB 2822.75

The International Encyclopedia of Educational Technology, LB 1028.3

International Encyclopedia of National Systems of Education, LB 43

International Encyclopedia of Teaching and Teacher Education, LB 1025.3

International Encyclopedia of the Sociology of Education, LC 191

Systems and Control Encyclopedia: Theory, Technology, Applications, QA 402

Philosophia
Books International Inc.
POB 605
Herndon, VA 22070-0605
703-435-7064; 800-359-7340; fax 703-689-
0660

Handbook of Metaphysics and Ontology, BD 111

Pocket
Pocket Books
1230 Avenue of the Americas
New York, NY 10020
212-698-7000; 800-223-2348

Alternative Health Care: The Encyclopedia of Choices in Healing, R 733

Praeger
Praeger Publications
see Greenwood

♦ Dictionary of Afro-American Slavery, E 441

Prentice-Hall
Prentice-Hall Press
240 Frisch Court
Paramus, NJ 07652-5240
201-909-6200; 800-947-7700; fax 800-445-
6991

American Women's History: An A to Z of People, Organizations, Issues, and Events, HQ 1115

Archaeological Encyclopedia of the Holy Land, BS 622

Dictionary of Twentieth-Century History, D 419

Encyclopedia Mysteriosa: A Comprehensive Guide to the Art of Detection in Print, Film, Radio, and Television, PN 3448

The Encyclopedia of Butterflies, QL 541.5

The Green Encyclopedia, GE 10

The Illustrated Encyclopedia of Birds: The Definitive Reference to Birds of the World, QL 672.2

The Parent's Desk Reference: The Ultimate Family Encyclopedia from Conception to College, HQ 769

Webster's New World Dictionary of Media and Communications, P 87.5

Prima
Prima Publishing
3875 Atherton Road
Rocklin, CA 95765
916-632-4400; fax 916-632-4405
www.primapublishing.com
primapub.com

College Football Encyclopedia: The Authoritative Guide to 124 Years of College Football, GV 956.8

♦ An Encyclopedia of Natural Medicine, RZ 433

Princeton Un
Princeton University Press
41 Williams Street
Princeton, NJ 08540
609-258-4900; 800-777-4726; fax 609-258-
1335
pup.princeton.edu/

♦ The New Princeton Encyclopedia of Poetry and Poetics, PN 1021

Pro-Action
Pro-Action Publishing
POB 26657
Los Angeles, CA 90026
213-666-7789; 800-567-7789; fax 213-666-3225

The Original Martial Arts Encyclopedia: Tradition, History, Pioneers, GV 1101

Pro-Ed
8700 Shoal Creek Boulevard
Austin, TX 78757-6897
512-451-3246; 800-397-7633; fax 512-451-8542
www.proedin.com/

Encyclopedia of Mental and Physical Handicaps, RC 570

Prometheus
Prometheus Books
59 John Glenn Drive
Amherst, NY 14228
716-691-0133; 800-421-0351; fax 716-691-0137
prometheusbooks.com
PBooks6205@aol.com

Dictionary of Science and Creationism, Q 123

The Encyclopedia of Biblical Errancy, BS 533

The Encyclopedia of the Paranormal, BF 1025

Raintree
Raintree/Steck-Vaughn
466 Southern Boulevard
Chatham, NJ 07928
973-514-1525; fax 973-514-1612
www.steck-vaughn.com

The Raintree Illustrated Science Encyclopedia, Q 121

Random House
Random House Inc.
201 E 50th Street
New York, NY 10022
212-751-2600; 800-726-0600; fax 800-659-2436
www.randomhouse.com

The American Medical Association Family Medical Guide, RC 81

The Dinosaur Society's Dinosaur Encyclopedia, QE 862

The Encyclopedia of Golf, GV 965

The Official NBA Basketball Encyclopedia: The Complete History and Statistics of Professional Basketball, GV 885.7

Safire's New Political Dictionary: The Definitive Guide to the New Language of Politics, JK 9

Spy Book: The Encyclopedia of Espionage, JF 1525

The Vampire Encyclopedia, GR 830

World War II: The Encyclopedia of the War Years, 1941-1945, D 743.5

Reader's Digest
Reader's Digest Association Inc.
260 Madison Avenue
New York, NY 10016-2401
212-850-7100
www.readersdigest.com

American Presidents, E 176.1

Foods That Harm, Foods That Heal: An A-Z Guide to Safe and Healthy Eating, RA 784

Illustrated Dictionary of Essential Knowledge, AG 5

Revell
Fleming H. Revell
6030 E. Fulton
Ada, MI 49301
616-676-9185; 800-877-2665; fax 616-676-9573
www.bakerbooks.com
tbennett@bakerbooks.com

Revell Bible Dictionary, BS 440

Rodale
Rodale Press Inc.
33 E Minor Street
Emmaus, PA 18098
610-967-5171; 800-527-8200; fax 610-967-8962
www.rodalepress.com

The Practical Encyclopedia of Sex and Health: From Aphrodisiacs and Hormones to Potency, Stress and Yeast Infection, RA 788

The Prevention How-to Dictionary of Healing Remedies and Techniques: From Acupressure and Aspirin to Yoga and Yogurt, RM 36

Prevention's Giant Book of Health Facts: The Ultimate Reference for Personal Health, RC 81

Rodale's All-New Encyclopedia of Organic Gardening: The Indispensable Resource for Every Gardener, SB 453.5

Rodale's Illustrated Encyclopedia of Perennials, SB 434

The Visual Encyclopedia of Natural Healing: A Step-by-Step Pictorial Guide to Solving 100 Everyday Health Problems, RC 81

♦ Women's Encyclopedia of Health and Emotional Healing, RA 778

Ronin
Ronin Publishing Inc.
POB 1035
Berkeley, CA 94701
510-540-6278; 800-858-2665; fax 510-548-7326
www.roninpub.com
roninpub@dnai.com

Psychedelics Encyclopedia, HV 5822

Rosen
Rosen Publishing Group
29 E 21st Street
New York, NY 10010
212-777-3017; 800-237-9932; fax 212-777-0277
rosenpub@tribeca.los.com

The Illustrated Encyclopedia of Active New Religions, Sects, and Cults, BL 80.2

Routledge
29 W 35th Street
New York, NY 10001-2291
212-244-3336; fax 212-563-2269
www.routledge.com

Companion Encyclopedia of Anthropology, GN 25

Companion Encyclopedia of Geography: The Environment and Humankind, G 116

Companion Encyclopedia of Psychology, BF 31

Companion Encyclopedia of the History and Philosophy of the Mathematical Sciences, QA 21

Companion Encyclopedia of the History of Medicine, R 133

Companion Encyclopedia of Theology, BR 118

Companion to Literary Myths, Heroes and Archetypes, PN 56

Compendium of the World's Languages, P 371

Dictionary of Ancient Near Eastern Mythology, BL 1060

Dictionary of Conservative and Libertarian Thought, JA 61

Dictionary of Ethics, Theology and Society, BJ 63

Dictionary of Global Climate Change, QC 981.8

Dictionary of Islamic Architecture, NA 380

A Dictionary of Philosophy, B 41

Dictionary of Race and Ethnic Relations, GN 496

Dictionary of the Modern Politics of South-East Asia, DS 518.1

An Encyclopaedia of Language, P 106

An Encyclopaedia of the History of Technology, T 15

♦ The Encyclopedia of Democracy, JC 423

♦ Encyclopedia of Government and Politics, JA 61

Encyclopedia of Post-Colonial Literatures in English, PR 9080

♦ Encyclopedia of Social and Cultural Anthropology, GN 307

Encyclopedia of the History of Arabic Science, Q 127

A Glossary of Contemporary Literary Theory, PN 44.5

International Companion Encyclopedia of Children's Literature, PN 1008.5

♦ International Encyclopedia of Business and Management, HF 1001

International Encyclopedia of Information and Library Science, Z 1006

Linguistics Encyclopedia, P 29

Routledge Dictionary of Language and Linguistics, P 29

◆ The Social Science Encyclopedia, H 41

A Student's Dictionary of Psychology, BF 31

The World Encyclopedia of Contemporary Theatre, PN 1861

Running
Running Press Book Publications
125 S 22nd Street
Philadelphia, PA 19103
215-567-5080; 800-345-5359; fax 800-453-2884
www.runningpress.com

The Illustrated Encyclopedia of Victoriana: A Comprehensive Guide to the Designs, Customs, and Inventions of the Victorian Era, NK 2115.5

Sage
Sage Publications
2455 Teller Road
Thousand Oaks, CA 91320
805-499-0721; fax 805-499-0871
www.sagepub.com

The Dictionary of Family Psychology and Family Therapy, RC 488.5

Salem
Salem Press
POB 1097
Englewood Cliffs, NJ 07632
201-871-3700; 800-221-1592; fax 201-871-8668
salem@is.netcom.com

American Indians, E 76.2

◆ American Justice, KF 154

Great Events from History: American Series, E 178

Great Events from History II: Arts and Culture Series, NX 456

Great Events from History II: Business and Commerce, HC 55

Great Events from History II: Ecology and the Environment Series, GE 150

Great Events from History II: Human Rights Series, K 3240

Great Events from History II: Science and Technology Series, Q 125

Great Events from History: North American Series, E 45

Great Events from History: Worldwide Twentieth Century Series, D 421

Magill's Medical Guide: Health and Illness, RC 41

Magill's Survey of Science: Applied Science Series, TA 145

◆ Magill's Survey of Science: Earth Science Series, QE 28

Magill's Survey of Science: Life Science Series, QH 307.2

Magill's Survey of Science: Physical Science Series, Q 158.5

Ready Reference, Ethics, BJ 63

Survey of Social Science: Economics Series, HB 61

◆ Survey of Social Science, Government and Politics, JA 61

Survey of Social Science: Psychology Series, BF 31

Survey of Social Science: Sociology Series, HM 17

◆ Women's Issues, HQ 1115

Saur
K. G. Saur Inc.
121 Chanlon Road
New Providence, NJ 07974
908-464-6800; 800-521-8110; fax 908-665-6707

Encyclopedia of World Problems and Human Potential, HN 1

Pre-Cinema History: An Encyclopedia and Annotated Bibliography of the Moving Image Before 1896, TR 848

Scarecrow
Scarecrow Press
4720 Boston Way
Lanham, MD 20706
301-459-3366; fax 800-338-4550
www.scarecrowpress.com
orders@scarecrowpress.com

Dictionary of American Immigration History, JV 6450

Historical Dictionary of Australia, DU 90

Historical Dictionary of Buddhism, BQ 130

Historical Dictionary of Ecumenical Christianity, BX 6.3

Historical Dictionary of Hinduism, BL 1105

Historical Dictionary of Human Rights and Humanitarian Organizations, JC 571

Historical Dictionary of Israel, DS 126.5

Historical Dictionary of Methodism, BX 8211

Historical Dictionary of Mormonism, BX 8605.5

Historical Dictionary of Terrorism, HV 6431

Historical Dictionary of the Civil Rights Movement, E 185.61

Historical Dictionary of the European Community, JN 15

Historical Dictionary of the Orthodox Church, BX 230

Historical Dictionary of the Republic of Korea, DS 909

The Jules Verne Encyclopedia, PQ 2469

Schirmer
Schirmer Books
1633 Broadway
Fifth Floor
New York, NY 10019-6785
212-654-8518; fax 212-654-4753

Encyclopedia of the Musical Theatre, ML 102

The Illustrated Encyclopedia of Musical Instruments, ML 102

Scholastic
Scholastic Inc.
555 Broadway
New York, NY 10012-3999
212-343-6100; 800-392-2179; fax 212-343-6930
scholastic.com

Encyclopedia of English Studies and Language Arts, PE 65

Scholastic Encyclopedia of the North American Indian, E 76.2

Scholastic Encyclopedia of Women in the United States, HQ 1410

Scribner's
Scribner's Reference
see Macmillan

Civilizations of the Ancient Near East, DS 557

◆ Encyclopedia of American Social History, HN 57

Encyclopedia of Arms Control and Disarmament, JX 1974

Encyclopedia of Latin American History and Culture, F 1406

◆ Encyclopedia of the American Constitution, KF 4548

Encyclopedia of the American Judicial System: Studies of the Principal Institutions and Processes of Law, KF 154

Encyclopedia of the American Legislative System: Studies of the Principal Structures, Processes, and Policies of Congress and State Legislatures Since the Colonial Era, JF 501

Encyclopedia of the American Military: Studies of the History, Traditions, Policies, Institutions, and Roles, UA 23

Encyclopedia of the Confederacy, E 487

◆ Encyclopedia of the North American Colonies, E 45

Encyclopedia of the Vietnam War, DS 557.7

The Middle Ages: An Encyclopedia for Students, D 114

Seven Stories
Seven Stories Press
140 Watts Street
New York, NY 10013
212-226-8760; 800-596-7437; fax 212-226-1411

◆ The article titles in this encyclopedia are indexed by keyword in Part II.

www.sevenstories.com
info@sevenstories.com

The Woman's Encyclopedia of Natural Healing: The New Healing Techniques of Over 100 Leading Alternative Practitioners, RX 461

Shambhala
Shambhala Publications
300 Massachusetts Avenue
Horticulture Hall
Boston, MA 02115
617-424-0030; fax 617-236-1563
www.shambhala.com
shambhala@mcimail.com

An Encyclopedia of Archetypal Symbolism, BL 603

The Encyclopedia of Eastern Philosophy and Religion: Buddhism, Hinduism, Taoism, Zen, BL 1005

Shambhala Encyclopedia of Yoga, BL 1238.52

Sharpe
M. E. Sharpe Inc.
80 Business Park Drive
Armonk, NY 10504
913-273-1800; 914-273-2106; fax 800-541-6563
www.mesharpe.com
mesinfo@usa.net

The Encyclopedia of the Republican Party/The Encyclopedia of the Democratic Party, JK 2352

Encyclopedia of World Terrorism, HV 6431

The Illustrated Encyclopedia of World History, D 9

Simon & Schuster
1633 Broadway
5th Floor
New York, NY 10021
800-223-1244; fax 212-698-7007

The Cat Fanciers' Association Cat Encyclopedia, SF 442.2

♦ The Christopher Columbus Encyclopedia, E 111

D-Day Encyclopedia, D 756.5

The Dictionary of Contemporary Politics of Central America and Caribbean, F 2183

Dictionary of Science, Q 123

Dictionary of the Napoleonic Wars, DC 147

Dictionary of World Politics: A Reference Guide to Concepts, Ideas and Institutions, JA 61

The Doctor's Vitamin and Mineral Encyclopedia, QP 771

Elements of Style: A Practical Encyclopedia of Interior Architectural Details from 1485 to the Present, NA 2850

Hugh Johnson's Modern Encyclopedia of Wine, TP 548

James Madison and the American Nation, 1751-1836: An Encyclopedia, E 342

Oz Clarke's Encyclopedia of Wine: An Illustrated A-to-Z Guide to Wines of the World, TP 546

Oz Clarke's New Encyclopedia of French Wine, TP 553

Smithmark
Smithmark Publishers
115 W 18th Street
5th Floor
New York, NY 10001
212-519-1310; 800-932-0070; fax 732-225-7588

The Encyclopedia of American Crime, HV 6789

The Encyclopedia of Flowers, SB 403.2

The Encyclopedia of Mythology, BL 715

South Asian Publications
POB 502
Columbia, MO 65205
573-474-0116; fax 573-474-8124

Encyclopaedia of Sikh Religion and Culture, BL 2017.3

India 2001: Reference Encyclopedia, HC 435

Springer-Verlag
Springer-Verlag New York Inc.
175 Fifth Avenue
New York, NY 10010
212-460-1500; 800-777-4643; fax 212-473-6272
www.springer-ny.com

♦ Encyclopedia of Aging: A Comprehensive Resource in Gerontology and Geriatrics, HQ 1061

Encyclopedia of Marine Sciences, GC 9

Springhouse
Springhouse Corp.
1111 Bethlehem Pike
Springhouse, PA 19477
215-646-8700; 800-346-7844; fax 215-646-4399
www.springnet.com
sph.publishing@springnet. com

Nurse's Quick Reference: An A-to-Z Guide to 1,001 Professional Problems, RT 51

St James
Saint James Press
835 Penobscot Building
Detroit, MI 48226-4094
313-961-2242; 800-347-4253; fax 313-961-6950

Contemporary Fashion, TT 505

Encyclopedia of Banking and Finance, HG 151

Encyclopedia of Consumer Brands, HF 5415.3

Guide to French Literature: 1789 to Present, PQ 226

International Dictionary of Architects and Architecture, NA 40

International Dictionary of Ballet, GV 1585

The International Dictionary of Films and Filmmakers, PN 1997.8

International Dictionary of Opera, ML 102

International Dictionary of Theatre, PN 2035

Political and Economic Encyclopaedia of the Soviet Union and Eastern Europe, JN 96

Political and Economic Encyclopaedia of Western Europe, JN 94

St Martin's
Saint Martin's Press
123 W 18th Street
Fifth Floor
New York, NY 10011
212-367-0180; 800-321-9299; fax 212-420-9314

The Sports Encyclopedia: Pro Football, The Modern Era 1972-1996, GV 955

Stackpole
Stackpole Books Inc.
5067 Ritter Road
Mechanicsburg, PA 17055
717-796-0411; 800-732-3669; fax 717-796-0412
www.stackpolebooks.com

Encyclopedia of the American Revolution, E 208

Sterling
Sterling Publishing Co. Inc.
387 Park Avenue, S
New York, NY 10016-8810
212-532-7160; 800-367-9692; fax 212-213-2495
www.sterlingpub.com
customersservice@ sterlingpub.com

The Battle Book: Crucial Conflicts in History from 1469 BC to the Present, D 25

Cassell's Encyclopedia of Queer Myth, Symbol, and Spirit: Gay, Lesbian, Bisexual, and Transgender Lore, BL 795

Encyclopedia of Twentieth Century Conflict: Land Warfare, D 25

The Illustrated Encyclopaedia of Costume and Fashion: From 1066 to the Present, GT 580

Stockton
Stockton Press
see Grove's

The Guinness Encyclopedia of Popular Music, ML 102

Longman Guide to Living Religions, BL 80.2

The New Palgrave Dictionary of Money and Finance, HG 151

Stoddart
Stoddart Publishing Co. Ltd.
34 Lesmill Road
Don Mills, ON M3B 2T6 Canada
416-445-3333; 800-387-0141; fax 416-445-
5967

The Spycatcher's Encyclopedia of Espionage,
UB 270

TAB
TAB Books
11 W 19th Street
New York, NY 10011

Amateur Radio Encyclopedia, TK 9956

Encyclopedia of Electronics, TK 7804

The Illustrated Encyclopedia of General Aviation, TL 509

Tauris
I. B. Tauris & Co.
see St. Martin's

Dictionary of Third World Terms, HC 59.7

Taylor & Francis
Taylor & Francis Publishing Inc.
1900 Frost Road
Suite 101
Bristol, PA 19007-1598
215-785-5800; 800-821-8312; fax 215-785-
5515

Encyclopedia of Human Rights, JC 571

Encyclopedia of the United Nations and International Agreements, JX 1977

Thames & Hudson
Thames & Hudson Inc.
500 Fifth Avenue
New York, NY 10110
212-354-3763; 800-233-2588; fax 212-398-
1252
www.wwnorton.com/thames

The Gods and Symbols of Ancient Mexico and
the Maya: An Illustrated Dictionary of
Mesoamerican Religion, F 1435

The Thames and Hudson Dictionary of Art and
Artists, N 31

The Thames and Hudson Encyclopaedia of Impressionism, N 6465

Time-Life
Time-Life Inc.
777 Duke St
Alexandria, VA 22314
703-838-7000; 800-621-702
www.timelife.com

The Alternative Advisor: The Complete Guide to
Natural Therapies and Alternative Treatments,
R 733

Trafalgar Square
POB 257
North Pomfret, VT 05053
802-457-1911; 800-423-4525; fax 802-457-
1913
tsquare@souer.net

Crime: An Encyclopedia, HV 6017

A Dictionary of Mind and Body: Therapies,
Techniques and Ideas in Alternative Medicine,
the Healing Arts and Psychology, R 733

Dictionary of the British Empire and Commonwealth, DA 16

Edinburgh Encyclopedia, DA 890

The Encyclopedia of Ghosts and Spirits,
BF 1461

Encyclopedia of Medieval Church Art, N 7943

The Encyclopedia of TV Science Fiction,
PN 1992.8

Transaction
Transaction Publications
Rutgers Un
Building 4051
New Brunswick, NJ 08903
732-445-2280; 888-999-6778; fax 732-445-
3138
www.transactionpub.com
transpub@idt.net

Encyclopedia of Soviet Life, JA 64

Trinity
Trinity Press International
POB 1321
Harrisburg, PA 17105
717-541-8130; 800-877-0012; fax 717-541-
8128
www.morehousegroup.com
morehouse@morehousegroup.com

A Dictionary of Biblical Interpretation, BS 500

A Dictionary of Judaism and Christianity,
BM 50

Un of Arkansas
University of Arkansas Press
201 Ozark Street
Fayetteville, AR 72701
501-575-3246; 800-626-0090; fax 501-575-
6044
www.uark.edu/-uaprinfo
uakrinfo@cavern.uark.edu

Encyclopedia of the Blues, ML 102

Un of California
University of California Press
2120 Berkeley Way
Berkeley, CA 94720
510-642-4247; 800-822-6657; fax 510-643-
7127
www.ucpress.edu
ucpress@ucop.edu

Los Angeles A to Z: An Encyclopedia of the City
and County, F 869

Toxics A to Z: A Guide to Everyday Pollution
Hazards, RA 1213

Un of Hawaii
University of Hawaii Press
2840 Kolowalu Street
Honolulu, HI 96822
808-956-8255; 800-956-2840; fax 800-650-
7811
www2.hawaii.edu/uhpress/UHPHome.html
chuns@hawaii.edu

Encyclopedia of Australian Art, N 7400

Un of Ill
University of Illinois Press
1325 S Oak St
Champaign, IL 61820
217-333-0950
www.press.uillinois.edu

Astronomy from A to Z: A Dictionary of Celestial Objects and Ideas, QB 14

The Graying of America: An Encyclopedia of
Aging, Health, Mind, and Behavior, HQ 1064

Un of Oklahoma
University of Oklahoma Press
1005 Asp Avenue
Norman, OK 73019-0445
405-325-5111; 800-627-7377; fax 405-325-
4000

Encyclopedia of United States Army Insignia
and Uniforms, UC 533

International Encyclopedia of Horse Breeds,
SF 291

Un of Pennsylvania
University of Pennsylvania Press
4200 Pine Street
Philadelphia, PA 19104-4011
215-898-6261; 800-445-9880; fax 215-898-
0404

Potter's Dictionary of Materials and Techniques,
TT 919.5

Un of Toronto
University of Toronto Press
340 Nagel Drive
Cheektowaga, NY 14225
716-683-4547
www.utpress.utoronto.ca/

♦ Encyclopedia of Contemporary Literary Theory:
Approaches, Scholars, Terms, PN 81

Encyclopedia of Music in Canada, ML 106

The Spenser Encyclopedia, PR 2362

♦ The article titles in this encyclopedia are indexed by keyword in Part II.

Un of Utah
University of Utah Press
101 University Services Building
Salt Lake City, UT 84112
801-581-6771; 800-773-6672; fax 801-581-
3365

Utah History Encyclopedia, F 826

Un Press of Kentucky
University Press of Kentucky
663 S Limestone Street
Lexington, KY 40508-4008
606-257-2951; 800-666-2211; fax 606-323-
4981
www.uky.edu/ UniversityPress
dlloy@pop.uky.edu

The Kentucky Encyclopedia, F 451

Un South Carolina
University of South Carolina Press
937 Assembly Street
Carolina Plaza-8th Floor
Columbia, SC 29208
803-777-5243; fax 803-777-7251
www.scarolina.edu/uscpress

U.S. Army Patches: An Illustrated Encyclopedia
of Cloth Unit Insignia, UC 533

Van Nostrand Reinhold
Van Nostrand Reinhold Co.
115 Fifth Avenue
New York, NY 10003
212-254-3232; fax 212-477-2719

The Astronomy and Astrophysics Encyclopedia,
QB 14

The Color Compendium, QC 494.2

Encyclopedia of Computer Science, QA 76.15

Encyclopedia of Minerals, QE 355

The Encyclopedia of Television, Cable, and
Video, P 87.5

The Larousse Encyclopedia of Precious Gems,
TS 722

Van Nostrand's Scientific Encyclopedia: Animal
Life, Biosciences, Chemistry, Earth and At-
mospheric Sciences, Energy Sources and
Power Technology, Q 121

VCH
VCH Publications Inc.
605 Third Avenue
New York, NY 10158-0180

Encyclopedia of Applied Physics, QC 5

Encyclopedia of Molecular Biology and Molecular Medicine, QH 506

Encyclopedia of Physics, QC 5

Encyclopedic Dictionary of Chemical Technology, TP 9

International Encyclopedia of Composites,
TA 418.9

VGM
VGM Career Horizons
see NTC

VGM's Careers Encyclopedia, HF 5382.5

Viking Penguin
375 Hudson Street
New York, NY 10014-3657
212-366-2000; 800-331-4624; fax 212-766-
2666

The Penguin Encyclopedia of Weapons and Military Technology, U 815

Visible Ink
Visible Ink Prfess
Div. of Gale Research
P. O. Box 35477
Detroit, MI 48232-5477
800-776-6265; fax 800-414-5043

Bud Collins' Modern Encyclopedia of Tennis,
GV 992

Voyageur
Voyageur Press
123 N Second Street
Stillwater, MN 55082
612-430-2210; 800-888-9653; fax 612-430-
2211
books@voyageurpress.com

The Whitehead Encyclopedia of Deer, QL 737

Walker
Walker Publishing
435 Hudson St
New York, NY 10014
212-727-8300; 800-289-2553; fax 212-727-
0984

The Encyclopedia of Career Choices for the
1990s: A Guide to Entry Level Jobs, HF 5383

Warner
Warner Books
1271 Avenue of the Americas
New York, NY 10020
212-522-7200; 800-759-0190; fax 800-286-
9471
www.warnerbooks.com

◆ The Fortune Encyclopedia of Economics, HB 61

Watson-Guptill
Watson-Guptill Publications, Inc
1515 Broadway
New York, NY 10036
212-536-5121; 800-451-1741; fax 212-536-
5359

The Encyclopedia of Sculpture Techniques,
NB 1170

Illustrated Encyclopedia of Architects and Architecture, NA 40

Westminster John Knox
Westminster John Knox Press
100 Witherspoon Street
Louisville, KY 402020
502-569-5055; 502-569-5113
www.pcusa.org/ppcl
annie.mcclure@pcusa.org

Dictionary of Feminist Theologies, BT 83.55

Westview
Westview Press
5500 Central Avenue
Boulder, CO 80301-2847
303-444-3541; 800-456-1995; fax 303-449-
3356

The Soviet Military Encyclopedia, U 24

Whitston
Whitston Publishing
POB 958
Troy, NY 12181
518-283-4363
www.capial.net/com/ whitston
whitston@capital.net

A Melville Encyclopedia: The Novels, PS 2386

Wiley
John Wiley & Sons Inc.
605 Third Avenue
New York, NY 10158-0012
212-850-6000; 800-225-5945; fax 973-302-
2300
www.wiley.com/compbooks/
info@qm/wiley.com

Arnold Encyclopedia of Real Estate, HD 1365

Concise Encyclopedia of Polymer Science and
Engineering, TP 1087

Concise Encyclopedia of Psychology, BF 31

Concise Encyclopedia of Special Education,
LC 4007

Concise International Encyclopedia of Robotics:
Applications and Automation, TJ 210.4

The Design Encyclopedia, NK 1370

Dictionary of Scientific Literacy, Q 123

Encyclopedia of Acoustics, QC 221.5

Encyclopedia of Antibiotics, RM 267

Encyclopedia of Architecture: Design, Engineering and Construction, NA 31

Encyclopedia of Chemical Technology, TP 9

Encyclopedia of Common Natural Ingredients
Used in Food, Drugs, and Cosmetics, QD 415

Encyclopedia of Energy Technology and the Environment, TJ 163.235

Encyclopedia of Food Science and Technology,
TP 368.2

Encyclopedia of Nuclear Magnetic Resonance,
QC 762

◆ Encyclopedia of Psychology, BF 31

Encyclopedia of Software Engineering,
QA 76.758

The Entrepreneur and Small Business Problem Solver: An Encyclopedic Reference and Guide, HD 62.7

The Family Encyclopedia of Child Psychology and Development, BF 721

The International Business Dictionary and Reference, HF 1359

Kirk-Othmer Concise Encyclopedia of Chemical Technology, TP 9

Wiley Encyclopedia of Energy and the Environment, TJ 163.235

Wiley Encyclopedia of Packaging Technology, TS 195

Wilson
H. W. Wilson Co.
950 University Ave
Bronx, NY 10452
718-588-8400; 800-367-6770; fax 718-590-1617
www.hwwilson.com

Facts About the States, E 180

World Book
525 W Monroe
20th Floor
Chicago, IL 60661
312-258-3700; 800-621-8202
www.worldbook.com

The World Book Encyclopedia of People and Places, AE 5

The World Book-Rush-Presbyterian-St. Luke's Medical Center Medical Encyclopedia: Your Guide to Good Health, R 125

Writer's Digest
Writer's Digest Books
1507 Dana Avenue
Cincinatti, OH 45207
513-531-2690; 800-289-0963

Writer's Encyclopedia, PN 141

Wyndham Hall
Wyndham Hall Publishers
POB 45
Kirkland, WA 98083-0045
206-224-2848

National Gangs Resource Handbook: An Encyclopedic Reference, HV 6439

Yale Un
Yale University Press
302 Temple Street
New Haven, CT 06511
203-432-0960; 800-987-7328
www.yale.edu/yup
yupmkt@yale.edu

The Encyclopedia of New York City, F 128.3

The Yale Guide to Children's Nutrition, RJ 206

Zondervan
Zondervan Publishing House
5300 Patterson Avenue, SE
Mail Drop B28
Grand Rapids, MI 49530
616-698-6900; 800-226-1122; fax 800-934-6381

Dictionary of Cults, Sects, Religions and the Occult, BL 31

◆ The article titles in this encyclopedia are indexed by keyword in Part II.

Ratings Index

◆ The article titles in this encyclopedia are indexed by keyword in Part II.

◆ The article titles in this encyclopedia are indexed by keyword in Part II.

◆ The article titles in this encyclopedia are indexed by keyword in Part II.

◆ The article titles in this encyclopedia are indexed by keyword in Part II.

♦ The article titles in this encyclopedia are indexed by keyword in Part II.

Feminism and Psychoanalysis: A Critical Dictionary, BF 175.4

3.82

The Blackwell Dictionary of Judaica, BM 50

3.81

Historical Encyclopedia of School Psychology, LB 1027.55

Labor, Employment, and the Law: A Dictionary, KF 3317

The Performing Arts Business Encyclopedia, KF 4290

3.80

A Dictionary of Biblical Interpretation, BS 500

The Encyclopedia of Amazons: Women Warriors from Antiquity to the Modern Era, U 51

Encyclopedia of Invasions and Conquests from Ancient Times to the Present, D 25

3.79

Broadcasting It: An Encyclopaedia of Homosexuality on Film, Radio and TV in the UK, 1923-1993, PN 1995.9

The HarperCollins Dictionary of Biology, QH 302.5

3.78

Larousse Encyclopedia of Wine, T 548

3.77

The HarperCollins Dictionary of Economics, HB 61

3.76

The Encyclopedia of Depression, RC 537

Encyclopedia of the Second World, D 847

A Herman Melville Encyclopedia, PS 2386

The MIT Encyclopedia of the Japanese Economy, HC 462.9

The UFO Encyclopedia, TL 789

3.75

The A-to-Z of Pregnancy and Childbirth: A Concise Encyclopedia, RG 525

Alternative Healing: The Complete A-Z Guide to More than 150 Alternative Therapies, R 733

Encyclopaedia of Sikh Religion and Culture, BL 2017.3

From Archetype to Zeitgeist: Powerful Ideas for Powerful Thinking, AG 105

Isms: A Compendium of Concepts, Doctrines, Traits and Beliefs from Ableism to Zygodactylism, JF 51

World Encyclopedia of Organized Crime, HV 6017

3.74

Virginia Woolf A to Z: A Comprehensive Reference for Students, Teachers and Common Readers to Her Life, Work and Critical Reception, PR 6045

Wizards and Sorcerers: From Abracadabra to Zoroastrianism, BF 1588

3.73

Cowboys and the Wild West: An A-Z Guide from the Chisholm Trail to the Silver Screen, F 596

The Disney Encyclopedia of Baby and Child Care, RJ 61

The Encyclopedia of African-American Heritage, E 185

The Family Encyclopedia of Child Psychology and Development, BF 721

3.72

An Encyclopaedia of the History of Technology, T 15

Encyclopedia of Angels, BL 477

Encyclopedia of Cat Health and Care, SF 447

Revell Bible Dictionary, BS 440

Shipwrecks: An Encyclopedia of the World's Worst Disasters at Sea, VK 1250

3.71

The Chess Encyclopedia, GV 1314.5

The Encyclopedia of Flowers, SB 403.2

Encyclopedia of Literary Epics, PN 56

The Encyclopedia of the Central West, F 351

3.70

A Student's Dictionary of Psychology, BF 31

World Encyclopedia of Twentieth Century Murder, HV 6515

3.69

Crimes of Perception: An Encyclopedia of Heresies and Heretics, BT 1315.2

♦ Encyclopedia of African-American Education, LC 2717

The Encyclopedia of Jewish Genealogy, CS 21

♦ Encyclopedia of Relationships Across the Lifespan, HM 132

Nurse's Quick Reference: An A-to-Z Guide to 1,001 Professional Problems, RT 51

Our Sunday Visitor's Catholic Encyclopedia, BX 841

A William Somerset Maugham Encyclopedia, PR 6025

3.68

A Dictionary for Psychotherapists: Dynamic Concepts in Psychotherapy, RC 475.7

Encyclopedia of Lasers and Optical Technology, TA 1509

Encyclopedia of Major League Baseball Teams, GV 875

Illustrated Encyclopedia of Architects and Architecture, NA 40

A Rousseau Dictionary, PQ 2042

3.67

The Vampire Book: The Encyclopedia of the Undead, GR 830

3.66

Concise Encyclopedia of Modelling and Simulation, QA 76.9

Concise Encyclopedia of Polymer Science and Engineering, TP 1087

A Dictionary of Cultural and Critical Theory, HM 101

Dictionary of Third World Terms, HC 59.7

3.65

Concise Encyclopedia of Special Education, LC 4007

Dictionary of Philosophy and Religion: Eastern and Western Thought, B 41

The Whitehead Encyclopedia of Deer, QL 737

3.64

The Blackwell Encyclopedia of Industrial Archaeology, T 37

The HarperCollins Dictionary of Statistics, QA 276.14

3.62

Encyclopedia of Global Industries, HD 2324

Political Parties of the Americas, 1980s to 1990s: Canada, Latin America, and the West Indies, JL 195

3.61

Encyclopedia of Applied Physics, QC 5

3.60

The Larousse Encyclopedia of Precious Gems, TS 722

3.59

Dictionary of Cults, Sects, Religions and the Occult, BL 31

The Grolier Student Encyclopedia of Endangered Species, QL 83

3.58

The Facts On File Encyclopedia of Black Women, E 185.96

Historical Dictionary of the Spanish American War, E 715

United States in Asia: A Historical Dictionary, DS 33.4

3.57

The American Civil War: A Multicultural Encyclopedia, E 456

Historical Dictionary of Australia, DU 90

3.56

Encyclopedia of World Terrorism, HV 6431

♦ Human Environments: A Cross-Cultural Encyclopedia, GF 4

♦ The article titles in this encyclopedia are indexed by keyword in Part II.

♦ The article titles in this encyclopedia are indexed by keyword in Part II.